PACIFIC
PAYBACK

OTHER BOOKS BY STEPHEN L. MOORE

Battle Surface!: Lawson P. "Red"
Ramage and the War Patrols of the USS Parche

Presumed Lost: The Incredible Ordeal of
America's Submarine Veteran POWs of World War II

Relic Quest: A Guide to Responsible Relic
Recovery Techniques with Metal Detectors

Savage Frontier: Rangers, Riflemen, and
Indian Wars in Texas. Volume IV: 1842–1845

European Metal Detecting Guide:
Techniques, Tips and Treasures

Last Stand of the Texas Cherokees:
Chief Bowles and the 1839 Cherokee War in Texas

War of the Wolf: Texas' Memorial Submarine,
World War II's Famous USS Seawolf

Savage Frontier: Rangers, Riflemen, and
Indian Wars in Texas. Volume III: 1840–1841

Spadefish: *On Patrol with a Top-Scoring*
World War II Submarine

Savage Frontier: Rangers, Riflemen,
and Indian Wars in Texas. Volume II: 1838–1839

Eighteen Minutes: The Battle of San Jacinto
and the Texas Independence Campaign

Savage Frontier: Rangers, Riflemen, and
Indian Wars in Texas. Volume 1: 1835–1837

Taming Texas: Captain William T. Sadler's Lone Star Service

The Buzzard Brigade: Torpedo Squadron Ten at War
(with William J. Shinneman and Robert W. Gruebel)

PACIFIC
PAYBACK

THE CARRIER AVIATORS WHO AVENGED
PEARL HARBOR AT THE BATTLE OF MIDWAY

STEPHEN L. MOORE

NAL
CALIBER

NAL Caliber
Published by the Penguin Group
Penguin Group (USA) LLC, 375 Hudson Street,
New York, New York 10014

USA | Canada | UK | Ireland | Australia | New Zealand | India | South Africa | China
penguin.com
A Penguin Random House Company

First published by NAL Caliber, an imprint of New American Library,
a division of Penguin Group (USA) LLC

First Printing, June 2014

LIBRARY OF CONGRESS CATALOGING-IN-PUBLICATION DATA:
Moore, Stephen L.
Pacific payback: the carrier aviators who avenged Pearl Harbor at the Battle of Midway/
Stephen L. Moore.
   p.   cm.
   Includes bibliographical references and index.
   ISBN 978-0-451-46552-8
   1. Midway, Battle of, 1942.   2. United States. Navy. Bombing Squadron Six.
3. United States. Navy. Scouting Squadron Six.   4. Dauntless (Dive bomber)   5. World
War, 1939–1945—Aerial operations, American.   6. World War, 1939–1945—Naval
operations, American.   7. Enterprise (Aircraft carrier: CV-6)   I. Title.
   D774.M5M66 2014
   940.54'26699—dc23   2013046133

Printed in the United States of America
10 9 8 7 6 5 4 3 2 1

Set in Sabon

Special thanks to aviation researcher Mark E. Horan, who generously shared his early Pacific War database. Mark collected interviews and personal papers from dozens of Dauntless airmen over the course of many years. His fresh material and editorial suggestions helped breathe fresh perspectives into the historic Battle of Midway.

CONTENTS

MAPS

PACIFIC
PAYBACK

PREFACE

One hundred and sixty-four feet below the surface of Lake Michigan, the aircraft slowly broke free from the muck in which it had been settled upright for more than fifty years. The plane bore the white side number B-7, and on its cowling was stenciled the name *Midway Madness*. Wrapped in cables attached by a diver, she was carefully lifted to the surface by a powerful crane, and thereafter went through a careful restoration process.[1]

The magnificent result is now a prized piece on display in the National Naval Aviation Museum in Pensacola, Florida. It is truly one of a kind. This Douglas SBD-2 Dauntless dive-bomber—thirty-three feet long and weighing more than three tons without fuel or ordnance—is the only extant SBD-2 that saw combat operation during the first six months of the Pacific War. What's more, this Dauntless, officially Bureau Number 2106, was parked on Ford Island in Pearl Harbor during the surprise attack by the Imperial Japanese Navy on December 7, 1941.

Having escaped destruction during that infamous onslaught, BuNo 2106 was soon embarked on the United States Navy's second aircraft carrier, USS *Lexington*, for offensive operations against the Japanese. Flown by Lieutenant (Junior Grade) Mark Whittier in March 1942, it participated in dive-bombing attacks against enemy shipping in the New Guinea harbors of Lae and Salamaua. Three months later, the Dauntless was flown by a Marine crew at the Battle of Midway, where the dive-bomber was riddled with more than two hundred bullet holes. BuNo 2106 was then returned to an Illinois air base to be used as a training aircraft. The plane was lost in June 1943 when its crew was forced to ditch it in the cold freshwaters of Lake Michigan.

The Douglas Dauntless dive-bomber made history for America during the first six months of World War II. This ruggedly built carrier bomber was in it from the first moments of war. *Pacific Payback* is the odyssey of two Dauntless squadrons—Scouting Squadron Six (VS-6) and Bombing Squadron Six (VB-6)—that were based on board the carrier USS *Enterprise*.

Dick Best and Earl Gallaher assumed command of these two SBD squadrons during the months following Pearl Harbor. Each man possessed a burning desire to pay back the Japanese for what they had done at Hawaii. The ultimate vengeance for carrier aviators like Best and Gallaher would be to destroy the very flight decks that had launched the Pearl Harbor strikes.

It was no small feat, however, to score a direct hit on a moving vessel with a dive-bomber. Dauntless pilots pushed over into their dives from a height of more than two miles above enemy warships. The initial descent was vertical—ninety degrees. The pilot generally pulled back the angle to seventy degrees as his SBD reached a point between five thousand and thirty-five hundred feet above the target, allowing him to safely toggle his bomb to clear the propeller. There was no use of the plane's tail rudder, which could cause the bomb to yaw and miss the target. The pilot kept his target ship in line simply by using the stick to spin the airplane like a corkscrew to line up the target's advance on the ocean floor below.

This effort more often than not took place as both the pilot and rear seat gunner were being subjected to murderous antiaircraft fire from below, while fighter planes slashed at them from behind and above. Even against practice targets, successful bomb drops required precise execution; in combat drops against enemy shipping while under fire, the pilots often did not exceed a twenty-five percent hit ratio.

Dive-bombing had first been practiced by U.S. Marine aviators in 1919, as they learned to release a bomb from a steeply descending aircraft. The first American aircraft carrier, USS *Langley* (CV-1), was commissioned in 1922, but it was another four years before the first true dive-bomber aircraft were tested. The Navy assessed new Vought 02U Corsair biplanes with mixed results. Improvements in bomb release equipment were made, and other dive-bombers were introduced during the 1930s, including the Northrop BT-1 and the Vought SB2U-1.[2]

In 1938, the entry of an innovative product from the Douglas Aircraft Factory would soon prove to be the clear winner for all-around efficiency in U.S. carrier operations. The new Douglas SBD-1 (Scout-Bomber by Douglas) began deployment operation with Navy and Marine squadrons in 1939, and the dive-bomber soon became popularly known by its brand name, "Dauntless."

The first Douglas SBDs to begin carrier operations were actually of the second model variety, the SBD-2, which were built with fifty percent more fuel capacity for extended flight time. The first carrier squadron to be completely equipped with the new SBD-2 had been Bombing Squadron Two on board the USS *Lexington* (CV-2) in 1941. Each plane sported twin .30-caliber machine guns for the pilot's use, which were mounted in the nose above the engine and fired through the propeller arc, plus a single .30-caliber machine gun mount in the rear cockpit for the use of the radioman. Deliveries began in March 1941 of a newer SBD-3 model, which had a top speed of 216 knots, or 250 mph, from each plane's thousand-horsepower Wright Cyclone engine—although actual cruising speed on combat missions was normally 140 to 160 knots to preserve fuel. The range of a Dauntless with a thousand-pound bomb was safely 200 to 225 miles, or 250 to 275 miles with a five-hundred-pound bomb.

The Douglas SBD Dauntless was a much improved dive-bomber for the Navy's use. Although some would later nickname the SBD "Slow But Deadly," it actually had an aerial speed superior to the German Junkers Ju 87 Stuka dive-bomber, and comparable to the Japanese Aichi D3A and the British Fleet Air Arm Blackburn B-24 Skua. Aside from any shortcomings the Dauntless might possess in aerial speed, it would prove to be the Navy's most successful dive-bomber of the Pacific War.[3]

The Dauntless was indeed a formidable aircraft, and in the hands of the skilled pilots and gunners of VS-6 and VB-6, it helped alter the course of World War II.

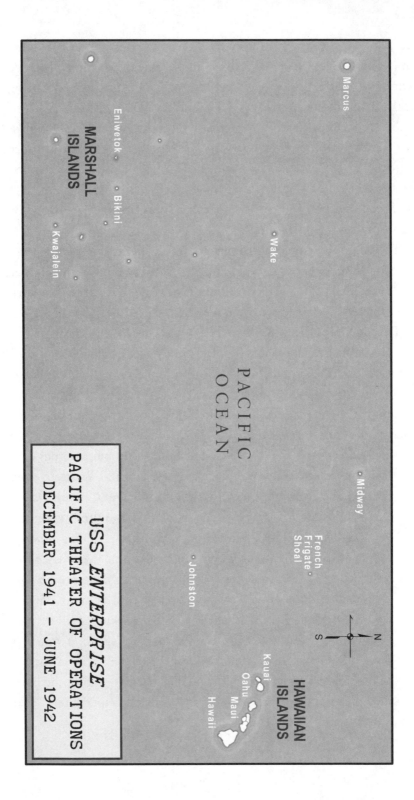

ONE

"We Would Have One Helluva Celebration"

This is it, he thought. One last flight. Then liberty. Then back to good ol' mainland USA.

In the predawn darkness, Jack Leaming moved with a purpose. Climbing around, under, and into the airplane assigned to him, the lean youth untied wing and tail lines; checked hinges, fasteners, and access doors; and assured that all was in proper order. Dozens of other men around him were similarly engaged in their own preparations, and although his eyes had not yet fully adjusted to the blackness topside, he could see enough to know they were there. Overhead, small patches of stars peeked through the partly cloudy skies.

The flight deck speakers crackled to life. "Stand by to man aircraft!"

The warm tropical breeze grew stronger on his face as Leaming felt the warship begin to swing into the wind. His dark, curly hair was pressed tight to his skull by a canvas flying helmet, whose straps whipped about his cheeks as he worked. Leaming was counting the hours to freedom. So far, things were looking good. He had just celebrated his twenty-second birthday the previous day, December 6, 1941. Even better, his four-year enlistment in the United States Navy would expire in two more days. With his boy-next-door clean-shaven good looks, healthy tan, and confident smile, he was sure to break young hearts back in the States.

Leaming, a native of Philadelphia, was one of many young men who had enlisted in the Navy in the late 1930s at a time when jobs were scarce for recent high school graduates. Within weeks of completion of his basic training in 1938, he had been assigned to the newest aircraft carrier in the fleet, USS *Enterprise* (CV-6).

Enterprise was only the sixth carrier built by the Navy. She had been commissioned on May 12, 1938, with Seaman Leaming being among her plank owners—those who helped bring the new vessel into naval service. The seventh American vessel to bear the name *Enterprise*, she was destined to become the most famous of that lineage. The big ship with the big name became affectionately known to her crew as "the Big E." Because the carrier's hull number was CV-6, her aircraft squadrons included the same number: Bombing Squadron Six (VB-6), Scouting Squadron Six (VS-6), Fighting Squadron Six (VF-6), and Torpedo Squadron Six (VT-6).

Each passing year since the Big E's commissioning day had brought the prospects of war ever closer. President Franklin Delano Roosevelt, a former assistant secretary of the Navy, could foresee the inevitable. Japan had displayed aggressive tendencies ever since attacking China in 1895, and her combative nature was spreading rapidly. Five years after Japan invaded Manchuria in 1931, the country denounced the 1922 Washington Naval Treaty, which limited the size of the Japanese, American, and British navies. World peace had continued to detriorate when Japan allied itself with Germany and Italy, and the Second World War finally commenced in September 1939.

FDR's administration imposed strict embargoes on Japan in 1940, prohibiting the export of oil, scrap iron, steel, and strategic minerals to the belligerent nation. It was only a matter of time before America would be drawn into the world war with Japan and her allies. When the United States asked Japan in the fall of 1941 to respect the sovereignty of all nations and to withdraw from China and Indo-China, the Japanese government and its powerful military machine were already working on plans to make a surprise attack on the U.S. Navy's Pacific Fleet at its advance base in Hawaii.

The prospect of America entering another world war prompted refinement in the traditional roles of naval operations as new sailors like Jack Leaming went through their early training in the late 1930s. The powerful guns of the fleet's battleships had ruled the seas during World

War I, but the emergence of the aircraft carriers held great potential. Some of the more visionary leaders of the U.S. Navy were beginning to see that checking the advance of the mighty Japanese military machine might just come from the air, not from the big guns at sea.

At first, each day was exciting for Leaming. Aviation was blossoming, and the use of aircraft in military roles was in its adolescence. Yet Leaming's initial months on the *Enterprise* were spent mess cooking, chipping paint, and doing other dirty jobs. *Why did I ever join the Navy?* he soon wondered as his early days of excitement melted into monotony. To help cure his blues, he made the most of his free time ashore when the carrier operated out of San Diego in the spring of 1939. He saved enough money to buy a 1932 Ford, in which he and his buddies would cruise up and down Broadway in search of dance halls and bars.[1]

His chance to escape the doldrums of remaining a "deck ape" finally came later that year, when he answered the call to attend radio school in order to become a qualified radioman. During his instruction, he learned how to interpret the coded dots and dashes of Morse code, a special radio language used by ships and aircraft to transmit messages. Soon after attaining the rating of radioman third class, Leaming was assigned to the dive-bomber squadrons on board *Enterprise* on February 9, 1940, along with companions Tom Merritt, Joe DeLuca, Lee Keaney, William Bergin, and Lee McHugh. In the year that followed, they learned aerial gunnery, as their new position entailed, in addition to their radio duties, riding in the rear cockpit of the Navy's newest carrier-based dive-bomber as rear seat gunners. Because of the cramped space in the gunner's backseat, most of Leaming's comrades were similarly small-framed youths of average height. Leaming himself weighed in at only one hundred and thirty pounds.

Leaming's first "hop" (Navy jargon for a flight) with his Scouting Squadron Six had been with Ensign Cleo Dobson. Experiencing his initial flights in Curtiss SBC-3 biplanes, Leaming found dive-bombing to be most impressive. "Hurtling earthward, straight down from fifteen thousand feet," he recalled, "was an awesome experience."[2]

Not all of Leaming's early hops were as awe-inspiring. On June 27, 1940, he and his pilot, Ensign Ben Troemel, narrowly survived their first catapult launch from *Enterprise*. As their plane left the deck, two large, balloon-shaped flotation bags—designed to keep the aircraft afloat for a short while in the event of a water landing—broke loose from the underside of the upper wing. Troemel struggled to keep their aircraft aloft with the unexpected drag. In the rear cockpit, Leaming inserted an auxiliary control stick that enabled him to assist his pilot in flying the plane. After sweating it out for twenty minutes, the pair managed to land their damaged warbird and avoid crashing into the ocean.

On another training flight off Oahu in January 1941, Leaming was embarrassed by a gunnery practice foul-up. As his pilot, Ensign Norm West, flew past a tow plane—another bomber rigged with a target sleeve—Leaming struggled to fire his gun when ordered. Realizing he had put the gun on "safe," he slid the safety sleeve over. He knew that Lieutenant Earl Gallaher, the VS-6 flight officer, was a stickler for doing everything right the first time, so Leaming feared asking Ensign West to make a second pass.

Instead, he aimed his machine gun in the general direction of the sleeve and pressed the trigger in desperation. Leaming lost control of his weapon in the process and three bullets ripped through their SBC's rear stabilizer.[3]

Ashamed and scared, he called over the intercom: "Mr. West, I think I shot three holes in the stabilizer."

"Think, goddammit, don'tcha know?" the pilot shouted back.

Leaming confirmed his mistake, and West radioed for immediate permission to land at the Ford Island Naval Air Station in Pearl Harbor. Back on the ground, Ensign West just looked at their damaged tail and walked away, shaking his head in disgust. Leaming felt as though he were at the bottom of the ocean. The Scouting Six executive officer, Lieutenant Ralph Dempsey Smith, chewed him out thoroughly, informing him that a new stabilizer would tax the squadron budget to the tune of three thousand dollars.[4]

Leaming was forced to write a letter to Smith, detailing how he had made such an error. Even worse was the endless ribbing he took from fellow radiomen Joe DeLuca and Tom Merritt. Fortunately for Leaming, it was only a matter of weeks before Merritt too managed to shoot up his own plane's tail, and he would not be the last.

Months of training hardened the young radiomen-gunners into

seasoned veterans. As spring passed into the fall of 1941, Scouting Six traded in their aged biplanes for the Navy's newest dive-bomber models. Even with faster and better planes, Leaming was ever mindful of the reason he and his comrades drew the extra hazard pay afforded to aviators. During a dive-bombing practice attack on Pearl Harbor, Lieutenant Smith and his gunner were killed when their automatic pilot feature locked in—something that was never desired in a terminal-velocity plunge.

The chidings the enlisted gunners showered upon one another for mindless screwups helped alleviate the stress of their demanding duties. Mistakes led to learning, and learning led to confidence. As 1941 drew to a close, the pilots and gunners of both Scouting Six and their sister squadron Bombing Six had refined their skills. They were precision teams, proud of their abilities, and ready for action.

"Pilots, man your planes!"

The predawn announcement blaring from the *Enterprise* loudspeakers sparked a stir of action. Leaming, checking over his dive-bomber, watched the plane handlers take their positions on the flight deck. They would help direct the movement of the aircraft from their parking areas to the engine run-up and takeoff areas. *Liberty*, he thought, *is just hours away.*

Eighteen warplanes were lined up in readiness for launch on the eight-hundred-foot-long teak flight deck. Beneath the nearly two acres of wood plank surface area were underplates of steel to help support the massive weight of so many men and machines. From the center of the starboard side of the deck, the hatch on the aircraft carrier's island superstructure burst open. The island operated like an airport's control tower, housing not only *Enterprise*'s navigation bridge but also the primary flight control station. Each pilot raced for his respective single-engine, propeller-driven plane, ducking under wings and sidestepping tails of others as they made for their mounts.

"Morning, sir," Leaming greeted his pilot. Lieutenant (Junior Grade) Hart Dale Hilton handed Leaming his chart board as he climbed up onto their plane's wing and into the cockpit to check his instruments. Radiomen new to their squadrons flew with a variety of pilots during their training period, but by December 1941, Jack Leaming was the regular radioman/gunner for Dale Hilton of Scouting Six. Hilton, seven years older than his enlisted partner, was as congenial and jovial as always as he ran through his flight check. A 1936 graduate of the University of Southern California, Hilton had gone through flight training at Pensacola, Florida. His first three years of flying had been in torpedo bombers with Torpedo Squadron Five (VT-5), but his transition into *Enterprise*'s scout bomber squadron had been smooth. He and Leaming had developed a mutual admiration for each other's abilities. "As my gunner and radioman, he was a great teammate," recalled Hilton. "No pilot could have had a better one."[5]

The peacetime training and routines of carrier operation had taken a new twist for Jack Leaming and his fellow *Enterprise* Air Group aviators one week earlier, on November 28, 1941, as their carrier prepared to depart Pearl Harbor in the Hawaiian Islands on a special mission. Vice Admiral William F. Halsey, the senior naval aviator in the Pacific Fleet, was on board *Enterprise* to direct the delivery of a Marine fighter squadron to U.S.-held Wake Island, some twenty-three hundred miles west of Oahu. Halsey was respected by the *Enterprise* air group. He was the only vice admiral in the Navy who was a certified naval aviator, even if he had earned his gold wings at age fifty-two. Now, nearly seven years later, he roamed the bridge of the carrier that served as the flagship for his task force. Halsey was later nicknamed "Bull" by the press, both for his fearless and often blunt persona and his bulldoglike facial features, but to his aviators, Admiral Halsey was gregarious and approachable. They felt that he truly cared about their safety and well-being.

Halsey had been less than pleased earlier, in the spring of 1941, when his flagship had been

U.S. Navy

Vice Admiral William F. Halsey.

tagged to assist with a new Warner Bros. film. The high-budget movie *Dive Bomber* was filmed at San Diego and Los Angeles with carrier footage captured on board *Enterprise*. The stars were Errol Flynn—a glamorous leading man known for his roles in such films as *The Sea Hawk* and *The Adventures of Robin Hood*—and Fred MacMurray, one of the highest-paid actors in Hollywood. Cameramen spent a week filming flight operations on the Big E.[6]

On the day shooting wrapped, a cranky Halsey yelled down to the film crews and the Hollywood actors to "get the hell off my ship!" In spite of the admiral's annoyance at the interruptions caused by the moviemakers, the Technicolor drama about Navy dive bomber pilots would be inspirational to many fledgling aviators. Among those who watched *Dive Bomber* in late 1941 was one Ensign Eldor Rodenburg. Fresh from earning his Navy pilot wings at Opa-locka NAS (Naval Air Station) in Miami on October 20, 1941, Rodenburg took his future wife to see the movie. Little could he expect that in a matter of months he would be just like Flynn—flying Navy dive-bombers and doing it from none other than the *Enterprise* itself.

There was no Hollywood glamour and glitz when the Big E departed Hawaii on November 28 on her special mission to Wake Island. That day, eighty-one aircraft from five squadrons took off from Oahu to fly out to *Enterprise* as she stood out to sea. Landing on board the 825-foot carrier were sixteen Grumman F4F Wildcat fighters of her own Fighting Six, plus another dozen F4Fs of Marine VMF-211. Also landing without incident were the eighteen Douglas TBD-1 Devastator torpedo bombers of *Enterprise*'s Torpedo Six. The other thirty-seven aircraft to land on the wooden flight deck were Douglas SBD-2 and SBD-3 Dauntless dive-bombers, the most modern carrier bombers assigned to the U.S. Pacific Fleet.[7]

An SBD was normally assigned to the *Enterprise* air group commander, while eighteen each were allocated to Scouting Six and Bombing Six. By midafternoon on November 28, the transfer of airplanes from Hawaii out to the Big E's flight deck was complete. Radioman Third Class Leaming and pilot Dale Hilton felt no indications or premonitions of any unusual events as they landed their VS-6 Dauntless.[8]

When the *Enterprise* aviators assembled in their ready rooms, however, they found that conditions had indeed changed. Mimeographed sheets from Admiral Halsey were distributed to each pilot. Orders from the carrier's skipper, Captain George Davis Murray, and from Halsey announced that *"Enterprise* is now operating under war conditions." The aviators must be ready for "instant action" both day and night and alert for hostile submarines at sea. The orders also included the advice, "Steady nerves and stout hearts are needed now."[9]

The many months of flight training endured by the pilots and their gunners would now be put to the test. A true life-or-death encounter with a hostile enemy would allow no room for mistakes.

With four years in the service, Leaming was well-versed in the ways of Navy life. Some of his younger enlisted comrades, however, were still learning the ropes in their respective dive-bomber squadrons. They hailed from big cities like Detroit and Milwaukee, and from map-dot towns such as Plainview, Texas, and Engelhard, North Carolina. Among them was nineteen-year-old Donald Laurence Hoff, who had just earned his rating of radioman third class with Scouting Six.

Hoff, a 1940 Mariposa, California, high school graduate, had started attending Coalinga Junior College in California that fall. He had made an agreement with his single mom that he would work part-time jobs to make payments on his pickup, but jobs proved to be scarce. In a council of war with his mother, Hoff agreed that it was best for him to join the Navy. The husky youth breezed through basic training and radio school with little problem, graduating near the top of his class.[10]

Hoff's commanding officer convinced him that aviation offered better financial rewards than what he could make in the ship's company radio gang. As a third-class radioman, he would be paid ninety dollars a month—a fifty percent increase over the sixty dollars a month he would make as a shipboard third-class petty officer. Hoff decided that he would like to fly in one of the big twin-engine PBY Catalina patrol planes, making scouting missions. Instead, he was assigned to Scouting Squadron Six on the carrier *Enterprise.* "Nobody ever explained to me that scouting squadrons do dive-bombing the same as bombing squadrons do," he related.

Hoff was dumbfounded the day he climbed out of a truck with his seabags and stared up at the massive warship moored near the wharf. He had never even seen a Navy ship in his young life. "What is that?" he asked.

A nearby old-timer replied, "That's the USS *Enterprise*."

Hoff boarded the Navy's newest carrier completely naive. He learned quickly not to ask stupid questions. He found that the old-timers enjoyed peppering greenhorns with sarcastic remarks and lies to confuse them. Don Hoff's first night on the massive ship was not a pleasant one. His bunk in the floating city of more than two thousand souls was in the enlisted men's quarters, deep within the Big E's bowels. Mentally exhausted by the time he reached his lower-deck berthing compartment, he found his lower-level bunk, dropped into it, and drifted off to sleep.[11]

Hoff was wearing only his shorts when he was startled awake around midnight by warm water splashing on his chest and stomach. As the liquid splattered onto his face, his eyes quickly found the source of the cascade—a thoroughly inebriated aviator who had stumbled back aboard from shore leave. The man was now urinating on Hoff and his bunk. *How long am I going to put up with this life?* Hoff wondered.

The younger radiomen/gunners like Hoff who had fewer flying hours were generally shuffled between different pilots. RM3c Stuart James Mason from Portland was assigned to Bombing Six's plane number eighteen, the one most often flown in rotation by the most junior pilots. Mason had been so eager to join the Navy that he first tried to enlist at age fourteen in 1935. When he walked into the local recruiting office, he immediately noticed a big sign that read: MEN, DON'T LIE ABOUT YOUR AGE. When a chief asked him his age, Mason replied, "Fourteen."[12]

"Let me see your muscle," the chief petty officer said.

Mason flexed his scrawny arm. The recruiter said, "Come back when you're seventeen."

In September 1938, he was back to pass the recruiting exams and to enlist in the U.S. Navy. Mason's initial experiences with his new military life were more pleasing than those of Don Hoff. When Mason arrived at his first training center in San Diego, he was served a lunch of Swiss steak, mashed potatoes, gravy, vegetables, salad, apple pie, coffee, and milk. A child of the Depression years, he immediately decided, *I've found myself a home.*

Stuart Mason's first seven months on board *Enterprise* had been strictly grunt work: mess cooking, cleaning compartments, and scrubbing the bilges of the carrier's forty-foot motor launch. His break came when he was transferred to the ship's radio gang, where he had to learn Morse code in a hurry. By the first of September, 1941, Mason had joined Bombing Six. After qualifying in gunnery, he became the low man on the totem pole. As such, he rotated flight assignments. The lack of a permanently assigned pilot was little matter to young Mason—it was still a hell of a lot better than chipping paint or scrubbing the motor launch.

The gunners were under the direction of a senior petty officer in each of the *Enterprise* bomber squadrons. Scouting Six fell under the direction of Radioman First Class Harold Thomas. Some of his teenage radiomen barely needed to shave, so Thomas at age thirty-five was truly a father figure to them. His weathered face would sport an engaging smile of patience when one of his youngsters made a mistake. Thomas would explain the serious nature of the situation and help the newer men work to prevent making the same error again.[13]

Chief Aviation Radioman James Francis Murray, as the senior gunner for Bombing Six, was a no-nonsense kind of guy. At age thirty-two, Murray found Navy life to be old hat. He had graduated from Lincoln High School in Tacoma, Washington, in June 1927 and enlisted in the Navy at the end of the summer. With more than fourteen years in the Navy, he had more experience than most of the commissioned officer pilots, and was older than most of them as well. He had spent time on two other carriers before joining *Enterprise*'s Bombing Six, and he was the only gunner whose uniform sported an insignia of the Submarine Service, a dolphin patch. Murray was serving as a radioman and sonar operator on board the submarine *Bass* (SS-164) when his orders had come to report to flight training.[14]

Jim Murray expected a lot of his men, but only because he expected the same level of performance out of himself. In the air, he was alert and dependable. On board ship, he was in charge of all the scheduling, evaluations, and various issues that came with directing a large group of young aviators, most of whom were fairly naive to the imminent nature of war.

When Admiral Halsey announced that *Enterprise* was operating under wartime conditions as she put to sea on November 28, radioman Don

Hoff still did not comprehend the seriousness of it. "Being as young and inexperienced as I was," he said, "I was assuming that they were practicing war games."[15]

On board his carrier, Hoff became familiar with the Marine fighter pilots who were hitching a ride to their new air base on Wake Island, some twenty-three hundred miles west of Hawaii. On Thursday, December 4, *Enterprise* dutifully launched the dozen Marine Wildcats fighters for Wake. Hoff flew in the rear cockpit of one of the Dauntless dive-bombers that escorted the planes. His carrier was already turning back east toward the Hawaiian Islands when he returned. In a matter of days, his new Marine friends would either be killed or taken as prisoners of war when the Japanese invaded Wake Island.

Her delivery mission completed, *Enterprise* was scheduled to arrive back at Pearl Harbor on Sunday morning, December 7. Hoff was anticipating the liberty he would soon enjoy on Oahu. One of his Scouting Six comrades, Jack Leaming, was excited about more than just the free time ashore. His four-year enlistment in the Navy would end on December 9.

U.S. Navy

Radioman Jack Leaming (*right*) with Scouting Six buddy Joe Cupples. Just weeks after this photo was taken in early 1943, Leaming's plane would be shot down.

In his downtime on board ship, Leaming had been learning how to weld under the tutelage of Erwin G. Bailey, an aviation machinist's mate also attached to Scouting Six. Both men's enlistments expired at the same time, and they already had plans to hire on at Rohr Aircraft in San Diego upon their return. But first, they hoped to live it up one last time in Hawaii with a squadron mate, RM1c Joe Cupples, who was also leaving the service. "We would have one helluva celebration," recalled Leaming of their return to Pearl Harbor.[16]

Harold Thomas and Jim Murray, as the most senior radiomen, always flew with their respective Dauntless squadron skippers. For the morning mission of December 7, Thomas would fly with his VS-6 skipper while Murray remained on board the carrier with his CO, waiting for flight orders as the day played out. Each of the two bombing squadrons had eighteen pairs of pilots and gunners. Thomas and Murray's enlisted aviation gangs generally included a few spare greenhorns who were learning the ropes, able to fill in for a sick or injured radioman if necessary. Stuart Mason and Don Hoff, both low on the enlisted totem pole, would get their chances at combat in due time. Jack Leaming's introduction to war would come even sooner.

Early on December 7, eighteen Douglas SBD Dauntless dive-bombers were spotted for launch on the *Enterprise* flight deck as the big carrier plowed into the wind to fling them skyward.

"Stand by to start engines!" blared from the loudspeaker.

Strapped into his rear cockpit seat, radioman Jack Leaming was happy that his SBD's plane captain was handling the inertia starter this morning. The hand crank took all of Leaming's one hundred and thirty pounds and all his strength "to get the damn thing turning fast enough to start the engine when the pilot engaged it."[17]

"Start engines!"

Across the flight deck, the high-pitched whines of inertia starters were followed by coughs and sputters from eighteen Dauntless engines. As the dive-bombers roared to life, their propellers became spinning disks of silver with painted yellow tips to help make them more visible to the flight deck personnel.

At 0618, the launching signal officer waved his flag in a circular motion to cue the first pilot to rev up his engine for takeoff. When the pilot nodded his head to indicate a proper engine run-up, the signal officer pointed the flag toward the bow of the carrier. The pilot released his brakes and the first SBD began accelerating down the flight deck's teakwood planks. As the Big E approached the Hawaiian Islands fresh from her Wake Island delivery, these eighteen scout bombers and their thirty-six airmen would scour the oceans ahead of their mother ship, looking for trouble.

The first dive-bomber off *Enterprise*'s flight deck was that of the commander, *Enterprise* Air Group (CEAG), Lieutenant Commander Howard Leyland Young. Forty-year-old Young was often called by the nickname "Brigham" by his fellow pilots. A graduate of the Naval Academy class of 1923, Young had taken over as the CEAG in April after having served two years in Fighting Six. He had won his wings in 1926, following several years aboard surface ships, and thereafter served in several aviation units, including VF-2 on board the carrier *Langley* and Bombing Two on board the carrier *Saratoga* (CV-3). Young was one of a select few who had been a member of the air detachments of both of the U.S. Navy's two helium-filled flying carriers, *Akron* (ZRS-4) and *Macon* (ZRS-5). Young and his fellow airmen were fortunately not on board when *Akron* was torn apart in a storm off the Atlantic coast in 1933 that killed seventy-three passengers and crewmen. He was not lost with the former airship because she departed on her final flight in 1933 without embarking her air detachment. Young had also been transferred prior to *Macon*'s loss in 1935. The air group commander was respected by his *Enterprise* aviators for his flying abilities and a demonstrated desire to take care of his men.[18]

Brigham Young's scouting flight was under orders to search out 150 miles from the northeast to the southeast ahead of *Enterprise*'s course toward Oahu. Each two-plane section was assigned a ten-degree sector along a set of spokes that ranged from 045 degrees true through 125 degrees true. At the completion of their searches, the pilots were to fly into Oahu and land on Ford Island's Naval Air Station (NAS) Pearl Harbor.

None of Young's blue-gray Dauntlesses had been loaded with bombs for this flight. The prewar conditions were also evident in the fact that none of the SBDs possessed protective armor plates or self-sealing gasoline tanks to guard against enemy gunfire. Each rear cockpit was generally occupied by an aviation radioman or aviation machinist's mate who was capable of manning both the SBD's radio gear and the .30-caliber machine gun. Yet the rear seat in Brigham Young's Dauntless was occupied this morning by Lieutenant Commander Bromfield Bradford Nichol, a tactical officer of Halsey's staff. Nichol, thirty-seven, was charged with personally reporting to Admiral Chester Nimitz on the success of the *Enterprise*'s recent delivery of aircraft to Wake Island.[19]

The majority of the pilots of Young's December 7 fly-in scout mission were from Scouting Six. The squadron's skipper, Lieutenant Commander Hallsted Lubeck Hopping, was flying the search sector adjacent to Brigham Young. From the academy class of 1924, Hopping was a strong, lean, six-foot-one man with natural flying abilities. He was considered brilliant by many of his pilots but also tough to maintain formation on as a wingman.

Many of the fliers were eager to see girlfriends or wives ashore. One of the few Bombing Six pilots making the morning search was Ensign Manuel "Manny" Gonzalez. His wife, Jo Dene, resided on Oahu, and Gonzalez had approached fellow pilot Lieutenant (Junior Grade) Edward Lee "Andy" Anderson to effect a swap of assignments for this flight in the hopes of getting some extra time with her. Anderson had no family on the island, so when Gonzalez asked to take his place, he relinquished his spot. Unbeknownst to Gonzalez, his wife and several other VB-6 wives had already sailed for the West Coast on December 5 aboard the passenger steamship *Lurline*.[20]

As the search flight broke up into teams of two to cover their respective sectors, some of the enlisted bachelors were anticipating their downtime that was but hours away. Jack Leaming was belted into his rear cockpit, facing aft behind his Browning .30-caliber single machine gun. The Pacific Ocean below was a brilliant blue, dotted with only small whitecaps. After lifting off from the carrier, he heard nothing over the radio during the first hour of his plane's scouting mission. The only audible distraction was the sweet music of his Dauntless's Wright Cyclone engine as it hummed along at 150 knots.

Only yards away, flying tight formation as wingman, was another dive-bomber, similarly painted with blue-gray upper surfaces and light gray lower surfaces. Just below the rising slope of the aircraft's tail was a large blue circle containing a white star with a red center, indicating that it was another U.S. Navy aircraft. Just forward of this painted star and just aft of the rear gunner's cockpit was the only visible difference in the other dive-bomber that Leaming could barely make out through the bright early morning sun. Painted in black was the plane number, 6-S-5. To those in the know, this indicated that it was plane number five of Scouting Squadron Six. Leaming's own bomber sported the black call sign 6-S-7.

The morning mission went without incident, and at the ends of their search sectors, each team turned toward Oahu. Brigham Young was flying in company with a twenty-five-year-old VS-6 ensign, Perry Lee Teaff from Oklahoma. Teaff was an able wingman who had earned his bachelor's degree from State Teacher's College in Springfield, Missouri, before being appointed as an aviation cadet in 1938. He was considered something of a prankster among his squadron mates, but he was serious about his flying business. Back in California, he had a young wife and newborn daughter to provide for. Teaff and Young passed over several ships as they approached Pearl Harbor, the first being the oil tanker SS *Pat Doheny*. Around 0740, Young next spotted the submarine *Thresher*, in company with the destroyer *Litchfield*.[21]

By 0800, Dale Hilton's section had made no contacts in his sector, so he called back to Leaming to obtain a radio bearing on KGU Honolulu. This radio station and another Honolulu station would serve as a homing beacon for incoming aircraft, including a flight of big Army B-17 bombers that was expected to fly into Hickam Field that morning. Hilton headed for Barbers Point in silence with Ensign Edwin John Kroeger, his VB-6 wingman.[22]

Kroeger, a former baseball and football player known as "Bud" to his fellow pilots, was a graduate of Purdue. He had flown gliders at age nineteen and was appointed a naval aviator in August 1938. Bud Kroeger had been only a standby pilot on December 7, but when VS-6 pilot Ensign Earl Donnell's 6-S-18 plane was given a "down" signal by the plane director, Kroeger had been quickly slotted to fly wing on Hilton. As the two SBD crews sped in toward the coast of Oahu, they had no premonitions of the chaos that was about to unfurl around them.[23]

Approaching Pearl Harbor at the same time as the *Enterprise* SBDs was a force of 183 Imperial Japanese Navy (IJN) warplanes. They had commenced launching around 0600, just as the Big E air crews were warming up on deck.

Watching them take off from the bridge of his flagship was the small, weathered, fifty-five-year-old former aviator who was commander of the Japanese First Air Fleet. As such, Vice Admiral Chuichi Nagumo was also the commandant of the IJN's First Mobile Striking Force, known in Japanese as the Kido Butai. Nagumo's imposing force comprised six aircraft carriers, two battleships, three cruisers, nine destroyers, plus accompanying fleet tankers. Submarines offered protection for the fleet, and were prepared to launch miniature subs as part of the coordinated attack plan.

Nagumo was a serious officer who could at times be abrasive. His dress uniform hung heavy with medals, a testament to his impressive career. Not every mission was one he relished, but Admiral Nagumo carried out the assignments from his superiors with his usual passion. The job at hand today was no exception: Although he had not been in support of it, Nagumo was the man in charge of executing the attack on the Hawaiian Islands masterminded by Admiral Isoroku Yamamoto.

As commander in chief of Japan's Combined Fleet, Yamamoto was determined to have the final say in Pacific war strategy, even if some of his actions made him and his staff unpopular at Tokyo's Imperial General Headquarters. He had insisted that if Japan's domination plans were to continue successfully, then the U.S. Navy headquartered at

U.S. Navy

Vice Admiral Chuichi Nagumo.

Pearl Harbor must be dealt a crippling blow. During a heated debate with Japan's military leadership, Yamamoto threatened that he and his staff would resign if they did not get their way. His ploy worked, and he entrusted Nagumo to take care of business. On the same day that the U.S. Pacific Fleet's main anchorage at Pearl was attacked, other Japanese military forces would strike against the British at Hong Kong and on the Malay Peninsula and American forces at Manila in the Philippine Islands.

During the predawn hours of December 7, Admiral Nagumo visited his strike commander in the operations room of his flagship carrier *Akagi*. Commander Mitsuo Fuchida had been handpicked months earlier to lead the aerial assault. "I have every confidence in you," Nagumo assured him before Fuchida's pilots headed topside for their aircraft. The Kido Butai carriers swung into the wind and commenced launching the first strikers toward Oahu. At 855 feet in length and displacing more than forty-one thousand tons, the flagship carrier *Akagi* was enormous— slightly longer and nearly twice the displacement of the USS *Enterprise*.

Steaming near Nagumo's *Akagi*, five other IJN flattops—*Kaga*, *Hiryu*, *Soryu*, *Zuikaku*, and *Shokaku*—also began hurling their warplanes into the skies. Commander Fuchida's first strike group launched about 230 miles north and slightly east of Oahu, even as the Big E's scouts were launching to the west of the island. Each Japanese aircraft sported a red circle, their Rising Sun national emblem, on their after fuselage and on their wings. The distinct red balls soon became known to American aviators as "meatballs."

Lieutenant Yoshio Shiga, leading a division of nine *Kaga* fighter pilots, had been so excited as the fleet approached the Hawaiian Islands the previous night that he finally went to the ship's doctor for some sleeping pills. The next morning, he dressed in his best uniform and enjoyed a ceremonial breakfast before his fighter lifted off with the first strike wave. Lieutenant Shiga was feeling nostalgic as his target area approached. From his cockpit, the coastline of Oahu was pleasantly familiar. Shiga had visited Honolulu in 1934 on a naval training cruise after his graduation from Japan's naval academy. One of his targets would be strafing the Marine field at Ewa and engaging any American aircraft that rose to greet his fellow pilots.[24]

Some of Japan's finest naval aviators were at the controls of this first wave of attackers. Although the Japanese planes were unfamiliar to the Americans, they would soon give each model a nickname. The Aichi D3A1 Type 99 carrier dive-bomber would shortly be referred to commonly as a "Val." The Mitsubishi A6M2 Type 00 carrier fighter plane would simply become the "Zero," and the Nakajima B5N2 Type 97 torpedo bomber would be referred to as a "Kate." Behind the first wave of Japanese carrier attack planes, a second wave of 167 aircraft was also launched with the intent of finishing off whatever cripples remained from the first assualt.

Commander Fuchida's strikers were unchallenged during the flights into Pearl Harbor. At 0749, he gave the order to attack to his squadron leaders, who were surveying the ninety-six American ships nestled in the tranquil harbor below. He was so confident that surprise had been achieved that at 0753, he keyed the prepared signal words back to Admiral Nagumo and the other carriers: "Tora, Tora, Tora." The U.S. fleet had been caught sleeping, and the seven prized battleships lazily moored near Ford Island along Battleship Row would pay the price.

Kate torpedo bombers swept in low to release their aerial torpedoes against the battleships and other key warships. Fuchida's Val dive-bombers split to attack both the plentiful American shipping targets and the Army and Navy airfields. Zero pilots strafed U.S. aircraft caught parked on the runways and were quick to engage unsuspecting planes in the sky. The Sunday-morning silence was replaced by the explosions of bombs and torpedoes as they began ripping open U.S. warships.

At 0758, an alarm finally sounded: "Air raid, Pearl Harbor. This is not a drill!"

Hell had fallen from a clear morning sky onto the U.S. Pacific Fleet. Lieutenant Shiga and his fellow pilots would have a field day against the unsuspecting American aviators.

TWO

"Our World Was Shattered"

CEAG Brigham Young and wingman Perry Teaff were among the first to encounter the Japanese strike planes. Young was passing Barbers Point to seaward of Oahu when he noticed a squadron of aircraft circling Ewa Field in column. He assumed them to be U.S. Army pursuit planes, and gave a wide berth. Decreasing his altitude to about eight hundred feet, he continued on toward Ford Island Field. Lieutenant Commander Brom Nichol, riding passenger in Young's rear seat, was appalled that the Army was apparently conducting training on a Sunday morning.

Ensign Teaff made no effort to maneuver as the first of these planes approached his tail. Seventy-five feet behind him, it opened fire. Teaff was stunned as he realized that 7.7-mm bullets from a Japanese Mitsubishi Zero fighter plane were glancing off his wing surfaces. His Dauntless was not severely damaged, although its horizontal stabilizer was holed. By the time the Zero came in for a second pass, Teaff was recovered enough to counter with a tight turn to starboard. His rear gunner, twenty-two-year-old Texan Edgar Jinks, opened up with a short burst from his .30-caliber machine gun.[1]

This burst was apparently enough to convince the Zero pilot to shift to the Dauntless of Brigham Young. The CEAG noticed antiaircraft fire ahead and put his SBD into violent maneuvers. Recognizing the Rising Sun insignia of one plane that had completed a dive on him, he dove his SBD toward the ground, zigzagging. He shouted back to Brom Nichol,

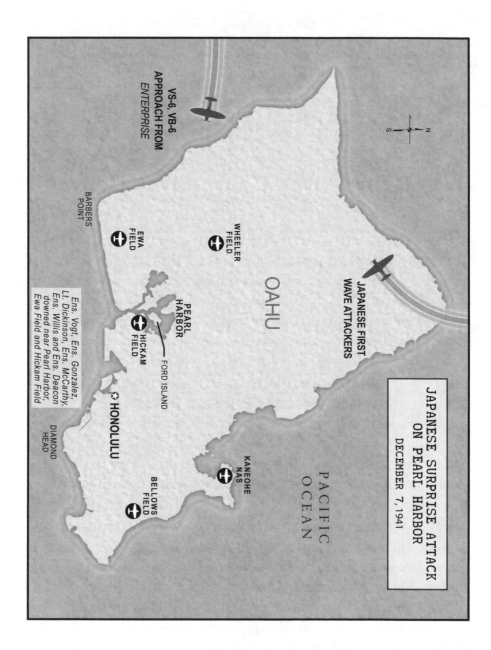

JAPANESE SURPRISE ATTACK
ON PEARL HARBOR
DECEMBER 7, 1941

OAHU

PACIFIC
OCEAN

JAPANESE FIRST
WAVE ATTACKERS

VS-6, VB-6
APPROACH FROM
ENTERPRISE

BARBERS
POINT

EWA
FIELD

WHEELER
FIELD

PEARL
HARBOR

HICKAM
FIELD

FORD ISLAND

HONOLULU

DIAMOND
HEAD

KANEOHE
NAS

BELLOWS
FIELD

Ens. Vogt, Ens. Gonzalez,
Lt. Dickinson, Ens. McCarthy,
Ens. Willis and Ens. Deacon
downed near Pearl Harbor,
Ewa Field and Hickam Field

N

S

"Get the gun out!" The staff commander, rusty on the use of the single .30-caliber, fumbled with unshipping the mount to get it into a firing position. He was unable to return fire. As for Young, his fixed guns were loaded and charged but he found no opportunity to use them.[2]

Teaff and Young managed to shake their attacker, but their evasive actions took them down low over a canefield north of Pearl City on Pearl Harbor's northwestern shore. Instantly they were met with antiaircraft fire. They did not have sufficient fuel to return to the *Enterprise*, even if they could get away from the island. Hoping that they would be recognized as friendly, Young decided to make a low approach to Ford Island Field and land. "I had no alternative," he recalled.

The *Enterprise* Dauntlesses were under heavy fire from American ships and shore gunners alike as they dropped their flaps and landing gear to attempt a landing at Ford Island. Everything airborne had suddenly become "enemy" to the rattled American soldiers and sailors. Their planes making their slow descent to the runway, Young and Teaff were subject to intense friendly fire. As Young's Dauntless rolled to a stop, he was greeted by the commander of the Naval Air Station, Captain James M. Shoemaker. As Shoemaker was driving over to meet them, Teaff pulled out of his landing approach and made a second pass on the field while still under heavy friendly fire. As Shoemaker approached their plane, Young and Nichol yelled, "What the hell goes on here?"[3]

Many of Brigham Young's junior pilots would not be so fortunate in their first encounters with the Japanese. Lieutenant Clarence Earle Dickinson's two-plane section was approaching Oahu around 0825 at fifteen hundred feet. Dickinson, a tall, lean twenty-nine-year-old flight officer of Scouting Six who hailed from North Carolina, was a 1934 academy graduate and one of the squadron's more experienced pilots. Because of his thin frame and excitable nature, Dickinson was called "Dickie Bird" by some behind his back.

The morning's launch from *Enterprise* was likely to be one of the last for Dickinson's rear seat man, RM1c William Cicero Miller, a twenty-year-old farm boy from Thomasville, North Carolina. Like others in his squadron, Miller's enlistment was about to expire, and he had plans to return to the States to marry his sweetheart. With three years of service

		USS *Enterprise* Morning Search Pearl Harbor: December 7, 1941		
PLANE	PILOT	REAR SEAT GUNNER/ PASSENGER	SECTOR
CEAG	Lt. Cdr. Howard Leyland Young	Lt. Cdr. Bromfield Bradford Nichol	085–095
6-S-2	Lt. (jg) Perry Lee Teaff	RM3c Edgar Phelan Jinks	085–095
6-S-1	Lt. Cdr. Hallsted Lubeck Hopping	RM1c Harold "R" Thomas	095–105
6-S-3	Ens. John Henry Leon Vogt*	RM3c Sidney Pierce*	095–105
6-S-4	Lt. Clarence Earle Dickinson Jr.	RM1c William Cicero Miller*	105–115
6-S-9	Ens. John Reginald McCarthy**	RM3c Mitchell Cohn*	105–115
6-S-7	Lt. (jg) Hart Dale Hilton	ARM2c Jack Leaming	115–125
6-B-5	Ens. Edward John Kroeger	RM2c Walter F. Chapman	115–125
6-S-11	Ens. Carleton Thayer Fogg	RM3c Otis Lee Dennis	125–135
6-S-8	Ens. Cleo John Dobson	RM3c Roy L. Hoss	125–135

6-S-10	Lt. Wilmer Earl Gallaher	ARM1c Thomas Edward Merritt	075–085
6-S-5	Ens. William Price West	RM3c Louis Dale Hansen	075–085
6-S-16	Lt. Frank Anthony Patriarca	RM1c Joseph Ferdinand DeLuca	065–075
6-S-15	Ens. Walter Michael Willis*	Cox Fred John Ducolon*	065–075
6-S-14	Ens. Edward Thorpe Deacon**	RM3c Audrey Gerard Coslett**	055–065
6-B-9	Ens. Wilbur Edison Roberts	AMM3c Donald H. Jones	055–065
6-B-3	Ens. Manuel Gonzalez*	RM3c Leonard Joseph Kozelek*	045–055
6-B-12	Ens. Frederick Thomas Weber	Sea1c Lee Edward John Keaney	045–055

*Killed in action December 7, 1941.
**Injured or wounded on December 7, 1941.

in VS-6, he had been flying with Dickinson since his pilot had joined the squadron in April 1941.[4]

Before he climbed into his rear cockpit that morning, Miller had remarked to Dickinson that his four years of sea duty ended soon and he was the only one of twenty-one fellow radio school students who had not yet crashed in the water. "Hope you won't get me wet this morning, sir," Miller joked.[5]

Dickinson reassured his gunner that all they had to do was get through the morning's flight. The first two hours were without incident until they approached Barbers Point. Soon, noticing antiaircraft bursts above Pearl Harbor and heavy smoke rising from Battleship Row, Dickinson assumed that some Coastal Artillery batteries "had gone stark mad and were shooting wildly" on a Sunday morning. "Just wait!" he said over his intercom mike. "Tomorrow the Army will certainly catch hell for that!"[6]

Dickinson motioned to his wingman, Ensign McCarthy, to close up alongside, and then led their section up to four thousand feet above Barbers Point. John Reginald McCarthy, a twenty-four-year-old graduate of the University of Minnesota, actually had more flight experience than his senior pilot Dickinson. Known as "Bud" or "Mac" to many, McCarthy was also nicknamed "Charlie" in reference to comedian and ventriloquist Edgar Bergen's dummy of the same surname. With his serious face and good-guy personality, McCarthy was the antithesis of his section leader, Dickinson.[7]

As they approached Pearl Harbor, the two American planes were jumped by a pair of Zeros from the carrier *Soryu*. The SBD pilots pushed over into steep dives as the Japanese fighters began firing into McCarthy's trailing 6-S-9, quickly setting ablaze his right main fuel tank and the right side of his engine. McCarthy continued strong evasive action, but the Zeros had thoroughly riddled his plane. His gunner, twenty-one-year-old RM3c Mitchell Cohn from New York, may have been killed by some of the 7.7-mm slugs, for he made no effort to escape his badly damaged aircraft.

McCarthy, realizing that his plane was mortally crippled, fought free from the cockpit and bailed out. His leg was badly injured when it struck one of the stabilizers—the fixed horizontal wing sections on either side of his SBD's tail. McCarthy's parachute barely opened at a mere two hundred feet. The crippled SBD slammed into the ground near Ewa Beach, about a mile off Ewa Field's southwest runway, with Cohn still aboard. McCarthy managed to land in a tree, but when he tried to climb free, he fell and broke his previously injured leg.[8]

Meanwhile, the Zero that had downed McCarthy zipped past Lieutenant Dickinson to his left. Dickinson rolled his plane to get a shot at him with his fixed guns. As the Zero pulled up in front of him and to the left, Dickinson saw painted on his fuselage a telltale insignia. *That red disk on his white wing looks like a big fried egg with a red yolk,* he thought. McCarthy's opponent escaped, but Dickinson was quickly beset by the fury of five more *Soryu* Zeros that locked onto his tail. Radioman Miller opened fire on the fighters with his single .30-caliber Browning tail gun and kept up constant reports to his pilot. A minute later, Miller calmly announced over the intercom, "Mr. Dickinson, I have been hit once, but I think I have got one of these sons of bitches."[9]

Miller's target was likely Seaman First Class Isao Doikawa, whose A6M2 was the only *Soryu* fighter to sustain bullet damage. Doikawa would return to his carrier claiming three aerial victories against American opponents.[10]

Dickinson looked aft and saw a Japanese plane on fire, then returned his attention to the other fighters shooting up the tail of his own plane. He turned aggressively to throw off their aim, but his SBD was taking a pounding. The Zeros' explosive and incendiary bullets "clattered on my metal wing like hail on a tin roof," Dickinson recalled. A line of big holes crept across his wing. One punctured his left wing's gasoline tank.[11]

As the wing caught fire, Dickinson called back to his gunner, "Are you all right, Miller?"

Miller replied that he had expended all six cans of his ammunition, then let loose with a horrifying scream as he was shot again. "It was as if he opened his lungs and just let go," Dickinson wrote. "I have never heard any comparable human sound. I believe that Miller died right then." When he called again to the rear cockpit, there was no reply.[12]

Dickinson's 6-S-4 was a flying wreck, its control cables shot away and its left wing in flames. As Zeros pulled into him again, his SBD refused to respond and instead went into a right spin less than a thousand feet above the ground. Dickinson unbuckled himself, ripped his radio cord free, grasped the sides of his cockpit, and pushed himself from his burning plane. He tumbled over and over before finally pulling his ripcord. He was in the air just long enough to hear his Dauntless—with Miller still aboard—explode as it crashed into the ground below. Dickinson struck a dirt road feet-first, followed by his rear end and finally his head. With the wind knocked out of him, he took a moment to untangle himself from his silk chute. A quick inspection found only a thorn embedded in his scalp from a bush and slight nicks on his anklebone where Japanese machine gun bullets had sliced his sock.[13]

I've got to get myself to Pearl Harbor! he thought. Dickinson alternately walked and ran a quarter of a mile to the main road that bordered Oahu's canefields. In the distance he could hear the booming of antiaircraft batteries, and he could feel the tremor caused by bomb explosions.[14]

He was able to flag down a middle-aged couple who raced him to Hickam Field even as Japanese planes strafed civilian vehicles around them. Dickinson thanked the couple hurriedly and took off in a full sprint to the entrance gate, eager to find his way to another airplane. Buildings, ships, and aircraft burned furiously in the distance. Less than an hour had passed since he had been shot down.

S couting Six's skipper, Lieutenant Commander Hal Hopping, had lost his wingman en route to Oahu. Like Brigham Young earlier, Hopping had encountered the tanker *Pat Doheny* making her way to Honolulu. He had advised Ensign Johnny Vogt to remain out of gun range while he investigated the ship's identity. When Hopping next looked for Vogt, his wingman was out of sight, so he continued on in alone.[15]

Vogt's plane would be the first SBD lost on December 7, when he collided in midair with a Japanese Zero. Both aircraft were seen crashing to the ground a half mile from Ewa Field. Neither Vogt nor his gunner, nineteen-year-old ARM3c Sidney Pierce from Texas, survived. Vogt had served nearly two years with Scouting Six, and his loss would be sorely felt by many.

Ensign Johnny Vogt.

At 0810, ensigns Manny Gonzalez and Des Moines native Fred Weber were about twenty-five miles from Oahu when Weber suddenly sighted a large group of planes milling around between three thousand and four thousand feet. He had been flying about five hundred yards on the starboard and five hundred feet above Gonzalez. When he looked for him again after studying the other planes, he found that Gonzalez was nowhere to be seen.

Gonzalez obviously mistook the Japanese strikers for Army planes. As his Dauntless suddenly came under Zero gunfire, the ensign issued an urgent radio call at 0833: "Do not attack me! This is Six Baker Three, an American plane!" His SBD was heavily riddled with 7.7-mm fire, and Gonzalez yelled to his rear

U.S. Navy

Ensign Manuel Gonzalez.

gunner, twenty-three-year-old RM3c Leonard Joseph Kozelek, "Stand by to get out the rubber boat!" It was too late. Six Val dive-bombers from the carrier *Shokaku* engaged the Dauntless and blasted Gonzalez and Kozelek to their deaths.

Weber banked to make a wide circle and commenced a series of S-turns while scanning for his section leader. He noticed a plane ahead of him at the same altitude and course. He tried to catch up with him, thinking that it was Gonzalez, yet was soon stunned to witness the plane flip around and begin a run on him. He finally spotted a large red circle on the other plane's port wing and realized it was a Japanese aircraft. Weber plunged down to about twenty-five feet off the water and applied throttle. The Zero made no attempt to follow. Weber told his gunner, Seaman First Class Lee Keaney, to switch from the Hawaiian radio station KGU's frequency to that of *Enterprise* as he set course for Barbers Point.

As Hal Hopping neared Oahu solo, he saw heavy smoke rising from the harbor. Once abreast of Ewa Field, he sighted the first Japanese planes attacking the base. He broadcast a report that Pearl Harbor was being attacked by Japanese aircraft, and dived in through the antiaircraft fire to land at Ford Island. Hopping made it down safely at 0845, just the third *Enterprise* pilot to land after Young and Teaff.

· · ·

The other five sections of *Enterprise* Dauntlesses en route to Pearl Harbor fared better than many of their comrades. In the search sector immediately to the south of that of Weber and Gonzalez was the team of VS-6's Ensign Edward Thomas Deacon and VB-6's Ensign Wilbur "Bill" Roberts. Twenty-six-year-old Roberts, a graduate of the University of Michigan, was a slight young man who would prove to be solid and steady under fire. He spotted about thirty planes flying low on the whitecaps as they approached Oahu. They were painted a shade of green similar to that used on Army planes, which Roberts assumed them to be.[16]

Ed Deacon thought perhaps they were Army P-40s. His rear seat man, twenty-year-old RM3c Audrey Gerard "Jerry" Coslett, spotted strange markings on the unknown aircraft. He said dryly to his twenty-seven-year-old pilot, "It looks like the Army's changed the markings on their planes."[17]

The American and Japanese planes passed one another by, but not before Bill Roberts watched one through his telescopic sight as it approached him head-on. He could clearly see the red meatballs painted on its sides. *How stupid of the Army to paint their planes like that for war games*, he thought. *Someone might take them for Japanese!* The approaching aircraft appeared to be a torpedo plane. Roberts briefly considered how good a shot he could have if only it were an enemy aircraft. The two opposing pilots each rocked their wings in salute to each other and continued on.[18]

Deacon and Roberts's radiomen, Jerry Coslett and AMM1c Donald H. Jones, found that they were unable to communicate with the Ford Island tower because of considerable voice chatter on the circuit. Their SBDs passed over Fort Weaver at low altitude, and Roberts felt several bullets strike his plane.

The friendly fire from below also hit Deacon's SBD, while two Zeros commenced a firing run on him. Bullets from the Army gunners tore into Deacon's 6-S-14 and knocked the .30-caliber machine gun from Jerry Coslett's grasp. Slugs cut Deacon's parachute straps at the cushion and nicked the pilot's thigh. Coslett was hit by additional rounds that struck his right shoulder, right wrist, and the right side of his neck.[19]

Roberts observed white smoke or gasoline pouring from wingman

Deacon's SBD, as well as gasoline pouring from his own left wing as friendly rounds struck his plane. His engine sputtering and losing power, Ed Deacon was furious that he and his radioman were the victims of American gunners. Just short of Hickam Field, he was forced to make an emergency water landing with his wheels up in about two feet of water. He clambered out of his cockpit to help Coslett, only to find himself under rifle and machine-gun fire from the beach some two hundred yards away. He used the rear seat radio cord as a tourniquet on Coslett's forearm, then broke out the life raft.

The wounded men remained under friendly fire as Deacon paddled for the beach. Coslett was bleeding heavily from the forearm, which had lost two inches of bone from a single bullet. Fortunately, an Army crash boat set out from the dock at Hickam and recovered them. The vessel remained under rifle fire as it returned. As Deacon helped his wounded radioman toward an aid station, an Army sergeant handed Coslett a half-pint bottle of Old Crow to help drown his pains.[20]

Donald Jones, rear gunner for Ensign Roberts, considered bailing out of his SBD. Gasoline streamed from its port-side wing, and bullets had torn through his pant legs without injuring him. He opted to remain on board, and Roberts effected a safe landing on Hickam Field. Roberts hurried to the administration building to issue a Teletype message warning and returned to his SBD to send out similar radio messages to other aviators. Jones remained in his rear seat, using his Browning machine gun to fire at diving Japanese planes. "He was fortunate not to have been hit," Roberts said. Two new bullet holes were punched from top to bottom through their plane's tail. Other bullets had pierced the left elevator, left aileron, engine cowling, and both left fuel tanks. It was a miracle that Roberts had brought his plane down safely.[21]

Lieutenant (j.g.) Frank Anthony Patriarca and Ensign Walter Michael Willis were both attacked by Zeros as they neared Ewa Field. Patriarca and gunner Joe DeLuca were unable to keep tabs on their wingman in their efforts to evade the fighters. No trace would ever be found of Willis—considered one of the best pilots of Scouting Six—or his SBD. Lost with him was Coxswain Fred John Ducolon, the thirty-six-year-old squadron master-at-arms.

U.S. Navy

Ensign Walter Michael Willis.

Another inbound VS-6 team was that of Lieutenant Wilmer Earl Gallaher, the squadron's executive officer, and his wingman, Ensign William Price West. Gallaher, a lean thirty-four-year-old who hailed from Wilmington, Delaware, had graduated from the Naval Academy in 1931. Known to friends by his middle name, Earl, Gallaher had flown fighters off the carrier *Ranger* and patrol planes from the carrier *Langley* before serving a two-year stint as a pilot trainer at Pensacola. Some of his comrades considered him cocky and a stickler for regulations. Gallaher had joined Scouting Six in June 1940 as its flight officer, or third senior pilot. During his flight training at NAS Pensacola, he had dated the daughter of the station commandant, Captain Bill Halsey. Now Gallaher was second in command of VS-6 and Admiral Halsey was in command of the entire *Enterprise* task force.[22]

Gallaher's wingman, solid and stocky "Willie" West, was athletic. A day shy of his twenty-eighth birthday, West had been a boxer and all-fraternity handball champion at the University of Minnesota before winning his wings in November 1940. Near Oahu, the search team noticed ten brightly colored planes with fixed landing gear. "Did we miss something on the board this morning?" Gallaher asked his radioman, Tom Merritt. "Are we supposed to have an exercise with the Army?"[23]

Gallaher and West were unable to get into Ford Island on their first attempt due to heavy antiaircraft fire, so they returned to the vicinity of Barbers Point. They were soon joined by the last section of VS-6 to launch from *Enterprise*, ensigns Carleton Fogg and Cleo Dobson. Other members of Gallaher's stunned squadron soon joined. "Our world was shattered," said Jack Leaming, when he heard the frantic pleas of Ensign

Gonzalez over the radio. He and his pilot, Dale Hilton, also sought refuge off Barbers Point with their wingman, Ed Kroeger.[24]

The first wave of Japanese attackers had done great damage on the shipping and shore installations at Pearl Harbor. They had also destroyed dozens of aircraft on the ground and had managed to shoot down five Dauntlesses from the *Enterprise* air group. A sixth had been downed by friendly fire. The fury over Oahu had taken the lives of three SBD pilots (Manny Gonzalez, Walter Willis, and Johnny Vogt) and five rear seat gunners (Leonard Kozelek, Fred Ducolon, Sidney Pierce, Mitchell Cohn, and William Miller). Two other pilots, Ed Deacon and Mac McCarthy, and radioman Jerry Coslett had been wounded or injured.

One third of the *Enterprise* SBDs had been lost by 0900. Four planes had managed to land at Ford Island under heavy friendly fire. Eight other *Enterprise* Dauntlesses remained in the air after 0900, uncertain of where to go, and with the Japanese follow-up strike still to come.

Don Hoff, the nineteen-year-old junior radioman of Scouting Six, was also airborne but close to the ship. He and his pilot, Ensign Earl Donnell, had originally been assigned to be part of the eighteen-plane scout group flying into Pearl Harbor, but a fussy engine had caused them to give their place to Bud Kroeger. Hoff and Donnell then launched with two other Scouting Six SBD crews to perform antisubmarine and inner-air patrol duties. As he heard radio transmissions erupting from the Oahu area, Hoff thought to himself, *Boy, they sure are making these war games really serious.*

The Bombing Six and Scouting Six aviators still on board ship heard enough over the radios to realize it was no drill. In the VB-6 ready room, Lieutenant Richard Halsey Best had been anxiously riding out the morning hours. His wife and four-year-old daughter were awaiting his arrival in Hawaii, where he was due to begin a six-day leave once *Enterprise* had docked. Dick Best was well seasoned in Navy life. Following his graduation from the Naval Academy, his fleet service had started on board the light cruiser *Richmond*. He was a member of Flight Class 76 in Pensacola, Florida, and thereafter was assigned to Fighting Two on the carrier *Lexington*.[25]

Best's proven abilities as a pilot landed him an instructor position at

NAS Pensacola in June 1938, then a session at the Navy Photographic School. In May 1940, Best was assigned to be the flight officer, or third in command, of *Enterprise*'s Bombing Squadron Six, then based in California flying Northrop BT dive-bombers. By the spring of 1941, VB-6 had received the SBD dive-bomber, Bill Hollingsworth had been promoted to skipper of the squadron, and Lieutenant Best had fleeted up to second in command.[26]

Best's squadron skipper was thirty-eight-year-old Lieutenant Commander William Right Hollingsworth, who was known to his contemporaries simply as "Holly." Born in Fort Meade, Florida, Holly was a 1926 Naval Academy graduate with a slow Southern drawl. He and one of his closest academy graduates, Bob Armstrong, had since married sisters Thelma and Mildred Stallworth. When America entered World War II, the brothers-in-law were each commanding a carrier-based Navy dive-bomber squadron—Holly Hollingsworth heading up VB-6 on *Enterprise* and Bob Armstrong in charge of VB-5 on the carrier *Yorktown*.[27]

Dick Best was feeling sore that the cruiser *Northampton*—struggling with damaged screws that slowed her speed—had already caused him to be one day late for his pending leave. Sitting in VB-6's ready room, Best was anxious. He knew that as the carrier went in, the air staff would retain a few planes to do antisubmarine patrol, and thus anticipated a further delay before his leave started.[28]

Shortly after 0800, the ready room talker announced the attack on Pearl Harbor. The ship was instantly put on alert, and all pilots were soon called to man their aircraft in preparation for a strike launch. The deck crews began arranging an attack group topside, loading them with thousand-pound bombs while awaiting orders on what to strike.[29]

Those not assigned to the morning mission could only wonder which of their squadron mates might not return. Ensign Benjamin Henry Troemel had lost two good buddies—his roommate Johnny Vogt and also Manny Gonzalez. Troemel had enrolled in the New York Merchant Marine Academy's cadet program and graduated in 1936. But his service as a licensed third mate did not fulfill his boyhood dream of being a pilot, and with the help of the academy's commander, Ben Troemel made it into the Navy's flight school at Pensacola in 1938. "They told us, 'If you don't make it, doesn't mean you can't learn to fly,'" Troemel recalled. "'We could teach a baboon to fly if we had enough time.'"[30]

Troemel had been given his first "down" signal that morning from the *Enterprise* launching officer due to a faulty spark plug. Several reserve SBDs had been warming up and available only if needed, so Ensign Bill Roberts had been launched in his place.[31]

By 0845, eight *Enterprise* SBDs from the morning search were still airborne. Scouting Six XO Earl Gallaher and Willie West attempted to make landings at Ford Island around 0900, but they too came under heavy American antiaircraft fire from ship and shore batteries. The second round of Japanese attackers had the area as stirred up as a kicked-over anthill. Gallaher and West returned to Barbers Point to wait, where by 0915 they had been joined by five other circling stragglers: VS-6 pilots Fogg, Dobson, and Hilton, plus VB-6 pilots Kroeger and Weber.

The second wave of Japanese attackers would complete their dives during the next half hour, leaving a terrible scene of destruction across Oahu. The battleships *Oklahoma* and *Arizona* were destroyed, while three others were completely wrecked. Numerous other ships were sunk or heavily damaged, and most of the Army's 231 aircraft had been wiped out or damaged. The Marines could not count any of their own aircraft serviceable by the end of the second raid, leaving only *Enterprise*'s surviving scout bombers available for further operation.

Earl Gallaher moved his seven SBDs out to sea to allow things to settle at Pearl. When he saw Japanese planes effecting a rendezvous southwest of Barbers Point, he went against protocol by opting to break radio silence.

"Pearl Harbor is under attack by the Japanese," he radioed. "This is no shit!"[32]

Gallaher proceeded toward Ford Island as soon as the antiaircraft fire had subsided. He, Dobson, and then West chose to land at Ewa Field because of lighter AA fire in that area. As Gallaher taxied up to the line, a Marine sergeant jumped up on the ramp and yelled, "Get the hell off the ground! Can't you see what's going on?"[33]

The trio took right back to the air and rejoined their other four VS-6 and VB-6 comrades to fly into Ford Island. Ship and shore batteries sent up a barrage, mistaking them for enemy aircraft. Willie West's plane took two or three rounds in the left wing in the process. Carl Fogg suffered a bullet hole in the main spar of his right wing and another round through his tail surfaces. As they approached the water tower on Ford Island, Gallaher dropped his wheels and landing gear per standard procedure, but some of the gunners on the island saw planes coming with wheels down and opened fire, assuming they were Japanese.

Earl Gallaher sat in his plane, ducking the incoming tracers. He knew that if he could see the tracers, they would not hit him, as the fire came from the rear ends of the bullets as they zipped by. With no other obvious choice, he bored straight in and landed as the American gunners continued firing at him.[34]

Tracers streaked by Cleo Dobson's plane thick and fast. The husky, athletic Oklahoman, who had played baseball, football, and basketball in college, was a "congenial, jovial old guy," according to squadron mate Jack Kleiss. "His mother really wanted a daughter and planned to call her Cleopatra. She didn't arrive, so when she had a son, she named him Cleo."[35]

One close shell burst off Dobson's right wing, throwing his plane upon its side. He dropped his seat down so he could hide behind his engine. He gunned his throttle and dived for the runway, worrying all the while that an eager gunner would shoot out one of his tires as his Dauntless settled in.[36]

Dobson stomped his brakes hard upon touchdown and groundlooped his SBD off the end of the landing mat. Handlers moved in to refuel and arm the carrier Dauntlesses, while the other four pilots—Hilton, Fogg, Kroeger, and Weber—landed at Ewa Field around 1000.

Only eleven of eighteen Dauntlesses had safely landed on Oahu, with Frank Patriarca of VS-6 still airborne. America's "day of infamy" was far from over for the shaken aviators of the *Enterprise* Air Group.

By 1000, the last planes of the second Japanese strike wave were heading for their carriers. Admiral Nagumo's fleet was steaming to the northwest of the Hawaiian Islands. Admiral Halsey's lone carrier task force was left chasing phantoms for the balance of the day.

Allen James Brost became one of the phantom chasers. The twenty-one-year-old Wisconsin youth had been assigned to *Enterprise* almost exactly one year prior. Radioman Brost and his pilot, Lieutenant (j.g.) John James Van Buren, had been kept on board ship to fly antisubmarine patrols. At 1020, *Enterprise* turned into the wind, launching a full strike group to investigate a report of two Japanese carriers some thirty miles south of Barbers Point. Brost was up on the flight deck with his gear on, watching the others take off. Van Buren ran out and yelled at him to get into the last unmanned SBD.[37]

Rear gunner Achilles Antonius Georgiou, a New Yorker whose parents had immigrated to the United States from Greece, had joined Bombing Six in the spring of 1941. Several of his buddies, also fresh from radio school, had joined at the same time: Alfred Stitzelberger, William Rothletter, and Mitchell Cohn, who all hailed from Long Island. Georgiou and Cohn had often made liberty together. Georgiou was on the hangar deck, stretched out on the wing of his SBD, blissfully unaware that his air group was under attack. When word of the attack came, he scrambled up on deck and helped his pilot ready their plane.

Hailing from the little country town of Hillsboro, Missouri, Ensign Tony Frederic Schneider was crushed when he heard Manny Gonzalez's final frantic pleas over the radio. He had shared his first stateroom on board *Enterprise* with Gonzalez. Schneider had been sitting in the ready room waiting for orders to man his dive-bomber to fly into Pearl Harbor for liberty. Just minutes later, he and his gunner were climbing into the air with a live thousand-pound bomb in their SBD's racks for the first time.[38]

Lieutenant Commander Holly Hollingsworth formed his dive-bombers over the task group. Yet Lieutenant Dick Best, heading up the second division of Bombing Six, soon became frustrated with the lack of immediate action. After an hour in the air, Hollingsworth's crew had made no enemy contacts. As he circled near his carrier, Best was thrilled to see that *Enterprise* had broken out her battle colors, her largest American flag. To Lieutenant Jim McCauley, VB-6's gunnery officer who was flying nearby, it was the largest and most beautiful American flag he had ever seen.[39]

Radioman Lee McHugh, flying rear seat for Best, noticed another radioman trying to get his attention. It was Harry Nelson, gunner for Jim McCauley. He transmitted Morse code on the side of his cockpit by hitting his fist down for a dot and using an open hand for a dash. McHugh told his pilot that their division had been ordered to investigate Japanese minisubs reported to be refueling southwest of Oahu.[40]

This report, and others received by Halsey, proved to be erroneous. Scouting Six had sent out thirteen aircraft in the morning, leaving only five on board ship. Only eight pilots remained, and three of them were not yet carrier qualified: ensigns Reid Stone, Daniel Seid, and Percy Forman. Three ready VS-6 aircraft were next sent to investigate a report of a Japanese tanker. The three most experienced VS-6 pilots still on the ship were assigned to this mission: Lieutenant (j.g.) Norman Jack Kleiss, Ensign John Norman West and Ensign Horace Irvin Proulx.

The senior pilot was Jack Kleiss, from Coffeyville, Kansas, a town known for its defiant stand against the Dalton Gang of bank robbers in 1892. He and gunner Johnny Snowden had but recently landed from a four-hour morning hop of flying inner-air patrol with two other VS-6 crews. Once his Dauntless was refueled, Kleiss was back in the air leading three Bombing Six pilots on the search, which also proved to be fruitless.

The *Enterprise* aircraft that had landed at Ford Island were refueled and armed with five-hundred-pound bombs. The erroneous report of Japanese carriers compelled Rear Admiral Patrick N. L. Bellinger to order one of the *Enterprise* SBDs out to investigate.

Hal Hopping departed at 1030 for a solo search, but found nothing. Dale Hilton, Ed Kroeger, and Fred Weber were sent out next to rendezvous with Army B-17s over Hickam Field, but were soon called back. At about the same time, Frank Patriarca—the last of the morning searchers still airborne—landed on the island of Kauai at the Army Air Corps' Burns Field after five and a half hours. His gunner, Joe DeLuca, was assigned to ground defense with his .30-caliber Browning and six cans each of a hundred rounds of ammunition.[41]

There was no rest, however, for the other weary Big E bomber crews at Ford Island. Rear Admiral Bellinger ordered Brigham Young to send out nine of his SBDs to scout 175 miles out from Oahu. Their mission was to investigate and bomb sampans and hostile enemy ships reported south of Barbers Point.[42]

The CEAG plane would be flown by Dick Dickinson, freshly returned from being shot down during the morning. Young was apparently un-aware of the VS-6 pilot's ordeal, and Dickinson did not complain. He had been pleased to see that his XO, Earl Gallaher, had also survived the morning's attack, and when they saw each other they shook hands in an effusive greeting and then just stood there, grinning at each other.[43]

The *Enterprise* group launched with a trio of three-plane sections: Hal Hopping with wingmen Perry Teaff and Ed Kroeger; Earl Gallaher with Willie West and Cleo Dobson; and Dickinson with Dale Hilton and Fred Weber. This flight sought the Japanese for more than three hours north of Oahu as foul weather began moving in.[44]

Teaff courageously maintained formation with his skipper through-out the search in spite of the fact that his 6-S-2 was struggling with a dangerously high oil temperature. Teaff and his gunner Edgar Jinks had made temporary repairs during the morning to their plane's dam-age, which included a bullet lodged in its engine and a busted hydraulic system.[45]

Hopping's nine SBDs returned to Ford Island at 1530. A few machine guns opened up on them near Wheeler Field, but at least the Ford Island gunners held their fire this time.

*E*nterprise in the meantime had landed her fifteen Dauntlesses from the luckless midmorning search group. Admiral Halsey promptly or-dered another search, and the ship turned into the wind at 1345. Nine SBDs departed to effect single-plane searches covering sectors to the east-southeast to south-southwest, out to 175 miles. This group included En-sign Clifford "Bucky" Walters, Ben Troemel, and Earl Donnell.

Lieutenant Commander Hopping's flight landed at Ford Island and immediately received orders to take off again for *Enterprise*. For many, it was their third flight of the day. For Hopping, Kroeger, Weber, and Hilton, it was already their fourth. As the crews manned their planes, VS-6 exec Earl Gallaher confronted gunner Jack Leaming, asking him if he still planned to ship out once his enlistment ended in two days.[46]

"Hell, no!" was Leaming's reply. He and his buddy E. G. Bailey would both extend their Navy enlistments by two years during the month, figuring that the war would be over soon enough.

Gallaher was furious. *Arizona* had been his first ship in the Navy, and now more than eleven hundred of her crew were dead, some men Gallaher had known. He was left with a burning desire to avenge their deaths by one day dive-bombing the very carriers that had destroyed her.[47]

When the SBDs arrived on the Big E, the airmen were peppered with questions about Pearl Harbor from their shipmates, yet they were promptly ordered back to Ford Island, the exhausted crews making their fourth or fifth flight of the day.

Around 1630, Bombing Six pilot Bucky Walters radioed that he had spotted Japanese warships. He also evaded what he believed be to a Japanese aircraft. Admiral Halsey, who later quizzed the young ensign, believed that Walters had actually seen an American ship and had likely encountered an Army A-20 or patrolling PBY patrol plane. In the afternoon craze of December 7, however, his report was concern enough to send the *Enterprise* air group into action once again. The excitement and stress of the Japanese surprise attack led to many such false sightings and hastily dispatched strike groups on December 7.[48]

"Pilots, man your planes!" blasted from the loudspeakers. From Scouting Six, Hod Proulx, Norm West, and Jack Kleiss had climbed into their SBDs with chart boards and gear, believing that they would merely be taxiing their planes forward. The Walters report that forced their sudden launch caught the VS-6 trio by complete surprise. They took off without a Point Option, wind data, enemy position, or even their own ship's position.[49]

The *Enterprise* attack force was led by Lieutenant Commander Gene Lindsey's torpedo-loaded Douglas TBD Devastator torpedo bombers. Scouting Six's only three pilots were launched with three Bombing Six planes under Dick Best and six Wildcats under Lieutenant (j.g.) Francis "Fritz" Hebel. The bomb loads on the SBDs had been replaced with 850-pound ferrous sulfate smoke tanks. The Navy doctrine at this time was to lay a smoke column for attacking torpedo planes. The "smokers" would drop their smoke tanks a thousand yards out from the target in preparation for the TBDs' torpedo runs.[50]

The SBDs flew at three hundred feet in gentle S-turns to avoid overtaking the slow TBDs. Failing to find a Japanese fleet at the designated point, Gene Lindsey spread his group into scouting sections to further scour the area. Once darkness set in, Dick Best found it quite a chore to keep his SBDs in tight formation. Lindsey turned command of the flight over to Lieutenant Best to lead them back to the carrier. This did not sit well with Best, five years junior to the torpedo squadron skipper. The two had had a run-in back in August 1941. "He came over to make a complaint to my squadron and we stood chest-to-chest, shouting at each other," Best remembered. "A junior to both of us tried to resolve by inviting both of us to a cocktail party."[51]

That confrontation only added to Best's frustration on December 7. *He's taken me out and lost me where I can't navigate by looking into my cockpit*, he thought. *He has cowardly turned over the lead to me without saying that is what he's doing. He's just crawling behind through this mishap of mine. Now he's saying, "We're lost; take us home."*

Best called to Lindsey on the radio. "Six Torpedo One, from Six Baker Ten. Are you leading or am I leading?"[52]

There was no response.

Best radioed, "I'm turning on running lights, dropping my smoke tanks, and returning to base."

The SBDs dropped their tanks, and Lee McHugh in Best's rear seat turned on the Zed Baker (ZB) homing device to help guide the group back in. Best was unaware at the time that McHugh's radio was malfunctioning, unable to broadcast or receive transmissions. He assumed for the time being that Lindsey had chosen to ignore his calls.

Fritz Hebel's Wildcats, low on fuel, opted to fly on to Ford Island to land. This left the SBDs and TBDs on their own to reach *Enterprise*. Best, for one, was afraid of the "duck shoot" that might ensue if his strike group tried to land at Pearl Harbor after dark on this most confusing of days.[53]

Enterprise did not want to take them on board, but Lindsey was insistent that his Devastators could not fly over the mountain range near Oahu. The TBDs began coming on board at 2038, although T-13 hit the barrier. It was the first time that torpedo planes had landed with live torpedoes, considered too precious to jettison this day, and the resulting crash of the Devastator sent its torpedo skidding wildly down the flight deck. The TBD fiasco forced the remaining planes to circle overhead in the darkness for another half hour while the deck was cleared. There were many near collisions, and the pilots lost sight of the task group several times while preparing to land. "It was one of the most nightmar-ish flights I ever made," said Ensign Irvin McPherson of VT-6.[54]

The last of the evening strikers was finally landed by 2113. Dick Best had logged 4.3 hours in the cockpit and considered this mission one of the roughest he ever made. His specialty on touching down was to catch the number one arresting wire, but in the darkness he made the worst landing of his career. Bombing Six pilot Jim McCauley literally kissed the flight deck upon landing with only eight gallons of fuel remaining in his tanks.[55]

Enterprise had brought aboard all of the Devastators and Daunt-lesses from her strike group, but her Wildcats were still aloft. Hebel's fighters, waved off from the *Enterprise*, proceeded to Ford Island to land. As they circled around to approach, nervous machine gunners from all over opened up on them. Ensign Herbert Menges's F4F was hit and crashed, killing the pilot—the first U.S. naval fighter pilot to die in the Pacific War. As the gunfire erupted, many of the *Enterprise* aircrews were trying to sleep in a hangar on Ford Island. Jack Leaming jumped up and grabbed his flight gear and ran outside in time to see a plane crash and explode north of Ford Island.[56]

Hebel's Wildcat was hit and he was fatally injured in a crash landing in a canefield. Ensign Gayle Hermann's Wildcat was slammed by bullets, but he made a crash landing on Ford Island's little golf course. Ensign David Flynn safely parachuted from his crippled F4F, but he badly wrenched his back during his landing in a canefield. Ensign James Dan-iels landed under gunfire, but had to dodge parked trucks set out to deter Japanese landings. Lieutenant (j.g.) Eric Allen also parachuted from his damaged fighter plane but later died from a rifle shot to his chest. Fight-ing Six's introduction to war was as deadly as that of Scouting Six: Four Wildcats had been destroyed and three fighter pilots killed.

The last *Enterprise* aviators still aloft long after dark on December 7 were two of the young ensigns who had made the long afternoon search, Ben Troemel and Bucky Walters. Unable to find *Enterprise* in the dark, both were so low on fuel that they opted to fly to NAS Kaneohe to land. Walters received permission to touch down, but he was unaware that the Marines had parked trucks and other vehicles on the landing mat at irregular intervals to prevent Japanese gliders from landing.

As he came in over the darkened runway, Walters touched down between two automobiles. Suddenly he spotted another vehicle in his landing lights. He managed to jump it by pulling back on his stick and then dropping back down into a ground loop. He and gunner Joe Ivantic were unharmed but had to taxi around various parked vehicles until they ended up face-to-face with a cement mixer.

Ensign Troemel arrived a half hour later over Kaneohe after more than five hours in the air, the fuel in his SBD nearly exhausted. He and gunner RM3c Alfred Stitzelberger also managed to avoid the parked vehicles. Leaving smoking rubber while dodging parked trucks and Walters's SBD, Troemel came to a halt nose-to-nose with the same concrete mixer. When daylight revealed the hazards on the runway the next morning, Walters said that he would have never attempted such a landing if he had seen the parked vehicles.[57]

Enterprise had lost ten planes and ten men on December 7. By nightfall, her remaining air group was badly scattered between bases on Oahu and those still on the ship. Scouting Six exec Earl Gallaher was unaware of the tragedy that took place on Ford Island that night when the *Enterprise* fighters attempted to land. He and his fellow VS-6 pilots stayed the night in the basement of the base's Bachelor Officers' Quarters. Some of the enlisted men slept on cots, but most of the naval aviators could manage little more than a few hours of sleep.

THREE
The Stuff

Nothing could have prepared the Dauntless aviators for the shock of December 7. Yet each pilot had already proven that he possessed "the stuff" needed to be a naval aviator. Some had considerable flight hours under their belts, whereas others had but recently been pinned with their coveted gold wings. But each man had survived his grueling flight school elimination training to make it into carrier aviation. Now all of their skills would be tested in the weeks to come as America entered World War II.

Twenty-four-year-old Lieutenant (j.g.) Jack Kleiss had held a desire to fly since age fifteen, when he was a cavalryman in the Kansas National Guard. During a mock battle in 1934, Army Air Corps biplanes swooped down on the guardsmen. Young Kleiss, caught staring in awe at one of the incoming planes, was quickly declared "dead" by one of the battle's referees.[1]

He decided right then and there that he would never be caught so helpless again; he would become a pilot. Kleiss mustered out of the Kansas National Guard, and was appointed to the U.S. Naval Academy in Annapolis.

Many of his classmates, such as Ralph Weymouth, had turned to the military to escape the Depression. Weymouth was the oldest of three brothers forced to become more independent when their mother had to get a job to help support the family. Weymouth passed the entrance exam in 1934 and joined Kleiss for four years of military schooling.

Kleiss and Weymouth graduated Annapolis in 1938 and commenced two required years of surface duty, joining the ranks of the "black shoe" Navy. Surface officers wore traditional double-breasted blue uniforms with gold stripes and black leather shoes. In contrast were the "brown shoe" officers—naval aviators—whose attire was markedly different. Their uniforms were forest green with black stripes while grounded, their shoes brown leather. Brown-shoe aviators donned fleece-lined leather jackets while aloft to protect them from the bitter cold faced in their open-air cockpits.

The role of aircraft carriers in the old battleship Navy was just coming to the forefront, and Kleiss and Weymouth both developed a strong desire to become a brown shoe. Weymouth, who had been interested in flying since he first hitched a ride in an Army aircraft as a youngster, served as a catapult officer in 1939, launching SOC biplanes from his cruiser. Some of the pilots appreciated his key position enough to have him ride rear seat in their floatplanes as they were fired into the sky. "I was bitten by the bug," Weymouth said.

Jack Kleiss's first assignment out of the academy was as a junior gunnery officer on board the heavy cruiser *Vincennes* (CA-44). While his ship was stationed at Long Beach, California, he ran into a friend from his hometown of Coffeyville. His buddy described Kleiss to a young woman he knew, telling her about a lonely sailor who needed some attention.

Jean Mochon, a tall, striking brunette who worked in Los Angeles as a stenotypist, agreed to go on a date with the young officer, who was immediately taken by her beauty and warm personality. "The first time I saw her, I said, 'She's the one for me,'" he remembered.

As a new ensign, Kleiss pulled in only $125 per month, barely enough to cover his room, board, uniforms, and other expenses. For only ten dollars he purchased a used car that he managed to tinker into working condition. Deciding to impress Jean by taking her on a drive up to Los Angeles, he was flustered when his left rear tire blew out, forcing him to struggle with changing the flat in the midst of busy L.A. traffic. He figured he had lost her interest.

Fortunately for Jack, Jean was equally smitten with him. He forged an immediate connection with her French-Canadian family and was encouraged that Jean's father took a liking to him. Jack had studied French at the Naval Academy, and even subscribed to a Quebec newspaper so he could practice reading. The Mochon family was impressed that he knew a little of their language.

Jack's developing relationship with Jean was soon tested. *Vincennes* was moved from her home port in Long Beach to the other side of the country in Norfolk, Virginia. The couple began writing to each other every week or two, a correspondence that would continue during the next two years as Kleiss served on his cruiser and two subsequent destroyer assignments. One day, his skipper on the destroyer *Yarnall* (DD-143) noticed Kleiss eyeing a photo of Jean. "Boy, she's pretty," he said. "Marry her before she gets away!"

That very thought had entered Jack's mind. But the Navy restricted academy graduates from marrying for two years after Annapolis. Complicating matters was that Jean's devotion to Jack had become equally strong. "I can't help but feel a little on the low side," she wrote to him after his departure. "For the first time in my life I'm sure of my feelings and then something like this has to happen."[2]

After two frustrating years in the surface Navy, Jack Kleiss's aviation dreams finally became reality when he commenced flight school in Miami in May 1940. Training began with three months of primary instruction in land-based aircraft. While at NAS Miami, Kleiss would pass through three separate squadrons, advancing from basic to advanced levels. His early training was in a three-hundred-horsepower-engined acrobatic biplane, the N3N "Yellow Peril," named not only for its bright shade of yellow paint but also for the high number of new aviation cadets (AvCads) who washed out of the program.

During the eleven-month training regimen, nearly forty percent of the cadets were killed in accidents or dropped out for physical or flight inabilities. Sunday memorial services were not uncommon. In order to progress to the second squadron, the AvCads were given tests or "checks" at twenty, forty, and sixty hours of flight time by instructors known as "check pilots," often recent AvCads who had drawn the less desirable instructor duties versus fleet squadron duty. They were hard to please.

For a "down" check, a cadet was assigned additional study time before being given a second chance to pass the flight test. If he failed, he washed out of the program. Jack received an "up" from his instructor and progressed to the second squadron for intermediate training. Along the way, AvCads advanced to flying the six-hundred-horsepower North American SNJ Texan single-wing trainer.

Jack learned instrument flying, aerial gunnery, dive-bombing techniques, fighter tactics, and formation flying during the more advanced third squadron training. He knew that he would leave the Florida flight training program in only one of three ways: with the coveted gold aviator wings on his uniform; washed out and disgraced because he did not possess "the stuff" to advance; or in a pine box shipped home to his family.

After eleven months of intense training, Kleiss was pinned with his naval aviator's gold wings in the spring of 1941 and ordered to California to join Scouting Six for service on the carrier *Enterprise*. While his ship was in San Diego, he had time to continue his courtship of Jean Mochon. On occasion, they would visit the home of Kleiss's shipboard roommate, Perry Teaff.

Unlike academy graduate Kleiss, Teaff was a reservist, and not bound by the two-year marriage rules. Teaff's wife, Maggie, kept their home in San Diego, where their family was already blossoming. When Jean and Jack visited for dinner parties, they found that Perry and Maggie Teaff were super pranksters. They enjoyed amusing their guests by asking them to check out their new shower. Upon pulling back the shower curtains in the bathtub, Jack was startled to see a baby alligator crawling about. "They kept it like a pet," he said. "It never bothered anyone."

When *Enterprise* and Scouting Six put to sea, Jack and Perry spent many hours talking about their significant others back in San Diego. In their stateroom, Jack took the top bunk. It was only three feet below the hangar deck. Planes rolled over his head both day and night, but he slept soundly. Kleiss noticed in the logbook that one of the duty petty officers once scribbled about him, "Hard to awaken."

Jack and Jean exchanged letters frequently when *Enterprise* was away from port. Jack shared his pleasant but grueling life as a pilot of Scouting Six. In one letter during the summer of 1941, he wrote that they flew so frequently "we've been considering putting coffeepots in the planes and bunks in the ready room."[3]

Kleiss found that squadron exec Earl Gallaher was a taskmaster.

Skipper Hal Hopping gave Gallaher free rein to work their men into an efficient fighting unit. Instead of liberty, the XO doled out extra time on gunnery practices, night flying, and every maneuver possible. Kleiss felt that Gallaher kept Scouting Six busier than any other squadron in the Navy.[4]

During qualifying training off Hawaii in June 1941, Kleiss earned a new nickname. He had been assigned to pull a gunnery tow sleeve off Barbers Point. In order to have his rear gunner John Snowden pack the target sleeve, Kleiss decided to land at nearby Ewa Field. Although the tower did not respond to his transmission, Kleiss took its displayed green landing light as an invitation to land. As his SBD approached the runway, he spotted Marine fighter planes lining up behind him for their own landing.[5]

Kleiss touched down and taxied off into a hard-packed red clay dirt field. As he tried to make room for the fighters, his prop blast sent up a huge cloud of red dust. The ensuing mushroom cloud covered the landing strip and rose a mile into the air, preventing the Marines from landing. Kleiss had Snowden quickly haul in their tow sleeve as the Ewa Field tower operator bellowed, "Unknown dust cloud, who the hell are you?"

Kleiss quickly returned to the paved runway and cleared the landing strip as Marine pilots swore at him over their radios. His air base "dusting" incident would not be quickly forgotten. Once back on board *Enterprise*, fellow pilot Cleo Dobson—who had seen everything from his SBD—greeted him with, "Hello, Dusty." And so, "Dusty" he became. The nickname would stick with him for life among his fellow aviators.

The *Enterprise* air group was filled with pilots who had long dreamed of becoming naval aviators. Ensign Tony Schneider of Bombing Six knew what was at stake. He had lost close friends in the Pearl Harbor attack.

Each first-time assignment in his relatively young career as a pilot had been a genuine rush. Tony had first become interested in flying as a teenager, although the opportunity to actually fly had never presented itself. He applied with his local congressman for an appointment to West Point and received an alternate appointment, but the principal appointee passed all his tests and was selected to attend. During his pursuit of a mathematics degree at Westminster College in Missouri, Tony first learned of the naval aviation program from his roommate and fraternity brother William Ross. After three years of college, Tony looked into the possibilities of joining the program. "I was advised by the Navy people to go back and finish college and that was a wise decision," he said.[6]

After graduating from Westminster in 1939, Tony entered the Navy's program while his friend William joined the Army Air Corps' program. They would remain close friends, however, as Tony had been introduced to William's beautiful sister Jean Ross. Tony's relationship with Jean would progress, and in time he and William would become brothers-in-law.

Thanks to the Naval Aviation Reserve Act of 1939, cadet aviators received both their gold wings insignia and commissions upon completion of flight training. Candidates had to be between the ages of nineteen and twenty-five and have an associate's degree or at least two years of college under their belts. Tony's training entailed three hundred flight hours and 465 hours of ground school in an eight-month period.

But to even have a chance at earning gold wings, aviation cadets like Tony Schneider had to get past "E-base"—elimination base training. His E-base took place in November 1939 at the U.S. Naval Reserve Aviation Base at Lambert Field in Robertson, Missouri. As a prospective aviation cadet, Tony was enlisted in the Navy Reserves as a seaman, second class petty officer. His dreams of flying would begin or end in the yellow, open-cockpit Stearman N3N biplane the pilots called the Yellow Peril. "The objective was to recruit promising young men to become naval aviators, give them ten hours of flight time leading up to a solo in a Yellow Peril," he said. At that point, the instructors decided whether each young man had "the stuff" to progress into full-fledged flight training.

Tony's initial flight with a regular Navy instructor was "thrilling" in that it was his first time to ever leave the ground. He progressed through his first nine hours of flight time, and on his tenth flight, he was able to solo successfully. One-third of his comrades had not been as fortunate.

After a short leave period back home, Schneider reported to Florida in March 1940 for the next step in his quest for gold wings at NAS

Pensacola. In addition to the Stearman Yellow Perils, Tony now began flying other naval trainers, including the single-wing North American AT-6 Texan trainer plane. The students were cautioned repeatedly and strenuously about the dangers of flying a low-wing monoplane, as opposed to the biplanes they had started in. "So we were on our toes," Tony said. "Every time I moved to a bigger and better airplane, it was a big thrill."

The 150 future pilots progressed through different stages of flight training at Corry and Saufley fields around Pensacola. Those who passed from Squadron One training moved to Squadron Two at Chevalier Field, NAS Pensacola's main field. There, Tony and his fellow students learned formation flying and instrument-controlled flying, both of which demanded coolness, sound judgment, and keen decision making by the pilots at all times.

Tony Schneider's next big thrill came in December 1940, when he completed his flight training and was finally pinned with his golden aviator's wings. Along with his new commission as an ensign in the U.S. Navy came a nice increase of pay (including a fifty percent flight pay bonus above the base pay rate), tripling the seventy-five dollars a month he had been making—and far above the thirty-six dollars a month he had been paid at E-base. He was assigned to Bombing Squadron Six at NAS North Island in San Diego, where he mastered the two-seat, single-engine Northrup BT-1 monoplane dive-bomber. It often leaked oil so badly that Tony flew with a rag to wipe the sludge off his windscreen. Bombing Six's transition to the Dauntless SBD was a godsend.

The Dauntless proved hardy and maneuverable. "It was an easy airplane to fly and it was tailor-made for the job to which it was assigned," said Tony. Lieutenant Dick Best, second in command of Tony's Bombing Six, would later describe the SBD as being "rock steady in a vertical dive, completely responsive to the controls, and ready to absorb punishment and still get you home."

Lieutenant Earl Gallaher, second in command of Scouting Six, believed the stout construction of the Dauntless kept his pilots and gunners alive. "Each time one of our Douglas Dauntless dive-bombers returned to the ship after having been damaged by gunfire, there was always someone who marveled at how rugged this plane was," Gallaher said. "It was always a comforting feeling to know how much they could take and still get us home."[7]

Another of the first pilots to fly the SBD was Lieutenant Commander Max Leslie, who was serving as skipper of *Saratoga*'s Bombing Three at the start of the war. "The Douglas Dauntless dive-bomber, in my opinion, possessed the most perfect combination of ruggedness, stability, ease of maintenance, combination of performance, speed, and endurance of any aircraft before or since," Leslie said. "Many other dive-bombers had been used by the Navy, but none was a close second to the Dauntless."[8]

Lieutenant Stanley "Swede" Vejtasa of *Yorktown*'s Scouting Five was among the pilots who were immediately impressed with the Dauntless. "From the start it proved to be one awfully fine aircraft because it responded well," he said. The SBD's split flaps enabled the pilots to exercise a fair amount of control in their normal seventy-degree dives during attacks. "This plane was designed in all respects about as perfect as a dive-bomber could be," Vejtasa added. Swede Vejtasa would put his Dauntless through radical maneuvers while using it to engage Japanese fighter planes during the first carrier battle in the Coral Sea in May 1942. "Every time I had an opportunity with a different plane, I didn't give a damn what it was, I used that plane to dogfight something," he said. Vejtasa's aggressive nature was well suited for flying the SBD, for his plane withstood every maneuver he put it through. He accounted for at least one Japanese kill while flying an SBD at Coral Sea, and, as a fighter pilot during the Guadalcanal campaign, Vejtasa would score at least seven more confirmed aerial kills.

The Dauntless weighed more than four and a half tons when it was fully loaded for combat. It was capable of carrying a lethal thousand-pound bomb for attacking capital warships, or smaller loads for attacking land-based targets or enemy submarines at sea with depth bombs. The SBD was also more automated than the obsolete Curtiss SBC-4 biplanes that Tony and other aviation cadets flew at times. "The flaps took about sixty turns with a big crank to move them up and down," said Ralph Weymouth of the SBC-4. "I think it was a hundred and twenty turns to get the wheels up and down." In comparison, the Dauntless had a two-man tandem cockpit with dual flight controls and hydraulically actuated perforated split dive-brakes (or "flaps").[9]

The young pilots had proven they had "the stuff" to make it into carrier aviation. Now they had the dive-bomber of choice to carry out their mission.

Tony Schneider's big dream was of serving at sea as a carrier-qualified pilot. He had his chance as he rode *Enterprise* out to the Hawaiian Islands in 1941 for advanced training. At Ford Island, he and other rookie pilots went through touch-and-go landings. The LSOs ran them through field carrier landing practice, forcing them to learn how to land in very tight marked spaces. Then it was time to make real traps (arrested landings) by engaging a wire on the Big E's flight deck with his SBD's hydraulic tail hook.

"I really didn't find that difficult to master," Tony said. "It came pretty easy for me." He fell right in with his new squadron and his fellow pilots. "I wanted to spend the rest of my life working with people like this," he said.[10]

The thrills of flight training were but distant memories as Schneider lay in his *Enterprise* bunk on the night of December 7. America had been sucker punched in the heart of its Pacific Fleet at Pearl Harbor. Ten of his fellow airmen were gone, and others were wounded. Others from his air group were ashore, scattered among various air bases on the Hawaiian Islands.

"Most of us knew the war was coming," he said. "The fact that they slammed Pearl first was a stunner, since all our preparations were for defending the Far East, not this sudden, bold strike in Hawaii."

Tony found that his carrier's crew and his fellow aviators reacted to the surprise attack with a mixture of shock and anger. His own reaction was a resolve to obtain vengeance.

While Schneider drifted off peacefully in his bunk, many of his Scouting Six comrades were far from comfortable. They tried to sleep in the new concrete Bachelor Officers' Quarters on Ford Island, which was also packed with scared civilians and wounded battleship sailors. Jack

Leaming, still shaken by the violent loss of the VF-6 pilots shot down by friendly fire, tossed fitfully on a rickety cot. The surprise attack brought out a mix of emotions for him—anger, fear, contempt, defiance, and retribution. *No son of a bitch is going to deprive me of my freedom!* he thought.

FOUR

"I Was Really Upset"

The weary aviators at Ford Island were roused at 0400 on December 8. Skipper Hal Hopping had his third officer, Dick Dickinson, gather the men before daybreak to disseminate information on the morning's scouting flights and relate orders to take off an hour before sunrise. The nine Navy Dauntless bombers were the only planes available for the early search, which was scheduled to extend past Diamond Head until an hour after sunrise to look for Japanese ships. As the VS-6 pilots warmed up their engines, a seaplane taxied up from the other side of the airfield and warmed up its engine to take off.[1]

Lieutenant Earl Gallaher watched the plane clear the ground with all its running lights on. To his amazement, antiaircraft guns opened fire. The seaplane's pilot frantically took his craft down low on the water and applied full throttle to clear the island and its trigger-happy gunners. Disgusted, Gallaher reached down and cut his engines. He climbed up on the wing of Hal Hopping's S-1. "Captain, I'm not gonna take off," he announced. "I'd rather have the Japs shoot up this plane on the ground than have these people shoot me down in the air."[2]

Hopping stomped into the command center to talk by telephone with some of the Ford Island staff. Gallaher later remembered that his skipper's voice was so loud he didn't need the telephone. "My planes are not gonna take off until these people got some fire control discipline!" Hopping shouted. In the end, CEAG Brigham Young held his SBDs for an

56

hour after first light to prevent shore batteries from firing on them again. Eager plane captains on board *Enterprise* later greeted the returning aviators, curious for the latest information on who had made it and who had not.

Enterprise's other Dauntlesses flew scouting missions from the carrier on December 8. Around 0800, Dick Best was ordered to take Admiral Halsey's chief of staff, Commander Miles Browning, into Pearl for a conference with Admiral Kimmel. Best, whose own middle name was Halsey, had high regards for the admiral. "Halsey was an inspirational leader," he said. "We come from the same family. It goes back to 1640 when they landed in Massachusetts." As for Halsey's chief of staff, Best considered Browning to be "a bully" who "got by bullying; not very bright."[3]

Before he took off, squadron mate Jack Blitch warned his exec that the trigger-happy shore gunners shot at anything that moved. As he flew in toward eastern Oahu with Admiral Halsey's aide, Best pondered why the air staff had sent him in without a wingman. *I guess they're willing to get rid of the best dive-bomber in the fleet if they can only get rid of Miles Browning.*[4]

Near Bellows Field, Best looked down and spotted what looked like a sampan with a little deckhouse in the surf's edge. It was actually a Japanese minisub, launched early on the morning of December 7 from the fleet submarine *I-24*. The minisub's commander, Ensign Kazuo Sakamaki, had gotten lost before he could launch his boat's two torpedoes at a U.S. warship. He had inadvertently beached his sub, forcing the crew of three to swim for shore. His two enlisted men

U.S. Navy

Lieutenant Dick Best.

drowned, but Sakamaki was captured, becoming America's first Japanese prisoner of war.[5]

"It looks like a midget submarine out there in the surf," Best called to Browning. "Can you see it?"[6]

"You young jocks wouldn't know a submarine from a galleon," Browning snapped back.

I despise him, Best thought. *What a typical bully put-down remark.*

Best flew in over the beached battleship *Nevada* and delivered Browning to Kaneohe, where he spent the better part of the day waiting on the admiral's chief of staff. Best joined local Marines to sip on some of the foulest coffee he had ever had in his life. The island's water lines were damaged and taking on salty harbor water, as well as anything else that seeped into the pipes.[7]

The second day of war proved to be challenging for some of VS-6's scouts. Dusty Kleiss flew a morning search with Earl Donnell as his wingman. Heavy cloud cover made navigating difficult. When he arrived at Point Option after his scouting leg, Kleiss was unable to find the ship. From a height of three hundred feet, he could not even see the ocean. He proceeded to *Enterprise*'s secondary Point Option, but again found no carrier. Kleiss spent the next hour flying square searches in hopes of finding his flight deck. Unable to reach the ship via radio, gunner Johnny Snowden finally reported that the radio in their 6-S-18 was out of commission. After another hour and nearing Oahu, Kleiss finally spotted *Enterprise* below through a tiny hole in the clouds. He dived straight down without flaps, reaching 240 knots by five thousand feet. He was at terminal velocity, making nearly eleven Gs, and was on the verge of passing out when he pulled out of his dive and leveled off at a thousand feet. His own formation's surprised destroyers opened fire on the diving SBD. "At that speed, I wasn't worried about AA fire," he wrote. "I gave signals, firing ceased, and I landed aboard with less than twenty-five gallons of fuel."[8]

To Scouting Six gunner Don Hoff, the Big E's return to Pearl was a somber affair. His carrier entered the channel at Pearl Harbor near dusk on December 8 and moored to her usual berth just ahead of the *Utah*. No brass bands awaited. The men who stood on the flight deck stared in silence at the devastation around them in the falling darkness. As *Enterprise* approached her berth, Hoff realized there was some resentment that their mighty carrier had not done more to stop the Japanese attackers. He heard a sailor on the dock shout up, "Where were you?"[9]

Ed Anderson was equally stunned by the wreckage at Hickam Field as *Enterprise* eased into port. He spotted the remains of Ed Deacon's 6-S-14 Dauntless lying in two feet of water near the entrance to the main channel of Pearl Harbor. The sobering realization of war continued to sink in as his ship passed the twisted steel corpses of battleships, destroyers, and other vessels that were still upside down or largely submerged in many cases. "It was a terribly disheartening sight," he wrote in his private diary.[10]

Edward Rutledge Anderson was born in 1917 in his family's home in Inglenook, a suburb of Birmingham, Alabama. He and his older sister, Inez, were very close to their mother, who was remarried to one of Teddy Roosevelt's Rough Riders when they were very young. Rutledge, as he was called by his mother, shared a sense of adventure with his new stepfather. The family settled just south of Los Angeles, where Rutledge attended high school, playing on both the varsity basketball team and on the school's championship football team.[11]

Rutledge Anderson scraped up enough money during high school to buy both a motorcyle and a sailboat. After graduating in 1936, he went to work for the California Automobile Association. He became known as "Ed" instead of Rutledge during this time. In July 1941, Ed received a high draft notice that gave him greater odds of being pulled into service. He had "little interest in marching around through the mud" with the Army, so he and a buddy decided to enlist in the U.S. Navy.

Ed jumped at the chance to take aviation radioman training. Graduating as radioman third class in September 1941, he reported on board the carrier *Enterprise* with two of his radio school buddies, Dave Craig and Doug Cossitt. Ed was fresh from learning Morse code, and had not even gone through a true basic training before he was sent to his new carrier. He crossed the quarterdeck with his seabag slung over his shoulder, and thus became a seagoing sailor who had no clue about shipboard protocols.[12]

Courtesy of Janice Anderson-Gram

RM3c Ed Anderson.

As he gaped at the rubble of Pearl Harbor, Anderson yearned to be fully qualified for air duty to help strike back against the Japanese. At the moment, however, he was assigned to the air group's ordnance department until he could qualify as an aerial gunner. His first job entailed servicing the SBDs' machine guns and bombs. His dream was to be in the skies as an aviation radioman/gunner. His reality, however, was being sent ashore that night to stand radio watch in the control tower at Luke Field while his carrier hastily took on provisions. Ed's dreams would have to wait awhile longer.

Hours ahead of the ship, the *Enterprise* air group had flown ashore to land on Ford Island in the late afternoon of December 8. As Jim McCauley overflew Pearl Harbor on his approach, he was stunned by the devastation below him. He found the burning battleship *Arizona* to be a pretty rugged thing to look at.[13]

Bombing Six rear gunner Allen Brost was equally shocked. The buildings at Hickam Field had roofs blown out, now left hanging over the side. He noted the ravaged battleships and other smoldering vessels. As Brost's pilot John Van Buren landed their dive-bomber, he was forced to dodge craters in the runway.[14]

Bombing Six landed at Hickam Field, where they spent the night in an old wooden temporary barracks. McCauley found that jittery gunners made it life-threatening to move around after dark. Around 2330, Army personnel came into the VB-6 barracks with a report that the Japanese were dropping paratroopers up in the hills of Oahu. Skipper Holly Hollingsworth was asked whether his dive-bombers could go up and attack. McCauley was pleased when his CO said it was an impossibility.

Hollingsworth told the Army that their infantrymen were to take care of the paratroopers.[15]

Enterprise remained in Pearl Harbor only long enough to take on provisions and fuel. The junior aviators who had stayed on board worked through the night to stock the ship. There was no sleeping now that war was on. "Everyone, and I mean officers and enlisted men, worked side by side to resupply the *Enterprise*, because we had been gone for a couple of weeks," said Don Hoff. Everyone toiled under "darkened ship" conditions, with all visible lights turned off during the loading process. Word was passed that the task force had to put to sea by daybreak on December 9 to avoid being spotted in the harbor by Japanese snoopers. "By dawn, there was no trace that we were [ever] there," remembered Hoff. "As far as anyone else was concerned, the *Enterprise* had never been in there."[16]

Scouting Six picked up a replacement pilot at Pearl Harbor to help offset the losses suffered on December 7. In addition, Mac McCarthy was in a Navy hospital with a badly broken leg that would sideline him from flight duty for many weeks. Joining Hal Hopping's squadron was Lieutenant Reginald Rutherford, a 1934 Naval Academy graduate with a wife and young child. Rutherford had earned his gold pilot's wings in July 1940, then had flown nearly a year and a half with *Lexington*'s Scouting Two before being detached on December 1 to Pearl Harbor to await transportation to new duties in the Asiatic Fleet. Everything changed with the Japanese surprise attack, and Hopping was happy to scoop up Reggie Rutherford as a new section leader for the upcoming actions he expected to face in the Pacific.

Shortly out to sea from Oahu on December 9, *Enterprise* landed her returning aircraft. Her SBDs were to be used for constant wartime patrolling, and they began making contacts on only their second day at sea.

The first submarine report came in from a Bombing Six pilot after dawn on December 10. Andy Anderson, in 6-B-17 with rear gunner Stuart Mason, was scouting forty miles ahead of *Enterprise* at three hundred feet when at 0617 he sighted the wake made by a Japanese submarine. Anderson could see its conning tower as he closed the distance. The I-boat was making a crash dive. Anderson pulled up to eight hundred feet over the submarine and released his thousand-pound bomb, which exploded approximately fifty feet aft and somewhat to port of the submerging

U.S. Navy

Ensign Clifford "Bucky" Walters.

conning tower. Anderson and Mason soon noted oil seeping across the water, and saw no further evidence of the I-boat.

Next to spot a Japanese submarine was Bucky Walters. In the bright sunlight, he could see that the sub was large, had no flag, and was traveling at about sixteen knots. Walters decided to attack in a shallow-glide bombing run, but the higher winds pushed him into a dive-bomb assault and with little flaps. He released his half-ton load at eighteen hundred feet and was unable to pull out until about six hundred feet because he was traveling at a speed of about 240 knots. As he did so, Walters's gunner, RM3c Joe Ivantic, strafed the conning tower with his .30-caliber Browning machine gun. The I-boat blew many bubbles during its crash dive as Walters banked around to attempt a run with his forward .50-caliber fixed guns. By the time he was in range, the submarine was gone, leaving no oil on the surface.

Around 1130, Admiral Halsey sent out three more SBDs to attack any surfaced submarines that were encountered. Ensign Perry Teaff in the group commander's SBD sighted another I-boat, later determined to be *I-70*. He dropped his bomb on the spot where she made a crash dive. Ensign Ed Deacon also made an attack on a submarine, but failed to cause any damage.

Lieutenant Dick Dickinson used the morning reports as a starting point for his hunt. He flew a search pattern for more than an hour with nothing in sight but sky and whitecapped waves below. Just as he reached the north corner of his rectangle, Dickinson and his gunner, Tom Merritt, finally spotted their target—a large submarine running on the surface. They had found Teaff's previously damaged *I-70*, fifteen miles to starboard. The lieutenant radioed a contact report to *Enterprise* and stated that he was attacking. *I-70* opened fire as Dickinson climbed from five hundred feet toward five thousand to commence his assault.[17]

It took precious minutes to close the fifteen miles to reach the proper diving position, and en route, Dickinson made ready. He flipped switches on the electrical distribution panel before him to arm his five-hundred-pound bomb by removing safety wires from the fuse—thereby preparing the explosive to properly detonate upon contact. Pilots who forgot to arm their bombs would risk their life only to drop a dud weapon. Antiaircraft shells burst around their Dauntless as Dickinson and Merritt bore in on the 343-foot-long *I-70*. The undersea vessel made no attempt to submerge, but merely turned to the right a few degrees. Dickinson felt certain that one of his fellow bombers had damaged the boat enough to prevent it from submerging.

In just over five minutes, Dickinson had surpassed five thousand feet altitude. His quarry was still racing ahead. Now was time to dive. He eased back on the throttle, pulling his SBD's nose slightly above the horizon, then grasped the diamond-shaped handle on his right to activate his split upper-wing surface dive flaps—his dive brakes. From this height, he would be in his dive less than fifteen seconds as his Dauntless settled into an angle of seventy degrees. As gravity lifted his rear end from his seat, he knew his vertical positioning was correct. Throughout his plunge, Dickinson eyed *I-70*'s deck through a telescopic sight.

He kept the sight's crosshairs properly aligned on the submarine while simultaneously using his left hand to adjust the rudder trim tab. Moving a small wheel on this indicator instrument held his Dauntless steady on target against the prevailing wind. If his plane skidded (slid laterally either to the right or left of the target), he knew his bomb would be released off-center of the I-boat below. For the second time in days, he watched the winking of machine-gun muzzles as he slanted down toward his quarry. As Dickinson reached seventeen hundred feet, he pulled back on the double-handled manual bomb release to his left. He quickly retracted his dive brakes and yanked back on the stick, pulling more than five Gs at high speed, low over the water below.

Dickinson's bomb hit close aboard the fourteen-hundred-ton sub amidships. The deck gunners were instantly silenced by the explosion and shrapnel. As he turned his SBD back around, he noted that the sub's forward progress had ceased and she appeared to be settling somewhat by the

Lieutenant Dick Dickinson.

stern. Forty-five seconds after his bomb struck, the sub slipped under the water. Right after it disappeared, Dickinson saw an eruption of oil and foam from her midships section.[18]

Seconds later, another eruption of foam and oil marked the end of Lieutenant Commander Takao Sano's *I-70*. "Looks like we got him, Mr. Dickinson," Merritt said from the rear seat. The pair made their return to *Enterprise* and Dickinson was immediately summoned to the bridge to relate the success of his attack to Admiral Halsey. Postwar records would credit Dickinson and Merritt with sinking the first combatant ship of World War II by U.S. forces.

Enterprise narrowly missed disaster on December 11, when a submarine torpedo passed within twenty yards of her stern. She returned to Pearl Harbor on December 16, having survived the crisis. Ashore, two VS-6 aviators were waiting. Lieutenant Frank Patriarca and gunner Joe DeLuca had landed on Kauai on December 7, where Patriarca had been hospitalized with fatigue. On December 11, he had gone on a scouting mission without a rear seat man, but during his return landing his Dauntless hit an obstruction placed near the runway. The SBD's wingtip was crumpled and the plane stood on its nose, bending the propeller. Patriarca and DeLuca were eventually transported on an interisland ferry back to Oahu, where they found that their flight gear had been packed up along with that of other missing men.[19]

During the week following Pearl Harbor, Brigham Young and his squadron leaders compiled reports from the surviving airmen. Hal Hopping singled out four VS-6 aviators for special commendations. Dick Dickinson received the Navy Cross for his actions on December 7, as well as a second for sinking *I-70* three days later. Perry Teaff received the

Navy Cross for bravely maintaining formation on patrol in the afternoon of December 7 with a damaged SBD. Ed Deacon received a Letter of Commendation for rescuing his wounded radioman after their crash landing. Gunner William Miller was posthumously recommended for heroism by the secretary of the Navy, and a new destroyer escort, USS *William C. Miller* (DE-259), was named in honor of the VS-6 radioman. Another destroyer escort, USS *Willis* (DE-395), was also commissioned during the war in honor of VS-6's lost Ensign Walter Willis.

Enterprise returned to sea on December 19 to operate south of Midway Island. At the same time, *Lexington*'s and *Saratoga*'s task groups were busy supporting planned reinforcement landings on Wake Island. The garrison's small band of defenders had gallantly repelled the first Japanese landing attempt on December 11 but were in desperate need of supplies, aircraft, and more soldiers. One day out from Pearl, Dauntless pilots from *Enterprise* mistakenly attacked the U.S. submarine *Pompano*, which had departed Hawaii two days prior. *Pompano* was four hundred miles from Pearl at 0705 on December 20 when Commander Lewis Smith Parks was forced to make a crash dive to escape an attacking Navy antisubmarine patrol plane. Back on the surface at 1410, *Pompano*'s skipper was again forced to crash-dive when three unidentified planes were spotted in attack formation. The strikers were three SBDs from *Enterprise*, called in to destroy the "enemy" submarine.[20]

Skipper Hal Hopping, Reggie Rutherford, and Cleo Dobson of Scouting Six all made drops on the diving boat. Dobson's bomb hit about thirty-five feet off the starboard beam as the sub was submerging. The conning tower was just visible as the bomb exploded. The trio saw an oil slick on the surface, proof enough to them that this undersea raider was damaged if not out of commission.[21]

The attack was a grave error, but fortunately did not prove fatal for *Pompano* and her crew. Dobson's blast damaged her fuel tanks, but skipper Lew Parks managed to continue his first war patrol. Six weeks later, Dobson happened to run into one of *Pompano*'s officers at the Royal Hawaiian Hotel on Oahu. As the submarine officer complained of being bombed by U.S. aircraft on December 20, young Dobson immediately realized his mistake. "He said the second bomb dropped (which was mine) burst an oil tank and they lost 2,500 gallons of fuel," Dobson wrote. "I am really glad we didn't get them but they didn't fire an identification signal. He said they were not afraid of the Jap planes but he was of these goddamn American aviator[s]."[22]

The Dauntless airmen logged endless hours of single-plane search flights during late December. Jack Leaming put in 76.1 hours of flight time for the month—four times his prewar rate.

The aviators learned the value of sharpening their individual navigation skills during their long scouting flights. Some logged as much as seven hours in the air during the two-hundred-mile searches, and found it was often no easy task to find their carrier upon completion. From Bombing Six, Jack Blitch and Andy Anderson each became lost on consecutive days and managed to safely find the Big E only after dark. In his diary, Dusty Kleiss logged for December 22 that Blitch had managed to sink either a "whale or sub with direct hit."[23]

During these patrols, squadron pilots were thoroughly indoctrinated into the use of the first six new Zed Baker homing devices being installed in their aircraft. This new navigational aid worked in conjunction with the YE transponder installed on *Enterprise*, which sent out a separate code letter for each sector in the 360-degree circle around the ship. The radiomen received the coded letter and were able to make their pilots aware of what sector they were in relative to the ship's position.[24]

Lieutenant Ward Powell of Torpedo Six took it upon himself to play Santa Claus for the *Enterprise* Air Group on Christmas Day at sea. Using red signal cloth to fashion a Santa suit with the help of the squadron's parachute man, Powell donned a white beard and went around the ship delivering presents—cigars, candy, and gift-shop goodies—to everyone.[25]

Admiral Halsey's task group returned to Pearl on December 31, having encountered no enemy opposition. Among the pilots burning with desire to strike back at the Japanese was Dick Best. The carnage at Pearl Harbor was still fresh in his mind, and there was no disguising the anger he felt for his new enemy. "All I could think of was those squinty-eyed little fat Japs sitting around their war room toasting with sake. If I could have gone in there with a samurai sword, I would have cut the heads off a whole bunch of them. I was really upset."[26]

As the Dauntless crews flew constant long patrols in search of enemy subs and other surface vessels, each man shared a common goal: to make the Japanese pay for their sneak attack on Pearl Harbor.

FIVE

"We Lost as Much as We Gained"

Dick Best savored the brief hiatus in Hawaii. Suspecting that more serious action was imminent, he used what little time he had to be with his wife and young daughter in Honolulu. Meanwhile, Cleo Dobson of VS-6 noticed that their carrier loaded more supplies and war matériel than ever before. Although no specific information was given, Dobson was told that he could expect more action on the Big E's next cruise.[1]

There were other indications that the ship meant serious business. During its time at Ford Island, Bombing Six received a few more Zed Baker homing devices and spare ZB accessories. To Chief Jim Murray, these were a godsend. This meant more SBDs could be equipped with the antenna and coax cables, necessitating only a shift in black boxes to meet flight schedule requirements.[2]

Bombing Six also received two sets of twin .30-caliber machine guns to replace the standard single .30-calibers currently used in its Dauntlesses. The doubled firepower units were installed in 6-B-1 and 6-B-10, the dive-bombers routinely flown by skipper Holly Hollingsworth and exec Dick Best. "All the gunners gathered around to inspect the 'twins' and wish we had more," said Murray. At least there was hope that more twins would soon replace the single .30s.[3]

The extra equipment was timely. Admiral Chester Nimitz, the commander in chief, U.S. Pacific Fleet (CinCPac), had decided that the pickings were ripe for his aircraft carriers to effect an offensive raid on

Japanese-held territory in the Pacific. His plan was to hit Jaluit and Mili in the southern Marshall Islands, as well as the new Japanese conquest of Makin Atoll in the northern Gilbert Islands.

Admiral Halsey's Task Force 8 sailed west from Pearl Harbor on January 11. *Enterprise*'s destination was still a mystery to her pilots, until Halsey finally announced that a major offensive strike was in the planning. "Looks like some fireworks," Cleo Dobson wrote in his diary.[4]

During the second morning at sea, gunner Jim Murray was enduring yet another long-range search flight. Before turning back, Lieutenant Commander Hollingsworth flew their 6-B-1 past the task force headed by the big carrier *Saratoga*, which was en route to Pearl Harbor.[5]

"Do you notice anything unusual about the *Sara*?" Hollingsworth asked over the intercom.

Murray swept his eyes over the length of the Navy's third aircraft carrier. "Yes, she's trailing a streak of oil behind her."

Saratoga had been hit by a torpedo fired by the Japanese submarine *I-6* the previous evening. She could still make sixteen knots by morning, but her planned rendezvous with Bill Halsey's *Enterprise* task force was canceled. The *Sara* was heading in for repairs that would sideline her for months. For the time being, the U.S. Pacific Fleet's carrier striking force had been cut to three—*Yorktown*, *Lexington*, and *Enterprise*.

Scouting Six had the morning search on January 13. Cleo Dobson was paired with a new pilot, Ensign Reid Stone, who had only recently become fully carrier qualified. They ran into bad weather 169 miles out and had to cut their search leg short by thirty-seven miles. Dobson had tense moments in leading Stone through the soup to find their flight deck again.[6]

Ensign Tony Schneider of Bombing Six had more difficulty. He was flying without one of the squadron's new Zed Baker homing units. When he got back through the foul weather to where the ship was supposed to be, *Enterprise* was nowhere to be found. Like Dobson, Schneider commenced ever-expanding square search patterns to find his ship. "I wasn't allowed to break radio silence and I wasn't about to do it," he said.[7]

Without the benefits of radar or radio, Schneider began to consider his options. He calculated the distance to the nearest of the Hawaiian Islands and his odds of being able to land on or near a beach. Good fortune was in his favor this day, however. Before he reached the point of no return, the ship radioed a "steer" (course correction) to him.

No contacts were made during the first days at sea, though the Dauntless airmen continued to hear the scuttlebutt of impending action with their new enemy. The weather was hot as Task Force 8 (TF-8) crossed the equator on January 15, and the days of routine patrolling soon turned disastrous. On January 16, Ensign Daniel Seid of Scouting Six crashed into the barrier upon landing his 6-S-2, killing the petty officer (ACMM George Frank Lawhon of Bombing Six) who was manning the arresting gear. Seid, one of the squadron's replacement pilots, escaped the tragedy with only a small cut over his left eye. His gunner, Dave Craig, was unhurt. Further loss came when ACMM Harold Frederick Dixon's TBD was forced to ditch at sea this day. He and his two VT-6 crewmen would drift some 750 miles in their rubber raft before finally reaching shore on Puka Puka Island.

The following day, Fred Weber of VB-6 ran out of fuel, suffering a broken jaw and lacerations to his lips during his water landing. A task force destroyer recovered him, but his gunner, Joe Ivantic, failed to escape from their sinking SBD. That afternoon, a somber funeral service was held on board *Enterprise* for her two casualties. Prayers were said for Ivantic, and Chief Lawhon's body was buried at sea.[8]

Reid Stone of VS-6 added to the SBD casualty list on January 18, when, during a landing, he plowed his dive-bomber into the crash barrier. Stone and his gunner were uninjured, but their Dauntless was totaled. "This makes four planes in three days, which is too many if we expect to conduct a good war," Cleo Dobson confided in his diary.[9]

Rear Admiral Frank Jack Fletcher's Task Force 17 received word of the offensive thrust on January 20 as his flagship *Yorktown* was just completing a mission of safeguarding the U.S. Marine landings on the island of Samoa. Admiral Halsey planned to carry out Nimitz's orders by utilizing the *Enterprise* and *Yorktown* task groups for simultaneous strikes against Japanese bases in the Marshalls and Gilberts on the morning of February 1. *Enterprise*'s air group would concentrate on the islands of Wotje, Maloelap, and Kwajalein, while Fletcher and *Yorktown*'s air group was to hit the islands of Jaluit, Mili, and Makin.

The assaults would be America's first chance to lash back at the mighty Japanese war machine. Admiral Nagumo's pounding of the Pacific Fleet at Pearl Harbor had come off almost flawlessly. Only twenty-nine Japanese planes were lost, plus the minisubs and the one fleet submarine sunk by Scouting Six's Dick Dickinson. At the same time, the Japanese had made attacks on Malaya, Hong Kong, Guam, Wake, Midway Atoll, and the Philippine Islands. Other Japanese forces operating from French Indochina had sunk a British battleship and battle cruiser on December 10.

Nagumo's Kido Butai returned to Japan unmolested on December 23, where his victorious pilots were showered with sake and praise for their surprise attack on America's great fleet. Not one to rest on his laurels, Admiral Yamamoto dispatched Nagumo's First Air Fleet carriers from the home islands in early January to the advance base at Truk Atoll in the Pacific. On January 20, Japanese carrier aviators began pounding Rabaul on New Britain and Kavieng on New Ireland in advance of their army's planned landings in these areas. The war news that filtered back to Halsey on the Big E gave him great incentive to do something to show that the U.S. Navy was in the fight as well.

The *Enterprise* squadrons continued to fly routine scouting hops en route to the Marshalls. Ed Kroeger of VB-6 had a few tense moments on January 26 when he encountered a big four-engine PBY flying boat out of New Zealand. His gunner, Achilles Georgiou, found that the PBY crew failed to answer his identification challenges. Kroeger responded by firing several warning shots under the plane's belly. "Everybody quickly stuck out their British flags and waved them back and forth after that," said Georgiou. Spotting the New Zealand flag, Kroeger flew up alongside the flying boat. The crew gave him the thumbs-up signal to indicate their safety, and the close encounter ended without damage.[10]

Scouting Six XO Earl Gallaher flew over to *Yorktown* on January 28 to deliver Admiral Halsey's latest plan of attack to Admiral Fletcher while both carrier task forces refueled. Three days later, Halsey brought his pilots up to speed. In an afternoon speech in one of the ready rooms, he said that radar had picked up a Japanese scouting plane coming out of Maloelap. Dick Best quickly realized that the snooper could jeopardize the entire mission. Halsey informed them that the strike would proceed as planned if the scout failed to report their force.[11]

Pilots of *Enterprise*'s Scouting Six in a photo taken on January 24, 1942. Ten of these men flew into Pearl Harbor on December 7. Seven would be killed in action or taken prisoner during the first six months of the Pacific carrier war in 1942: (*front row, left to right*) Lieutenant (j.g.) Dale Hilton, Lieutenant Reggie Rutherford, Lieutenant Earl Gallaher (XO), Lieutenant Commander Hallsted Hopping (CO), Lieutenant Clarence Dickinson (FO), Lieutenant Frank Patriarca, and Lieutenant (j.g.) Dusty Kleiss; (*standing, left to right*) Ensign Percy Forman, Ensign Willie West, Lieutenant (j.g.) Ben Troemel, Ensign Daniel Seid, Ensign Reid Stone, Ensign Earl Donnell, Lieutenant (j.g.) Norm West, Lieutenant (j.g.) Ed Deacon, Ensign Cleo Dobson, Lieutenant (j.g.) Perry Teaff, and Lieutenant (j.g.) Carlton Fogg.

The radiomen/gunners of Scouting Six. Ten would die or be taken prisoner during the first six months of fighting in the Pacific: (*front row, left to right*) RM2c Jack Leaming, RM3c Donald Hoff, RM3c Alfred Stitzelberger, RM3c John Snowden, and RM1c William Bergin; (*middle row, left to right*) AM3c Erwin Bailey, RM1c Joe Cupples, RM3c Earl Howell, RM1c Thomas Merritt, RM3c Otis Dennis, and RM3c Louis Hansen; (*standing, left to right*) RM3c Porter Pixley, RM3c David Craig, RM2c William Stambaugh, RM1c Joe DeLuca, RM1c Harold Thomas, RM3c John Dance, RM3c Edgar Jinks, and RM3c Roy Hoss.

Mark Horan Collection, courtesy of Lieutenant Commander James Murray

Pilots of *Enterprise*'s Bombing Six in January 1942 before the Marshalls strike: (*front row, left to right*) Lieutenant Harvey Lanham, Lieutenant Lloyd Smith, Lieutenant Dick Best (XO), Lieutenant Commander Holly Hollingsworth (CO), Lieutenant Jack Blitch (FO), Lieutenant Joe Penland, and Lieutenant Jim McCauley; (*middle row, left to right*) Lieutenant (j.g.) Leonard Check, Ensign Norm Vandivier, Ensign Tony Schneider, Lieutenant (j.g.) Edwin Kroeger, Lieutenant (j.g.) Edward Anderson, Lieutenant (j.g.) John Van Buren, Ensign Bucky Walters, and Ensign Bill Roberts; (*back row, left to right*) Ensign John Doherty, Ensign Arthur Rausch, Ensign Fred Weber, Ensign Delbert Halsey, Ensign Keith Holcomb, and Ensign Thomas Ramsay.

Mark Horan Collection, courtesy of Lieutenant Commander James Murray

The radiomen/gunners of Bombing Six: (*front row, left to right*) RM2c Lee McHugh, RM3c Achilles Georgiou, RM3c Gail Halterman, RM2c Harold Heard, AOM3c Ernest Hilbert, AOM3c Will Hunt, RM3c Stuart Mason, RM2c Parham Johnson, and AMM3c William Steinman; (*standing, left to right*) ACRM Jim Murray, RM3c Edward Garaudy, AMM3c Herman Caruthers, ARM1c Harry Nelson, RM3c Lee Keaney, RM3c Glenn Holden, RM1c Carl J. Schlegal, RM3c Allen Brost, RM1c James M. Shea, and RM3c Jay Jenkins. Of this group, Hunt was lost during the Marshalls strike and Brost was wounded. More than three-quarters of these men would be lost during the first half of 1942.

Gallaher learned Scouting Six's first target in the Marshalls was to be a Japanese airfield on tiny Roi-Namur Island. "We had a really old map of the Marshall Islands and it showed just a little dot on the thing, which was Roi Island," he said. Such intelligence was only slightly better than nothing.[12]

Cleo Dobson described the eager discussions among the pilots as similar to the banter before a big basketball game in college. Their excited chatter, however, soon became more philosophical. His VS-6 buddy Ben Troemel could not bear the thought of killing, saying, "It isn't right." In his diary, Dobson was less concerned with the prospect. "Kill or be killed, say I."[13]

The weather began to turn nasty as the two American carrier forces approached the Marshalls and Gilberts. Staff aerologists called for foul weather again on the morning of February 1, but the *Yorktown* and *Enterprise* strikers were committed to America's first offensive carrier strikes, good weather or bad. The operations orders written by Commander Thomas P. Jeter, the Big E's executive officer, made things clear for all. "We can take pride in being privileged to participate in the first offensive engagement of the Pacific Fleet, and in the first naval action in which an American aircraft carrier has taken part," Jeter's memo concluded. "Remember Pearl Harbor."[14]

Dick Dickinson was awakened at 0300 on February 1. The VS-6 flight officer was among the dozens of *Enterprise* pilots and gunners scheduled for action. He dressed and headed to the wardroom, where he found a certain eagerness among his shipmates. Khaki-clad aviators shoveled in their food, some excitedly chatting about the day's prospects. Dickinson's mouth was so dry he could not even swallow his fried egg. He instead crammed a piece of toast in his mouth, washed it down with a swig of water, and headed for the ready room to prepare.[15]

Flight quarters sounded at 0345. Jim Murray went to the flight deck to check over his 6-B-1 while his skipper, Holly Hollingsworth, remained below with the pilots. Enlisted radiomen did not attend pilot briefings, and did not know what strike plans were ordered unless their pilots briefed them. Topside, it was pitch-black as the moon ducked behind low clouds, with no wind and calm seas. Murray proceeded with preparing the skipper's Dauntless and inspecting his new twin .30-caliber machine guns, anxiously awaiting the call to action.[16]

Below the flight deck in Scouting Six's ready room, twenty-one chairs

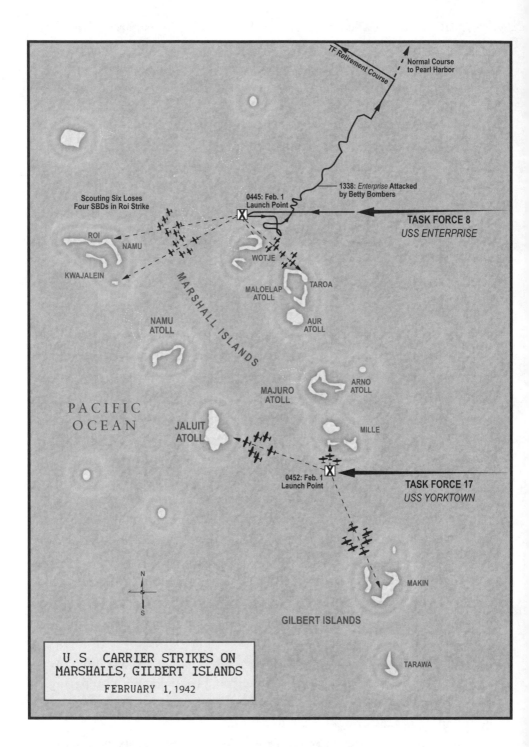

TF Retirement Course

Normal Course
to Pearl Harbor

1338: *Enterprise* Attacked
by Betty Bombers

Scouting Six Loses
Four SBDs in Roi Strike

0445: Feb. 1
Launch Point

TASK FORCE 8
USS ENTERPRISE

ROI

NAMU

WOTJE

KWAJALEIN

MARSHALL ISLANDS

MALOELAP
ATOLL

TAROA

NAMU
ATOLL

AUR
ATOLL

ARNO
ATOLL

MAJURO
ATOLL

PACIFIC
OCEAN

JALUIT
ATOLL

MILLE

0452: Feb. 1
Launch Point

TASK FORCE 17
USS YORKTOWN

N

S

MAKIN

GILBERT ISLANDS

TARAWA

**U.S. CARRIER STRIKES ON
MARSHALLS, GILBERT ISLANDS**
FEBRUARY 1, 1942

were neatly arranged in rows of threes. There, the pilots copied down all prestrike intelligence that was available from skipper Hal Hopping, plus the critical Point Option—where the Big E was expected to be found upon their return from the mission. The room smelled of coffee, consumed by the gallon by the pilots, and cigarette smoke, which hung like a haze throughout the compartment. In the ready rooms of Bombing Six, Torpedo Six, and Fighting Six, the pilots repeated the process.

Cleo Dobson had known for two weeks that his Dauntless would be carrying special camera equipment to document the initial action. It was a duty he did not cherish, running the risk of being shot down while flying low to allow his rear seat gunner to snap pictures. In the hours prior to launch, Dobson found his fellow VS-6 pilots to be tense but "in the mood."[17]

"Pilots, man your planes!" Soon after 0400, the awaited order was broadcast throughout the carrier.

Holly Hollingsworth climbed into his cockpit without offering many specifics to Jim Murray. Some pilots gave their radiomen a hint of what could be expected. Dick Best made it clear to rear gunner Lee McHugh prior to takeoff that they would not be taken as prisoners of war if their SBD was shot down over the Japanese base. "Your job is to get those twin .30-calibers and the ammunition cans available to me," he told McHugh in the event they had to crash-land on a beach. "We're going to put our backs into a sand dune and we're going to kill Japanese until they have to kill us to get the guns."[18]

The flight deck was washed with moonlight. Restless pilots anticipated the launch process like marathon runners awaiting a shot from a starter pistol. Starters fired and engines roared to life, their blue exhaust drifting aft in the breeze. As he pushed his throttle forward to taxi down Enterprise's deck, Dick Dickinson felt the same tension he had experienced long ago at Pensacola when he took off on his first solo flight.[19]

The morning's combat air patrol (CAP) fighters began launching at 0445, followed by thirty-seven dive-bombers, eighteen each from Bombing Six and Scouting Six, plus Brigham Young in the CEAG plane. Enterprise next sent up nine bomb-armed Devastators of Torpedo Six. Only one dive-bomber, Daniel Seid's 6-S-6, struggled with engine trouble, but he too managed to launch shortly after 0500 and chase after the main strike group.[20]

Bombing Six and Scouting Six circled close to each other as their divisions grouped. Dickinson, leading VS-6's third division, felt the unpleasant rocking of another plane from VB-6 passing close enough above to shake him with its prop wash. "I'll never know how we avoided crashing into each other," he said.[21]

The only loss for the *Enterprise* Air Group came when Ensign Dave Criswell's F4F crashed during takeoff. The fighter pilot sank into the dark waters with his Wildcat.

Commander Young's formation climbed to fifteen thousand feet in the predawn darkness, and by 0645, the attackers had arrived at a point twenty miles northeast of Roi-Namur Island, Kwajalein Atoll. The *Enterprise* strikers arrived over Roi fifteen minutes before dawn. The Japanese below heard the passing engines and were ready by the time Young recognized the island through dense ground fog. Dick Best was startled when guns suddenly broke loose and began firing behind him. A Scouting Six plane had suffered a mechanical failure, causing its guns to go into automatic fire when the pilot tried to charge them.[22]

Whereas Scouting Six was specifically assigned to pound the Roi airfield, Bombing Six was operating on a freelance basis and would reserve their munitions for shipping or shore installations deemed most worthy of attack. *We know very little about this place*, pilot Tony Scheider thought as he eyed the island below. *Nobody knows what we'll find here. We're going in with no aerial reconnaissance info or anything. If I make it out of here, I'll be able to draw a better map of Kwajalein than this one they gave us.*

The morning sun was just peeking over the horizon as Hal Hopping led Scouting Six in first from fourteen thousand feet. Japanese Type 96 fighters (Mitsubishi A5M "Claudes") were scrambled from the Roi airfield while AA gunners took their stations. Hopping ordered an echelon to the right. In such formation, each SBD was stationed behind and to the right of Hopping's leading bomber. Each pilot allowed enough space between his own and the plane ahead of him to retain a good view of the target airfield below. As VS-6's first division pushed over at 0705 in glide bombing runs on Roi, the sky quickly darkened with menacing black bursts of AA fire.[23]

Hopping glided over the beach and released his bombs over the airfield—the first American ordnance to explode on Japanese soil during World War II. By this time, ten Type 96 fighters from the local Chitose Air Group had gotten airborne to challenge the SBDs. One of the Japanese fighters bored in on Hopping's tail as he recovered low and level over the island. As witnessed by several of his junior pilots, Hopping's Dauntless was pounded by both shore gunners and the Claude on his tail. He and gunner Harold Thomas returned fire, but their fight was brief. Heavily damaged, their SBD spun into the Pacific northeast of Roi, killing both Scouting Six's skipper and senior radioman.[24]

Perry Teaff and Ben Troemel, close behind their skipper, both dumped all three of their bombs in their excitement. Most pilots opted to save their five-hundred-pound bomb for possible shipping targets to be encountered later. Dale Hilton, with wingmen Cleo Dobson and Percy Forman, followed the skipper's first section. For gunner Jack Leaming, it was his first experience being seated backward facing the SBD's tail during a dive. Hurtling downward about three hundred miles an hour, he could not see where in the hell he was going. Leaming watched the altimeter spin like a top as their SBD screamed into its dive. When it read fifteen hundred feet, he called, "Mark!" over the ICS. Hilton then released their bomb and pulled out of the dive. As the nose of the plane swung up and the horizon sprang into view, Leaming emptied a can of .30-caliber bullets, strafing the airstrip at low altitude.[25]

Lieutenant Earl Gallaher felt that Hopping's speed had appeared to be too slow in the face of considerable antiaircraft fire from shore batteries. He led his second and third divisions in a circle at an altitude of about ten thousand feet while allowing the first division to clear out. The Claude that shot down Hopping then started up toward Gallaher.[26]

He and his opponent traded fire as they approached each other head-on. Gallaher found later that only one bullet pierced his cowling in the exchange. As they flashed closer together, the Claude finally pulled up. Rear gunner Tom Merritt squeezed off a few .30-caliber bursts at the passing fighter.[27]

Gallaher, with wingmen Carl Fogg and Willie West, pressed into dives that reached speeds in the neighborhood of two hundred knots. Fogg, twenty-four, had graduated from the University of Maine and was a tall, dashing bachelor admired by the ladies for his looks. His 6-S-11 was hit by flak during his bombing approach and he never fully recovered from his dive. He continued across the island and crashed into the sea about a half mile north of Roi. Neither Fogg nor his gunner, RM3c Otis Lee Dennis, survived.

The next section of Reggie Rutherford, Dusty Kleiss, and Earl Donnell dropped only their small wing bombs. Kleiss landed his hundred-pounders on a parked plane while he strafed the ground. Upon pullout, as he tried to join with his section, Kleiss saw a Japanese fighter slide past him, latch onto the tail of Donnell's 6-S-18, and open fire.

From his rear seat, Jack Leaming looked over his shoulder just in time to see Donnell's starboard wing blow off, and then the plane spiraled upward through the air as the rest of the aircraft dropped straight down. Donnell and his rear seat man, AMM2c Alton John Travis, both perished in the crash. It all happened in a split second directly in front of Hilton's SBD, but too fast for Leaming to identify who had been hit. *Our own hide is too important to devote too much attention to others*, he thought.[28]

Kleiss's rear gunner, John Snowden, opened up with his .30-caliber. As the squadron educational officer, Kleiss had handpicked Snowden to be his rear seat man because of his shooting ability. "I grabbed him before anyone else had the chance to know how good his gunnery was," he said. "He was the best, I'm sure, of our radiomen-gunners." Snowden stitched lead into the Claude fighter; then Kleiss saw the enemy dive past his SBD at the point-blank range of twenty feet. He too fired a short burst, lost sight of him, and two seconds later spotted the Claude in flames.[29]

Kleiss watched the Japanese fighter plunge a thousand feet down into the sea. Its pilot did not bail out. Snowden was credited by the squadron with the kill. Another pair of Claudes jumped Willie West as he roared across Roi. His gunner, AMM3c Milton Wayne Clark, was credited with shooting down one of his opponents. West witnessed a second Claude receive full gunfire attention from Clark. This plane was last seen to roll over onto its back, apparently out of control, but West, fully engaged in evasive action, was unable to see whether the fighter crashed.

Next in was Dick Dickinson's six-plane third division. One of his wingmen, Dan Seid, was hit by either AA fire or by a Japanese fighter.

Seid's 6-S-6 was last seen making an extremely fast, but controlled, downwind landing on the water about one mile north of Roi. Neither Seid nor his gunner, AMM3c David Franklin Grogg, were to be seen again.

Dickinson dropped his pair of wing bombs toward a bunch of buildings on the airfield and kicked his tail around quickly, glancing back in time to see his ordnance explode into one of the buildings. His wingman, Norm West, dropped his bombs right next to the same building on what was apparently an ammunition storehouse. "It went up with a tremendous bang and a gigantic flare," said Dickinson. "That was quite gratifying."[30]

Either Dickinson or West may well have been the pilot who put a bomb through the roof of the atoll headquarters. The resulting blast claimed the Imperial Japanese Navy's first flag officer of the war, killing Rear Admiral Yatsushiro Sukeyoshi—who was celebrating his fifty-second birthday.[31]

Several VS-6 crews circled around to make secondary runs in the face of intense machine-gun and AA fire. Hilton dropped his load and pulled away as Leaming strafed a building where soldiers were running out of a door. A shiny brass shower of spent cartridges flew through the rear cockpit and out into 6-S-7's slipstream as Leaming mowed down the Japanese soldiers.[32]

During his second attack, Willie West was wounded in the right shoulder by gunfire from an enemy fighter. Yet his 6-S-12 remained intact, so the injured pilot turned his Dauntless back toward *Enterprise*, where he and Clark were recovered safely. Scouting Six paid a heavy price in its first attack on Japanese-held soil, losing four SBDs and their crews. In return, they claimed six planes destroyed on the ground, two fighters killed in aerial combat, two hangars bombed or strafed, one large building destroyed, six storehouses destroyed, and damage to shore installations.

Reid Stone's 6-S-15 was hit by AA fire during its bombing run over Roi, ripping a large hole in his right main fuel tank. He rendezvoused with Perry Teaff and Ben Troemel for the return toward *Enterprise* and they were soon joined by Dale Hilton, Pat Patriarca, and Ed Deacon. Earl Gallaher felt that if Scouting Six's Dauntlesses had been equipped with leakproof tanks, Stone's plane would have been able to continue the assault and expend his five-hundred-pound bomb.

After his first attack, Dusty Kleiss joined formation on Dickinson and Cleo Dobson. As the trio circled around to make another attack, they were jumped by three fighters. Joe DeLuca, rear gunner for Dickinson, found his machine gun difficult to manage due to his slight weight. When his plane was charged by a Claude, DeLuca pressed the foot release to lower the gun and it instantly fell all the way to the bottom. He struggled to bring it to bear but was not able to get off a shot against the fighter.[33]

Curiously, the Japanese pilots did not force their attacks. Dickinson watched in amazement as two enemy fighters climbed away and proceeded to perform aerial stunts. "They looped together and followed with an elegant slow roll," he remembered. "They just sat up there and did what we call 'flat-hatting,' a term for all kinds of stupid, show-off flying."[34]

Dobson suddenly found a Japanese fighter coming at him from about a thousand feet above and in front. The two planes were on a collision course, and both fired at each other for all they were worth. Dobson saw three puffs of white smoke in the fighter's engine before it went by, missing a collision by mere yards. From Dobson's rear seat, RM3c Roy Hoss saw that the Claude was losing altitude and weaving around after he flashed past their SBD.[35]

From Holly Hollingsworth's VB-6 command plane, Jim Murray had watched Scouting Six commence its attack on Roi. The dawn air had erupted with colorful red tracers that clawed angrily at the plunging war birds. He saw Hal Hopping's Dauntless burst into flames and head for the water. Suddenly he heard Torpedo Six skipper Gene Lindsey open up on the radio: "Targets suitable for heavy bombs at Kwajalein anchorage."

Japanese shipping! Another of the torpedo boys had mistakenly taken one of the enemy vessels for a carrier off Kwajalein Island. Brigham Young at 0705 ordered Hollingsworth to take his Bombing Six and attack. As his squadron approached Kwajalein from fourteen thousand feet, Murray thought, *It looks like the state of Florida.* The island's outline was formed by small coral islets, with Roi and Kwajalein being the largest.[36]

Below him in the anchorage, Murray could make out freighters, tankers, a few submarines, and a light cruiser. He knew now was the time to make good on paying back the Japanese for Pearl Harbor. Commander

Bombing Six (VB-6) Tactical Organization
Marshall Islands Attack: February 1, 1942

FIRST DIVISION

PLANE	PILOT	REAR SEAT GUNNER
6-B-1	Lt. Cdr. William Right Hollingsworth	ACRM James Francis Murray
6-B-2	Lt. Harvey Peter Lanham	ARM2c Edward Joseph Garaudy
6-B-3	Lt. Lloyd Addison Smith	AMM2c Herman Hull Caruthers
6-B-7	Lt. James Wickersham McCauley	RM2c Harry William Nelson Jr.
6-B-8	Ens. Keith Haven Holcomb	AMM2c Lloyd E. Welch
6-B-9	Lt. (jg) Wilbur Edison Roberts	AMM1c James H. Shea Jr.

SECOND DIVISION

PLANE	PILOT	REAR SEAT GUNNER
6-B-10	Lt. Richard Halsey Best	RM2c Lee Thomas McHugh
6-B-11	Lt. (jg) Edwin John Kroeger*	RM3c Achilles Antonius Georgiou
6-B-12	Lt. (jg) John James Van Buren	RM3c Allen James Brost*

*Wounded in action on February 1, 1942.   *(continued)*

Bombing Six (VB-6) Tactical Organization
Marshall Islands Attack: February 1, 1942 (cont.)

SECOND DIVISION

PLANE	PILOT	REAR SEAT GUNNER
6-B-16	Lt. (jg) Leonard Joseph Check*	ARM2c Stuart James Mason Jr.
6-B-17	Lt. (jg) Edward Lee Anderson	ARM2c Parham Screeton Johnson
6-B-18	Ens. Delbert Wayne Halsey	AOM2c Arie Turner Alford

THIRD DIVISION

PLANE	PILOT	REAR SEAT GUNNER
6-B-4	Lt. John Devereux Blitch	AMM2c William Burr Steinman
6-B-5	Ens. Norman Francis Vandivier	S1c Lee Edward John Keaney
6-B-6	Ens. Tony Frederic Schneider	RM3c Glenn Lester Holden
6-B-13	Lt. Joe Robert Penland	ARM2c Harold French Heard
6-B-14	Ens. Clifford Raymond Walters	AMM2c Wilbur Thomas Thompson

| 6-B-15 | Ens. John Joseph Doherty | AOM3c William Evan Hunt |
| CEAG | Cdr. Howard Leyland Young | CRM John Murray O'Brien |

*Wounded in action on February 1, 1942.

Scouting Six (VS-6) Tactical Organization Marshall Islands Attack: February 1, 1942		
FIRST DIVISION		
PLANE	**PILOT**	**REAR SEAT GUNNER**
6-S-1	Lt. Cdr. Hallsted Lubeck Hopping*	RM1c Harold "R" Thomas*
6-S-2	Lt. (jg) Perry Lee Teaff	RM3c Edgar Phelan Jinks
6-S-3	Lt. (jg) Benjamin Henry Troemel	RM3c William Hart Bergin
6-S-7	Lt. (jg) Hart Dale Hilton	RM2c Jack Leaming
6-S-8	Ens. Cleo John Dobson	RM3c Roy L. Hoss
6-S-9	Ens. Percy Wendell Forman	RM2c William Henry Stambaugh

(continued)

Scouting Six (VS-6) Tactical Organization
Marshall Islands Attack: February 1, 1942 (cont.)

SECOND DIVISION

PLANE	PILOT	REAR SEAT GUNNER
6-S-10	Lt. Wilmer Earl Gallaher	RM1c Thomas Edward Merritt
6-S-11	Lt. (jg) Carleton Thayer Fogg*	RM3c Otis Lee Dennis*
6-S-12	Ens. William Price West*	AMM3c Milton Wayne Clark
6-S-16	Lt. Reginald Rutherford	RM3c Earl Edward Howell
6-S-17	Lt. (jg) Norman Jack Kleiss	RM3c John Warren Snowden
6-S-18	Ens. Earl Roe Donnell Jr.*	AMM1c Alton John Travis*

THIRD DIVISION

PLANE	PILOT	REAR SEAT GUNNER
6-S-4	Lt. Clarence Earle Dickinson Jr.	RM1c Joseph Ferdinand DeLuca
6-S-5	Lt. (jg) John Norman West	RM3c Alfred R. Stitzelberger

6-S-6	Ens. Daniel Seid*	AMM3c David Franklin Grogg*
6-S-13	Lt. Frank Anthony Patriarca	RM1c Ferdinand Joseph Cupples
6-S-14	Lt.(jg) Edward Thorpe Deacon	RM3c Louis Dale Hansen
6-S-15	Ens. Reid Wentworth Stone	AM3c Erwin G. Bailey

*Shot down and killed on February 1, 1942.
**Wounded in action on February 1, 1942.

Jeter's orders for February 1 seemed most appropriate: "An eye for an eye, a tooth for a tooth, this Sunday it's our turn to shoot."

At 0725, Bombing Six was over the Kwajalein area. From high altitude, they found the report of a carrier to be in error. Holly Hollingsworth saw several large ships in the lagoon putting up a heavy barrage of antiaircraft and machine-gun fire, but no aircraft carrier was present. Hollingsworth knew that his brother-in-law, Lieutenant Commander Bob Armstrong, was likely getting in his own licks at this very minute. Armstrong, skipper of *Yorktown*'s Bombing Five, was leading his SBDs into dives on Japanese ships in the harbor of Jaluit Atoll at 0725. Back home on Coronado Island near the San Diego Naval Air Station, Hollingsworth's and Armstrong's wives lived just blocks from each other.

In the center of the anchorage position was a large ship that VB-6's pilots believed to be an antiaircraft cruiser. The ship was actually the former cruiser *Tokiwa*, which had been converted to a minelayer. Hollingsworth gave the signal to attack at 0727, and his divisions separated for their dives, selecting a shipping target for their five-hundred-pounders. Hollingsworth selected the cruiser for his own target. "As we went into our dive, all hell broke loose on the cruiser," said Jim Murray. "The ship looked as if it was on fire with all their guns blasting away."[37]

As Murray called off the descending altitude, his eyes darted from his rear seat altimeter to the ack-ack buzzing past their wings. Murray saw their bomb land on the port side of *Tokiwa*'s fantail, and the aft end of the cruiser jumped out of the water from the explosion's force. Harvey Lanham and Lloyd Smith achieved near misses on a nearby tanker.

Dick Best, leading VB-6's second division, decided he would drop his five-hundred-pound bomb first, then make a second run to unleash his twin hundred-pound wing bombs. He had read that a large bomb would suppress the effect of a smaller bomb when dropped at the same time. "Everybody else dropped in salvo, and got the hell out of there," said Best. "If I'd had any sense, that's what I'd have done." He dropped his five-hundred-pounder on the transport *Bordeaux Maru* and circled to make another run.[38]

Lieutenant (j.g.) Leonard Check led the second section of VB-6's second division in as Best prepared for his second run. Check's rear gunner, ARM3c Stuart Mason, felt the G-forces pressing against him as they dived on a merchant ship anchored in Kwajalein's lagoon. As they pulled out, their Dauntless was hit by antiaircraft fire that punched a big hole in the starboard inboard tank and left Check with minor shrapnel wounds. They lost a quarter of their fuel and barely made it back to the ship. "More attacks were made but Check and I didn't fly anymore," said Mason.[39]

Dick Best was lining up a second merchant ship when another Dauntless flew right through his line of sight. He pulled out over the harbor with his SBD under heavy fire from a column of Japanese warships. Although his engine was struggling and sputtering oil, Best was able to coax his Dauntless back to the Big E from his first combat bombing mission.[40]

Jack Blitch, leading the third division, landed a direct hit on a cargo vessel off Roi. His wingman, Norm Vandivier, added a near miss. Joe Penland was credited with damaging another large cargo vessel and Jack Doherty landed a direct hit with his five-hundred-pound bomb. Tony Schneider watched the decks of a cargo vessel grow larger in his telescopic sight before making his drop. Schneider's gunner, Glenn Holden, announced that their bomb was a miss right alongside their target freighter.[41]

As Holly Hollingsworth circled the lagoon, Jim Murray saw several ships burning and smoking from bomb hits. Their Dauntless passed close by a seaplane hangar and ramp, where Murray spotted two huge Mavis four-engine flying boats sitting wingtip to wingtip. "Boy, did my eyes light up and my trigger finger became itchy," he related.[42]

"Captain," he called over the intercom. "Do you want to make an overhead run so I can test my twin .30s on the flying boats?"

"Hell, no!" Hollingsworth snapped. "We want to get the hell out of here!"

Scouting Six had lost four SBDs in the attack over Roi, and now the remaining planes realigned into new formations. Dusty Kleiss swept in over Kwajalein with Dickinson and Dobson flying to his left side as they prepared to attack the shipping from an altitude of eighty-five hundred feet. Numerous ships dotted the water below, but Dusty focused on what looked to be a large cruiser anchored in the Kwajalein harbor.

There're no fighters around, he thought. *Oh, boy, this is great!*

He knew, however, that dive-bombing a ship was much different from the glide-bombing runs the scouts had made on the airfield at Roi. A mile and a half above the harbor, Dusty proceeded into his dive. Pulling his plane's nose up slightly, he then dropped it straight down. As his angle increased to seventy degrees, he used his dive brakes to help check his descent rate. The Dauntless reached terminal velocity at about 240 knots, or 276 miles per hour. It would take only twenty seconds from the start of his dive until he would make his pullout above the warship.

The longer he waited before pulling out, the greater his odds were of scoring a direct hit. But the lower the release point, the greater the odds his plane would be caught in the bomb's fragmentation pattern, or his SBD would slam into the harbor at terrific speed. Somewhere in there— generally around two thousand feet or slightly less—the Dauntless pilots knew there was a happy median that offered both personal safety and a higher chance of a direct bomb hit. Dusty had already unloaded his wing bombs. He now had one chance to make his dive count with the larger five-hundred-pound bomb.

Just above his instrument panel was the three-powered telescope that he squinted through to keep his target lined up throughout his dive. If Dusty allowed his Dauntless to "skid"—drift laterally right or left—his sight would be off the flight path and his bomb would not hit where his sight indicated. Even if he released as low as fifteen hundred feet above target, one degree of skid would throw his bomb off about twenty-eight degrees. For the cruiser centered in his sights below, even that much off would cause his bomb to move from dead center to a near-miss alongside the vessel. He held his aim until his altimeter passed two thousand feet.[43]

Then Dusty pulled the bomb release. He began a sharp pullout, closing his dive brakes at the same time. He felt pressure six times the force of gravity as his SBD pulled six g's. A "g-meter," an instrument showing the force of gravity, indicated pressure that was immediately obvious to the pilot. At six g's and higher, Dusty knew that he would go into some stage of blackout. At lower stages, it became difficult to see. At higher stages, vision went away altogether until he eased back on the stick to flatten out his pull-up. The length of the time, the severity of the pullout, and the pilot's physical conditioning all factored into how severe a blackout stage he experienced.

This time, the blackout feeling was not severe. Dusty pushed his control stick forward to get right down on the water to escape the AA fire. From his rear seat, Johnny Snowden blasted away at the cruiser even as their bomb exploded dead center on the Japanese ship. Dusty roared across Kwajalein, passing directly over a radio station near the shoreline, and squeezed the trigger on his stick, lacing the building with machine-gun fire from his .50-caliber forward guns. Snowden then strafed it with his .30-caliber Browning from the rear.

Separately and almost simultaneously, Dick Dickinson and Cleo Dobson had pushed over into their own attacks against other prime targets at about 0743. Dickinson set his sights on a large *Yawata*-class liner—likely the large submarine depot ship *Yasukuni Maru*—which had a seaplane perched on its stern. He aimed right for the plane on her deck, and his aim was good—his five-hundred-pound bomb struck the stern and the blast wrapped the ship in flames. Dickinson looked back to see Dusty Kleiss's bomb strike the large cruiser. His other companion, Dobson, was credited with landing his big bomb squarely on a submarine tied up alongside a tender.[44]

Dobson could see only the tender at first, but as the distance narrowed, he made out the submarine through his bomb site. He saw his load hit squarely on the tail of the submarine. "It really blew the ass end of the sub and the last I saw he was sinking," Dobson logged.[45]

. . .

Upon completion of his first assault on Roi-Namur Island, Earl Gallaher joined up with Percy Forman, Norm West, and Reggie Rutherford and proceeded to Kwajalein Island. The foursome initiated a
dive-bombing attack from twelve thousand feet at 0748, sweeping in on
the shipping below. Gallaher did a figure eight coming down on this dive
to avoid antiaircraft fire. He felt certain that his five-hundred-pounder
was a direct hit on the stern of a cruiser—likely the former cruiser
Tokiwa—while Forman missed a supply ship with his load. West scored
a direct hit on a tanker. Rutherford claimed a possible hit on another
large tanker and then strafed the radio station at Enubuj Island before
Gallaher's four Dauntlesses turned for home.[46]

The pilots continued to attack targets of opportunity until each of
their three bombs had been expended. Various smaller ships, seaplanes,
a radio installation, three submarines, and shore installations were additionally strafed. Several VS-6 planes strafed a Japanese motor launch,
forcing its crew to dive overboard and leave the launch running about in
circles. Jim McCauley and Leonard Check were largely credited with
destroying several seaplanes discovered floating in the lagoon.

Japanese records indicate that Air Group Six had sunk the transport
Bordeaux Maru and left auxiliary subchaser *No. 2 Shonan Maru* in a
sinking condition. The submarine *I-23* was damaged by near misses and
strafing, although the other Japanese submarines managed to submerge
during the attack—likely appearing to be "sinking" to some of the aviators. The 11,933-ton submarine depot ship *Yasukuni Maru* was hit by
one bomb in her after turret and was further damaged by near-miss
bomb fragments that struck her stern. Other Japanese vessels damaged
by *Enterprise* SBDs and TBDs to varying degrees on February 1 were the
tanker *Toa Maru*, tanker *Hoyo Maru*, army cargo ship *Shinhei Maru*,
minelayer *Tokiwa*, and auxiliary netlayer *Kashima Maru*.[47]

The heavy presence of Japanese ships off Kwajalein compelled Bill
Hollingsworth, VT-6 skipper Gene Lindsey, and his second section
leader, Lieutenant (j.g.) Arthur Ely, to radio back to the ship for more
Devastators. The remaining nine TBDs on *Enterprise* had been loaded
with torpedoes, and were quickly launched under command of the VT-6
exec Lieutenant Lance Edward "Lem" Massey.

The first aerial torpedo attackers in American history quickly encountered a barrage of Japanese gunfire. The Devastators struck two tankers and one merchant vessel, claiming hits on all three. The final three-plane section, under Lieutenant (j.g.) Paul "Pablo" Riley, set their sights on the light cruiser *Katori* as she attempted to escape. Riley and Irvin McPherson released from within a thousand yards, as did third pilot Ensign Glenn Hodges. McPherson noticed that *Katori* was stopped and down at the stern in shallow water.[48]

For its part, Bombing Six suffered no lost planes or injured personnel, although six aircraft were damaged by shrapnel and machine-gun fire. At 0745, the attack was completed and the squadron returned to the ship in small groups, joining up en route. For Scouting Six, the aircraft and personnel losses were a tough pill to swallow. *It was not a real successful attack*, Dusty Kleiss thought. *We lost as much as we gained.*

The surviving planes returned to *Enterprise* low on fuel, but the aircrews were eager to get back into the fight. The first survivors from Scouting Six—Patriarca, West, Hilton, and Deacon—landed at 0905. West's 6-S-12 and Patriarca's 6-S-13 had been damaged enough by gunfire that they were hauled down to the hangar deck for repairs. Holly Hollingsworth and six of his VB-6 planes touched down right behind them.

Hollingsworth raced to the bridge to report to Admiral Halsey, while gunner Jim Murray remained with their 6-B-1 as it was refueled and rearmed. Reports from VF-6 Wildcat pilots said that enemy Type 97 fighters were airborne over the newly constructed military airfield and base on Taroa Island. "Mr. Hollingsworth had hardly returned from the bridge when flight quarters sounded," Murray said.[49]

The first of the reserviced Dauntlesses were launched again for a second strike at 0935. Dale Hilton and Ed Deacon of Scouting Six flew with seven pilots from Bombing Six: Holly Hollingsworth, Bucky Walters, Lloyd Smith, Jack Blitch, Norm Vandivier, Tony Schneider, and Joe Penland. Despite the presence of enemy fighters over the target areas, the aircrews found that there would be no Wildcats available to escort them. They departed immediately for Taroa Island, climbing to nineteen thousand feet for a planned up-sun strike position.

The remaining ten SBDs of Scouting Six were recovered by *Enterprise* around 1000. Three of the bombers—Dickinson's 6-S-4, Forman's 6-S-9, and Stone's 6-S-15—had been damaged by gunfire and were stuck belowdecks for repairs. "Most of us as we came aboard piled down into the wardroom, grabbed sandwiches, tomato or pineapple juice or coffee, and then ran to our various ready rooms fairly wild to see who was there and who was not," Dickinson said. With his damaged plane out of service, Dickinson settled into Air Plot to listen to the morning's excitement coming in over the radio.[50]

Jim Murray felt like his plane had hardly gotten into the air when suddenly they were over the Taroa military airfield. The Big E was operating only about ninety-five miles from the Japanese bases. At 1032, Hollingsworth and Jack Blitch led their sections down on Taroa in a high-speed, nose-down approach. The skipper counted a dozen two-engine bombers parked in a single row on the edge of the north–south runway. Five fighters were parked in front of the north hangar and another six sat at the south end of Taroa's main runway. Two bombers were parked to the northeast of the runways, separated from the rest of their group. Hollingsworth dropped a ripple salvo of all three bombs, destroying two large bombers and setting two others afire. He also spotted three small fighter planes catching fire from the explosions.

As Hollingsworth retired from the area, Jim Murray could see black puffs of the bursting shells about one thousand yards behind and above their 6-B-1. Suddenly, Jack Blitch came on the radio, excitedly screaming, "Captain! The AA had a bead on you! You'd better get out of there!"[51]

Murray, facing aft to watch for fighters, was already keeping his skipper apprised of every black puff of AA fire. *I guess Lieutenant Blitch must think I've lost my eyesight!* he sneered to himself.

Bucky Walters, second to dive, dropped his big bomb on a hangar that likely housed aviation fuel. The resulting explosion sent flames high into the sky. Walters proceeded to Ollot Island, where he landed each of his hundred-pound bombs on additional structures. Lloyd Smith demolished three parked Japanese fighters. The Japanese machine gunners finally came to life as Lieutenant Blitch led in the second section next. His first wing bomb hit demolished a large bomber and set two fighters on fire. Blitch then set ablaze an oil storage tank with his five-hundred-pounder and headed for Ollot to dump his final hundred-pounder on an antiaircraft emplacement. A series of white smoke bursts erupted around the emplacement as Japanese ammunition cooked off. Blitch's 6-B-4 escaped the action with only a single bullet hole in his right aileron.

Norm Vandivier dropped all his bombs in the initial dive and blasted a small barracks. Tony Schneider ripped open a T-shaped barracks building with his toggled load. Following their pullouts, Vandivier and Schneider strafed a small boat seen proceeding toward a pier on Ollot. Schneider was just pulling out of his strafing run when he suddenly saw tracers streaking past his plane. From the rear seat, RM3c Glenn Holden shouted out the obvious: "There's a fighter on our tail!"[52]

"Well, shoot him!" Tony hollered back.

Schneider did not have time to announce the presence of fighters over the radio to his comrades. Holden hammered away with his .30-caliber until he swung the gun too hard on its tracking ring and busted a bearing in the mounting. "Sir! The thirty can't traverse!" Holden called over the intercom.[53]

"Do your best and get it up!" Schneider hollered back.

With his rear guns out of commission, Tony knew escape lay in his hands only. "He had a better plane than I did for dogfighting, and every time we would make a scissors turn, he would gain a little on me," said Schneider. He also noticed another enemy fighter sitting up above on his perch. *He wants to get into this fray, too, but he doesn't know how*, Tony thought.[54]

The Japanese fighter on his tail did not push his attack home. Still, the wily pilot seemed willing to display the maneuverability of his plane and fire outside of gun range. "When you're pissed off and you have someone behind you that wants you dead, you can suddenly work magic," Schneider said. "I wanted that guy to work for his money." Schneider felt that his radical turns were more than enough to frustrate his opponent, who was unable to put bullets in the Dauntless. The frantic pursuit took them to within three hundred feet of the wave tops before Tony was able to force his opponent to break off. He was amazed to see the Japanese pilot fly right by his starboard side and shake his fist at the American before departing.

"I could see the expression on his face," Tony said. "He was that close." As the Japanese pilot broke off, Schneider slammed his canopy shut and pushed his throttle to full bore. He had gotten separated from Lieutenant Blitch's division and it was time to get the hell out of the area. He headed for home independently, avoiding more enemy fighters that passed by overhead.

Joe Penland hit the southern hangar with his five-hundred-pound bomb and dropped his small bombs in salvo near parked planes. The eighth pilot in order, Dale Hilton of VS-6, released his full load in a ripple salvo, aiming at the northern hangar. Ed Deacon, flying tail-end Charlie of the Taroa strike group, landed his bombs between the two hangars.

"It seemed that our group had stirred up a hornets' nest at Taroa," said Jim Murray of the fighters who engaged Bombing Six. Holly Hollingsworth retired to the northward with his eight comrades following. When he was about six miles north of Taroa's airfield, he was attacked by a diving Japanese fighter. He took evasive action and escaped with no bullet holes in his plane.[55]

Two of Hollingsworth's pilots became separated from the group but finally managed to join the other seven SBDs before arriving back over Enterprise. Upon landing, the second-strike aviators were told to report to sick bay for a shot of whiskey to calm them down.[56]

Admiral Halsey was eager to keep pounding the Japanese installations on the Marshalls. Enterprise turned into the wind at 1015 and began launching a third bomber strike on Taroa Island of Maloelap Atoll. This nine-plane group, led by VB-6's executive officer, Dick Best, included Dusty Kleiss of VS-6 and seven VB-6 pilots making their second attacks: Bud Kroeger, Harvey Lanham, Jim McCauley, Keith Holcomb, Bill Roberts, John Van Buren, and Jack Doherty. McCauley considered it grim going in without fighter protection when enemy fighters were reported to be in the air.[57]

"When we got in from the morning raid, they wouldn't let us get out of our flight gear or go below to talk things over," Bud Kroeger said. "They were rushing the rearming and the refueling and shoving cold sandwiches at us." Flight leader Best sent his gunner, Lee McHugh, racing to grab a better map of Taroa before they departed.[58]

Best's group climbed steadily while swinging to the east toward Maloelap. His engine was still having problems, and he could not climb above fourteen thousand feet. He led his flight down to the windward, wanting to get around the sun line in position before attacking.[59]

About fifteen miles from the island, Jim McCauley signaled that he had spotted a section of Japanese fighters over Maloelap. These were the Mitsubishi A5M4 Type 96 "Claude" carrier fighters of the Chitose Air Group. Best also spotted the planes, and urged his pilots to level off in order to gain speed. He was due east of Taroa as he saw the Claudes turning toward his formation. *We must attack at once before they can attack us*, he decided. As he swung his group to the left, the fighters were now broad on his starboard bow, in naval jargon.[60]

The *Enterprise* Dauntlesses went into two-hundred-knot power glides, as the four fighters closed from their above quarter. The ground gunners also commenced firing in a steady barrage on the nine American dive-bombers. Best pushed over around 1130, and landed his five-hundred-pound bomb right on a large hangar. The whole south side of the building erupted into smoke and flames. "I was just admiring my handiwork when, damn! A Japanese fighter came whizzing by shooting at me from the tail," said Best. He found himself in a fierce dogfight as the balance of his pilots completed their bomb runs.[61]

Bud Kroeger hit a hangar with his big bomb and took out a lumber pile or stores pile with one of his small loads. Jim McCauley scored a five-hundred-pound bomb hit at the door of Taroa's north hangar, adding to the general conflagration started by Best. Harvey Lanham dropped his hundred-pound bombs on an administrative building west of the landing field. Bill Roberts destroyed a twin-engine bomber with his salvo.[62]

Dusty Kleiss had three fighters on his tail for ten miles, eluding his pursuers by splitting his flaps and chopping his throttle, before he pushed over from seventeen thousand feet. The Claudes flashed past him and Kleiss released his five-hundred-pound bomb and one wing bomb on a large hangar.[63]

Bringing up the rear were John Van Buren and Ensign Jack Doherty, a young pilot fresh from Pensacola. Just prior to diving, Doherty flew under and just ahead of Van Buren. As they went over into their dives,

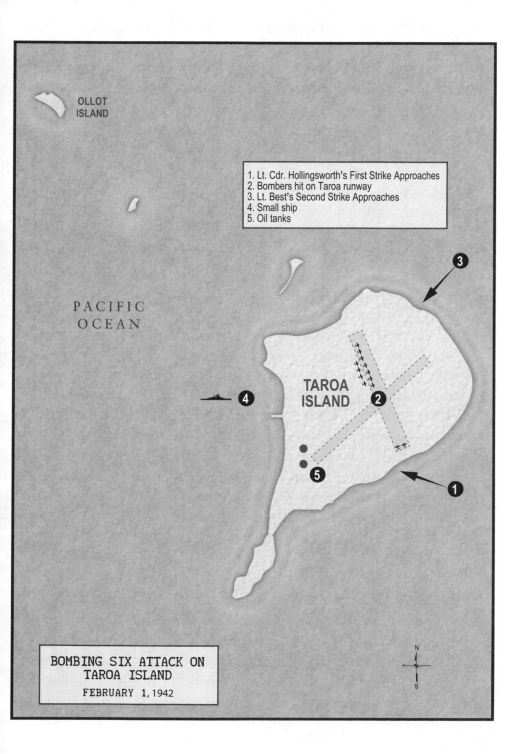

OLLOT
ISLAND

1. Lt. Cdr. Hollingsworth's First Strike Approaches
2. Bombers hit on Taroa runway
3. Lt. Best's Second Strike Approaches
4. Small ship
5. Oil tanks

PACIFIC
OCEAN

TAROA
ISLAND

BOMBING SIX ATTACK ON
TAROA ISLAND
FEBRUARY 1, 1942

N
S

Van Buren, spotting a Japanese fighter on the tail of Doherty's 6-B-15, opened fire with his two fixed .50-caliber guns and was credited with shooting down the enemy plane. Doherty held doggedly to his dive and delivered his bomb on the flying field.

Bud Kroeger noted the Claudes attacking Doherty and Van Buren. As one of the fighters came across his nose, Kroeger pulled up with the speed he had left from his dive. He intended to make the Japanese pilot turn off before popping his SBD into cloud cover. Instead, the fighter pulled up directly in front of Kroeger, who stayed right on his tail until both aircraft were reaching their stalling points. Kroeger poured lead into the Mitsubishi and saw his target fall off on a wing. Dodging through the clouds, Kroeger emerged with another enemy fighter right in front of him. "I gave it to him as long as I could and then ducked back into the cloud once more," he said.[64]

Kroeger then announced to his gunner, Achilles Georgiou, that he was going back in to drop his last wing bomb. *I've been training for years for just this situation and I don't plan to go home without unloading it*, Kroeger thought. Noting that Taroa Field was bounded by two large cloud formations, he decided to pop out of one side, deliver his bomb, and then zoom back into the other. Kroeger made his drop on what he deemed to be either a large barracks or a storehouse.[65]

During pullout, the planes were engaged by a low-level fighter patrol. In their defensive maneuvering, the Dauntlesses were unable to make an effective rendezvous. "We all got jumped on that hop and got shot up," said McCauley. The action broke up into individual dogfights. Gunner Allen Brost called out to his pilot, Van Buren, that fighters were approaching from astern. Their slow pullout speed allowed the fighters to catch them quickly. Brost got off only four shots before his gun jammed. In the process of standing to clear the jam, he was shot through the left arm by a bullet that cut a nerve and a tendon. He could not raise the arm, which streamed blood down across his hand.[66]

Yet Brost somehow managed to unjam his gun. As he took his seat again, more fighters were blazing away at his tail. Using only his right hand, he steadied his .30-caliber and poured lead into the second fighter following his SBD. "I emptied the gun on him and he went down," Brost said. He quickly reloaded with his right hand and began firing again at the persistent fighters.

Brost managed to score more hits on a second fighter until it began passing underneath their Dauntless. He called up to Van Buren to nose over to take a shot. Van Buren squeezed off several rounds until the fighter moved out of range. Brost turned his attention to a third fighter which remained on their tail. "I took a little better aim on him," he said. "I hit him and he turned right around and went the other way. He had enough."

The SBD pilots made defensive use of the excellent cloud layer that lay between two thousand and four thousand feet. Achilles Georgiou correctly believed that his attackers looked like old Type 97 fighter planes—often mistaken by U.S. pilots to be German Messerschmitts. His pilot, Bud Kroeger, jinked desperately to throw off the aim of two pursuing fighters. "Each time they made a firing run, I gave them the poorest possible shot," he said. "I was plenty scared and really kicking that plane around." Georgiou opened up with his single .30-caliber, claiming one of the Japanese planes, which he saw spiral away toward the ocean. A second fighter in the meantime riddled Georgiou and Kroeger's Dauntless.[67]

Bullets punctured their fuel tanks. One slug entered the front cockpit, hit the dashboard, and ricocheted off the plate containing the ignition switch. The bullet tore through Kroeger's left foot, breaking several bones and splattering blood throughout his cockpit. Georgiou knew his pilot had been hit but had no idea how serious it was. Kroeger felt a sharp initial pain but then lost all feeling in his foot as it spurted blood. "I'd lost my helmet, goggles, and earphones in the mess, and the airplane was riddled," he said. Kroeger found that his radio, controls, and engine were still okay, so he dived for the clouds and managed to elude the other Japanese fighters.[68]

Jack Doherty was less fortunate. The son of Irish immigrants who had settled into the projects of St. Francis Parish in Charlestown, Massachusetts, Doherty had joined the Navy in 1940 as an aviation cadet while his younger brother became a seaman on the cruiser San Francisco.

Clean-cut with a serious manner, Doherty was said by Dick Best to possess "a real go-get-the-bastards attitude" toward war. Off duty, Best found the young man to be just as fun-loving as most of the others. The only problem Best had with his junior pilot had been when Doherty was caught by the shore patrol running nude out of the old Moana Hotel in Waikiki. Doherty's shipboard roommate, Tony Schneider, said his friend had "decided to go skinny dipping on the beach behind the old Moana and then run bare-ass through the lobby."[69]

Bombing Six's exec had covered for Doherty when the young pilot was called before Lieutenant Commander Hollingsworth, and never had another problem from him. "He never swore in public, maintained a sharp uniform, and stopped to do the sign of the cross before slipping into his plane," Best remembered.

Doherty and gunner Will Hunt failed to return from their second strike. Their SBD was last seen twisting and turning under fire from three Nakajimas as Doherty raced frantically into cloud cover. Squadron mates heard his last radio call: "These goddamn Japs will never get me!"[70]

Dusty Kleiss fought through AA fire after making his drops and then was jumped by three fighters before he could reach cloud cover. One fighter came in close and offered his rear gunner an excellent shot. Johnny Snowden, however, had used all his ammunition while strafing Taroa and was in the process of reloading. The fighters' guns punctured Kleiss's two right wing tanks and nicked Snowden's right leg with shrapnel. Dusty pulled into a tight wingover and traded short-range head-on shots. The Claude pilot quickly turned and headed back for base, as did his two wingmen. Dusty was greatly relieved: He had only fifty rounds left in his forward guns.[71]

His SBD was a mess. Dusty watched gasoline stream from his starboard fuel tanks until they were empty. His bigger concern was with the oil spraying onto his Plexiglas windshield from his shattered engine cylinder. Kleiss was forced to stand periodically and wipe the misty oil from his windshield during the return flight to the *Enterprise*.

Dick Best felt the Japanese fighters were largely reluctant to finish off their prey. Their longer-range sniping had caused some damage, but more determined fighter pilots could have scored more kills. The first fighter to buzz Best's tail overshot him as he pulled out of his dive. The Claude then

turned and made two more runs on his SBD. A former fighter pilot of
Lexington's VF-2, Best dodged his opponent by employing his fighter
tactics. As the Japanese plane approached, he pulled up with all the speed
he had built up and turned in to his opponent with guns blazing. At
length, his violent maneuvers gave rear gunner Lee McHugh a good shot
that produced black smoke from the enemy aircraft.[72]

Best did not witness the kill. To McHugh's disappointment, he therefore did not let his gunner take credit for it. The second fighter was less
aggressive as Best continued sharp countermaneuvers over Maloelap's
harbor. He then ducked into a cumulus formation, and immediately turned
sharply ninety degrees to break free in a new location. Best dodged in and
out of the clouds several times until the fighter was gone.[73]

As he headed north to clear the lagoon, Best spotted a big gas plume
spurting out of his right wing. *A lucky and wild shot must have gotten
that one*, he thought. He had intended to go back to Wotje to use the two
bombs that he had not released, but the brush with Japanese fighters and
the newly discovered fuel leak ended these thoughts.

"Mr. Best, we're on fire!" yelled McHugh.

Best glanced quickly to the starboard wing, where McHugh was
pointing. "Dammit, McHugh!" he hollered. "That's our gasoline leaking. Don't you ever scare me like that again. I'm using that right tank."

Best's strike group had lost Jack Doherty and suffered two other airmen wounded—pilot Ed Kroeger in the left foot and gunner Allen Brost
in the left forearm. Three planes—those of Best, Kroeger, and Van
Buren—had sustained numerous bullet holes and punctured fuel tanks.
Kleiss's VS-6 plane had bullet holes punctured in both right-hand fuel
tanks, and other holes. After landing, Best demanded that any further
strike groups being sent out should do so only with appropriate fighter
escorts. He and McHugh were credited with destroying two Japanese
fighters, and Best would receive, months later, the Distinguished Flying
Cross for his actions.[74]

Gunner Achilles Georgiou was concerned, uncertain how Kroeger
would be able to land their Dauntless with a crippled left foot. Kroeger
reached the landing circle but found that *Enterprise* was not yet ready to
take him aboard. As he circled around, Georgiou penciled him a note that
read, "What do you think you are? Superman? Let's land!" Kroeger was

waved off by LSO Robin Lindsey on his first pass. His second approach was rather wild and fast, without brakes or hydraulic controls. He had just enough fluid left to let the flaps down with the use of his hand pump. Kroeger struggled to ride the brakes with his mangled foot after his tail hook was disengaged from the arresting wire. Georgiou motioned to the flight crew to help stop the plane. Then he scrambled from his rear cockpit to see that Kroeger was properly assisted to sick bay for attention.[75]

Dick Best was in the ready room when he heard that Jack Doherty's SBD did not return. "Every loss hurt, as it rightly should," he said. Skipper Holly Hollingsworth wrote out a citation and personal letter for Doherty's parents. The lost pilot's roommate, Tony Schneider, added his own letter to the family describing their friendship. "I cursed, I cried a little; then I calmed down," Schneider remembered. "If you allowed yourself to go numb over the deaths of your friends, you'd join them." He had lost another early roommate, Manny Gonzalez, weeks earlier over Pearl Harbor, and knew their occupation came with a harsh necessity. "We said our good-byes; then we got back into the war," Schneider said.[76]

Allen Brost was hustled to sick bay and remained under care until *Enterprise* made port again. Back at Pearl Harbor, his left arm was operated on, but the nerve and tendon damage was enough to put the VB-6 gunner out of commission. He was shipped to California for another operation and remained on limited shore duty for the rest of the war.[77]

Forty-five minutes after Lieutenant Best's Taroa strikers departed, *Enterprise* launched a fourth bombing mission of eight SBDs to strike Wotje Island and its shipping. CEAG Brigham Young took off at 1115 leading Andy Anderson of VB-6 and six pilots from VS-6—Earl Gallaher, Cleo Dobson, Reggie Rutherford, Norm West, Perry Teaff, and Ben Troemel. They took off in company with nine torpedo bombers of Torpedo Six.

Ten miles southeast of Wotje, Young turned the lead over to Lieutenant Gallaher. Scouting Six's acting commander started a high-speed approach at 1215. Five miles south of the island, he spotted a large cargo ship anchored near the shore inside the lagoon. Gallaher and his four pilots claimed four hits and one near miss. Lieutenant Commander Young, with wingmen Teaff and Troemel, bombed a building on the south side of Wotje. Gallaher's division climbed back to eight thousand feet and made secondary dives to strafe targets of opportunity and unload their hundred-pound wing bombs on the shipping.

Torpedo Six's nine TBDs, led by squadron XO Lieutenant Lem Massey, encountered intense and sustained AA fire. It was a new experience for ARM2c Ronald Graetz, rear gunner for Ensign Severin Rombach. His plane had been given a "down" for the first strike of the morning. Now Romback was roaring over a Japanese merchant ship's bow. Graetz saw a gunner on the deck starting to swing his weapon toward his plane and unleashed a long burst of machine-gun bullets to discourage the Japanese AA man. "I really did not feel that I was nervous, at any time, over the flight, but I used the 'P-tube' and relieved myself four times on the way out and five times on the way back," said Graetz. "I guess I was more nervous than I had realized."[78]

The cargo ship attacked by Gallaher's dive-bombers was burning fiercely in Wotje's harbor when this *Enterprise* strike finally turned for home. All eight planes were recovered at 1315 without damage. Cleo Dobson, having avoided Japanese fighters, felt this mission was not nearly as exciting as his first morning hop to Roi.[79]

Perry Teaff received ribbing from his buddies for engaging two Claudes near the Marshalls. He had immediately headed in pursuit of the Japanese fighters, expecting fellow VS-6 pilots Dobson and Norm West to join him. Teaff allowed one of the fighters to come closer to him as he led his opponent into a gradually tighter, lower, and slower turn. The Claude eventually plunged toward the water when last seen by Teaff. "Perry was a super pilot," said his roommate, Dusty Kleiss. Back on *Enterprise*, Dobson quizzed his buddy on why he would undertake such a "stupid" maneuver.[80]

"Why didn't you follow?" Teaff asked. "We had them outnumbered!"

Ed Anderson had never worked harder in his life than he did on February 1. He had been waiting since the Pearl Harbor attack for his chance to become qualified as an aviation gunner for Bombing Six. Instead, on January 9 he had been reassigned from ordnance work on the SBDs to fill a vacancy in the flight deck plane-handling crews.[81]

He had since spent long days helping to push aircraft from one end of the flight deck to another to help facilitate the countless takeoffs and landings. His days began at 0330, and would often stretch to 1930 or later. He rarely had more than two hours off on any given day. "Throughout the day, every time flight quarters go, you are constantly harassed, bullied, cursed at and generally kicked around by the chief, Jew Prather," he wrote in his diary.

Anderson's flight deck boss, ACMM Vern A. Prather, worked his plane handlers at a brutal pace for good reason. On February 1, his handlers' efforts made the difference in keeping the Big E's planes going back out time and time again against the Marshalls. His young sailors like Anderson rearmed, refueled, and repositioned planes continuously during a fourteen-hour stretch. "I can honestly say that no one on our ship worked as hard," Anderson wrote in his diary.

Ed, who had just celebrated his twenty-fifth birthday several days prior, had been encouraged by his girlfriend Margie's latest letter. He resolved to record more of his daily events in his little diary, though he found it almost impossible to do so on most nights. The temperature in his enlisted bunk area was always above a hundred degrees, making sweat pour from his face and hands while he was writing. Most nights, he would awaken to find his sack and pillow dripping wet.[82]

When he was finally relieved of flight deck duty on February 1, he was too exhausted to even write. "I thought my legs would give out, but somehow they kept going," he said. Ed finally enjoyed two sandwiches and tried to relax, his thoughts turning to liberty back at Pearl Harbor. Deep down, he felt damned proud to have done his part in America's first offensive against Japanese forces.

Enterprise at last prepared to hightail it out of the action zone. Ed Anderson and Chief Prather's other plane handlers spotted the last of the returning SBDs forward on the flight deck. Bombing Six skipper Holly Hollingsworth believed that any further strikes might be pushing their luck this day. On the bridge, Holly gave Admiral Halsey a play-by-play recap of his second strike mission, then asked, "Admiral, don't you think it's about time we got the hell out of here?"[83]

"My boy, I've been thinking the same thing myself," Halsey replied. His task force had circled for some ten hours in the same square of ocean, but he now directed his group to retire north at thirty knots. Only fifteen minutes after Brigham Young's last SBDs had returned, *Enterprise*'s radar picked up a troubling blip. From Taroa's battered airfield, the Japanese had sent out five big twin-engined Type 96 "Nell" bombers.

Fighting Six Wildcats made contact with the big bombers about fifteen miles from *Enterprise*, but gun failures allowed the Nells to race past the U.S. fighters at 250 knots. At 1338, the Japanese planes released their bombs from three thousand feet while every ship in the task force sent up heavy flak. Captain George Murray handled his big carrier spectacularly, throwing her into a hard turn to port that saved his flight deck. The nearest 250-kilogram load exploded only thirty yards to port, sending fragments tearing into *Enterprise*.

One damaged Nell bomber, piloted by Lieutenant Kazuo Nakai, suddenly turned sharply left and circled back toward *Enterprise*. Nakai was apparently intent upon crashing his crippled plane into the aircraft crowded forward on the Big E's flight deck—thus making him the first Japanese kamikaze pilot faced by the U.S. Navy in World War II. Anti-aircraft guns blazed away at the Japanese bomber as it made a beeline toward *Enterprise*'s flight deck.[84]

Aviation Machinist's Mate Third Class Bruno Peter Gaido decided he must do something. The young member of Scouting Six's flight deck plane-handling crew had watched the Nell bomber attack from the flight deck catwalk. Lieutenant Nakai's crippled bomber was heading for his ship, so Gaido sprinted across the deck to help. Willie West's 6-S-5 was the rearmost Dauntless spotted forward, and Gaido leaped into the rear cockpit. He swung the .30-caliber machine gun toward the incoming Nell and began blasting away at the massive aircraft.

Admiral Halsey and dozens of others watched Gaido pour lead into the flaming

AMM3c Bruno Peter Gaido.

Nell. His fire was perfect; his bullets may well have killed the fanatical pilot. *Enterprise* was saved by Gaido's actions and a violent turn to starboard by Captain Davis. Nakai's big bomber failed to score a direct hit, but its right wing sliced right through the fuselage of the Scouting Six SBD from which Gaido was firing. The Nell's wing skidded into the port catwalk, while West's broken Dauntless was knocked toward the after edge of the flight deck. Gaido stood in the SBD's torn tail section and depressed the .30-caliber gun to hammer tracers into the wreckage of the Japanese bomber as it hit the ocean astern of *Enterprise*.[85]

The flight deck crews sprang into action and extinguished the gasoline fires. Lieutenant Dickinson and others raced from the VS-6 ready room to the flight deck. They gaped in awe at the sheared-off SBD. There was Bruno Gaido, standing in the plane's severed tail, looking around for something else to shoot.[86]

In Bombing Six's ready room, Dick Best had realized how serious the situation was up on deck when he heard .50-caliber machine-gun fire. *They must be in our laps by now*, he thought. At that moment, *Enterprise* had gone into a violent turn, followed by an explosion and a shudder above. Holly Hollingsworth beside him gasped. "My God, that one got us!"[87]

When Best looked around the ready room, he found himself seated alone. The pilots were pressed up against the rear bulkhead for protection. The only exception was Tony Schneider, who had his helmet over his face with his feet up, fast asleep.

After the action, Admiral Halsey called Gaido to the bridge and asked him his name.[88]

"What is your rate, Bruno?" the admiral then asked.

"Aviation Machinist's Mate Third Class, sir," said Gaido.

"Well, Bruno, you are now Aviation Machinist's Mate First Class," said Halsey with a smile.

That afternoon, Dusty Kleiss and other Dauntless airmen visited sick bay. There, the staff dispensed "medicinal" bourbon to those aviators needing a remedy to calm their nerves and promote sound rest. Kleiss retired to his stateroom to resume a letter to sweetheart Jean Mochon. "I wish I could tell you some of the places I've been and what we've been doing," he wrote. "But just now all I can say is that our men have got more guts and our gunners have a better eye than those of any other country."[89]

Halsey was thrilled with his *Enterprise* pilots' performance and handed out awards liberally for those involved in the first carrier strikes of the Pacific War. Bombing Six skipper Holly Hollingsworth was awarded a Navy Cross. The Distinguished Flying Cross was given to pilots Best, Doherty, Blitch, Kroeger, McCauley, and Van Buren of VB-6, and to Dobson and Kleiss of VS-6. Air Medals were later awarded to pilots Deacon, Dickinson, Donnell, Fogg, Patriarca, Rutherford, Seid, Stone, Teaff, Troemel, and West of VS-6, and to pilots Anderson, Check, Halsey, Holcomb, Lanham, Penland, Roberts, Schneider, Smith, Vandivier, Walters, and Weber of VB-6. Air Medals were later awarded to some of the rear gunners, including Allen Brost, Ed Garaudy, Jim Murray, and Harold Heard of Bombing Six.

Enterprise's Kwajalein attack had sunk one transport and damaged nine other ships. Many aircraft were destroyed, and buildings and facilities had been hit. Two Wildcats and five SBDs, along with their crews, had been lost in action. The long-term effects to Japan's military efforts from this raid were minimal, but it marked the first serious attack on the Japanese since the war had started. *Enterprise* proceeded to race clear of the Marshalls area as other Japanese aircraft and submarines attempted, without success, to strike back at the American carrier force. Dick Best and others ruefully termed their ship's hasty retreat "hauling ass with Halsey."[90]

SIX
Island Raiders

"We are about the luckiest people ever," Cleo Dobson confided in his diary. Much of *Enterprise*'s time retiring from the Marshalls was under weather so foul that the daily scouting hops were canceled for two days. The rains prevented the Japanese from finding the U.S. task forces again, and gave the aviators some much-enjoyed rest. During these two days, Dobson noted that the Dauntless crews had plenty of time to "swap lies about each other's experiences."[1]

Yorktown's air group had carried out its own surprise attacks against Japanese installations in the Marshall/Gilbert islands on February 1 at the same time the *Enterprise* SBDs were in action. The *Yorktown* aviators damaged two merchant ships and destroyed shore installations and aircraft, at the cost of two SBDs and four TBDs lost. The *Enterprise* task force steamed into Pearl Harbor on February 5, freshly returned from the first American carrier offensive of the Pacific War. Evidence of the morale boost the raid had provided was abundant as workmen and sailors on other ships cheered the force. The *Enterprise* Air Group flew in ahead of the carrier, with Earl Gallaher leading VS-6 as its acting skipper, following the loss of Hal Hopping over Roi.

From Ford Island, Chief Jim Murray watched Task Force 8 make its triumphant entrance flying huge battle flags. Ships in the harbor blew their whistles and sirens. Even the *Enterprise* airmen ashore cheered for "Wild Bill" Halsey and the Big E. "What a sight and what a choked-up feeling it gave you," said Murray. For plane-pusher Ed Anderson, it was the thrill of a lifetime. "As we passed each ship in the harbor, the crews on deck would give us three cheers and we would return them," he wrote in his diary.[2]

Two of the wounded pilots, Bud Kroeger and Willie West, were put on board the hospital ship *Solace* for surgery. Doctors removed most of the shrapnel from Kroeger's foot but were concerned about his ability to fly again. West's bullet wound was even more serious. "The slug hit him at a spot awfully close to vital organs," said Irvin McPherson of VT-6. "Half an inch lower or half an inch more to the left, it would have been fatal. Even so, it took out a big hunk of flesh in its exit."[3]

While Dick Best enjoyed a brief reunion with his wife and daughter, other men endulged in a little luxury for a change. Flight personnel were allowed to go ashore for three days' R & R at the Royal Hawaiian Hotel, a plush rental on Waikiki Beach that had been leased by the Navy for the war's duration for the exclusive use of naval aviators and submariners in between combat cruises. Known affectionately as the "Pink Palace," the Royal Hawaiian could accommodate 150 officers and a thousand enlisted men at a time. *Those beds really feel good*, thought pilot Cleo Dobson. *Big, deep mattresses with no pitch or roll*. Jim Murray enjoyed the fact that guests of the Royal Hawaiian did not have to be off the streets until 2200. Ship and shore station personnel had to report back by 1800. Ed Anderson feasted on a steak dinner with a buddy at the Wagon Wheel restaurant and drank gallons of pineapple juice. Joe Cupples and Jack Leaming of Scouting Six shared a room that normally rented for $78 per night. Leaming spent an evening enjoying music and drinks with a young lady he had previously met in Hawaii.[4]

Dusty Kleiss and his roommate Perry Teaff made the most of the luxurious Pink Palace. Since their abrupt thrust into the war two months prior, there had been no time to really relax. Now Kleiss was content to just smoke cigarettes, sip a drink, and stare out past the palm trees at the calm Pacific surf off Waikiki. *When you have the chance to relax, you must do it*, he thought. The return to combat would come quickly enough.

Enterprise underwent normal upkeep in port as her air group operated ashore. The pilots found a cure for the prevailing rationing of liquor by making scouting hops to other island bases to draw their weekly rations. Replacement SBDs were drawn from the spare dive-bombers operating from Oahu to bolster the losses suffered during the strike on the Marshalls. Scouting Six had suffered the most severe losses during the early months of war, including four aircrews killed over Roi.

Lieutenant Gallaher fortunately found a surplus of pilots to fill his vacant roster slots. From *Yorktown*'s Scouting Five, he received Lieutenant Charlie Ware and Ensign Bill Hall on temporary assignment to VS-6. Soft-spoken and genuinely likable, twenty-eight-year-old Hall was the son of a mining family from the little Utah boomtown of Storrs. Although slender and only five-foot-five in height, he was athletic: He had excelled on the Redlands University track team and was a bantam-weight boxer. The other side of red-haired, blue-eyed Bill Hall lay in his performing arts abilities. He had majored in music at his California college and was teaching music when he joined the Navy in 1938 to take part in the naval aviation cadet training program.

Thirty-year-old Charles Rollins Ware had fallen in love with military service while in the ROTC at Knoxville High School. Unable to obtain a congressional appointment from Tennessee to the Naval Academy, he

Lieutenant Charlie Ware.

had studied for six months to pass the entrance exams. Ware joined the Navy as a seaman, second class, and one year later received his "at large" appointment to the academy. A crack shot on the Annapolis rifle team, he had graduated in 1934 and first served on the battleship *Texas*.[5]

Charlie Ware was a dashing bachelor who had his own secondhand Buick for escorting his dates around the Pensacola area during his flight training in 1940. He became the second-oldest pilot of Scouting Six— with a receding hairline to go with more than seven years of military service—when he joined Earl Gallaher's lineup in Hawaii. The flight experience of Ware and Hall, both fresh from action against the Gilbert Islands on February 1, was much appreciated by Gallaher to offset his losses.

Gallaher found other pilots in Hawaii to rebuild his unit. Bombing Squadron Three had been cast upon the beach in January following torpedo damage to their carrier *Saratoga*. Ensign Austin "Bud" Merrill, who had entered flight training in 1940 while at Long Beach Junior College in California, was eager to get into action. He, his former *Saratoga* roommate Bob Campbell, and Ensign Alden Hanson answered Gallaher's call for volunteers from VB-3 to fill in for *Enterprise*'s next war cruise.

Scouting Six received ten replacement SBDs, all in need of new guns and overhauls. Squadron gunnery officer Cleo Dobson found this "a hell of a job." He noted in his diary, "Oh, well. That's the Navy. Since we got a 48-hour rest they are going to get it back by working us 25 hours a day."[6]

Holly Hollingsworth's Bombing Six was similarly busy. His unit received several more twin .30-caliber gun mounts, which were installed in the section leaders' planes. The squadron's metalsmiths equipped all eighteen SBDs with armor plating for the pilots' seat backs. Jim Murray was pleased to see the installation of enough ZB homing devices to complete VB-6's requirements. In terms of personnel changes, Bombing Six lost Allen Brost due to his injuries, and Dick Best's regular gunner, Lee McHugh, was transferred to flight training at NAS Pensacola. Ed Anderson was excited to be moved from his plane handler duties back into squadron radio work. He managed to make two hops on Oahu as a passenger, which gave him hope that he was one step closer to regular flight duty.[7]

When *Enterprise* sailed from Pearl again on Valentine's Day, Halsey's carrier force was redesignated as Task Force 16. The original plans called for *Enterprise* to rendezvous with Admiral Fletcher's *Yorktown* force to conduct raids on Wake Island and Eniwetok, but *Yorktown* was soon detailed to join *Lexington* for raids on coastal positions in New Guinea. Instead, Halsey's force received orders to proceed independently for strikes against Wake Island. *Enterprise* sailors cheered the orders, as they remembered the Marine pilots they had delivered to Wake in December—men who had fallen when the Japanese captured the island.[8]

Admiral Halsey earned high marks with his aviators by halting his whole task force on February 18 to search for a downed Torpedo Six crew. Lieutenant (j.g.) Thomas Eversole had become disoriented in a weather front and ditched his TBD some sixty miles from the carrier. The next morning, Ensign Bob Campbell made contact with their life raft, and the destroyer *Dunlap* was sent to fetch the downed men. Dusty Kleiss, best friends with Eversole, flew out with Cleo Dobson to help lead the destroyer to Eversole's crew with smoke bombs.[9]

Upon returning to the Big E, Dobson was called to the bridge to see Admiral Halsey. For his work in helping to direct the destroyer, Dobson was pleased to receive a "very well done." Halsey's compassion for making every effort to locate the downed airmen was uplifting to everyone who faced the possibility of being lost at sea.[10]

Two days of bad weather helped to mask TF-16's approach to Wake Island.

Flight quarters sounded at 0430 on February 24.

The hot, humid air quickly created problems for the pilots. The airplanes' rapidly turning propeller blades produced tremendous friction, condensing the moist air. Clouds of light bluish vapors spiraled backward and enveloped each plane. "Sometimes it was a problem because in the early morning darkness, the flame from the exhaust was reflected by it," explained Jack Leaming. "This restricts the vision of the pilot and may disorient him."[11]

Shortly before 0600, the first CAP Wildcats began launching. Behind them on deck were spotted eighteen SBDs of VS-6, another eighteen from VB-6, and Brigham Young's CEAG bomber. Each Dauntless was loaded with a five-hundred-pounder and two wing bombs. Third division leader Dick Dickinson recalled the disorientation as he awaited his turn to taxi forward: "I was just peering into nothing, preparing to roll off the equivalent of a fast-moving six-story building out in the middle of the Pacific; and I couldn't even see the Pacific. Actually, each of us was manufacturing his own fog."[12]

Earl Gallaher, as the new skipper of the scouts, was first to launch and therefore had the shortest takeoff distance. He couldn't see a thing through the eerie halo effect. The signal officer pointed toward the bow

Scouting Six (VS-6) Tactical Organization Wake Island Raid: February 24, 1942		
FIRST DIVISION		
PLANE	**PILOT**	**REAR SEAT GUNNER**
6-S-1	Lt. Wilmer Earl Gallaher	ARM1c Thomas Edward Merritt
6-S-2	Lt. (jg) Perry Lee Teaff*	RM3c Edgar Phelan Jinks*
6-S-3	Ens. William Edward Hall	AMM1c Bruno Peter Gaido
6-S-16	Lt. Charles Rollins Ware	ARM2c William Henry Stambaugh
6-S-7	Lt. (jg) Hart Dale Hilton	ARM2c Jack Leaming
6-S-8	Ens. Percy Wendell Forman**	AMM1c John Edwin Winchester**
SECOND DIVISION		
PLANE	**PILOT**	**REAR SEAT GUNNER**
6-S-10	Lt. Reginald Rutherford	RM3c Earl Edward Howell
6-S-11	Lt. (jg) Norman Jack Kleiss	RM3c John Warren Snowden
6-S-12	Ens. Robert Keith Campbell	AMM2c Milton Wayne Clark

(continued)

Scouting Six (VS-6) Tactical Organization
Wake Island Raid: February 24, 1942 (cont.)

THIRD DIVISION

PLANE	PILOT	REAR SEAT GUNNER
6-S-4	Lt. Clarence Earle Dickinson Jr.	RM1c Joseph Ferdinand DeLuca
6-S-5	Lt. (jg) John Norman West	RM3c Alfred R. Stitzelberger
6-S-6	Ens. Alden Wilbur Hanson	AMM2c Floyd Delbert Adkins
6-S-13	Lt. Frank Anthony Patriarca	ARM1c Ferdinand Joseph Cupples
6-S-14	Lt. (jg) Edward Thorpe Deacon	RM3c Louis Dale Hansen
6-S-19	Ens. Milford Austin Merrill	AOM2c Thurman Randolph Swindell

PHOTOGRAPHIC PLANES

PLANE	PILOT	REAR SEAT GUNNER
6-S-17	Ens. Cleo John Dobson	RM3c Roy L. Hoss
6-S-9	Lt. (jg) Benjamin Henry Troemel	RM2c William Hart Bergin
6-S-15	Ens. Reid Wenworth Stone	AM3c Erwin G. Bailey

*Crashed on takeoff; only injured pilot recovered.
**Shot down over Wake; aviators taken POW and executed.

Bombing Six (VB-6) Tactical Organization Wake Island Raid: February 24, 1942		
FIRST DIVISION		
PLANE	PILOT	REAR SEAT GUNNER
6-B-1	Lt. Cdr. William Right Hollingsworth	ACRM James Francis Murray
6-B-2	Lt. Harvey Peter Lanham	ARM2c Edward Joseph Garaudy
6-B-3	Lt. Lloyd Addison Smith	AMM2c Herman Hull Caruthers
6-B-7	Lt. James Wickersham McCauley	ARM2c Parham Screeton Johnson Jr.
6-B-8	Lt. (jg) John James Van Buren	RM3c Achilles Antonios Georgiou
6-B-9	Ens. Arthur Leo Rausch	RM3c Gail Wayne Halterman
SECOND DIVISION		
PLANE	PILOT	REAR SEAT GUNNER
6-B-10	Lt. Richard Halsey Best	ARM1c Harry William Nelson Jr.
6-B-11	Lt. (jg) Edward Lee Anderson	RM3c Jay William Jenkins
6-B-12	Ens. Wilbur Edison Roberts	AMM1c James H. Shea Jr.

(continued)

Bombing Six (VB-6) Tactical Organization
Wake Island Raid: February 24, 1942 (cont.)

SECOND DIVISION

PLANE	PILOT	REAR SEAT GUNNER
6-B-16	Lt. (jg) Leonard Joseph Check	ARM2c Stuart James Mason Jr.
6-B-17	Ens. Keith Haven Holcomb	AMM2c Lloyd E. Welch
6-B-18	Ens. Thomas Wesley Ramsay	AMM2c Sherman Lee Duncan

THIRD DIVISION

PLANE	PILOT	REAR SEAT GUNNER
6-B-4	Lt. John Devereaux Blitch	AMM2c William Burr Steinman
6-B-5	Ens. Norman Francis Vandivier	Sea1c Lee Edward John Keaney
6-B-6	Ens. Tony Frederic Schneider	RM3c Glenn Lester Holden
6-B-13	Lt. Joe Robert Penland	ARM2c Harold French Heard
6-B-14	Ens. Clifford Raymond Walters	AMM2c Wilbur Thomas Thompson

6-S-18	Ens. Delbert Wayne Halsey	AOM2c Arie Turner Alford
GC	Cdr. Howard Leyland Young	CRM John Murray O'Brien

with his flag, and Gallaher shifted to instruments. He had never launched from a carrier flying solely on instruments.[13]

Perry Teaff in 6-S-2 was second to launch, and the blue exhaust fog foiled his vision. His SBD's left wheel dropped into *Enterprise*'s port-side catwalk and his left wing struck a five-inch gun mount that catapulted his plane over the carrier's side. Plane guard destroyer *Blue* raced in and used her searchlights to help recover the crew from the sinking Dauntless. Sailors hauled on board Teaff, whose face had been severely injured in the crash. Rear gunner Edgar Jinks, who had survived the Japanese attacks on his plane on December 7, was not as fortunate. Although Jinks was heard calling out in the darkness, *Blue*'s sailors were unable to find him. Teaff was given swift medical attention, but the crash cost him his right eye.[14]

The loss of Teaff's SBD created a delay in the launching process. Gallaher flew circles alone in the soupy weather, hoping to never again experience a launch like this one. Finally, the air group resumed launching at a slower pace. The last TBD of Torpedo Six's first division lifted off at 0647.[15]

Commander Young led his fifty-one planes toward Wake Island, with VT-6 lumbering ahead in the lead. For a change, the torpedo bombers flew high, since they each carried a dozen hundred-pound bombs instead of a torpedo. "The result of that was to relieve the pressure of my head cold for a time, but drive it right back in when we descended," Irvin McPherson remembered. The dive-bombers climbed to eighteen thousand feet during the 110-mile flight to the prearranged deployment area just west of the Japanese-held, arrowhead-shaped island.[16]

As Holly Hollingsworth approached Wake, he saw a rapidly expanding AA barrage more than twenty miles ahead. It took an hour from departure from the task force for the carrier planes to arrive over Wake's main island and its two small additional islands, Peale and Wilkes. The long delay in launching and rendezvous caused the *Enterprise* strike group to arrive over Wilkes after the heavy cruisers *Northampton* and *Salt Lake City* had started shelling the island.

At 0750, Brigham Young radioed to his air group, "Attack. Attack." Holly Hollingsworth took his lead division of VB-6 in first. He focused on targets on Peale: a radio station, seaplane ramps, any aircraft present, or an adjacent oil tank. Gunner Jim Murray watched with satisfaction as the skipper's three bombs blasted huge holes right in the middle of the runway.[17]

John Van Buren, fifth to dive, had a new rear gunner, Achilles Georgiou. His own gunner, Allen Brost, had been seriously wounded during the Marshalls raids, while Georgiou's normal pilot, Ed Kroeger, was still recovering from a bullet wound in the foot. Georgiou saw their big bomb create a large hole in the runway. The antiaircraft fire had intensified by this point, and the gunner was relieved when his new pilot opted to clear the area.

Hollingsworth's men destroyed a four-engined seaplane moored just south of a pier on Peale Island. Lloyd Smith made a glide-bombing attack that destroyed a second seaplane on a barge. Scouting Six began hitting Wake Island's airfield as the first division of VB-6 was still diving down on Peale. Earl Gallaher plunged from twelve thousand feet in an easterly direction with his first division.

Reggie Rutherford's second division of VS-6 dropped their bombs in a ripple effect from altitudes between four thousand and two thousand feet. Dusty Kleiss hit an ammunition magazine and started a fire with his load. Dick Dickinson, leading the third division, created another explosion when he dropped on what was supposed to be an underground hangar or storehouse. The scouts then strafed Japanese gun positions along Wake's eastern shores.[18]

Dickinson's "tail-end Charlie" pilot was Bud Merrill, one of the VB-3 replacements new to Scouting Six. He was unsatisfied with his dive and opted to hold his bomb. Merrill pulled up and went back up by himself to make another dive from ten thousand feet. *This is crazy*, he thought as he made his solo bombing run.[19]

Cleo Dobson, Ben Troemel, and Reid Stone—flying the three VS-6 photo planes—joined Brigham Young and VT-6 for a composite bomb-

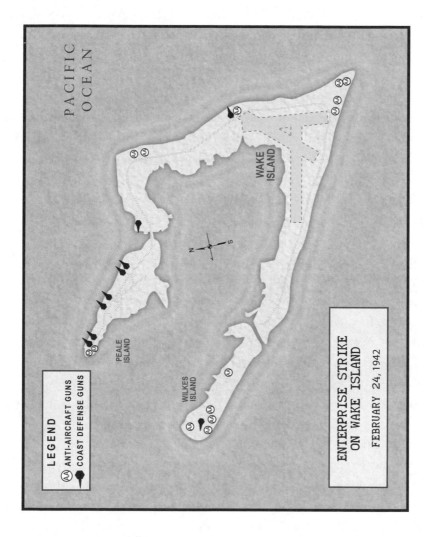

LEGEND
ⒶⒶ ANTI-AIRCRAFT GUNS
⬛ COAST DEFENSE GUNS

PACIFIC OCEAN

WAKE ISLAND

PEALE ISLAND

WILKES ISLAND

N ⟵ ✦ ⟶ S

ENTERPRISE STRIKE
ON WAKE ISLAND
FEBRUARY 24, 1942

ing attack. They dropped their bombs in salvo, and Dobson was credited with blowing up an oil tank. The Dauntless trio then proceeded to make a mapping run across the island as their rear seat men snapped photos while under AA fire.

Some of the SBDs scoured the area for Japanese ships after making their initial drops. "We didn't find an awful lot at Wake," said VB-6's Jim McCauley. Squadron mate Ensign Delbert "Pete" Halsey (no relationship to Admiral Halsey) had dropped his big bomb and was strafing gun positions while deciding upon where to unleash his small wing bombs. He came upon another of the four-engined Kawanishi Type 97 flying boats airborne about five miles east of Wake. Halsey opened up on his radio to report the big plane before attacking with his forward guns. The Kawanishi poured on the throttle, leaving Halsey to report to Commander Young that he couldn't catch up.[20]

Young radioed to the fighter division leader, Lieutenant Commander Clarence Wade "Mac" McClusky, "Take that seaplane, Mac." McClusky and two of his wingmen caught the Kawanishi near the U.S. cruisers off Wilkes Island and exploded it in dramatic fashion at 0835. Debris from the violent blast left a chunk of shrapnel from the Japanese seaplane embedded in the left wing of Lieutenant Roger Mehle's F4F.[21]

Rutherford and Dickinson's VS-6 divisions found a small, 120-foot patrol vessel near their rendezvous point. "We hit him with everything left," said Dusty Kleiss. He had two hundred-pound wing bombs remaining, but Kleiss rushed the job of aiming and missed the violently maneuvering patrol boat with both. He swung back around to blast the little vessel's waterline and bridge with his forward .50-caliber guns, as did many other excited SBD pilots.[22]

"We weren't taking turns," said Dickinson. "It was everybody for himself and devil take the hindmost. The wonder is we didn't shoot each other." The patrol vessel was left abandoned, spewing oil and turning in aimless circles. As his pilot Dale Hilton made two strafing runs on the boat, gunner Jack Leaming thought, *Those poor sons of bitches.*[23]

U.S. surface vessels closed in later, sank the ship, and took four prisoners of war. For its part, Scouting Six had damaged Wake's runway, destroyed four magazines or underground hangars, shot up the patrol vessel, and also demolished several small buildings and one coastal

defense gun on the island's eastern edge. Three VS-6 planes suffered bullet holes—those flown by Gallaher, Rutherford, and Pat Patriarca.

Ensign Bill Hall saw another VS-6 Dauntless smoking badly upon
retirement to the east of Wake. It was Percy Forman's 6-S-8. When Hall
approached, he could not see any holes in Forman's fuel tanks or other
vital areas, but his plane had obviously been crippled by antiaircraft fire.
Forman was never seen again by his shipmates. He ditched his damaged
SBD near Wake and both airmen were captured by the Japanese. Forman
and his gunner, AMM2c John Winchester, were interrogated on Wake
and then placed on board the freighter *Chichibu Maru* for transportation
back to Japan. The VS-6 aviators perished when the U.S. submarine *Gar*
torpedoed and sank the merchant ship on March 13.[24]

Three SBDs of Bombing Six were also damaged. Lloyd Smith's 6-B-3
was hit in the right wing and fuselage, and Pete Halsey sustained several
bullets through the left wing of his borrowed Scouting Six Dauntless.
Tony Schneider's 6-B-6 took armor-piercing .50-caliber bullets in the
belly and floorboards of the rear cockpit, shattering Glenn Holden's radio transmitter and tearing holes in the thin metal shelf above it. His
protective head plate deflected another bullet that might well have killed
Schneider. The work of the VB-6 metalsmiths at Pearl Harbor in install-
ing the new armor plates had already proven its value. A crewman who
inspected Tony's SBD later handed him a .50-caliber slug that had come
to rest in the floorboard of his plane.

By 0945, the fifty planes of the *Enterprise* Air Group began to land back
on their ship. Scouting Six had lost another two SBDs in the Wake strike.
Three of Earl Gallaher's aviators were dead or prisoners of war, and pilot
Perry Teaff faced life with only one eye. Cleo Dobson's diary entry for the
Wake strike summed up the VS-6 losses: "It looks like the scouts take it on
the nose every time. . . . All told we have lost nine pilots and eleven rear seat
men since Dec. 7. From that figure, we can expect only about 2½ months left
and by God I don't like it. I am ready to turn in my suit."[25]

Task Force 16 retired under cover of a sheltering rainstorm as Commander Young's aviators detailed the results of their strike to Halsey's
and Murray's staffs. The majority of Wake's fuel tanks had been destroyed,
effectively crippling enemy efforts from this island for some time.

The bombardment force rejoined *Enterprise* on February 25 as the carrier withdrew northeastward from Wake. That evening, Bill Halsey received an urgent message from his commander in chief, Nimitz: "Desirable to strike Marcus if you think it feasible." The task force obligingly turned west toward lonely Marcus Island, located only a thousand miles from Tokyo.[26]

That afternoon, the destroyer *Blue* returned Perry Teaff back to *Enterprise*. Dusty Kleiss found that his buddy was taking it pretty well in spite of the crash that had cost him an eye. Teaff joked that he would get two new glass eyes, a "sporty" version for weekdays and a slightly bloodshot one for the "morning after." Cleo Dobson visited Teaff in sick bay and also found his buddy to be in jovial spirits. Teaff's first comment to him was, "Dobbie, do you think a one-eyed farmer can plow a straight furrow?"[27]

Bombing Six lost another Dauntless the following day. Leonard Check was taking off with a group of searchers for a two-hundred-mile scout on February 26. Unable to maintain altitude, he crashed into the sea a few hundred yards forward of *Enterprise*'s port bow.

Gunner Stuart Mason narrowly escaped. His belt was quite loose, a normal practice for Mason to remain free to move with his .30-caliber as needed. His body lurched forward upon impact with the ocean and the young aviator was knocked out. When he came to, his Dauntless had already bubbled under the water. He had practiced what he would do if his plane ever went into the drink. Mason unbuckled his belt, shucked his parachute, and reached the surface gasping for air.[28]

Plane guard destroyer *Ralph Talbot* raced in to rescue Check and Mason, but the tin can's speed caused the ship to overshoot the men. *Ralph Talbot*'s skipper backed down but slid past them again. The destroyer pulled forward once more and thrice overshot the mark. An injured and frustrated radioman Mason finally shouted up, "Stop the son of a bitch and we will swim over!"

Ralph Talbot eventually hauled the SBD crew aboard, where Check moved in with the destroyer's executive officer. Mason was given dry clothes, but began vomiting up all the ocean water he had ingested during his escape from the sinking Dauntless. The next morning, he had to be helped from his bunk. A big bruise covered his entire chest, and both thighs were bruised.[29]

Mason passed time on board *Ralph Talbot* by standing watches in the radio shack. Three days later, Check and Mason were returned to *Enterprise* as she refueled from a tanker. In addition, the destroyer sent over another recovered Big E fighter pilot, Ensign Joseph R. Daly, in exchange for the customary payment. *Enterprise* signaled that she would reciprocate with fifteen gallons of ice cream and two hundred pounds of bread once her airmen were transferred. "Send the ice cream and bread first, else no pilots and radioman," *Ralph Talbot*'s skipper signaled back. The traditional payment was made and the three fliers found themselves back on board the Big E. "The flight surgeon grounded Check but didn't bother to look at me," said Mason. "Sometime later, I learned my sternum had been broken."[30]

Enterprise headed for the 740-acre island of Marcus during the closing days of February. Halsey intended to launch a strike group against the Japanese base from 175 miles away on the morning of March 4. Few of the aviators had any idea where Marcus Island was located. "Wish we knew how many fighters and AA they have there," Dusty Kleiss penned in his diary, "or if they have a landing field. Wish we had a spy system."[31]

Jim Murray listened to the scuttlebutt running through his Bombing Six enlisted gunners as they grumbled about making yet another island strike.[32]

"What the hell?" asked one. "Is the Big E the only ship that is going to fight this war?"

Others bitched that *Saratoga* was back in the States to repair her torpedo damage while *Lexington* and *Yorktown* were nowhere to be seen. Murray appreciated the healthy banter. *If a sailor is not griping, he is not happy*, he thought.

The Marcus mission was jeopardized on March 2, when *Enterprise* broke radio silence to help guide the morning's search planes back to the ship through an ugly rainstorm. The inner-air patrol SBDs made two different submarine sightings during the day and attacked both times. The target was actually the U.S. submarine *Gudgeon*, outbound from Midway Island. *Gudgeon* was able to crash-dive and avoid the "friendly

Bombing Six (VB-6) Tactical Organization
Marcus Island Raid: March 4, 1942

FIRST DIVISION

PLANE	PILOT	REAR SEAT GUNNER
6-B-1	Lt. Cdr. William Right Hollingsworth	ACRM James Francis Murray
6-B-16	Lt. Harvey Peter Lanham	ARM2c Edward Joseph Garaudy
6-B-3	Lt. Lloyd Addison Smith	AMM2c Herman Hull Caruthers
6-B-7	Lt. James Wickersham McCauley	AMM2c Benjamin W. Boyd
6-B-14	Ens. Clifford Raymond Walters	AMM2c Wilbur Thomas Thompson
6-B-9	Ens. Arthur Leo Rausch	RM3c Gail Wayne Halterman

SECOND DIVISION

PLANE	PILOT	REAR SEAT GUNNER
6-B-10	Lt. Richard Halsey Best	ARM1c Harry William Nelson Jr.
6-B-15	Lt. (jg) Edward Lee Anderson	RM3c Jay William Jenkins
6-B-12	Ens. Wilbur Edison Roberts	AMM1c James H. Shea, Jr.

6-B-8	Lt. (jg) John James Van Buren	RM3c Achilles Antonios Georgiou
6-B-17	Ens. Keith Haven Holcomb	AMM2c Lloyd E. Welch
6-B-18	Ens. Thomas Wesley Ramsay	AMM3c Sherman Lee Duncan

THIRD DIVISION		
PLANE	**PILOT**	**REAR SEAT GUNNER**
6-B-4	Lt. John Devereaux Blitch	AMM2c William Burr Steinman
6-B-5	Ens. Norman Francis Vandivier	ARM2c Stuart James Mason Jr.
6-B-6	Ens. Tony Frederic Schneider	RM3c Glenn Lester Holden
6-B-13	Lt. Joe Robert Penland	ARM2c Harold French Heard
6-S-18	Ens. Delbert Wayne Halsey	ARM2c Parham Screeton Johnson

fire" incident, reaching eighty feet before one of the SBD's five hundred-pound bombs exploded above her starboard quarter. This mistake marked the second attack on a U.S. sub by *Enterprise* bombers in only ten weeks.[33]

The bad weather also took its toll with another *Enterprise* SBD loss. Lieutenant Charlie Ware of VS-6 ran out of fuel during his final approach in the rain and made a forced landing of his 6-S-16 just astern of the carrier. Ware's first encounter with the ocean had been two days

Scouting Six (VS-6) Tactical Organization
Marcus Island Raid: March 4, 1942

FIRST DIVISION

PLANE	PILOT	REAR SEAT GUNNER
6-S-1	Lt. Wilmer Earl Gallaher	ARM1c Thomas Edward Merritt
6-S-7	Lt. (jg) Hart Dale Hilton*	ARM2c Jack Leaming*
6-S-2	Ens. William Edward Hall	AMM1c Bruno Peter Gaido
6-S-4	Lt. Clarence Earle Dickinson Jr.	ARM1c Joseph Ferdinand DeLuca
6-S-6	Ens. Alden Wilbur Hanson	AMM2c Floyd Delbert Adkins

SECOND DIVISION

PLANE	PILOT	REAR SEAT GUNNER
6-S-10	Lt. Reginald Rutherford	RM3c Earl Edward Howell
6-S-11	Lt. (jg) Norman Jack Kleiss	RM3c John Warren Snowden
6-S-12	Ens. Robert Keith Campbell	AMM2c Milton Wayne Clark
6-S-13	Lt. Frank Anthony Patriarca	ARM1c Ferdinand Joseph Cupples

| 6-S-14 | Lt. (jg) Edward Thorpe Deacon | RM3c Louis Dale Hansen |
| 6-S-3 | Ens. Milford Austin Merrill | AOM2c Thurman Randolph Swindell |

PHOTOGRAPHIC PLANES		
PLANE	PILOT	REAR SEAT GUNNER
6-S-9	Ens. Cleo John Dobson	RM3c Roy L. Hoss
6-S-8	Lt. (jg) Benjamin Henry Troemel	RM2c William Hart Bergin
6-S-15	Ens. Reid Wentworth Stone	AM3c Erwin G. Bailey

CEAG		
PLANE	PILOT	REAR SEAT GUNNER
CEAG	Cdr. Howard Leyland Young	CRM John Murray O'Brien

*Ditched near Marcus; became POWs.
6-S-5 Lt. (jg) West/ RM3c Stitzelberger aborted with engine trouble.

before Christmas, when his SBD crashed during a takeoff from *Yorktown*. This time he had enough control to make a good water landing. Ware's gunner, ARM1c Bill Stambaugh, was slightly injured in their ditching. Both men were picked up by the cruiser *Northampton*, but they would not be returned in time for the Marcus strikes. *Lucky Charlie!* Kleiss wrote in his journal. *Or is he? He'll miss out on all the fun.*[34]

During the evening of March 3, *Enterprise* and two escort ships picked up speed for a run in toward Marcus Island. In the chief petty officers' quarters, Jim Murray felt the vibrations of the ship as the pace increased. *We are making our final run-in and another reveille is in the offing*, he thought.[35]

"If anything should ever happen to me, my biggest regret would be not getting to see you again," Dusty Kleiss wrote to his girlfriend Jean that night. "Always my last thoughts and words will be to you."[36]

Jack Leaming would never forget Ash Wednesday, March 4, 1942. He was sleeping soundly when reveille sounded for the airmen at 0330. He dressed quickly and completed his breakfast. While the pilots were being briefed, Leaming checked his equipment, chatted, and kidded with other gunners about the day's mission as they sipped their coffee.[37]

"Pilots, man your planes!" The call came at 0435 with the clanging of the ship's general alarm.

The moon was still shining as the aviators poured out of the island structure at a full run. Leaming ran excitedly to 6-S-7, clutching his pilot's chart board as he climbed into the rear cockpit. He passed the board to Dale Hilton, fastened his earphones to the ICS, and awaited the order, "Start engines!"[38]

Hilton's plane captain offered to man the inertia starter that fired the engine. Leaming asked him to hold the key to his locker until he returned, not wanting any extra clutter in his flight suit. "Don't get any ideas about that money and my wristwatch in my locker!" Leaming hollered.[39]

Leonard Check remained grounded and thus would miss the Marcus Island strike. His regular gunner, Stuart Mason, however, had been cleared for flight duty with VB-6 junior pilot Norm Vandivier. Dusty Kleiss was happy with the "God-sent moonlight" that offered the *Enterprise* strikers the opportunity to launch with less drama than they had experienced during the previous week's Wake strike.[40]

Brigham Young was first off the deck at 0446 in his command SBD. He was followed by Earl Gallaher's Scouting Six—down to just fourteen operational planes. Holly Hollingsworth's VB-6 added another seventeen dive-bombers, followed by six of Wade McClusky's Wildcat fighters. By 0525, Commander Young's thirty-eight-plane flight departed for Marcus Island, located 128 miles distant. The full moon had eased the formation process, but a heavy overcast prevailed.

Dick Dickinson struggled to see his wingmen in the fog. His division climbed up through the two-mile layer of cloud cover, but the *Enterprise* units were already split up. Scouting Six became separated from Bombing Six, and they lost track of the few fighters going in with them. Dickinson's squadron could not even maintain formation within its own divisions.[41]

Jim Murray's nerves were on edge. Bombing Six's rendezvous and departure were equally stressful. *The position lights on our rudder don't mean a thing in these clouds*, Murray thought. *I'm lucky to see our own tail in this fog, let alone an approaching SBD or F4F!*[42]

Young's dive-bombers climbed to sixteen thousand feet but struggled to stay on course to Marcus. The overcast grew increasingly denser as they approached the island. Lieutenant John Baumeister, the *Enterprise* radar officer, tracked the strike planes on his radar scope and communicated to them via the carrier's superfrequency YE homing transmitter. Young's gunner, CRM John O'Brien, intercepted the code dispatch and relayed to the CEAG that their planes were five miles north of the correct course. The new technology of radar guided the *Enterprise* Air Group to its objective, and Marcus was spotted at 0630 through a break in the clouds.[43]

Holly Hollingsworth had informed his Bombing Six that their primary target was aircraft on the field. Secondary objectives were any installations sighted, with particular regard for radio stations, fuel tanks, hangars, and AA batteries. Forty minutes remained before full sunrise, but Marcus Island's three shining runways could be seen paralleling the coastlines. Commander Young knew that surprise would be lost if his dozens of planes circled about the island waiting for full sun.[44]

Young pushed over. He was followed by the VS-6 photo plane division of Dobson, Troemel, and Stone. Dobson planted his five-hundred-pounder dead center in the runway and then flattened a hangar with his wing bombs. The darkness and heavy cloud cover made accurate bombing difficult, although VB-6 planes dropped parachute flares to help illuminate the target. Hollingsworth's first planes pushed over at 0640 and released their bomb loads in ripple effect from three thousand to two thousand feet. Antiaircraft fire was intense and uncomfortably close. Hollingsworth felt that the smaller-caliber fire was much more accurate than any previously encountered. Tracers were close aboard even as planes retired as far as five miles away. *The first four to dive succeeded in waking up the Japanese gunners,* thought Jim Murray.[45]

The Marcus airfield appeared to be under construction. Heavy AA fire made it difficult, if not impossible, for pilots to ascertain the results of their bombing runs. Several buildings and an oil storage tank were set aflame, and a string of explosions was seen in one area. Jack Blitch, leading VB-6's third division, took out a radio transmitter building located between a pair of radio towers. Two fires on Marcus burned brightly enough that they could be seen thirty miles away as the first SBDs retired.

Reggie Rutherford's second division of scouts was next to attack. They approached at 0650 from an altitude of seventeen thousand feet. Dusty Kleiss was rocked by eight AA bursts all around his Dauntless. *Best shooting I've seen yet,* he wrote in his journal. *I skimmed through the cloud fringe of the hole in the clouds at five thousand feet and laid my eggs in the center of a group of wooden barracks beside the runway.* His two hundred-pound incendiaries sparked impressive fires, but his five-hundred-pound bomb hung up in the rack. Kleiss was forced to shake it off over the ocean during his return.[46]

Bud Merrill, last to dive of his division, saw tracers coming up at his plane and cracked open his canopy to get a better view of his target. The wind force suddenly pulled the goggles from his head and tugged in the wind with such ferocity, Merrill feared they might pull him from his cockpit. The hold-down straps broke at last as he flattened out from his dive.[47]

Earl Gallaher's first division of VS-6 was the last to attack at about 0700. His five planes had become lost in the heavy cloud cover and spent considerable time circling about to find their target. On his wing, Gallaher had Dale Hilton and one of his loaner pilots, Bill Hall, as they ducked down underneath some clouds and finally gained sight of the island. Bringing up the rear of the division was Dick Dickinson with another VB-3 loaner pilot, Ensign Al "Oley" Hanson, on his wing. Marcus Island's defenders had the best AA installations and gun control Dickinson had encountered. "I was convinced each was shooting straight at me," he said.[48]

Dickinson dived past two hundred feet through the overcast and smoke to release his bomb on a wooden structure near the hangar area.

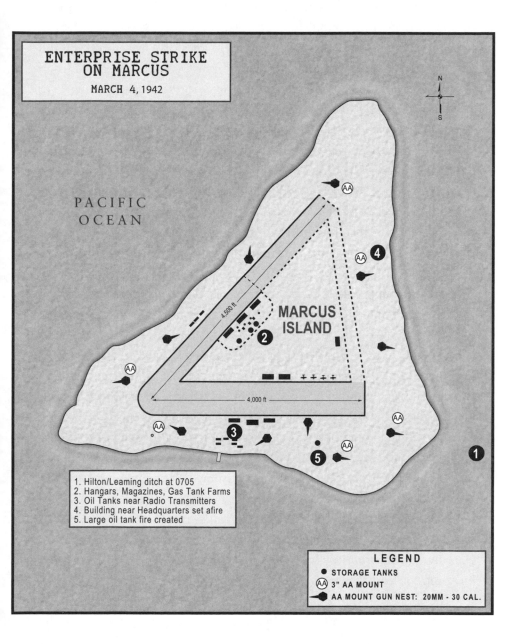

ENTERPRISE STRIKE
ON MARCUS
MARCH 4, 1942

PACIFIC
OCEAN

N
S

MARCUS
ISLAND

4,500 ft

4,000 ft

1. Hilton/Leaming ditch at 0705
2. Hangars, Magazines, Gas Tank Farms
3. Oil Tanks near Radio Transmitters
4. Building near Headquarters set afire
5. Large oil tank fire created

LEGEND
● STORAGE TANKS
AA 3" AA MOUNT
AA MOUNT GUN NEST: 20MM - 30 CAL.

As he pulled out, he and gunner Joe DeLuca felt that every single Japanese gunner was aiming their red tracer bullets at them. Somehow, Dickinson's plane was unscathed. His roommate, Dale Hilton, in 6-S-7 ahead of him, was less fortunate.[49]

Jack Leaming had been watching the planes dive ahead of him and noticed an AA battery that began firing on his plane. Lieutenant Hilton made his dive at approximately a forty-five-degree angle, coming over and parallel to the runway on the island. Leaming watched the altimeter spin down and yelled, "Mark!" into his mike as they reached fifteen hundred feet. Their three bombs were released and Hilton streaked across the narrow edge of the island to escape under heavy AA fire. Leaming felt like they were aiming at his crotch, and he was soaked with sweat.[50]

Hilton jinked his SBD about to avoid the streams of machine-gun fire stitching the sky ahead of him. He figured that maintaining a straight course only made his plane a steadier target for the heavier-caliber batteries below. Several close bursts tossed his Dauntless about like a toy. And then it happened. Hilton's plane was slammed hard by a large-caliber round and Jack Leaming heard a loud *r-r-r-rrup* sound that rose above the flight noise. *It sounds like a steel plate being dragged over concrete*, he thought. *Jesus Christ! There goes our landing gear.*[51]

At the same instant, a hot clip from Leaming's spent .30-caliber machine gun dropped into his boot. He thought for a second he had been hit. He glanced at his plane's starboard side and was alarmed. A boiling mass of red and blue flames crackled through a four-inch hole in the upper structure of the wing. The sixty-five gallons of aviation fuel in Hilton's starboard tank were quickly consumed as fire ate up his wing.

What the hell is all this for? thought Leaming. *It must be for something. It has to be! All this sacrifice, this misery, this terror. I have listened to much chatter and have been in some very tight spots. From experience, I feel that the last word or expletive a flier utters before disintegrating with his plane is SHIT!*[52]

The airspeed of Hilton and Leaming's SBD only increased the rate at which the fire spread up their wing. Pieces of aluminum flew off into the slipstream as Leaming watched, joining the plume of fire and smoke that trailed his plane.

"Is the radio okay?" Hilton asked over the ICS.

"Yes, sir, all set," Leaming replied.

At 0705, Hilton opened up on his radio and announced to *Enterprise* that his plane was afire. "I am going to land east of the island, but I am all right," he reported.

Hilton's dilemma was witnessed by others. Dick Best was retiring to the southeast, watching flaming balls flying up at him like oranges from a distant shore battery. Best suddenly saw a flash in the sky and realized that an *Enterprise* plane had been hit. Dick Dickinson caught a glimpse of Hilton's Dauntless as he passed by underneath. His roommate's plane seemed to be completely ablaze, except for its left wing. The engine was wrapped in fire, and flames streamed back twenty feet from the right wing. *There's not even a chance that Dale can hold her together long enough to make a water landing*, Dickinson thought.[53]

But somehow, Hilton managed to win the fight. He kept his blazing SBD aloft until about ten miles east of Marcus Island. Jack Leaming could see the ocean coming up fast as they prepared to ditch. Their 6-S-7 hit the water, bounced, then hit again, skidded over the surface, and came to a sudden stop. The bomber's nose went under and its tail rose into the air. Leaming scrambled out onto the port wing and removed their rubber boat.

Hilton was momentarily stunned. His face had hit the gunsight, opening a deep gash under his left eye and other lacerations on his forehead. The little finger on his left hand was bent outward. Leaming followed his pilot's directions and helped pull the broken finger back into place. He then climbed into the rubber raft. Hilton, still dazed and his face bleeding profusely, floundered around in the ocean, unable to climb on board or even inflate his Mae West. Leaming finally convinced him to pull his flotation handle to lift his face out of the water before his blood loss attracted sharks.[54]

Several SBDs passed overhead as Hilton finally flopped into their rubber boat. Dick Best saw the VS-6 aviators waving to him and giving the thumbs-up signal before he departed. Jim Murray in 6-B-1 also spotted Hilton's crew and realized there was nothing he could do to help other than advise his ship of their location. Murray was troubled when he learned the downed pilot's identity; he and Hilton had both served prewar in *Yorktown*'s Torpedo Squadron Five.[55]

The American planes overhead soon departed, leaving Hilton and Leaming drifting near Marcus Island. They had only their .45 pistols, two canteens of water, and some scant rations. Leaming was in favor of unloading both clips on the first Japanese that approached them, but his pilot convinced him that they were better off being taken prisoner than dying in their raft. "We are not going to win the war today, but we will certainly win it ultimately," Hilton said.[56]

Both men reluctantly tossed their guns in the ocean. Leaming rowed toward the island burning in the distance while Hilton nursed his swollen face. As they neared shore, the swirl of angry breakers convinced Hilton that they should row toward the calmer southern side of the island to avoid the nasty coral reefs. A short time later, a thirty-foot boat with a small motor came chugging out toward them.[57]

The boat of Japanese soldiers pulled up alongside their raft. The Scouting Six aviators knew that fighting was useless. The soldiers were shouting angrily in their native language and were brandishing rifles affixed with bayonets. *Staring at death is a sensation that is extremely difficult to accept, because you are looking into eyes that seem to reflect the same feeling you are experiencing*, Leaming thought. The Americans were blindfolded and guarded at either ends of the little boat as it chugged back to the island. There, they were herded into a waiting truck and driven down a bumpy, shell-covered road. Leaming and Hilton were interrogated by a squad of armed soldiers bearing fixed bayonets.[58]

The senior commander of the island began asking questions, which were relayed by an interpreter in his best broken English. "If you do not answer my questions truthfully, I will kill you," he said. Leaming was quizzed on what ship he had flown from. Because of the remote location of Marcus Island, the Japanese certainly knew that they were carrier aviators, so Leaming stated that they were from the carrier *Yorktown*. He thought, *I am not going to tell these sons of bitches the truth. The hell with them!*[59]

The Scouting Six fliers were thereafter trucked to a building where they were placed in an eight-foot-square prisoner cell. Hilton and Leaming were given white jumpsuits, typical Japanese sailor work clothing, to wear. As they sat in their cement-floored cell, they realized their short time at war was over. Life had now reverted to maintaining a will to survive as prisoners of war. "Our predominant thoughts centered on what the future held for us," Leaming said.[60]

The Marcus Island strike had been completed twenty minutes before it was even scheduled to begin. Because of the lack of light, no photos were obtained by the three VS-6 photo planes. Bombing Six escaped without damage to any of its aircraft. Scouting Six was stung again by the loss of the Hilton/Leaming crew. Brigham Young's remaining planes withdrew to the southeast from Marcus and returned to *Enterprise* at 0845.

The damage caused at Marcus was hard to assess, aside from a gasoline storage tank, the radio transmitter, and many new holes in the coral runway. "It is regretted that more valuable targets could not be found," Commander Young wrote. The raid had, however, served notice to Japan of how close the American carrier groups were approaching to their home islands. "We gave it a fairly good working over for the number of planes we had," VB-6's Jim McCauley said of the Marcus strike.[61]

During retirement on March 5, the task force was shrouded with weather so foul that all planes were grounded. Cleo Dobson passed the time playing bridge with a quartet in Perry Teaff's sick bay room. Despite the loss of his right eye, Teaff remained upbeat, anxious to return home to his wife, Maggie. "He is looking forward to a lifetime with his wife and family," Dobson wrote, "which is a lot more than I can look forward to."[62]

The Dauntless crews flew almost constant missions during the following days as the task force headed for Hawaii. Fatigue began to catch up. Lieutenant Dickinson was so exhausted from long scouting flights by March 6 that he nearly cracked up his SBD upon landing. The flight surgeon, Lieutenant J. M. Jordan, advised Earl Gallaher to ground him temporarily from flying. For once, Dickinson decided not to argue.[63]

The *Enterprise* air group had become the most bloodied of the American carrier task groups, with raids on the Marshalls, Wake, and Marcus now under their belts. *Lexington*'s Task Force 11 had attempted a raid on Rabaul in late February, but she had been snooped out by Japanese aircraft en route. Two waves of Japanese Mitsubishi "Betty" bombers had attacked *Lexington*, stymied only by the valiant efforts of her fighter and SBD airmen. Lieutenant (j.g.) Edward "Butch" O'Hare of Fighting Three became an ace in a day by downing five Bettys, earning the Congressional Medal of Honor in the process.

Enterprise entered Pearl Harbor on March 10, with her air group landing on Oahu ahead of her. The pilots and gunners of VS-6 and VB-6 secured their planes and headed for the Royal Hawaiian Hotel to enjoy a well-deserved week's rest. There, they found that Admiral Halsey had furnished five bottles of good whiskey, a luxury almost impossible to obtain on Oahu by this time of the war.[64]

SEVEN
Arrival of the "New Boys"

As *Enterprise* was slipping into Pearl Harbor on March 10, two of her Scouting Six aviators were being loaded on board a Japanese merchant ship bound for Yokohama on Japan's mainland. Dale Hilton and Jack Leaming, forced to ditch off Marcus Island, had spent the better part of a week as prisoners of war.

Leaming endured the Japanese interrogations but soon found a great dislike for the seaweed, kelp, rice, and tiny fish that provided his only nutrition. On the third day, Hilton was taken away for questioning and was beaten when his answers did not please his interrogators. On the morning of March 10, the Dauntless crewmen were put on board the 12,755-ton transport ship *Argentina Maru* for passage to Japan. They arrived on Friday the thirteenth, and were moved ashore to a home for extensive questioning.[1]

In their new place of internment, they met six POWs from *Yorktown*'s Torpedo Five who had been lost during the February strikes on the Gilberts. They were Lieutenant Harlan Johnson, Ensign Herbie Hein, and their enlisted crewmen James "Ace" Dalzell, Charles Fosha, Joe Strahl, and Marshall Windham. Leaming exchanged information with the *Yorktown* radiomen using Morse code to tap out words with their fists and open hands when the guards were not looking.[2]

Leaming, Hilton, Fosha, Dalzell, Windham, and five POWs captured from Wake Island were transferred on April 6 to the newly completed secret interrogation camp of Ofuna. Bathing was allowed only twice a week and most meals were of rice and some type of preserved fish. Leaming was smart enough to hide his high school ring under the flooring in his barracks. He pretended to have lost it when one of the guards demanded he hand it over. He convinced the guard that it was missing, but he received a terrible beating in the process.[3]

Shortly after the Doolittle raid of April 18, the VS-6 prisoners were placed on a train and moved from Ofuna to the camp at Zentsuji on the island of Shikoku. The food rations were barely enough to sustain life, and the prisoners were forced to perform slave labor six days a week, whether sick or well enough to work. According to Leaming, survival meant consuming anything the POWs could beg, barter, or steal.[4]

The first ray of hope came a month after their arrival at Zentsuji. During an inspection of the camp by the Red Cross, both *Enterprise* aviators were allowed to take part in a propaganda broadcast back to the United States. Dale Hilton and Jack Leaming found some relief in the knowledge that their families knew that they were still alive. The war was far from being decided, however, and it would be years before either Dauntless aviator would touch American soil again.[5]

As *Enterprise* was making her way into Pearl Harbor on March 10, the air groups of *Lexington* and *Yorktown* carried out a surprise attack against Japanese forces concentrated in New Guinea. They flew through a 7,500-foot pass in the rugged Owen Stanley mountains, and then descended upon shipping targets anchored off the towns of Lae and Salamaua. They sank three merchant vessels and a converted minesweeper and killed or wounded 375 Japanese men. In addition, they damaged a light cruiser, three destroyers, and a seaplane tender with their bombs and torpedoes. The Lae-Salamaua strikes by the *Yorktown* and *Lexington* aviators inflicted the heaviest losses on the Imperial Japanese Navy since the start of the war.[6]

Admiral Yamamoto's Navy had enjoyed an almost unchecked string of victories in the past month. During mid-February, Admiral Nagumo's First Air Fleet had conducted carrier attacks on Port Darwin on Australia's coast. They sank the old World War I–era U.S. destroyer *Peary*, along with two American troopships and several other Allied vessels. In all, three warships and five Allied merchant vessels were destroyed and another ten ships were damaged. Commander Mitsuo Fuchida, who had led the first Pearl Harbor attack on December 7, was again head of the carrier aviators from *Akagi*, *Kaga*, *Hiryu*, and *Soryu* that pounded the shipping at Darwin on February 19. That afternoon, the Kido Butai's carrier warriors attacked two American supply ships bound for the Philippines and sank both.

The darkest of months for the Allies continued a week later. A Japanese cruiser force near Surabaya pounded an Allied surface fleet in the Battle of the Java Sea on February 27. Three British and Dutch destroyers were sunk, along with two Dutch cruisers. On the same day, the U.S. seaplane tender *Langley*—America's first aircraft carrier—was caught at sea by Japanese bombers and finished off. Further bad news came on March 1: The U.S. heavy cruiser *Houston* and Australian light cruiser *Perth* were lost in the Indian Ocean in Sunda Strait in a battle with Japanese landing force warships.

Nagumo's Kido Butai was not to be left out of this victorious period. Between late February and the first week of March, Commander Fuchida's carrier pilots attacked and sank eight merchant ships and several warships in the Indian Ocean south of Java. American losses to the First Air Fleet planes included the destroyers *Edsall* and *Pillsbury*, along with the oiler *Pecos*. It was only the surprise attack by *Yorktown* and *Lexington* carrier planes at New Guinea on March 10 that caused Japanese command to pause, postponing planned invasions of Port Moresby and Tulagi in the Solomon Islands for a month. During the time it took Japan to formulate new offensives in the Pacific, the American carrier air groups saw little action of significance.

Much of this time was spent in replacing lost aircraft and training new pilots. *Yorktown* remained at sea battle cruising, while *Lexington* enjoyed a short overhaul at Pearl Harbor. *Enterprise* remained in the Hawaiian Islands during late March, as Admiral Halsey had received orders to await the arrival of the new carrier *Hornet*, en route from the East Coast to the Pacific.

During the interim, the *Enterprise* Air Group shuffled personnel during mid-March. Commander Brigham Young was detached to new duties. His place as CEAG was filled by Lieutenant Commander

Wade McClusky, the former skipper of Fighting Six and an Academy classmate of VB-6's Holly Hollingsworth and VB-5's Lieutenant Commander Bob Armstrong. Hollingsworth also received new orders, and turned command of Bombing Six over to his capable XO, Lieutenant Dick Best. Four other experienced VB-6 pilots were transferred to other duties during this period: Jack Blitch, Jim McCauley, Keith Holcomb, and Leonard Check, the latter receiving orders to help teach at NAS Corpus Christi.

Bombing Six also lost three rear seat men to transfers: Jim Shea, Achilles Georgiou, and Carl Schlegal. In return, the squadron received a whole new batch of enlisted radioman-gunners to be trained for active flight duty. Dick Best also received seven rookie ensigns to bolster his pilot losses—Stephen Hogan, Don Ely, Harry Liffner, George Goldsmith, Bert Varian, Lewis Hopkins, and Gene Greene. The time ashore proved to be much needed for Best to work with his green young pilots on their bombing practice against land targets.[7]

Ed Anderson finally got his chance. On March 10, he was placed on VB-6's tactical organization along with the unit's eight new radiomen. He became the regular rear seat man for rookie pilot Lew Hopkins. Bombing Six operated for several weeks from Ewa Field, the Marine air base on Oahu. Anderson felt that the Marine chow, served family-style, was excellent. Best of all, he was gaining practical experience with all the training hops.[8]

Some of his first flights were more hair-raising than others. Ensign Hopkins forgot to open his dive flaps during one practice dive. They managed to pull out at only five hundred feet, screaming down at terminal velocity—estimated by Anderson to be around 350 knots. Pilot and gunner both enjoyed a good laugh over it later, but it had been a close call.

Earl Gallaher's VS-6, sent ashore to NAS Kaneohe for training, was given a surprise on March 18. Their place on *Enterprise* was being temporarily assigned to Lieutenant Commander Max Leslie's Bombing Three, which had been operating from Oahu since *Saratoga* had returned stateside for repairs. As disappointing as the news may have been to some, the time ashore would be well used by Gallaher in reshaping his depleted scouting unit. In the past month, he had lost the services of

U.S. Navy

The pilots of *Yorktown*'s Bombing Three photographed in April 1942 while on temporary duty on *Enterprise*: (*front row, left to right*) Ensign John Roberts, Lieutenant Ralph Arndt, Lieutenant Dave Shumway (XO), Lieutenant Commander Max Leslie (CO), Lieutenant Syd Bottomley, Jr., and Ensign John Lough; (*standing, left to right*) Lieutenant (j.g.) Gordon Sherwood, Ensigns Roy Isaman, John Butler, John Bridgers, Bob Elder, Carl Peiffer, Charlie Lare, Randy Cooner, Bob Campbell, Paul Schlegel, and Frank O'Flaherty. Roberts, Lough, Peiffer, and O'Flaherty were on temporary duty with VB-3 at the time, but all flew with VS-6 at Midway, and all were lost in action.

three pilots—one killed in the Wake raid, one taken POW at Marcus, and Perry Teaff, who had lost an eye in an SBD crash.

In addition, Lieutenant Reggie Rutherford, the VS-6 executive officer who had joined in December, was transferred during the weeks at Pearl Harbor, and the three loaner pilots from Bombing Three—Oley Hanson, Bob Campbell, and Bud Merrill—were reunited with skipper Max Leslie. Another temporary pilot, Lieutenant (j.g.) Bill Hall, would soon transfer into *Lexington*'s VS-2 to take the place of a pilot lost during the Lae-Salamaua strikes. Finally, VS-6 pilots Cleo Dobson and Ed "Deke" Deacon were assigned as assistant landing signal officers in training under senior *Enterprise* LSO Lieutenant Robin Lindsey at Kaneohe.

The personnel losses and reassignments left skipper Gallaher with only eight other veteran VS-6 pilots: Dick Dickinson, Reid Stone, Charlie Ware, Dusty Kleiss, Pat Patriarca, Norm West, Willie West, and Mac McCarthy, the latter two only recently returned from injuries sustained in the first part of the war. Doctors had completed skin grafts on Willie West's chest to patch the chunk of flesh that had been ripped away by a bullet in the Marshalls raid. "He had the doctors make a design on his tummy with a 'V' and then a dot, dot, dot, dash," said his buddy Irvin McPherson. The symbols spelled out the International Morse Code symbol for V, as in *victory*.[9]

Dickinson fleeted up to become Gallaher's XO and Charlie Ware became flight officer, the third-senior pilot. Scouting Six's veterans would spend the next month checking out new dive-bombers and training new men. Fortunately, a fresh crop of rookie pilots had just arrived in Hawaii at the first of March from the Advanced Carrier Training Group (ACTG). Prior to the return of *Enterprise*, many of the fresh faces were blended into Lieutenant Commander Leslie's shore-based VB-3 squadron. Among the new arrivals were ensigns John Butler, John Quincy Roberts, John Lough, Elmer Maul, Frank O'Flaherty, Raymond Miligi, John Bridgers, and Carl Peiffer. Most of these fresh aviators would become very familiar with the flight deck of USS *Enterprise* in the next three months.

Max Leslie—with more than four thousand accumulated flying hours—was one of the most experienced dive-bomber aviators in the Pacific Fleet. He had won his wings in 1929 and reported on board the battleship *Oklahoma* as an observation pilot. He had since flown patrol planes and fighters before switching to dive-bombers. In comparison, many of Leslie's new ACTG arrivals had less than four hundred flight hours.[10]

Ensigns John Bridgers and Carl Peiffer, both from the Tarheel state of North Carolina, were representative of Leslie's new junior pilots, whose lean flight hours were often made up for in their eagerness. Bridgers had received his naval aviator wings in Miami in November 1941 and had spent some of his early training at NAS Norfolk. "When you reported into ACTG, you were a 'new boy' and remained so designated until another batch of 'new boys' reported," Bridgers said. "That could be a week or a month, and then the prior 'new boys' became 'old boys.'"[11]

The Norfolk training period included many hard lessons. Peiffer, an "old boy" slightly senior to Bridgers, was making a touch-and-go landing one afternoon when he decided he would bring his plane to a halt. Peiffer realized too late that his brakes could not stop him in the short distance and that he had lost sufficient speed to take off again. As he reached the far end of the field—still with considerable ground speed—he pulled back on the stick. Peiffer jumped the perimeter fence, whereupon his Dauntless flipped onto its back, straddling a ditch in the backyard of one of the homes surrounding the field.

His passenger began shouting from the rear cockpit, where he was suspended upside down by his belt. In the confusion of trying to figure out what had happened, Peiffer released himself and dropped on his head. The woman of the house chastised the pilot for making so much noise and waking her husband, who worked nights at the nearby Newport News naval shipyard.

The soft-spoken Peiffer could only

Ensign Carl Peiffer.

mutter, "I'm sorry, ma'am. I brought her in as quietly as I could."

Bridgers and his fellow new boys had become carrier-qualified by making three landings in an SB2U on the Navy's first jeep carrier, *Long Island* (ACV-1), as she plied back and forth in Chesapeake Bay. They arrived at Pearl Harbor on board the troop transport ship SS *President Hoover* and had their first look at the U.S. Fleet's damage. They would soon have their chance to help even the score with the Japanese Navy.[12]

The thirty-odd new pilots were distributed among squadrons on Oahu, many being temporarily assigned to Max Leslie's VB-3. The next days were spent becoming familiar with the Douglas SBD Dauntless. It was a dive-bomber, said Ensign Bridgers, "none of us had previously seen, much less flown."[13]

Lieutenant Robin Lindsey, the regular LSO for *Enterprise*, worked with the newer dive-bomber pilots. The month was tough on Lindsey, tough on the newer pilots, and hell on their SBDs. On March 31, Ensign Harry Warren Liffner—a new pilot for Dick Best's Bombing Six—made a forced landing at sea off Hawaii during bombing practice. He and his gunner, AMM3c Peter William Altman, were safely recovered.

The mishaps escalated when *Enterprise* put to sea on April 1 for two days of training exercises and carrier qualification landings. New gunner Ed Anderson recorded his first carrier flight hours in his logbook that day after Lew Hopkins successfully trapped his tail hook. Ensign Ray

Miligi, one of the ACTG pilots, hit the barrier upon landing. His face was badly cut and he was sent to the Pearl Harbor hospital to recover. Two more SBDs were lost on April 2 as the Big E was entering port. Two of the new-boy pilots, Harry Liffner and Stephen Hogan of Bombing Six, collided in midair when one of them failed to see their formation going into a right turn. Only the pilots managed to parachute to safety. Ed Anderson was stunned by the loss of two buddies—Peter Altman and Wilbur Thompson. The crash occurred at only about a thousand feet, and neither gunner was able to extricate himself in time. "With twin guns that weren't designed for the plane, and armor plate in the seat that folds in front of your chest and stomach, you haven't got much chance to bail out at that altitude," Anderson said.[14]

The following day, Ensign Johnny Lough of VB-3 cracked up yet another Dauntless beyond repair while landing on Oahu. Bombing Six and Scouting Six each received some new SBD-3 model Dauntless aircraft while in Hawaii. Compared to their older SBD-2 planes, the newer models were impressive to the crews. Chief Jim Murray, now assigned to VB-6's new skipper Dick Best, marveled at his new 6-B-1. It came fully equipped with radio gear, an Identification Friend or Foe (IFF) transmitter, a Zed Baker homing device, self-sealing fuel tanks, and armor plating to protect the pilot. Even better, Murray found the biggest "morale booster" to be an additional armor plate mounted on the twin .30-caliber machine guns to protect the radioman/gunner.[15]

The trials and tribulations for indoctrinating new pilots soon came to a close. The *Enterprise* Air Group was put on a two-hour sailing notice on April 7, as the new carrier *Hornet* approached Hawaii. Together, the two flattops would embark on a mission the likes of which their airmen could scarcely have dreamed to be possible.

The *Hornet* Air Group was the newest arrival to the Pacific Fleet during April 1942. The Navy's eighth aircraft carrier had a full war load displacement of 29,100 tons, making her slightly larger than her sister flattops *Yorktown* and *Enterprise*.

The *Hornet* Air Group's flight crews were scattered in and around the naval air station at Norfolk, Virginia, when war commenced for America on December 7, 1941. Ensign Roy Philip Gee of Bombing Eight, a conservative Mormon raised in Salt Lake City, was at a Washington Redskins and Philadelphia Eagles football game with his roommate, Ensign Grant Teats of Torpedo Eight, when they first heard of the Pearl Harbor attacks on a portable radio. They raced back to Norfolk to join their air group as war was declared. "The *Hornet* pilots were like a group of racehorses chomping at the bit," Gee said.[16]

Hornet's green air group conducted extensive training during the next three months as the carrier was prepared for combat duty in the Pacific. The Commander, *Hornet* Air Group, was Lieutenant Commander Stanhope Cotton Ring, whose official CHAG acronym soon informally became "Sea Hag" to many of his pilots.

Not all of the men were confident in the Sea Hag's leadership. Ensign Kenneth White of Bombing Eight recalled that Commander Ring became lost while leading a training flight in the Gulf of Mexico during January 1942. Ring had to be escorted back to the *Hornet* by Lieutenant Gus Widhelm in what was considered to be good weather. "He scared me," said White. "To his credit, he looked like a naval officer; tall, handsome. He wore his uniform well." Stan Ring had been the first pilot to make a landing on *Hornet* after the new carrier's commissioning. Yet even this historic honor had not gone well for the Sea Hag as he settled into the groove with one of his air group's SBC-4s. Ensign Troy Guillory of VB-8 was riding as the CHAG's rear seat. Ring came in "high and fast," according to Guillory, and his SBD barely caught the last arresting wire and slammed into the barrier.[17]

U.S. Navy

Lieutenant Commander Stanhope Cotton Ring, known to the men as Sea Hag.

Hornet transited the Panama Canal on March 12 en

route to the Pacific, and she docked at San Diego on March 20. There, Sea Hag learned his ship would serve temporary duty as the training base for the Navy's second graduating class of ACTG pilots. Some of these new boys would soon be mixed into *Enterprise*'s two Dauntless squadrons. The eager aviators were truly a cross section of America, hailing both from rural farming families and from wealthy inner-city upbringing.

Ensign Eldor Rodenburg would never forget his carrier qualification landings on the brand-new *Hornet*. Rodenburg hailed from the farmlands near Davenport, Iowa, and had spent summers on a tractor while studying civil engineering at the University of Nebraska. In December 1939, Eldor enlisted in naval aviation training and progressed to Pensacola for aviation cadet training. His twenty-hour check ride on June 20, 1941, had been given by a Marine major named Gregory Boyington, who would go on to become the famous Congressional Medal of Honor–winning fighter pilot known more affectionately as "Pappy" Boyington.[18]

Rodenburg earned his Navy pilot wings on October 20, 1941, and was soon part of the advanced carrier training group based at the NAS on North Island in San Diego. He and his fellow trainees were still learning the Dauntless dive-bomber when Pearl Harbor was attacked. On a day off from flying in January 1942, "Rodey" Rodenburg was introduced to a young woman named Virginia Nell Tipsword. They were married weeks later on March 1.[19]

Rodenburg and three dozen rookie ACTG pilots were ordered to pack their bags and board *Hornet* on March 23. It would be a short cruise to qualify them in carrier landings under the tutelage of landing signal officer Lieutenant Ray Needham. For many of them, it was their first experience aboard a Navy vessel, much less the newest and largest aircraft carrier in the fleet.[20]

Hornet put to sea and Lieutenant Needham took his post on the aft LSO platform with his circular paddles as eight SBDs were cued up for the rookies. A large group of bystanders gathered on the island structure ("Vulture's Row") to witness these takeoffs and landings. Lieutenant (j.g.) Paul Holmberg landed too far to port and his left wheel nearly dropped over the edge of the flight deck. Ensign Bob Edmondson smashed his SBD into the island structure and a crash barrier on his second landing.

Ensign Ralph Goddard landed far right of center, crumpling his right wing and breaking a wheel shaft as his bomber dropped into a bank of antiaircraft guns.[21]

There were more crashes the next day and even planes that went over the side. Ensign Tom Durkin watched an escort destroyer rescue the second pilot to cartwheel his aircraft into the ocean. "Only two more, and they'll have enough for bridge over there," he said to his buddy Fred Mears.[22]

Hornet returned to port after four days of breaking in the fleet's newest replacement pilots. Their training was complete. The new boys knew they might never see their hometowns again. Jim Shelton, who hailed from Great Falls, Montana, spent his last free hours with pilot Freddy Mears discussing their situation in their favorite bar. Ensign Jim Dexter from Seattle pounded down 150-proof rum with his girlfriend while talking over their future together. Ensign Bill Pittman also spent his last hours ashore with his girlfriend, Natalie.

Pittman was twenty-four and held a degree from the University of Florida. The young officer's rugged good looks could have turned heads with the local ladies in the clubs. But his heart had been won by young Natalie, whom he intended to marry after his tour of duty in the Pacific. As a naval reservist, he was not bound by the two years of nonmarried status that the academy men faced. Pittman enjoyed his time with his girlfriend but felt an obligation to let off some final steam with his ACTG buddies.

On the night before shipping out from Coronado, he joined Dexter, Mears, and Shelton to breeze through the last of their pocket money. Broke, they had to write a check for the taxicab back to base. En route, Pittman found one last dollar bill his pocket and the four ACTG buddies tore it into four parts. Each stuffed a quarter of the dollar bill into their wallets as a good-luck piece. "These talismans were not very effective," wrote Mears. "Only two of us ever saw the States again."[23]

Stan Ring's *Hornet* Air Group made final preparations to ship out to war. Five of the new ACTG pilots were added to Fighting Eight to help fill roster slots. For the moment, *Hornet*'s Scouting Eight and Bombing Eight had but twenty-four planes between them, and her Torpedo Eight had only ten TBDs.[24]

The reason for the shorthanded torpedo and dive-bomber squadrons soon became apparent. Captain Marc Mitscher moved his carrier from San Diego to NAS Alameda in San Francisco on March 30. There, sixteen Army B-25 Mitchell medium bombers were hoisted on board and arranged over most of the flight deck. *Hornet*'s Task Force 18 sailed with her deck so loaded with Army planes that any fighters able to launch could not be recovered again. Scuttlebutt ran rampant about the big bombers being transported to the Pacific. Few on *Hornet* knew the truth—their carrier's first war duty was to deliver Lieutenant Colonel James Henry "Jimmy" Doolittle's B-25s directly to Tokyo!

Admiral Halsey's Task Force 16 departed Pearl Harbor at noon on April 8 to rendezvous with Marc Mitscher's inbound *Hornet* force. The *Enterprise* Air Group had new faces. Max Leslie's Bombing Three landed on board that afternoon as the temporary replacements for Lieutenant Gallaher's Scouting Six. Leslie had pulled half a dozen rookies from the first class of ACTG aviators—who had arrived in Hawaii in early March—to help fill out VB-3. Among them were John Bridgers and his fellow Tarheel buddy Carl Peiffer, both recommended to skipper Leslie by Lieutenant Robin Lindsey based on their aptitude at Kaneohe. Bridgers made his flight out to the Big E as rear seat passenger in the SBD flown by Ensign Bob Elder.[25]

Elder had been assigned to Bombing Three in June 1941, after earning his wings at Pensacola. He had been running track at his Milwaukie, Oregon, high school in 1935 when a Boeing F4B landed on the football field. The recruiting pilot who climbed out of the cockpit had already completed his mission. Elder never even considered another career path after that day.[26]

During his carrier qualifications, Elder had to return with his SBC-4 to NAS San Diego due to engine problems. Once the engine was fixed, Elder jumped into his cockpit and flew out to sea to make his first carrier landing on *Saratoga*. His virgin foray into the groove was a success, but Elder was startled to suddenly see his rear canopy slide forward. Instead of the expected load of sandbags in his passenger seat, out climbed an Army colonel, a guest of skipper Max Leslie.[27]

"Well done, lad." The colonel grinned. "My first experience of landing on an aircraft carrier."

"Mine too, sir!" quipped the young pilot.

Bob Elder proceeded to prove his merit as a first-class dive-bomber pilot in the months that followed. His attitude was all business when word made the rounds about the attack on Pearl Harbor. *Now we're going to do what we were trained for*, he thought. His part in the war effort had been sidelined by *Saratoga*'s torpedo damage in January. At long last, Elder and his untested fellow VB-3 pilots were at sea on *Enterprise*, heading straight for Japan.[28]

Customarily, the captain or Admiral Halsey would offer some inkling of their mission over the ship's intercom, but this night was different. No details were given after dinner on the first evening at sea. Most decided that the *Enterprise* air group was destined for some top-secret, highly important strike. *So the rumormongers will have a field day*, thought Bombing Six's Jim Murray.[29]

Enterprise made this war cruise with the unique distinction of sporting two dive-bombing squadrons—VB-3 and VB-6—and no scouting squadron. Lieutenant Best had made the most of his weeks at Oahu, and now at sea, he continued training his new Bombing Six replacement pilots.

Among them was Ensign Lewis Hopkins from the small farming community of Luthersville, Georgia. "Everybody was dirt-poor," he said. "You didn't know it because everybody was the same way." Hopkins worked the hard life of a farmer's son and completed high school by age fifteen. He worked his way through Berry College in Rome, Georgia, and graduated in 1939. Hopkins went to work for Sears, Roebuck in Atlanta and then as a junior salesman with the Royal Typewriter Company before joining the Navy in 1940.[30]

He completed his training in September 1941, and was among the ACTG pilots shipped to Pearl Harbor on the first of March. Temporarily assigned to VB-3 at Kaneohe, Hopkins joined *Enterprise*'s Bombing Six just before the ship departed Hawaii for Tokyo. He found his new squadron to be quite experienced. His new skipper, Dick Best, was a "wonderful guy" who "was so interested in each of us becoming proficient."

On the morning of April 13, *Hornet*'s task force appeared on the horizon, her deck crowded with the Army B-25s. As Dick Best returned from a search flight, he could not tell what was on the carrier's flight deck. *It looks like construction equipment, odd shapes, maybe tractors,* he thought at first. From his rear seat, Jim Murray realized the shapes were large Army bombers. He assumed the new carrier was ferrying them to some advance base. *One thing is for sure,* Murray thought. *Once they leave that flight deck they are not going to land back on board.*[31]

Admiral Bill Halsey finally dispelled all rumors that evening by announcing that the task force was proceeding to a point five hundred miles east of Tokyo. There, Colonel Jimmy Doolittle's B-25s would be launched to bomb the Japanese mainland. "Halsey even said that a medal given to him by the Japanese government was being returned to them, strapped to one of the bombs that would be dropped," said Murray. "With that, the crew went wild."[32]

The Tokyo-bound carriers crossed the international date line en route and skipped April 14. A strong storm was encountered on April 17, which helped to mask their approach. The Doolittle raiders were scheduled to launch the following day against mainland Japan.

The weather had grown noticeably colder, and the aircrews drew winter clothing to help keep them more comfortable on their scouting flights. Radioman Ed Anderson was well pleased with a package he received while *Enterprise* was refueling at sea. In it was a sweater knitted for him by a woman with the local Red Cross unit back home. "It couldn't have come at a more opportune moment," he wrote in his diary.[33]

Lieutenant (j.g.) Ozzie Wiseman.

Enterprise conducted all the flight duties on the morning of April 18. Heavy seas caused water to cascade across her flight deck as the morning CAP fighters launched at 0508. They were followed by three SBDs of VB-3— piloted by Lieutenant (j.g.) Osborne "Ozzie" Wiseman, Ensign Charlie Lane, and Ensign Oley Hanson—to conduct a two-hundred-mile search to the west. A fourth Dauntless piloted by Ensign John "J. Q." Roberts was launched for an inner-air patrol to the westward.

It would be an eventful day, to say the least.

At 0558, Wiseman sighted a small patrol craft forty-two miles from *Enterprise*. In accordance with his orders, he did not attack. He returned to the ship and dropped a beanbag message reporting his contact and stating that he believed he had been sighted by the vessel. At 0738, *Hornet* lookouts also spotted the ninety-ton whale catcher *No. 23 Nitto Maru* just ten miles away. The little Japanese picket boat spoiled Admiral Halsey's element of surprise by sending out radio reports of American carriers approaching. By 0744, *Enterprise* lookouts had also spotted *Nitto Maru*, just five miles off her port quarter.[34]

Halsey detailed the cruiser *Nashville* to sink the boat and passed orders to Captain Mitscher on *Hornet* to prepare his Army B-25s for launching immediately. Jimmy Doolittle's pilots were now forced to fly some 650 miles in to their target instead of the four hundred miles planned.

The *Enterprise* SBDs found plenty of action with several picket boats as the B-25 crews hustled to begin taking off. Wildcats from Fighting Six began strafing *Nitto Maru* and a second vessel, the eighty-eight-ton converted fishing boat *Nanshin Maru*. The second boat had been spotted by J. Q. Roberts of VB-3 about twenty miles from *Enterprise* at 0745. Roberts tried to dive on the 125-foot-long metal boat but had to abort his first run when an F4F got in his way. On his second approach, his five-hundred-pound bomb sailed about a hundred feet over the target. Roberts and AMM2c Clarence Zimmershead in his rear seat both stitched the vessel with bullets.[35]

Ed Anderson was sitting in the rear seat of his 6-B-12 on the flight deck. The little Japanese picket boat was barely visible to him on the horizon. Anderson, manning the machine guns while the ship was at general quarters, watched the cruiser *Nashville* turn and open fire at 0823. *The Nashville is really throwing a lot of steel*, he thought. Jim Murray was equally surprised when the cruiser opened fire. He had been seated in his SBD's rear cockpit, hoping to tune in to a Japanese radio station with his radio direction finder. The luckless *Nanshin Maru* was pounded under the waves in short order as Anderson and Murray watched.[36]

Bud Merrill of Bombing Three was topside as Jimmy Doolittle's raiders began lifting off *Hornet*'s flight deck shortly after 0900. He saw the seventh big Army B-25, piloted by Lieutenant Ted Lawson, dip below the flight deck and then slowly crawl for altitude. On *Hornet*, Ensign Ben Tappan watched the launch from a flight deck gun tub with VS-8 buddy Helmuth "Lefty" Hoerner. Tappan had to jump up and down to maintain his view as the carrier pitched in the heavy gale. John Bridgers felt that all of them rushed to get into the air. He was surprised none of them hit the rising bow as they pulled up early.[37]

By 0920, the last of the sixteen Army bombers was lumbering toward Tokyo. Admiral Halsey promptly turned his task force around and increased speed to twenty-five knots. The next two hours passed quietly, as both carriers dispatched fighters and patrol planes. At 1130, *Enterprise* additionally sent out thirteen Dauntlesses to patrol astern two hundred miles. Of this group, ensigns Bob Elder, Bob Campbell, and Johnny Butler of VB-3 were sent out singly to search to the southwest. Another group, Lieutenant Ralph Arndt of VB-3 with VB-6 ensigns Tom Ramsay and Tony Schneider, was sent to attack enemy surface vessels reported about fifty-eight miles from the carriers.[38]

Twenty minutes after taking off, Campbell made two glide-bombing attacks on a 150-foot gray picket vessel. His bomb missed but he and gunner Harman Bennett took turns strafing the little vessel. At 1226, Arndt, Ramsay, and Schneider attacked another Japanese picket, a single motor patrol boat about seventy-five feet long with one radio mast. "I didn't sink him but I lifted him out of the water and reversed his course," said Schneider.[39]

At 1245, Johnny Butler made three glide bombing attacks on a 125-foot metal vessel towing a small white boat. Between their bombs and bullets he and gunner David Berg sank the towed boat, collecting three small-caliber bullets in their SBD in the process. Task force lookouts spotted more Japanese patrol vessels near the retiring carriers at 1400, and *Enterprise* fighter planes and returning scouts continued to pound them. Lieutenant Andy Anderson and gunner Stuart Mason bombed and then strafed one little vessel. Their Bombing Six skipper, Dick Best, even joined in on the action. He and his gunner, Jim Murray, never used seniority to skip out on routine flight duties. Best also preferred that no one else fly his 6-B-1 command Dauntless, so he took part in whatever mission was launched based on where his plane was spotted on deck.[40]

Best attacked a forty-foot Japanese trawler in his search sector, trying to hit the careening small ship by throwing his five-hundred-pound bomb at the last second. It fell short, and Best was further frustrated when his forward guns jammed and prevented him from even firing back at the bow gunner on the vessel.[41]

Murray in his rear seat saw that some of the patrol boats they passed over had radios and even guns on board. The temptation was too much for him.

"Captain, can I take a few shots at these boats?" he asked.

"No!" Lieutenant Best snapped.

Murray eventually decided his skipper was correct in not chancing the loss of their plane to such minor targets. But at the moment, he was left smarting. At the Marshalls, skipper Holly Hollingsworth had denied Murray the chance to shoot up two Mavis flying boats sitting on a seaplane ramp. *I may go through this war without ever getting a chance to fire my guns at the enemy*, he thought.

Ed Anderson had better luck with his pilot. He called over the intercom to Ensign Hopkins, "Let's get in on the fun!"

Hopkins dived in and sprayed a Japanese trawler with his .50-calibers. He then made a hard right turn to bring Anderson's .30-calibers to bear. "I poured 200 rounds of incendiary bullets from stem to stern in that Jap sampan," he wrote. The seas were so rough when Hopkins landed back on *Enterprise* that the impact buckled the body of his Dauntless. The landing gear was damaged enough that Hopkins and Anderson's bomber would be out of commission for days.[42]

Lieutenant Lloyd Smith participated in the strafing, but suffered the misfortune of an accurate Japanese machine gunner who hit his 6-B-4 square in the engine. Smith nursed his SBD back to the task force and made a forced water landing at 1503. The cruiser *Nashville*, in the area to help shoot up the picket boats, picked up Smith and AMM1c Herman Caruthers within fifteen minutes.[43]

Doolittle's B-25 pilots reached Tokyo, bombing industrial and military targets near the port. Ensign Stanley Holm of VS-8 knew that they had made it when the Tokyo radio station went off the air. Holm was standing in *Hornet*'s Air Plot, which was so crowded that he could hardly move about. The long-term damage was not significant, but the use of long-range bombers fooled and completely shocked the Japanese. *Enterprise*'s pilots and the cruiser *Nashville* had also finished off five Imperial Navy picket boats, at the cost of one SBD lost.[44]

Hornet and *Enterprise* rotated flight duty each day as they retired toward Pearl Harbor. During one of *Enterprise*'s down days, Lieutenant Commander Max Leslie took the opportunity to carrier-qualify some of his rookie pilots, including Frank O'Flaherty, Johnny Lough, John Bridgers, and Carl Peiffer. Vulture Row had a larger-than-usual crowd of onlookers gathered to watch from the walkways and in the gun sponsons on the island. The rookies were on the money this day, as they became qualified for carrier operations as dive-bomber pilots.[45]

Bombing Three's only plane loss of the trip came on April 20 during the return of her dozen morning scout bombers. Ensign Liston "Larry" Comer, an ACTG new boy from California, lost control and his SBD plunged over the port side. He and his gunner, AMM1c J. A. Browning, launched their rubber raft and were quickly picked up unhurt by the destroyer *Ellet*.

Hornet's Bombing Eight was less fortunate the following day, when Lieutenant (j.g.) Gardner Durfee Randall became lost during his scouting mission. Randall made a water landing about a hundred yards from the destroyer *Meredith*. He and his gunner, RM2c Thomas Alvin Gallagher, were unable to escape their sinking plane and thus became VB-8's first wartime casualties.

On April 25, the carriers entered Pearl Harbor. The *Enterprise* Air Group flew ahead to Ford Island, while the *Hornet* Air Group landed at Ewa Field. Ed Anderson had finally gotten in a full month of flying during the trip and had logged his first thirty-five hours of carrier flight duty. He had gotten little sleep, so the three days of R & R at the Royal Hawaiian Hotel were appreciated. "I had a good time," he wrote. "Plenty of good chow and a bottle of good scotch."[46]

Max Leslie's VB-3 would remain ashore in Hawaii, after having spelled Earl Gallaher's Scouting Six during the delivery of Doolittle's To-kyo raiders. Lieutenant Gallaher and his XO, Dick Dickinson, were frus-trated by the time Scouting Six finally reported back to *Enterprise*. Near the end of April, they had but four SBDs remaining under their charge. "Fourteen more were issued to us," said Dickinson. "We labored mightily getting them to satisfy our finicky taste." Once they were almost satisfied, their planes were pulled out from under them and assigned to another squadron. "We swore and grumbled, drew eighteen more and worked on those all night, only to have them taken away," Dickinson wrote.[47]

As equally troubling as obtaining aircraft for Gallaher and Dickin-son was the fact that Scouting Six had only seven other veteran pilots by late April. By month's end, they would inherit a dozen new pilots. The most experienced of the newbies were Carl Peiffer, John Roberts, Frank O'Flaherty, and Johnny Lough, who had been temporarily assigned to Leslie's VB-3 for the Doolittle mission. Scouting Six's other eight new pilots—Eldor "Rodey" Rodenburg, Bill Pittman, Clarence Vammen, Jim Dexter, Tom Durkin, Dick Jaccard, Jim Shelton, and Vernon Larsen "Mike" Micheel—had never spent time at sea on a carrier.

The latter eight were among thirty-four pilots of the second ACTG class to reach Pearl Harbor. The group had boarded the transport *President Hoover* at San Diego on April 8, and arrived in Pearl Harbor on April 16. Rodey Rodenburg was disturbed by the sight of the capsized battleship *Oklahoma*. He would long be bothered by the thoughts he had of the sailors who perished when their warship had rolled over. One of his companions, Mike Micheel, quickly got over his initial wave of sad-ness at seeing the battered American shipping, replaced by desire to exact revenge on the Japanese.[48]

Ensign Micheel, a former Iowa dairy farmer, had entered the Navy's flight program in 1940, when he learned of his impending draft. He was still in ACTG training at North Island when the war started. Micheel was in danger of washing out after cracking up an SNJ trainer in De-cember. His senior training officer grounded him from flying for three weeks.[49]

The thirty-two new pilots were moved to NAS Kaneohe and then farmed, based upon their training, to various carrier squadrons in need of replacements. Eight went to Gallaher's Scouting Six. During the shuffling of pilots, Lieutenant (j.g.) Bill Hall was transferred to *Lexington*'s VS-2. Hall, who had attacked the Gilberts with *Yorktown*'s VS-5 and had most recently flown from *Enterprise* for the Wake and Marcus strikes, was something of a grizzled veteran. He became known as "Pappy" to his new VS-2 comrades.[50]

Earl Gallaher worked with the ACTG arrivals who joined his VS-6 ashore. Two of Gallaher's new recruits, Bill Pittman and Dick Jaccard, had been carrier-qualified on *Saratoga* at the start of the war. "Our individual flight time totaled about four hundred and fifty hours, with each having four to six carrier landings," Pittman said. "Since we had no previous combat nor definite fear of what war was like, we were more interested in adventure. It was apparent that as young ensigns, we were not thinking beyond each day."[51]

Gallaher was only too happy when *Enterprise* put to sea for training on April 30 and his Scouting Six returned home. During the previous week, a VT-6 enlisted man had slugged a shore patrol officer while drunk and caused a mess of Navy routine and paperwork. Dusty Kleiss, for one, reflected of his squadron's return to *Enterprise*: "The stupid court-martial and training of new pilots and alerts have worn us out, although this was supposed to be a rest. Back to ship and damn glad of it."[52]

While the new boys were being checked out, the old boys enjoyed a bit of a breather. Lieutenant Charlie Ware, VS-6's third senior pilot, took the chance to write to his grandmother while the Big E was at sea for training. Nearly eight years out of the Naval Academy, he joked to her, "I'd better start looking around for a wife and some kids—or some kids and a wife." Ware asked his grandmother to "scout around the hills a bit" in Tennessee for "a good-looking widow with some insurance."[53]

Enterprise and *Hornet* both conducted training exercises northwest of Oahu. Mike Micheel found himself rooming with Bill Pittman, who had been on *Enterprise* at the start of the war but still had no combat experience either. Micheel was also happy to be reunited with Johnny Lough, with whom he had gone through flight school since their preflight days in Iowa.[54]

Gallaher and his fellow squadron commanders began carrier-qualifying their newest pilots the next morning. The rookies made a series of landings and takeoffs on April 30 in order to prove their abilities. For Ensign Micheel, it had been a month since he had made his four qualification landings on board *Hornet*. Micheel's log showed that he had a cumulative 371.9 hours of flight time in his career when he became fully qualified that day.[55]

Johnny Lough was the only one to smash up an SBD. The fuselage of his 6-S-2 broke at the forward cockpit, releasing two parachute flares that burned fiercely on the flight deck. Neither Lough nor gunner Johnny Snowden was injured.[56]

Once the "car-qual" process was completed, the *Hornet* and *Enterprise* aviators learned that they would not be returning to Pearl Harbor again. Their task force was instead ordered into the South Pacific. On board *Enterprise* were twenty-one Wildcat fighters of Marine VMF-212, destined for delivery at an advanced Pacific base. The Dauntless squadrons of the two flattops rotated daily scouting duties as they moved toward Palmyra Atoll. Dispatches were received from Rear Admiral Fletcher's Task Force 17 about carrier strikes having been carried out on Tulagi Harbor in the Solomons. Admiral Halsey realized that action was brewing in the Coral Sea, and he raised the speed of the *Enterprise* and *Hornet* force to race toward what he hoped to be a rendezvous with Imperial Japanese Navy forces.[57]

EIGHT

"Something Big Was in the Works"

"Same old thing," Cleo Dobson noted in his diary for May 2, 1942. "The SBDs made their usual scouting hops and the fighters keep up inner air patrol." Dobson had recently moved from being a regular pilot of Scouting Six into the position of *Enterprise*'s assistant LSO. His confidence received a hefty boost on May 4 when he used his wands for the first time to direct in the landing of fifteen scout bombers without cracking up a single one. "I got a big thrill from it," Dobson wrote that night. "I felt just about the same as I did when I first flew a plane aboard."[1]

Dobson's plane-landing experience was the only excitement he would see in early May. His *Enterprise* task force was racing for the Coral Sea action that was beginning to brew. The Japanese navy had been unstoppable during April. On April 5, the carriers *Akagi, Soryu, Hiryu, Shokaku,* and *Zuikaku* launched attacks against the British bases of Colombo and Trincomalee on Ceylon. That afternoon, Admiral Nagumo's carrier bombers destroyed the British heavy cruisers *Dorsetshire* and *Cornwall,* and four days later they sank the carrier *Hermes* and her escorting destroyer, *Vampire.*

Even as Nagumo's Kido Butai returned to Japan in late April for a rest and refit, his boss was at work on new plans. Admiral Yamamoto was unquestionably the mastermind and driving force behind the IJN's offensives. Yet Yamamoto had been stunned by the boldness of Jimmy Doolittle's Army bombers when they made their Tokyo raid on April 17.

It became clear to him that in order to rule the Pacific, he must first smash the American aircraft carriers that had escorted this strike and had conducted offensive assaults against Wake, Marcus, and the New Guinea areas of Lae and Salamaua. He allowed plans to proceed for an invasion of Port Moresby on New Guinea's southern coast and Tulagi in the southeastern Solomon Islands. The invasion fleet was covered by the light carrier *Shoho* and two of the Pearl Harbor sneak attack fleet carriers, *Shokaku* and *Zuikaku*.

The U.S. learned of the invasion plans through signals intelligence. Admiral Chester Nimitz sent a joint carrier force under Rear Admiral Frank Jack Fletcher to oppose the offensive. The Japanese forces invaded and occupied Tulagi during the first days of May, but their shipping came under assault on May 5 from *Enterprise*'s sister carrier *Yorktown*. In a series of dive-bombing and torpedo attacks, the *Yorktown* Air Group demolished a Japanese destroyer, sank three small minelayers, destroyed four seaplanes, and inflicted damage to several other ships.

The Japanese fleet entered the Coral Sea intent upon destroying the Allied naval forces. The world's first battle between opposing carrier forces—the ships never within sight of their enemy—played out during the next three days. Admiral Halsey caught only snatches of the action via messages he received daily from admirals Fletcher and Aubrey Fitch. On May 7, the *Lexington* and *Yorktown* aviators found the light carrier *Shoho* and put her under the waves. In the action that continued throughout the next day, the larger carrier *Shokaku* was damaged, but the Japanese managed to sink *Lexington*, a U.S. tanker, and a destroyer, and also heavily damaged the carrier *Yorktown*. The Americans suffered heavier losses in terms of shipping, but it was a strategic victory for the Allies, turning back the Port Moresby invasion and knocking the

U.S. Navy

Admiral Isoroku Yamamoto.

big carriers *Zuikaku* and *Shokaku* out of Admiral Yamamoto's next big master plan.

Yamamoto decided against directly attacking the U.S. base at Pearl Harbor. He instead selected Midway Atoll—at the extreme northwest end of the Hawaiian Island chain—as the centerpiece for his scheme to draw the American carriers out into a showdown. Midway, located some thirteen hundred miles from Oahu, was America's most vital forward base in the Pacific for staging bomber attacks and for refueling patrolling submarines. Yamamoto thus proposed a complex ploy to lure out the U.S. flattops into battle. He would send out a full invasion force, including two small carriers, to seize two of the Aleutian Islands, a chain of rocky isles that spread from Alaska across much of the North Pacific. At the same time, another invasion force supported by Vice Admiral Nagumo's Kido Butai would assault Midway and seize the two little islands. When the American carrier task forces arrived to attack the Japanese forces, Yamamoto planned to position an invasion force under Vice Admiral Nobutake Kondo to become the bait. Kondo's group would consist of two battleships, four heavy cruisers, a light cruiser, eight destroyers, and the light carrier *Zuiho*.[2]

Yamamoto hoped that the U.S. fleet would move from Pearl Harbor and head north to ambush Kondo's invasion force. Once the Americans were detected, two powerful Japanese forces would move in to assault the U.S. carriers. Nagumo's main carrier force would be supported by another group, known as the main body, under Admiral Yamamoto himself. His forces included Japan's largest battleships, two seaplane tenders, a light carrier, and various other warships. Between the Midway and Aleutians operations, Japan planned to send out nearly its entire navy, including all of its carriers and battleships.

The one thing Isoroku Yamamoto had not taken into account in his detailed planning was the fact that Chester Nimitz's cryptanalysts had broken the Japanese navy's secret code. Commander Joseph Rochefort and his analyst team at Station Hypo in Hawaii managed to confirm that Midway Atoll was the main target of an impending Japanese strike. Rochefort's team determined that the date of the attack would be either June 4 or June 5, while additionally providing Nimitz with a complete Japanese order of battle. The intelligence teams continued to unravel the complex enemy plans during May.

It soon became clear to Texas-born Nimitz that his only hope of averting this latest Japanese threat rested primarily with his carrier aviators.

As *Yorktown* retreated from the Coral Sea to lick her wounds, Admiral Halsey carried out his assigned mission of delivering Marine Fighter Squadron 212 to Efate Island east of Australia on May 11. New *Enterprise* Air Group Commander Wade McClusky and Cleo Dobson in two SBDs, plus a Marine in an SNJ training plane, flew to Efate to check out the airstrip. After Dobson had photographed the harbor, village, and landing field, the group landed and met with the local Marine detachment. "We found the field too small for the Marine fighters to land and so we reported to the ship," Dobson wrote. "I would like to have spent two weeks there. It really looked good for a short vacation." *Enterprise* instead flew off the twenty-one Marine Wildcats to Noumea in New Caledonia that day.[3]

Task Force 16 remained south of Efate for several days while Halsey sent out scouts in hopes of catching some of the retiring Japanese carrier forces. Dick Best rotated his pilots equally into scouting flights each day at sea. He also flew usual rotation, opting as always to never use his rank to skip out on an assigned flight. SBD pilots served as carrier pigeons, dropping or landing various messages to help keep their task force's location a secret from Japanese searchers.

Enterprise finally headed north on May 13. Two of her scouts failed to return that afternoon from a two-hundred-mile search mission. Ensign Tom Durkin in 6-S-9 reported at 1725 that he and his gunner, AM2c Erwin Bailey, were making a water landing as darkness fell. Nothing at all was heard from the lost Bombing Six plane, 6-B-16, which was manned by Ensign Bucky Walters and ARM2c Parham Johnson Jr. Lieutenant Best felt responsible for Walters's loss. He had refused to accept the ensign's attempt to resign from aviation in late 1941. Walters had received transfer orders soon after he had survived his hair-raising night landing at Pearl Harbor on December 7. Best consulted with skipper Holly Hollingsworth on the matter, and decided that Walters was more valuable as a pilot than he realized. He was a popular member of VB-6 and served as the unit's gym instructor, maintaining physical fitness among the pilots. Best tore up Walters's discharge papers and threw them over the side of the ship.[4]

Enterprise launched twenty-one SBDs at dawn on May 14 to search the sectors where Durkin and Walters were believed to have been lost. No signs of Walters or Johnson were ever found. Ensign Durkin and Bailey had gone down northeast of the New Hebrides. The pair began to lose hope after five days of drifting on the open ocean in their rubber raft. Durkin tried to inject humor by removing $220 from his wallet that he had won in poker the night before they were lost. He amused himself by counting it in front of Bailey and estimating how many milk shakes it would buy at fifteen cents per shake.[5]

Durkin was tough—a former boxer during his first two years at Notre Dame—but watching search planes twice pass them by without seeing them was brutal. The VS-6 crew consumed the last of their water after ten days adrift. Fortunately, they spotted the island of Espiritu Santo the following day and regained hope. Durkin and Bailey finally reached shore after fourteen days in the ocean, and Bailey killed an eel for their first meal. They survived on coconut milk and shellfish for three more days until friendly natives found them and helped effect their return to the nearest Navy base. Long written off as lost, Tom Durkin and Erwin Bailey would finally make their return to Pearl Harbor suffering from sun exposure three weeks after their loss at sea. A devout Catholic, Durkin told a buddy that he had made so many vows saying his rosary during the fourteen days bobbing in the Pacific that he would have a tough time living up to them the rest of his life.[6]

Enterprise's string of bad luck continued. Ensign Bill Pittman put another dive-bomber in the drink on May 15. He was taking off with a VS-6 inner-air patrol group that morning, but he struggled to get his 6-S-16 above the waves. There was only a single knot of wind to aid with lift, and it wasn't enough. Pittman crashed off the port bow, but both he and gunner Floyd Adkins were picked up by the plane guard destroyer *Ellet*.

That afternoon, one of VF-6's Wildcats crashed overboard while landing after CAP duty. The pilot was recovered, but yet another crash occurred a quarter hour later. Ensign Walter Hiebert of Fighting Six attempted to land, but his Wildcat's tail hook failed to snag an arresting wire. Radioman Ed Anderson was walking aft on the starboard side of the flight deck at the time. He and others ducked as the F4F's wings sailed over their heads. Hiebert's fighter plowed into the crash barrier, damaging other planes and injuring sailors in the process. "I am surely living on borrowed time," Anderson wrote in his diary.[7]

Enterprise and *Hornet* feinted a run toward Tulagi in the Solomons to confuse Japanese snoopers. The anticipation for real action grew when Admiral Halsey received orders from his boss, Admiral Nimitz, to expedite the return of Task Force 16 to Hawaii. Once *Enterprise* was recalled to Pearl Harbor, Lew Hopkins of VB-6 found that their scouting flights were conducted under strict radio silence. For Hopkins, hitting the flight deck with the beanbag messages proved to be quite a challenge. "You were going a lot faster than the ship and you had to drop the beanbag before you got over the ship. Everybody usually missed on their first try. The deck crew began to keep score of our drops."[8]

Task Force 16's SBD loss jinx continued on May 18 as *Hornet*'s air group conducted the two-hundred-mile searches. Ensign Roy Gee of Bombing Eight made a forced landing alongside *Hornet*, but both he and gunner Donald Canfield were recovered by a destroyer. It was *Enterprise*'s turn next on May 20, as a group of sixteen SBDs was cued up for a scout mission.

Dick Best was first to launch. He quickly realized that the SBDs were being sent off without sufficient airspeed. When he got to the bow, instead of lifting off, his left wing dropped. *I'm stalling*, Best thought. He managed to fight his aircraft up over the waves and gain altitude before he opened up on his radio and called to the carrier to cease launching at her reduced speed.[9]

Best's warning came too late, for other SBDs were already rolling down the deck. Willie West of Scouting Six failed to get airborne. His 6-S-2 smacked into the ocean just off the Big E's port bow at 0530. West, who had survived the Pearl Harbor attack and was wounded during the Marshalls strike, struggled to get free of his sinking Dauntless. Cleo Dobson saw West's head and shoulders finally pop up close to the tail of the plane. Then a wave dashed over the SBD and West, and they both disappeared. The destroyer *Conyngham* picked up West's rear gunner, AMM2c Milton Clark, uninjured. Dusty Kleiss considered the loss of his buddy Willie West "one of the greatest shocks of the war. I was on deck, about two hundred feet away, when the sinking aircraft dragged him down. A very special friend."[10]

For Dobson and Mac McCarthy, this loss was very painful. All three pilots had survived rough experiences over Pearl Harbor on December 7 and had become close. As he and McCarthy surveyed West's personal effects, Dobson found "it was one of the hardest jobs I have had since I came into the Navy. It doesn't seem right for a man whose every idea and thought was so pure and good should have to go as he did. I guess when your number is up, you have to go."[11]

Enterprise had lost four SBDs and three men in only a week's time. The following day, May 21, Ensign Louis John Muery of *Hornet*'s Bombing Eight failed to return from a scouting mission. No contact was made and subsequent searches conducted by other *Hornet* aviators failed to find any trace of Muery or his gunner, ARM3c Walter Max John Richter.[12]

Much later, it was learned that Muery's engine had failed while he was on the extreme end of his search leg. The VB-8 airmen drifted and sailed for twenty-three days before reaching a small island. Their boat capsized in the rough barrier reef surf, and Richter drowned. Muery used the boat's paddle to dig a grave for his gunner. Natives found Muery and helped nurse him back to health until Navy ships could come rescue him. The Texan returned home and immediately married his girlfriend.[13]

Task Force 16 made seventeen knots on a steady return course to the Hawaiian Islands. Fighting Six pilot Gayle Hermann, who had survived being shot down on December 7, was killed in a takeoff crash from *Enterprise* just one day short of making port. "This makes the trip a most unhappy one," Dusty Kleiss wrote in his diary of the loss of Hermann and Willie West. "Two of my best friends."[14]

The *Hornet* and *Enterprise* air groups flew into Oahu on Tuesday, May 26, shortly ahead of the task force warships. The *Enterprise* Air Group landed on Ford Island and received the welcome word from Lieutenant Commander Wade McClusky that the air group could enjoy thirty-six hours of R & R at the Royal Hawaiian Hotel. In contrast, *Hornet*'s air group settled at Ewa Field, but the fifty-mile flight took two hours "due to eternal circling necessary to rendezvous and stagger in behind the CHAG and the torpedo planes," recalled VF-8's Ensign

Elisha "Smokey" Stover. The CHAG, Commander Stan Ring, then told his pilots that they would not be getting two days' liberty at the Royal Hawaiian like the *Enterprise* pilots. Instead, they would remain on continual alert at the base until their ship sailed again.[15]

This resulted in a near mutiny against the *Hornet* group commander. Several SBD pilots got into trouble for excessive griping and for expressing their opinions of CHAG to his face. The unpopular Sea Hag even grounded Lieutenant George Ellenburg of VB-8 from flying at Midway for his part in the vocal outbursts.[16]

The *Hornet* fliers turned to several bottles of whiskey to pass the night ashore. Some of the pilots became inebriated and ended up in semi-friendly fistfights and wrestling matches on the beach. Clay Fisher of Bombing Eight found that no one was seriously hurt, but the next morning he spotted some lacerated faces and black eyes among the pilots. No hard feelings existed among the aviators. Instead, they shared an increased camaraderie after having unleashed some of their frustrations with the Sea Hag.[17]

Yorktown was still trailing fuel oil from her bomb-damaged fuel bunkers when her TF-17 sortied from the port of Tongatabu in the Tonga Islands on May 19. There would be no stateside rest for her crew and most of her air group. The carrier was instead ordered to Pearl Harbor to refuel and repair. Admiral Fletcher congratulated his crew on the fine spirit they had displayed during a hundred straight days of battle cruising.[18]

When *Yorktown* made port on May 27, Fletcher went ashore for a conference with Admiral Nimitz. He was told that *Yorktown* would be sent back to sea almost immediately to defend Midway Atoll. Further shocking news came when he learned that Admiral Halsey, his senior, had been sent ashore for treatment of a skin ailment. Command of the *Hornet* and *Enterprise* carrier TF-16 would instead fall upon the shoulders of Rear Admiral Raymond Ames Spruance—the previous TF-16 cruiser commander—at the recommendation of Halsey. Admiral Fletcher of *Yorktown*'s TF-17 would remain the senior carrier task force commander and overall carrier commander.

Spruance and his carrier aviators faced steep odds. He was briefed that a major Japanese force intended to occupy Midway Atoll, located about thirteen hundred miles northwest of Pearl Harbor. If they succeeded, the Hawaiian Islands would become an easier next target for Japanese occupation in the Pacific. The Americans scrambled to ready forces on Midway and at sea around the atoll; the Japanese war machine was already in motion.

Two powerful armadas sortied from the Japanese island toward the two strategic assault areas of Midway and the Aleutians. The Aleutians force was divided into a number of concentrated groupings of warships, landing ships, and submarines. It total, it comprised the smaller carriers *Ryujo* and *Junyo*, four battleships, ten cruisers, twenty-four destroyers, six submarines, three oilers, three supply ships, four support vessels, three minesweepers, and two minelayers. The larger force being dispatched toward Midway was similarly divided into distinct tactical formations. Admiral Yamamoto's main body included the light carrier *Hosho*, three heavy battleships, one light cruiser, nine destroyers, an oiler, two tenders, and a supply ship. Vice Admiral Takeo Kurita's close support group was comprised of four cruisers, two destroyers, and an oiler. Vice Admiral Kondo's Midway invasion force included the light carrier *Zuiho*, two battleships, five cruisers, eight destroyers, four oilers, and a supply ship. Rear Admiral Raizo Tanaka's transport group numbered one light cruiser, ten destroyers, and thirteen transport and supply ships. Fifteen submarines were deployed to the area from five divisions.[19]

Finally, there was Vice Admiral Nagumo's deadly first carrier strike force, the Kido Butai. His main striking force was built around the fleet carriers *Akagi* (his flagship), *Kaga*, *Hiryu*, and *Soryu*—four of the perpetrators of the December 7 surprise attack on America at Pearl Harbor. The Kido Butai also included two battleships, three cruisers, twelve destroyers, and five small oilers to refuel the fleet. Nagumo's carriers sortied for Midway on May 27 with great confidence. It was Navy Day, the thirty-seventh anniversary of Admiral Heihachiro Togo's great 1905 victory over the Russians at Tsushima. Sailors lined the rails of their ships in the Hashirajima anchorage in Japan's Inland Sea to cheer and wave their caps.[20]

In contrast, the U.S. Navy would do well to scrape together three aircraft carriers, eight cruisers, seventeen destroyers, three oilers, and nineteen strategically placed submarines. Counting all of the invasion force and battle groups steaming from Japan toward Midway and the Aleutians, Nimitz's thirty-one surface vessels and nineteen submarines faced 168 enemy vessels. On paper, it would be no contest.

That the Americans would even put three carriers to sea was not a certainty on May 27. *Yorktown* was rushed into a dry dock at Pearl Harbor for emergency repairs to her Coral Sea bomb damage. Admiral Nimitz, sloshing through the water with Captain Elliott Buckmaster and Admiral Fletcher to inspect the hull, said that he must have the carrier back in operation in three days' time. More than a thousand yard workers swarmed over the battle-damaged ship around the clock to meet the deadline.[21]

The most troubling news for Fletcher and Buckmaster was that their *Yorktown* air group would be broken up to help fill out other newly forming squadrons. Her Fighting Forty-two, Torpedo Five, and Scouting Five squadrons were ordered to remain ashore when *Yorktown* completed her repairs. Only Lieutenant Wally Short's Bombing Five would be retained for the upcoming action. Three-quarters of the *Yorktown* Air Group would be replaced by squadrons from *Saratoga*'s displaced air group: Lieutenant Commander Max Leslie's Bombing Three, Lieutenant Commander John Smith "Jimmy" Thach's Fighting Three, and Lieutenant Commander Lem Massey's Torpedo Three.

Bombing Five mechanics scrambled to organize combat-ready Dauntlesses. They had only five of their own but drew two spares from the Hawaii fleet aircraft pool, six from VS-5, and another five from the *Lex*'s orphaned VS-2. Most of the SBDs still had to be hurriedly equipped with the dual .30-caliber machine-gun mounts. "We were all refitted at a most feverish pace," said rear gunner Lynn Forshee.[22]

Wally Short was equally strained to assemble his flight personnel for VB-5 in just a few days. Ten of his veteran pilots stayed on. One other veteran was added to Short's mix in the form of Lieutenant Charlie "Tex" Conatser, who had been sidelined from Bombing Five in January to undergo stomach surgery for an umbilical hernia. He had arrived at Hawaii weeks before *Yorktown*—a "naval officer without a navel"—and had spent his time living with Jimmy Thach learning fighter tactics. Lieutenant

Short was pleased to welcome Conatser and his experience back into his squadron for the impending battle.[23]

To this lot of veteran VB-5 pilots were added an equal mix of untested young ensigns: Carl Horenberger, John Bridgers, John Ammen, Bob Gibson, Larry Comer, Ray Kline, Dick Wolfe, Jerry Richey, Ray Miligi, and Spike Conzett. Of these "new boys," only Comer and Bridgers had flown temporary duty with VS-6 on *Enterprise* since the end of March.

The second Dauntless group to operate on *Yorktown* for the coming battle was up to the task. Max Leslie's VB-3 had spelled Scouting Six for the Doolittle raid. The *Enterprise* air group was by far the most combat-blooded unit to prepare for action off Midway. Dick Best, who had flown with the squadron since the Pearl Harbor attack, retained command of Bombing Six. He had a mix of veteran pilots and many new replacement pilots, some of whom had flown with other carriers. Best's gunner, Jim Murray, found that Ford Island was "a beehive of activity" as all types of aircraft were hastily prepared for action.[24]

Lieutenant Harvey Lanham, gunnery officer for Bombing Six, had a little more insight than others. His shipboard roommate was Lieutenant Gilvin M. Slonim, a Japanese-language interpreter assigned to the admiral's staff. "Although Gil was very closemouthed, in true intelligence officer fashion, I wormed enough from him to know that the Japanese fleet was putting to sea and we were planning to meet them," Lanham said.[25]

Earl Gallaher still led Scouting Six. He had been there since the start of the war, and he had inherited the unit early on when his skipper went down. Now he and his number two man, Dick Dickinson, had their hands full. They received new planes at Pearl Harbor to make good on the recent losses. Many of their new pilots had no combat experience. Old-timers like Charlie Ware were golden in teaching the new boys about sectional and divisional tactics.[26]

The newer ACTG pilots of Scouting Six stuck together. On board ship, they spent more time in the ready room than did the seasoned veterans. One of VS-6's untested young pilots, Bill Pittman, had no real idea what type of battle he was heading into. "Rumors were always plentiful and we believed anything," he said. He and buddy Dick Jaccard talked at length with the "old-timers," pilots who had two or three island raids under their belts. They learned how they could dive away from a trailing Zero by not opening their dive flaps. Pittman respected his section leader, Pat Patriarca. He said that Patriarca "always appeared cool to anything (including rumors) but was nervous until he became airborne. Then he was steady and like having the Rock of Gibraltar guiding the section."[27]

New air group commander Wade McClusky had been a fighter pilot during the previous months. Now flying an SBD as CEAG, McClusky had had little time to practice his dive-bombing doctrine. His handiwork as a fighter pilot was acknowledged during a brief awards ceremony on the flight deck of *Enterprise* on May 27. McClusky received a Navy Cross for his actions as VF-6 skipper during the Marshalls strike. Dusty Kleiss and Cleo Dobson of Scouting Six also received Distinguished Flying Crosses. Kleiss was not notified until that morning that he was being given the DFC for his direct hit on a ship at the Marshalls.

Kleiss felt great honor as he stepped forward to be pinned with the cross by Admiral Nimitz. The moment was also uplifting for Dobson, who had spent the morning helping Nancy West secure transportation back to the United States. Her husband, Willie, had been killed the previous week when his SBD crashed on takeoff. Dobson and Mac McCarthy had done their best to comfort the grieving widow. "What burns me up is that none of the officers in the squadron called on her while we were in there," he confided in his diary.[28]

The *Enterprise* Air Group received word their carrier and *Hornet* would be getting under way on the morning of May 28. The enlisted men heard plenty of scuttlebutt about what the fleet was setting out to meet, but little specific intelligence had been given to them. "We all knew something big was in the works," VB-6 gunner Stuart Mason said.[29]

The three carriers sported 112 total Dauntlesses as they headed for Midway. The *Hornet* Air Group was the least experienced group in terms of previous Pacific combat. Lieutenant William "Gus" Widhelm, XO of Scouting Eight, was almost left behind when the big fly-out took place on May 28. Air group commander Stan Ring could not get his SBD to launch due to fouled plugs, so he commandeered Widhelm's bird and took off.

Gus was able to get the Dauntless to fire up but the engine was missing badly. He finally left the errant SBD behind. Ensign George "Tex" Gay from Texas was preparing to take off in the last Devastator of

Torpedo Eight. Widhelm jumped into the middle seat of Gay's TBD and narrowly made it out to the carrier.[30]

The *Enterprise* air group suffered a plane loss during its carrier landings when Lieutenant Commander Gene Lindsey's TBD stalled and slammed into the ocean near the carrier. The torpedo bomber crew was quickly rescued, but skipper Lindsey suffered serious injuries to his face and chest.

Task Force 16 headed for Midway. Admiral Spruance planned to rendezvous with *Yorktown*'s TF-17 on June 2 some 350 miles northeast of the atoll. *Hornet*'s Scouting Eight suffered another plane loss on May 29, when Ensign Richard Milliman and ARM3c Tony Roger Pleto failed to return from a scouting mission. Ensigns Gus Devoe and Joe Auman circled the scene but saw nothing more than a floating cushion and a fuel tank. Coupled with the CHAG plane that was left at Pearl Harbor, the carriers were thus down to 110 SBDs before they even reached Midway.[31]

The *Enterprise* Air Group commanders held a conference on the morning of May 29. Wade McClusky, Earl Gallaher, Dick Best, Jim Gray, and Gene Lindsey gathered in Admiral Spruance's cabin as Captain Browning detailed the intelligence of how the Japanese were planning to attack. Best thought the intelligence was phony. *They can't tell us where the Japanese are going,* he thought. *They sure as hell don't know that the attack on Midway planned for the third of June isn't a diversionary attack.* Best, of course, wasn't informed enough to know that intelligence specialists had broken the Japanese code.[32]

Best still held no good feelings toward Miles Browning, the staff officer he had long considered to be a bully. At the conclusion of the briefing, Browning asked if there were any questions. Best, thinking of his wife and daughter back in Honolulu, replied, "Suppose they don't attack Midway? Suppose they keep going east and hit Pearl again and maybe Honolulu?"[33]

Browning narrowed his eyes and stared coldly at the young lieutenant for almost a full minute. He finally said, "Well, we just hope they don't."

The hastily patched *Yorktown* slipped out of dry dock on May 29. When her squadrons flew out to the carrier the next day, nearly half the

VB-5 pilots were making their first carrier landings. The air group still had no idea what exactly they were in for. Lieutenant Syd Bottomley, flight officer for VB-3, knew something must be in the wind, but he knew nothing about the Japanese designs on Midway. "It was a well-guarded secret up to then," he said.[34]

Bombing Three's enlisted men did not have time to worry. They had been tapped at the last hour to replace Scouting Five on *Yorktown*, and they were kept busy. There had been plenty of scuttlebutt, but rear gunner Joe Godfrey said, "Few of us paid much attention to it."[35]

The Dauntless landings on *Yorktown* went smoothly on the first day out from Pearl. One of the VF-3 rookies, however, bounced upon touchdown and smashed into the back of another Wildcat. His propeller chopped through the cockpit of Lieutenant Don Lovelace's F4F, killing the fighter squadron executive officer. Ensign Charlie Lane of Bombing Three felt Lovelace's loss had "a sobering effect" that calmed some of the nervous tension felt by everyone rushing toward combat with the Japanese. Lane had been in a group with Lovelace swimming at Waikiki only the day before.[36]

Yorktown's Bombing Five and Bombing Three quickly became an issue for air staff, pilots, radiomen, and deck personnel. Orders to "spot bombers for launch" were confusing. Loudspeaker announcements for bomber pilots to proceed to their ready room left Max Leslie and Wally Short's men wondering which group was being summoned. To settle the matter, Captain Buckmaster temporarily designated Bombing Five as Scouting Five for this cruise, a move that did not sit well with the VB-5 aviators.[37]

Earl Gallaher, having been briefed by Spruance's staff on the upcoming operation, decided to enlighten his senior pilots on the pending showdown off Midway. He called together division leaders Dick Dickinson and Charlie Ware; section leaders Dusty Kleiss, Norm West, and Pat Patriarca; and trusted combat veterans Mac McCarthy and Reid Stone. Once they entered the Scouting Six ready room, Lieutenant Gallaher locked the door behind them.[38]

"You must not give what I say to anyone!" he demanded. "There are only two exceptions."

Gallaher's two exceptions were more preparation-based necessities than they were intelligence-related issues. His key pilots were urged to practice with their regular radiomen on how to quickly switch out coils for the YE-ZB homing device in each SBD. Once the rear gunner had swapped the coils, each pilot was to immediately record the ZB's Morse code signal that offered the distance and course back to *Enterprise*. This data could mean the difference between making it back or not from such a long-range mission. Once the information was quickly logged before the attack, the SBD crew was to switch back to the normal radio and gunnery coil.

The only other allowance Gallaher offered his key pilots involved their working with maintenance personnel on the homing equipment, the SBDs' electrical controls, and any changes vital to the top performance of their dive-bombers. No other details of his briefing were to be shared with anyone. "There are *no* other exceptions!" he barked.[39]

Dusty Kleiss soaked up the fine points as his skipper began diagramming the area around Midway. Gallaher indicated where the Japanese carriers were expected to be approaching from and the approximate area where Midway's scout planes would hopefully spot them. The carrier-based dive-bombers would then be launched from about 180 miles away. This extreme range would likely exceed the fuel limitations of both escorting Wildcat fighters and the lumbering Devastator torpedo planes. "We knew that only SBDs could be used for this plan," Kleiss recalled.[40]

"None of what I have told you is to be given to others," Gallaher warned again. "Not even to our own pilots."

The three U.S. carriers rotated search duties each day en route to Midway. From the atoll, Marine and Navy scouts also flew out daily in search of the Japanese. The new pilots in each squadron were broken in during these two-hundred-mile scouting missions. Lieutenant (j.g.) Paul "Lefty" Holmberg of *Yorktown*'s VB-3, who had joined the squadron only in May at Kaneohe, was highly nervous. He was so apprehensive about his first long-range searches, about takeoffs and landings, and more, that he was too busy to fear the impending battle.[41]

The task forces built around *Enterprise*, *Hornet*, and *Yorktown* finally made a rendezvous on the afternoon of Tuesday, June 2. Admiral Spruance's next anticipated rendezvous would be near Midway with

U.S. Navy Photo, Mark Horan Collection

Enterprise's Scouting Six pilots just weeks before Midway: (*seated, left to right*) Lieutenant (j.g.) Norm West, Lieutenant Frank Patriarca, Lieutenant Charlie Ware (FO), Lieutenant Earl Gallaher (CO), Lieutenant Dick Dickinson (XO), Lieutenant (j.g.) Dusty Kleiss, and Ensign John McCarthy; (*standing, left to right*) Ensigns John Roberts, Carl Peiffer, Jim Shelton, Bill Pittman, John Lough, Vernon Micheel, Eldor Rodenburg, Tom Durkin, Jr., Dick Jaccard, Frank O'Flaherty, Clarence Vammen, Jr., Jim Dexter, Reid Stone, and Willie West.

Mark Horan Collection, courtesy of Captain John Goldsmith

Enterprise's Bombing Six pilots, photographed on June 3, 1942, at Midway: (*seated, left to right*) Lieutenant (j.g.) Andy Anderson, Lieutenant Harvey Lanham, Lieutenant Lloyd Smith (XO), Lieutenant Dick Best (CO), Lieutenant Joe Penland (FO), Lieutenant Horace Moorehead, Jr., and Lieutenant (j.g.) John Van Buren; (*standing, left to right*) Ensign Gene Greene, Ensign George Goldsmith, Ensign Stephen Hogan, Jr., Ensign Norm Vandivier, Ensign Don Ely, Lieutenant (j.g.) Bill Roberts, Ensign Lewis Hopkins, Lieutenant (j.g.) Ed Kroeger, Ensign Delbert Halsey, Ensign Fred Weber, Ensign Tom Ramsay, Ensign Tony Schneider, Ensign Bertram Varian, Ensign Arthur Rausch, and Ensign Harry Liffner.

Admiral Nagumo's Imperial Japanese Navy. The *Enterprise* dive-bomber squadrons paused long enough in the afternoon to take squadron photos of both the pilots and gunners of each unit.[42]

On *Hornet*, Lieutenant John Lynch wrote a letter home to his wife that afternoon. Lynch, a graduate of Boston College, was a senior pilot of Bombing Eight. *Sometime this week we expect to see some decisive action. I shall do my best,* he wrote. Lynch could not tell Ginnie what the action was, but he did offer a hint. *We believe that it should deal a telling blow in the outcome and length of the war.*[43]

Yorktown handled the air search and CAP duties on June 3. Her twenty SBD searchers turned up nothing, but during the day a Midway-based PBY flying boat spotted the Japanese transport force some seven hundred miles west of Midway. The next morning was certain to bring combat.

Ensign John Bridgers of VS-5 made only his second flight over open ocean as part of the scouting force. What he remembered most about that particular flight was the thin parachute cushion on which he sat. Bridgers suffered such discomfort during that four-hour flight that he worried little over his pending second carrier landing in an SBD. "I just wanted to be able to stand up and ease the pain in the seat of my pants," he said.[44]

Lefty Holmberg of Bombing Three flew the search as Max Leslie's wingman. On the return leg of his flight, the rookie pilot was chagrined to not find *Yorktown* in the place he expected her to be. His confidence was further shattered when gunner George LaPlant announced that he could not get the "damned receiver" to work on their YE-ZB homing device. Holmberg attracted the attention of Lieutenant Commander Leslie and turned the lead back over to the skipper. During the course of his flight, Holmberg changed courses many times to avoid patches of fog and low clouds.[45]

Following supper back on board *Yorktown* that evening, Holmberg was given a lecture and a gentle scolding from Leslie for changing courses so many times. The skipper reminded his wingman that this was a sure way to get lost and that Bombing Three needed every aircraft for the battle expected the next day.

Admiral Fletcher decided to follow up on the PBY contact reports by sending out another ten of his SBDs in the afternoon. The morning search had gone two hundred miles; the afternoon search went on 175 miles in the same sector covered in the morning, but again found nothing.[46]

Fletcher swung *Yorktown* southwest in order to be about two hundred miles north of Midway at dawn on June 4. Wally Short's newly designated Scouting Five drew the duty of flying the morning scouting missions again the next day. Orders were posted for new ensigns Jerry Richey, Bob Gibson, and John Bridgers to wake up the other pilots forty minutes before their flight time. Howard W. Johnson, plane captain for Wally Short, performed a special ritual that night. Although he would not be flying into combat, he stashed a twenty-dollar bill in each of VS-5's SBDs, giving him special equity in each flight.[47]

This is really it, thought Charlie Lane of VB-3. *We have been given the U.S.'s best naval equipment, all possible support of our country, and it is now up to us to do a vital job.*[48]

On *Hornet*, Ensign Clay Fisher of Bombing Eight spent time talking with his roommate, Ken White, of their slim chances of surviving the looming battle. Fisher wrote letters to his wife, Annie, and to his mother, telling them, "I had resigned myself to whatever fate had in store for me. If we lost the battle and I died, I knew our country would eventually defeat the Japanese."[49]

On *Enterprise*, many of the Dauntless aircrews were restless. Bill Roberts of Bombing Six had felt apprehension before each of the previous strikes against the Marshalls, Wake, and Marcus. But this time, as he waited for the confrontation with Japanese carriers off Midway, Roberts had a strange feeling of elation at the prospect of catching the Japanese off guard.[50]

Despite his initial doubts, Dick Best had gained confidence in the intelligence reports that he now believed would put his aviators in the right place at the right time for some good old-fashioned payback. *It's in the bag. Here we are, behind the garden gate with an ax in our hand, and the poor little innocent Jap is waltzing through with flowers in his hand and having lunch. We're going to get square for Pearl, because Pearl was humiliating.*[51]

"Every fresh word of information increased our tension," wrote Dick Dickinson of Scouting Six. That night, many of the aviators struggled with their nervous energy. "It was difficult for any of us to take ourselves off to bed, important as we knew that night's sleep to be," remembered Dickinson. "All of us fully realized that we were getting a chance to change the whole character of the war in the Pacific." [52]

Dusty Kleiss was another who still had visions of the carnage that Scouting Six had experienced on December 7. *Tomorrow is likely to be a big day*, he wrote in his diary that night. [53]

Kleiss and Dickinson's skipper had the same feelings of anticipation. Earl Gallaher knew "that we were really gonna have the chance of paying them back for Pearl Harbor." He had lost many pilots and enlisted men in the previous six months of the Pacific War. On the morning the war started, he had lost more than eleven hundred former shipmates when the battleship *Arizona*—his first ship to serve on—had been blown to the bottom of Pearl Harbor. With any luck, the following day would be his chance to settle a lot of old scores. With his resolutions thus set, Gallaher's night before the battle was unlike most of his junior pilots'. He recalled, "I had no trouble whatsoever going to sleep that night." [54]

NINE

"God, This Is It!"

Breakfast came early for the carrier air groups on June 4, 1942.

At 0200, a messenger tapped Dusty Kleiss on the arm and said, "It's time to wake up." After years at sea, Kleiss was able to sleep blissfully in a few minutes, hypnotized by the gentle rocking of his big ship. At the messenger's touch, he rolled out of his bunk, just three feet below the flight deck, dressed, and headed for the officers' mess.[1]

"I don't think anybody was particularly hungry that morning," said Lew Hopkins of Bombing Six. "I think everybody just kinda pushed their eggs around." Walt Rodee, skipper of *Hornet*'s Scouting Eight, sat down beside Torpedo Eight skipper Jack Waldron to eat his scrambled eggs. "Walt, this is what we've been getting flight pay for," Waldron said of the day's important mission. Rodee agreed, adding, "Let's be sure and get there."[2]

Chief Jim Murray, the leading radioman of Bombing Six, found the usual mealtime laughing and joking to be absent among the air group CPOs, including chiefs Wilson Sandefer and Charles Grenat of VT-6 and John O'Brien of VF-6. O'Brien, in addition to his Fighting Six duties, had long flown with the air group commanders, dating back to his flight with Brigham Young at the beginning of the war. O'Brien was now slated to fly with Wade McClusky, but he stopped by breakfast to say that he had lost his glasses and would be unable to fly.[3]

O'Brien then casually mentioned that he had made his own arrangements for ARM1c Walter Chocalousek to take his place without consulting his superior. "This upset me to no end," Murray said. Chocalousek, fresh from aircraft gunnery school, had just joined VB-6 at Ford Island the previous week and had been assigned to serve as Murray's on-deck maintenance man for the SBDs. Murray informed O'Brien in no uncertain terms that he would assume responsibility for all VB-6 on-deck radio maintenance in Chocalousek's absence.

By 0400, the *Enterprise* aviators were in their ready rooms. The pilots had plotted the carrier's position and had recorded wind and other data. *Yorktown*'s VS-5 handled the morning scouting. At 0430, ten of Wally Short's SBDs departed to search a northern semicircle out to a hundred miles. Lieutenant Tex Conatser, as flight scheduler for the squadron, had penciled himself in with those being held for the morning strike and placed Lieutenant Sam Adams on the morning scout mission. Adams, who held rank on Conatser, called for a switch of their positions. Short's and Conatser's SBDs formed on wing lights and blue exhausts in the darkness before fanning out to scout. The ready-room Teletypes began clattering with the first word from Midway's search planes minutes after the Yorktown scouts departed. A PBY flying boat reported shortly after 0440 that a night torpedo attack had been made on an enemy transport force. The next report did not come until 0534, and it was frustratingly brief: "Enemy carriers."[4]

Dick Dickinson was seated in the front of VS-6's seven rows of chairs between skipper Gallaher and third officer Charlie Ware. To him, their smoke-filled room had never been so quiet. "Yet the confidence was something one could feel," he said. Dusty Kleiss reached into the locked cabinet underneath his front-row seat and pulled out his chart board as Gallaher began printing vital information on the squadron's chalkboard.[5]

With a belly full of steak and eggs, Dusty was ready for action. Under his flight suit, he wore his girlfriend Jean's sweater for extra warmth at high altitude. In his upper left arm pocket were several sharpened pencils for plotting data on his chart board. In his chest pockets were a small flashlight and a lipstick-size container of Vaseline and ephedrine. The flight surgeon had long instructed each pilot to take a whiff of ephedrine if either nostril was not fully open before diving to save his eardrums. Kleiss's leg pockets included a spare flashlight, new batteries, wool cloths to clean his chart board, and another cloth to wipe his SBD's windshield.[6]

On *Yorktown*, ARM3c Lloyd Fred Childers felt, "God, this is it!" As he had dressed that morning, Childers placed his wallet and wristwatch on a shelf in the locker by his bunk that he shared with his brother, AMM3c Wayne Childers. The fourth of June was Lloyd's twenty-first birthday, but as one of Torpedo Three's radiomen/gunners, he was a realist. "Wayne," he said, "if I don't come back from this flight, these are yours."[7]

Flight officer Joe Penland conducted the squadron briefing in Bombing Six's ready room. His brown eyes flashed as the short North Carolina native gave the operational orders. Aside from the air group commander, there would be no switching of planes for VB-6's launch this day, to eliminate confusion. If anyone received a "down" for their SBD's launch, they were simply out for this important strike. Ensign George Goldsmith, one of VB-6's rookie pilots, could see a difference in the ready room. The rookies had a certain excitement not present in the faces of the unit's combat-seasoned veterans.[8]

In Scouting Eight's ready room, Benny Moore leaned over to his division leader.

"How'd you make out in the poker games last night, Gus?" Moore asked in his Texan drawl.

"I got a shellacking," Widhelm said.

Knowing his exec's deep superstitions, Moore replied, "Then you should have a good day today." Gus Widhelm had long felt that it was bad luck to win big before an important mission.[9]

Nearby in Bombing Eight's ready room, Roy Gee heard the Teletype machine steadily clicking away. He diligently copied the navigational data to his chart board, as did the other VB-8 pilots. One of Gee's squadron mates, Thomas Wood, was feeling confident. "I was very young and aggressive," he later said. "I boasted before the battle that I would sink the flagship *Akagi*."[10]

Clay Fisher learned that he had been "volunteered" to accompany the Sea Hag for the big mission. Fisher was totally devastated to be flying wing on Commander Ring. He normally flew the ninth position in VB-8's order. He wanted to be in his own squadron's formation with all the rapid-firing, twin .30-caliber rear guns from eighteen dive-bombers protecting their tails. Fisher feared that his lead section would probably be attacked first by Zeros.[11]

After three months on board Hornet, Stan Ring still had not endeared himself to his men. Before the war, Ring had been attached to a British carrier and had learned much of their snobbish ways. He had retained some English mannerisms, including his peculiar wearing of immaculately tailored dress uniforms and even a swagger stick as a show of authority. Bombing Eight pilot James Vose felt that the CHAG was "the epitome of the picture of the ideal naval officer."[12]

The deciding hours at Midway were at hand. Neither Admiral Fletcher nor Admiral Spruance could fathom how even the giant naval matchup odds had become. Admiral Yamamoto's Imperial Japanese Navy had put to sea with a staggering number of warships and landing vessels to facilitate the planned offensives against both the Aleutians and Midway. However, on the morning of June 4, only two of his formations were within a day's steaming distance of Midway—Rear Admiral Tanaka's transport group of transport ships and destroyers and Vice Admiral Nagumo's first carrier striking force. Yamamoto himself was in his main body of warships farther behind, and essentially out of the main picture.

Nagumo's Kido Butai was thus the only serious threat to the American carrier as the morning of June 4 unfolded. Nagumo had twenty warships—four fleet carriers, two cruisers, two battleships, and a dozen destroyers—against twenty-five U.S. warships. Fletcher and Spruance had three flattops, plus the air strength of a fourth "flight deck" in the form of the unsinkable Midway airstrip. They were thus not facing overwhelming odds, but merely a contest of which opponent would be first to shut down the other's flight decks.

At 0552, another PBY reported two carriers and battleships 175 miles away from the American carriers. Fletcher signaled Spruance at 0607 to attack the enemy carriers as soon as they were definitively located. Yorktown would follow after recovering Lieutenant Short's search planes. As Task Force 16 steamed away, word was prematurely passed on Enterprise for the pilots to man their planes. In Scouting Six's ready room, the pilots stood and shook hands. They filed out of the squadron meeting room and headed for the flight deck. The loudspeaker abruptly halted them. "Belay that. All pilots return to the ready room."[13]

On *Hornet*, there was also a false start order for all strikers to man their planes. Captain Mitscher then held a conference on the bridge with his air group leaders—Ring, Jack Waldron, Pat Mitchell, Walt Rodee, Ruff Johnson, air officer Commander Apollo Soucek, and Lieutenant Commander John Foster, the air operations officer. Waldron pleaded for fighters to help cover his Torpedo Eight TBDs, but Mitscher told VF-8 skipper Mitchell to "go out and stay with the bombers."[14]

In the meantime, the Japanese were already making their own strike. Shortly after 0600, Midway's radar picked up the first blip of approaching aircraft. As U.S. aircraft tangled with the incoming enemy, Midway launched strike groups toward the Japanese carriers. On board *Enterprise*, Admiral Spruance decided to launch his strike planes at 0700, but failed to pass the word along immediately to *Hornet*. Task Force 16 split into two groups to give the air groups ample room to form up before departing. Wildcat fighters were launched for combat air patrol duties by both carriers before the SBDs were taxied into takeoff positions.

The radiomen-gunners were still not included in the pilots' ready rooms for prestrike briefings as of June 1942. Jim Murray felt somewhat in the dark when the orders came to man their planes. As his skipper, Dick Best, climbed into the cockpit of their 6-B-1, he said only, "Well, Murray, this is it."[15]

Enterprise's deck was spotted with three dozen Dauntlesses of VS-6, VB-6, and the CEAG section. Dick Best's eighteen-plane contribution from Bombing Six was reduced to fifteen when three SBDs—Harvey Lanham's 6-B-10, Lloyd Smith's 6-B-4, and Arthur Rausch's 6-B-17—failed to start or maintain power and were struck below on the elevators. The fact that the *Enterprise* strike group had been spotted on deck for a full day without launching did not help the mechanical snafus of the morning.

AOM3c Harold Llewellyn "Lew" Jones was beyond disappointed. He had been busy for days working the bugs out of his squadron's new twin .30-caliber rear guns, some of which shook so much during firing that they would jam. Everything looked good when Ensign Rausch turned up their engine and pulled 6-B-17 to the takeoff line. Then the starter suddenly gave their plane a "down" signal. "Rausch took the power off and shut down," said Jones. "I just couldn't believe that my plane wasn't flyable."[16]

Scouting Six was spotted forward on the flight deck, and with a shorter takeoff distance the first six SBDs carried only a five-hundred-pound bomb. Earl Gallaher led off the procession in his 6-S-1 at 0706. Dickinson, turning up at the head of VS-6's second division, thought to himself: *This is the big day.*[17]

Frank Patriarca missed his chance to avenge Pearl Harbor this day. The starter found that his engine sounded questionable when he turned up to full power. He taxied to the side and his 6-S-13 was taken to the hangar deck for servicing.[18]

The last nine SBDs of VS-6, with a little more takeoff distance, had been armed with additional hundred-pound bombs under each wing. Pilot Mike Micheel was apprehensive of launching with seven hundred pounds of bombs, twice the weight of the 350-pound depth charge he had carried on scouting missions. Micheel had made a ritual of saying a prayer before each flight; today he just might need it more than usual. The flight officer dropped his flag and pointed it toward the bow. Micheel released his brakes and throttled full-speed down *Enterprise*'s flight deck.[19]

Scouting Six departed in three five-plane divisions under Gallaher, Dickinson, and Charlie Ware. Behind them was the CEAG section of Wade McClusky and his two VS-6 wingmen, ensigns Bill Pittman and Dick Jaccard. The latter two were assigned to fly the squadron's only two photo aircraft to document the mission. They were simply instructed how to turn the cameras on and off. "They were fixed cameras located in the belly of each aircraft to focus vertically as the aircraft flew in a level altitude," said Pittman.[20]

Dick Best's Bombing Six, armed with thousand-pound bombs, launched behind the CEAG section. Due to his heavy load, Best's Dauntless dropped below flight deck level upon launching. Jim Murray watched as sailors rushed to the bow to see whether Lieutenant Best could fight his bomber back above the waves. He did, and his division was followed by the five-plane second and third divisions of lieutenants Joe Penland and John Van Buren.[21]

Ensign Lew Hopkins was spotted far back in the pack of planes. He was worried about making his first launch with a live bomb, and the largest load he could carry at that. Rear gunner Ed Anderson gripped the sides of his cockpit tightly, ready to bail out if necessary. Their Dauntless sped forward and dropped off the flight deck with its heavy load, wobbling about dangerously low. *Let's go!* Anderson thought until their airspeed built up enough for them to climb above the waves. Stuart Mason was riding as gunner for Lieutenant Andy Anderson in the next-to-last VB-6 dive-bomber to launch. He felt great relief to see a long takeoff run for their full fuel tanks and thousand-pound bomb load.[22]

McClusky's thirty-three SBDs circled the task force, waiting for the torpedo planes and fighter planes to launch. His only instructions had been to make a group attack on the enemy force and to maintain radio silence until the enemy ships were sighted. No information had been given to McClusky as to how Stan Ring, the *Hornet* air group commander who was technically his senior, was to coordinate with him. In addition, no information was received by McClusky to indicate how the *Yorktown* group was to participate.[23]

Another twenty minutes passed and still nothing appeared to be happening on *Enterprise*'s deck below. The flight deck crews were busily hauling up Gene Lindsey's torpedo-laden Devastators, which would need the full deck length to launch. Dick Best could appreciate their need, as he had used the full deck to launch VB-6 with their thousand-pound bombs.[24]

The launching and formation went smoother on *Hornet*.

In Scouting Eight's ready room, Gus Widhelm stood up and announced, "Widhelm is ready; now prepare the Japs!" It would become his trademark slogan. "Everyone was gung ho to go," remembered Ben Tappan of VS-8. Bombing Eight pilot Roy Gee noted that everyone wished one another good luck as they left the ready room for the climb to the flight deck and their SBDs.[25]

The *Hornet* rear seat gunners waited for hours for their call to action, standing ready in the radio shack on the port side of the carrier near the after end of the island structure. Among them was ARM3c Earnest Ray Johnston, a twenty-four-year-old from Virginia who had been drafted one year prior. The Scouting Eight radioman had heard from

Morning Carrier Strike Group
Enterprise Strike Group: June 4, 1942

CEAG SECTION

PLANE	PILOT	REAR SEAT GUNNER
GC	Lt. Cdr. Clarence Wade McClusky Jr.	ARM1c Walter George Chocalousek
6-S-8	Ens. William Robinson Pittman	AMM2c Floyd Delbert Adkins
6-S-11	Ens. Richard Alonzo Jaccard	RM3c Porter William Pixley

SCOUTING SIX (VS-6), FIRST DIVISION

PLANE	PILOT	REAR SEAT GUNNER
6-S-1	Lt. Wilmer Earl Gallaher	ACRM Thomas Edward Merritt
6-S-2	Ens. Reid Wentworth Stone	RM1c William Hart Bergin
6-S-3	Ens. John Quincy Roberts*	AOM1c Thurman Randolph Swindell*
6-S-7	Lt. (jg) Norman Jack Kleiss	ARM3c John Warren Snowden
6-S-9	Ens. Eldor Ernst Rodenburg**	Sea2c Thomas James Bruce**
6-S-18	Ens. James Campbell Dexter	RM3c Donald Laurence Hoff

SCOUTING SIX (VS-6), SECOND DIVISION		
PLANE	PILOT	REAR SEAT GUNNER
6-S-10	Lt. Clarence Earle Dickinson Jr.*	ARM1c Joseph Ferdinand DeLuca*
6-S-15	Ens. John Reginald McCarthy*	ARM2c Earl Edward Howell*
6-S-12	Ens. Carl David Peiffer*	ARM3c Frederick Charles Jeck*
6-S-16	Lt. (jg) John Norman West	ARM2c Albert R. Stitzelberger
6-S-17	Ens. Vernon Larsen Micheel	RM3c John Dewey Dance
6-S-14	Ens. John Cady Lough*	RM3c Louis Dale Hansen*
SCOUTING SIX (VS-6), THIRD DIVISION		
PLANE	PILOT	REAR SEAT GUNNER
6-S-4	Lt. Charles Rollins Ware*	ARM1c William Henry Stambaugh*
6-S-5	Ens. Frank Woodrow O'Flaherty*	AMM1c Bruno Peter Gaido*
6-S-6	Ens. James Arnold Shelton*	RM3c David Bruce Craig*

(continued)

Morning Carrier Strike Group
Enterprise Strike Group: June 4, 1942 (cont.)

BOMBING SIX (VB-6), FIRST DIVISION

PLANE	PILOT	REAR SEAT GUNNER
6-B-1	Lt. Richard Halsey Best	ACRM James Francis Murray
6-B-2	Lt. (jg) Edwin John Kroeger	RM3c Gail Wayne Halterman
6-B-3	Ens. Frederick Thomas Weber	AOM3c Ernest Leonard Hilbert
6-B-5	Lt. (jg) Wilbur Edison Roberts	AMM1c William Burr Steinman
6-B-6	Ens. Delbert Wayne Halsey*	RM3c Jay William Jenkins*

BOMBING SIX (VB-6), SECOND DIVISION

PLANE	PILOT	REAR SEAT GUNNER
6-B-7	Lt. Joe Robert Penland*	ARM2c Harold French Heard*
6-B-8	Ens. Tony Frederic Schneider*	ARM2c Glenn Lester Holden*
6-B-9	Ens. Eugene Allen Greene*	RM3c Samuel Andrew Muntean*

| 6-B-11 | Ens. Thomas Wesley Ramsay* | ARM2c Sherman Lee Duncan* |
| 6-B-12 | Ens. Lewis Alexander Hopkins | RM3c Edward Rutledge Anderson |

BOMBING SIX (VB-6), THIRD DIVISION		
PLANE	**PILOT**	**REAR SEAT GUNNER**
6-B-13	Lt. (jg) John James Van Buren*	ARM1c Harry William Nelson Jr.*
6-B-14	Ens. Norman Francis Vandivier*	Sea1c Lee Edward John Keaney*
6-B-15	Ens. George Hale Goldsmith	ARM3c James William Patterson Jr.
6-B-16	Lt. (jg) Edward Lee Anderson	ARM2c Stuart James Mason Jr.
6-B-18	Ens. Bertram Stetson Varian Jr.*	ARM3c Charles Robert Young*
Fighting Six (VF-6): 10 F4Fs under Lt. James Seton Gray Jr.		
Torpedo Six (VT-6): 14 TBDs under Lt. Cdr. Eugene Elbert Lindsey		

*Shot down or ditched during June 4, 1942, morning strike.
**Forced to return to ship.

skipper Walt Rodee that a major sea battle was imminent and yet he felt no apprehension. "I was as ready as I'd ever be," said Johnston.

For Bombing Eight radioman Oral Lester Moore from Denver, there was an awful lot of waiting. He passed the time chatting with his two best friends, ARM2c Dick Woodson of Scouting Eight and ARM2c

Ronnie Fisher of Torpedo Eight. Moore was lean and the tallest of his squadron at six-foot-four inches, and was appropriately known to all as "Slim."[26]

Slim had worked a variety of odd jobs after graduating from East Denver High School in June 1939. One morning, his hometown buddy Ronnie Fisher came to visit him after Moore had completed a shift parking cars in an all-night garage.

"Slim, I'm going to join the Air Force," Fisher announced. "There's trouble in Europe and I think we ought to get a head start."

Slim had always wanted to become a naval aviator, although he had never seen the ocean. He convinced his buddy Ronnie to join the Navy with him instead and they proceeded to boot camp together. After aviation radio school, Moore was assigned to floatplanes on the heavy cruiser *Salt Lake City*, while Fisher went to a utility squadron on Ford Island in Pearl Harbor. As fate would have it, the hometown boys were reunited in 1942 as part of the new *Hornet* Air Group.

The call finally came to man their planes at about 0640. Fisher, Moore, and their close buddy Dick Woodson (who also hailed from Denver) exchanged offerings of good luck before racing up the steel ladder to the flight deck. Slim felt a sense of nervous excitement. After months of training and endless scout flights, he and his buddies now had a chance to experience real combat.

Stan Ring was senior aviator of the three carrier groups and was senior pilot launched from Task Force 16. At this time, carrier operation orders did not call for him to take overall tactical command of both *Hornet*'s and *Enterprise*'s strike planes. Even if such a doctrine existed, the hastily organized plans of June 4 would not have permitted him to oversee both air groups. Instead, Ring would command the forty-five-plane *Hornet* strike group.

Hornet launched thirty-four dive-bombers, half of the SBDs armed with five hundred-pound bombs and the other half with thousand-pound loads. Lieutenant Commander Walt Rodee took off first with fifteen dive-bombers of VS-8, followed by the Sea Hag with his VB-8 wingman. Lieutenant Commander Ruff Johnson followed with his seventeen SBDs of Bombing Eight.[27]

The CHAG section was spotted behind their F4F escorts on the deck.

Clay Fisher was surprised when *Hornet*'s chief photographer climbed up on his right wing just after he started his engine. The chief was frantically pointing at something behind Fisher's head. He finally understood that his 8-B-9 was equipped with an aerial camera mounted in the plane's belly and that he would have to flip a switch just below his headrest to activate the camera during an attack. "My plane was selected because I was supposed to be the last plane to dive," Fisher said.[28]

Roy Gee met his VB-8 rear gunner, ARM1c Donald Canfield, at their assigned Dauntless to go over the mission and inspect their plane. "As I sat there waiting for the signal to start engines, I suddenly got the same feeling of apprehension and butterflies in the stomach that I got before the start of competition in high school and collegiate athletics," remembered Gee. Behind his plane in the second division of Bombing Eight was Troy Guillory. He was disturbed that one of his squadron's senior pilots had refused to fly his own mechanically challenged dive-bomber, leaving Guillory with a dud SBD for this important mission.[29]

In the air, Stan Ring directed the Dauntless pilots to assume a group parade formation with his command section at the head of a giant vee of vees. Scouting Eight and Bombing Eight deployed in huge vee formations to either side of the CHAG section, VS-8 on the right and VB-8 on the left. Pat Mitchell's Wildcat fighter section took station in three groups as the dive-bombers slowly climbed toward nineteen thousand feet.[30]

With the deck clear of SBDs, *Hornet*'s air department brought up the last nine TBDs of Torpedo Eight. They began launching and *Hornet*'s deck was clear by 0742. The early PBY's contact report placed the Japanese carriers about 155 miles distant. Ring led his procession into good flying weather with bright sunshine and only scattered clouds at about fifteen hundred feet.[31]

Thirty-nine minutes after the launch had started, Wade McClusky's *Enterprise* dive-bombers were still orbiting their task force, waiting on the fighters and torpedo planes to take off. Tony Schneider of Bombing Six was becoming frustrated as his division slowly climbed and circled endlessly above the Big E. "We stayed there and stayed there until it seemed like an eternity," he said. At high altitude and at high blower, his SBD was burning up precious fuel in a hurry.

Admiral Spruance knew from his radio intelligence officer Gil Slonim

Morning Carrier Strike Group
Hornet Strike Groups: June 4, 1942

CHAG SECTION (2 SBDS)

PILOT	REAR SEAT GUNNER
Cdr. Stanhope Cotton Ring	ARM2c Arthur M. Parker
Ens. Clayton Evan Fisher	ARM3c George E. Ferguson

SCOUTING EIGHT (VS-8) (15 SBDS)

PILOT	REAR SEAT GUNNER
Lt. Cdr. Walter Fred Rodee	ACRM John Lenzy Clanton
Lt. (jg) Ivan Lee Swope	ARM2c Harmon L. Brendle
Ens. Paul Edmond Tepas	ARM3c Moley J. Boutwell
Lt. Ray Davis	ARM1c Ralph Phillips
Lt. Laurens Adin Whitney	ARM2c Angus D. Gilles
Lt. (jg) Jimmy McMillan Forbes	ARM3c Ronald H. Arenth
Lt. Ben Moore Jr.	ARM2c Richard Cusack McEwen
Ens. Stanley Robert Holm	ARM2c James H. Black Jr.
Lt. (jg) Albert Harold Wood	ARM3c John Louis Tereskerz

SECOND DIVISION, VS-8	
PILOT	**REAR SEAT GUNNER**
Lt. William John Widhelm	ARM1c George D. Stokely
Lt. (jg) Donald Kirkpatrick, Jr.	ARM2c Richard Thomas Woodson
Ens. Don "T" Griswold	ARM1c Kenneth Cecil Bunch
Lt. Edgar Erwin Stebbins	ARM2c Ervin R. Hillhouse
Ens. Benjamin Tappan Jr.	ARM3c Earnest Ray Johnston
Ens. Philip James Rusk	ARM2c John H. Honeycutt
BOMBING EIGHT (VB-8), 17 SBDS	
PILOT	**REAR SEAT GUNNER**
Lt. Cdr. Robert Ruffin Johnson	ACRM Joseph G. McCoy
Ens. Philip Farnsworth Grant	ARM2c Robert H. Rider
Ens. William Douglas Carter	ARM2c Oral Lester Moore
Lt. James Everett Vose Jr.	ARM2c Joseph Yewonishon
Ens. Roy Philip Gee	ARM1c Donald L. Canfield
Ens. Joe Wiley King	ARM3c Thomas M. Walsh
Lt. (jg) Fred Leeson Bates	ARM1c Clyde S. Montensen
Ens. Arthur Caldwell Cason Jr.	ARM3c Alfred D. Wells

(continued)

Morning Carrier Strike Group *Hornet* Strike Groups: June 4, 1942 (cont.)	
SECOND DIVISION, VB-8	
PILOT	**REAR SEAT GUNNER**
Lt. Alfred Bland Tucker III	ARM1c Champ T. Stuart
Ens. Gus George Bebas	RM3c Alfred W. Ringressy Jr.
Ens. Don Dee Adams	ARM2c John B. Broughton Jr.
Ens. James Austin Riner Jr.	ARM2c Floyd Dell Kilmer
Lt. John Joseph Lynch	ARM1c Wilbur L. Woods
Ens. Troy Tilman Guillory*	ARM2c Billy Rex Cottrell*
Ens. Kenneth Broughton White	ARM3c Leroy Quillen
Ens. Thomas Junior Wood*	ARM3c George F. Martz*
Ens. Forrester Clinton Auman*	ARM3c Samuel P. McLean*
Fighting Eight (VF-8): 10 F4Fs under Lt. Cdr. Samuel Gavid Mitchell	
Torpedo Eight (VT-8): 15 TBDs under Lt. Cdr. John Charles Waldron	

*Ditched during June 4, 1942, morning strike.
Note: *Hornet* aircraft assignments unknown for Battle of Midway. Scouting Eight composition for this flight based upon the research of Mark E. Horan.

that a Japanese scout plane pilot had radioed a contact report of the American force. He finally sent orders to McClusky via signal light at 0745: "Proceed on mission assigned."[32]

Hornet's strike force was no longer in sight when McClusky departed. In what would prove to be the most important mission of the war ever launched from American carrier decks, each carrier's strike force was departing independently—and each air group was not even cohesive.

Torpedo Six was the last of the *Enterprise* group to launch around 0800. Lieutenant Commander Gene Lindsey, still battered from his water landing several days prior, had to be helped into the cockpit of his Devastator. Radioman Ron Graetz stood on the starboard aft catwalk with his buddy Dick Butler to watch their squadron depart. Graetz, freshly returned from gunnery schooling, had been reassigned from Lieutenant (j.g.) Severin Rombach's crew to that of a newer pilot. As his familiar 6-T-9 rolled up the deck, Graetz and Butler saw their friend Wilburn Glenn facing aft, with his guns already in position. Glenn looked like a victorious boxer. He kept alternately giving the two-thumbs-up sign and the hands-clasped-over-his-head signal all the way up the deck. It was the last Graetz would ever see of Glenn or Rombach.[33]

It had taken nearly an hour to completely launch the *Enterprise* Air Group, but by 0800 the strike groups from *Hornet* and *Enterprise* were both on their way. The collective force numbered 116 aircraft: sixty-seven dive-bombers, twenty-nine torpedo planes, and twenty fighters.[34]

Bombing Six had three planes that had failed to launch, but Earl Gallaher's VS-6 had its own difficulties. Pat Patriarca, leader of the second section of Scouting Six, had been unable to take off due to mechanical problems. His wingman, Johnny Lough, formed up on the tail end of Dick Dickinson's second division, leaving Charlie Ware's third division of VS-6 with only three planes.

Ensign Rodey Rodenburg found his thirteenth carrier mission to be unlucky. The VS-6 rookie climbed for altitude with his squadron as Wade McClusky led them out from *Enterprise*, but his SBD was uncooperative. Rodenburg could not shift his engine into high blower for high-altitude operation. He gave it full throttle, full rich-fuel mixture, and full low-prop pitch, but his 6-S-9 steadily fell behind.[35]

Rodenburg was forced to stay at lower altitude as the *Enterprise* bombers climbed to twenty thousand feet, where the air became much colder. Section leader Dusty Kleiss was comforted by his girlfriend's sweater that he wore under his flight suit—as much for warmth at altitude as a good-luck charm.[36]

Nearly a hundred miles out, Ensign Rodenburg could not climb his SBD above eight thousand feet. "I had two choices," he said. "One was to fly at much lower altitude to keep up and run out of gas, or return to the *Enterprise*. I know I'm alive today because I made the latter decision." Rodenburg slipped into the cloud cover to dodge two Japanese planes during his lonely return leg while gunner Thomas Bruce used the *Enterprise* ZB homing beacon to locate the carrier. Once back on board, Rodenburg's 6-S-9 was struck down to the hangar deck, where the mechanics began work on its faulty high blower.[37]

Other SBDs were also struggling along. Tony Schneider eased up alongside division leader Joe Penland shortly into the flight and hand-signaled that he was fighting a balky engine and excessive fuel consumption. Penland acknowledged the report and Schneider eased back into position. "I knew before I headed for the enemy that I wasn't going to get back," said Schneider. Bombing Six's Bill Roberts decided to break a cardinal rule. Normal protocol was for the SBD pilots to always climb for altitude with their fuel mixture control in the "auto-rich" position. Roberts knew this helped to avoid overheating the engine and possible damage from resultant detonation. Yet for this mission he climbed in the "auto-lean" position because of the lower fuel consumption. "I felt that the engine would hold together during this one flight, and if it was unusable thereafter, I didn't care," Roberts said. "We had plenty of spare engines aboard ship."[38]

Lieutenant Best had his pilots switch to oxygen as Bombing Six climbed past twelve thousand feet. He quickly found that he had a bad oxygen canister in his cockpit. He only had two of them, and each was good for two hours. Best had stripped his Dauntless of unnecessary weight for this flight, removing his first-aid kit and extra oxygen containers. "I had to breathe it through and choke it through the caustic soda, the element that took out the moisture and heated up the air," he said. He was finally able to breathe clearly through his bad container, but the fumes he had inhaled would later have dire consequences on his body.[39]

The other *Hornet* and *Enterprise* aviators enjoyed a clear view of an open Pacific Ocean as they flew at eighteen-thousand- to twenty-thousand-foot altitudes toward the Japanese fleet.

Commander Stan Ring's air group was the first to take departure from TF-16. His thirty-four SBDs and ten F4Fs joined in formation above *Hornet*, then started a slow climb toward nineteen thousand feet. The aircrews also switched to oxygen masks upon reaching high altitude, and Clay Fisher soon discovered he was collecting ice inside his mask from cold air leaking in that mixed with his warmer breath. He had difficulty breathing and removed his mask periodically to clear the accumulating ice.[40]

Jack Waldron, one-eighth Sioux Indian and nicknamed "Redskin" at the Naval Academy, claimed his heritage gave him a kind of sixth sense. His Torpedo Eight flew at lower altitude and slower speed, remaining in the tail of the procession for the first half hour. Ring led his *Hornet* pilots out on a heading of 265 degrees true from the carrier for the first sixty miles. Ensigns Ben Tappan and Troy Guillory were concerned with their fuel situation due to how long their SBDs had circled the task force before departing. To further complicate the situation, a disagreement soon ensued between VT-8 skipper Waldron and Ring over their air group's course.[41]

At 0816, Guillory heard Waldron open up on the radio to tell the Sea Hag that they were flying in the wrong direction. There was no reply, but Tappan soon heard Waldron announce, "I know where the damn fleet is."[42]

Ring snapped, "You fly on us. I'm leading this formation. You fly on us."

A minute or two later, Tappan heard Waldron's voice again: "The hell with you." At 0825, Torpedo Eight began turning to the southwest as Waldron chose his own solo course toward where he sincerely believed Nagumo's carriers would be found. The sudden turn of the Devastators was noted by several of the SBD rear gunners, including Dick Woodson in Ensign Don Kirkpatrick's VS-8 plane.[43]

Woodson watched VT-8 veer to the left of Commander Ring's heading. "Where is Torpedo Eight going?" he asked his pilot.[44]

"I have no idea," Kirkpatrick replied, keeping his SBD tight in formation. Commander Ring continued doggedly on, with Pat Mitchell's Wildcats in company. "We took the given course. I don't know what he took," Walt Rodee said of Waldron. Torpedo Eight was on its own.[45]

The *Hornet* SBD pilots saw nothing but empty ocean during the first hour of their westward flight. By 0900, Ensign John McInerny was concerned enough about his fuel to twice fly up alongside Mitchell and point to his gauge. Lieutenant Commander Mitchell angrily gestured for him to fall back into position, but McInerny instead finally swung around and headed east with his F4F wingman. Mitchell reluctantly turned right, gathered his other eight Wildcats, and headed east behind his two junior pilots.[46]

The SBD pilots were dismayed to see their fighter escorts suddenly turn and depart just 160 miles out from *Hornet*. Ring maintained his westerly heading of 265 degrees, but no ships appeared at the point where the Japanese fleet was expected to be. Nagumo's carriers, having learned of the location of the American carriers, had turned toward Midway and had then been forced to dodge American land-based attacks during the morning. Pilot Roy Gee felt that they were getting close to the point of no return without seeing any sign of the Japanese fleet.[47]

Around 0920, at least one of the VB-8 plane crews heard snippets of radio chatter from Torpedo Eight, which had apparently located the Japanese carriers. Fuel was becoming a serious issue at this point for *Hornet*'s SBDs. Lieutenant Moe Vose, leading one of VB-8's sections, later said, "I knew that we would never make it back to the ship. We flew the whole route in tight parade formation! I can well recall whacking off the throttle, then putting it back on, and at times very nearly spinning out in order to keep position." Ben Tappan tried to maintain altitude on Commander Ring with very low power, with it leaned out so bad that his engine was coughing. *If this guy keeps on going this direction, we're never going to get back to the ship*, Tappan thought of Ring.[48]

Ensign Thomas Wood, flying in VB-8's last section, advised section leader Ken White of his fuel status. White in turn advised division leader Abbie Tucker by hand signal and received a nod in reply. White turned back to Wood, shrugged his shoulders, and kept going. Wood grinned back, told his radioman George Martz, "Horseshit, here we go again, Marty," and stayed with the pack. Wood assumed his senior officers felt that they were going to find the Japanese fleet one way or another. The availability of fuel to make it back home was apparently an afterthought.[49]

Not everyone was in agreement with Sea Hag's left turn. John Lynch of VB-8 felt from his own navigation that a right turn was more logical at this point. Stan Ring took his thirty-four dive-bombers out some 225 miles before he led them into a wide left turn in order to head south. His wingman, Clay Fisher, was in the process of trying to attract the attention of Lieutenant Commander Rodee. Fisher, noting the CHAG's sudden turn, attempted to reverse course to rejoin him but saw only empty sky. Alone and vulnerable, Fisher followed in the wake of Scouting Eight, lagging some distance behind them.[50]

The cohesive structure of *Hornet*'s dive-bombers began to crumble. Ring completed his 180-degree turn and set course east for Task Force 16, using his Zed Baker to home in on the fleet from high altitude. Walt Rodee's fifteen VS-8 bombers also turned east after only a few minutes on a southerly heading. Ruff Johnson, however, led VB-8 farther south before finally turning back with his squadron on its own. By turning for home and flying east, Ring missed the chance to happen upon the Kido Butai to the south. Johnson's VB-8 actually flew too far south of Nagumo's carriers before he decided to swing east for TF 16. The *Hornet* SBDs thus unwittingly missed the Japanese carriers on both sides before turning back.[51]

The true events of the *Hornet*'s air group during its June 4 attempt to hit Nagumo's carriers would never be recorded by Stan Ring or any of his four squadron commanders. Instead, *Hornet*'s skipper, Captain Marc Mitscher, would file an action report on behalf of all of his aviators. In it, he stated that the *Hornet* Air Group had flown a course of 239 degrees and therefore missed Admiral Nagumo's carrier fleet. If *Hornet*'s SBDs had actually flown a course of 239 degrees, they would likely have found the carriers.[52]

Hornet's aviators would admit decades later that Stan Ring had taken them on a course of 265 degrees—regardless of what their action report claimed. *Hornet*'s radar, in fact, had tracked her outbound strike group on a course of 265. The truth may never be known. Was the Sea Hag such a poor navigator that he missed Nagumo by twenty-five degrees? Or did Mitscher send Ring out specifically to try to locate the two

Japanese carriers that had not yet been reported? Squadron reports from each *Hornet* unit would have exposed court-martial-worthy charges against pilots and even squadron commanders for abandoning the Sea Hag at Midway.[53]

In the end, Captain Mitscher allowed only one report for June 4 to be submitted. Ring, Rodee, Johnson, and all of *Hornet*'s SBDs missed finding the Japanese fleet. The only ones who would find the enemy carriers were Waldron's VT-8 Devastators, who broke away early in the mission on their own course. They left all of Ring's SBDs and F4Fs on a frustrating mission that would later be called the "flight to nowhere."[54]

This is a hell of a way to fight a war, wandering around all over the ocean and not even finding them! thought VB-8's Slim Moore in Doug Carter's rear seat. "What a fine morning for such a mess," said Lieutenant (j.g.) Ralph Hovind of Scouting Eight. His skipper, Walt Rodee, agreed. "We were lucky the fiasco turned out so well for us and so poorly for the Japs."[55]

*Y*orktown's strike group was the last of the three American carriers to launch on June 4. She had recovered Wally Short's morning searchers by 0645, falling out of sight of *Hornet* and *Enterprise* in the process. "We had landed before the strike planes took off," said John Iacovazzi, gunner for Ensign John "Blackie" Ammen. "They pushed our planes down below to rearm them."

Squadron leaders Max Leslie, Lem Massey, and Jimmy Thach met with CAG Oscar "Pete" Pederson and air officer Murr Arnold about the mission. Arnold worried about Pederson leading the strike without strong fighter cover, so he was retained aboard to serve as a fighter director. The other three senior *Yorktown* Air Group leaders would proceed with their squadrons.[56]

Bombing Three's aviators were eager to experience their first big mission. Joe Godfrey, rear gunner for Ensign Oley Hanson, felt that he and some of his buddies were as excited as little boys going on their first campout and fishing trip. Pilot Charlie Lane felt a normal mix of anticipation, excitement, and some apprehension.[57]

Yorktown's pilots began manning their planes at 0830. Lieutenant Commander Lem Massey's twelve TBDs of Torpedo Three would be last

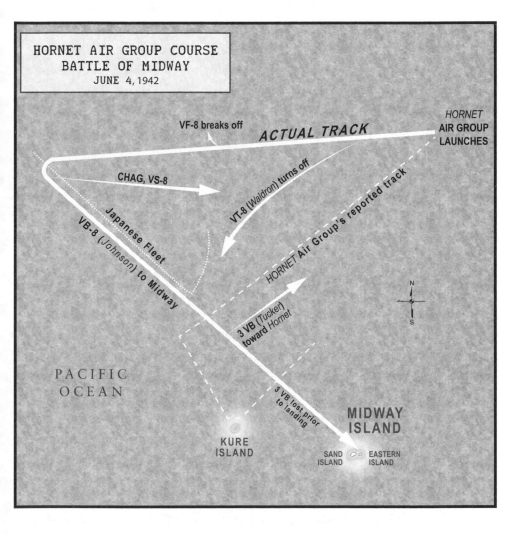

HORNET AIR GROUP COURSE
BATTLE OF MIDWAY
JUNE 4, 1942

to launch. Fighting Three skipper Jimmy Thach was allowed an insufficient number of Wildcats to cover the *Yorktown* strike group: Only a two-plane section and a four-plane division to divide between torpedo planes and bombers. Max Leslie took off first with seventeen SBDs of Bombing Three, and circled the task force for twelve minutes to allow VT-3 to get a good head start on them. Lefty Holmberg struggled to control his Dauntless and the thousand-pound bomb load he was carrying for the first time. Skipper Leslie made a slow turn to the left ahead of him, allowing Holmberg to rapidly overtake him. Holmberg caught his slipstream and nearly spun into the water.[58]

The *Yorktown* strikers departed Task Force 17 at 0905, eighty minutes behind Wade McClusky and his *Enterprise* SBDs. The cruiser *Astoria* blinkered a farewell message to the *Yorktown* aviators: "Good hunting and a safe return."[59]

Yorktown's flight deck was respotted with a dozen Wildcats of VF-3 and all seventeen serviceable SBDs of Scouting/Bombing Five. John Bridgers manned his plane on the rear of the flight deck, eager to be flying wing on Tex Conatser, who had been a strong influence on his flight career. When Bridgers and his companions reached the takeoff spot, however, their planes were simply taxied forward and they were ordered to return to the ready room. Admiral Fletcher decided to hold Lieutenant Short's squadron on board ship for a follow-up strike or in case the first groups came up empty-handed. Short's pilots figured they would get their chance eventually. Max Leslie, on the other hand, headed into battle assuming that Short's squadron was trailing behind him.[60]

Commander Walter "Butch" Schindler, Admiral Fletcher's staff gunnery officer, was among those missing out. He had flown five SBD missions as a rear gunner at Coral Sea, yet Admiral Fletcher expected surface action and ordered him to remain in the flag plot. Schindler had already made arrangements about an hour before to fly with VS-5's Lieutenant Sam Adams. He was now resigned to glumly await further developments with Short's crews.[61]

Bombing Three climbed for altitude and caught up to Massey's slower Devastators in short time. About a half hour into his flight, Lieutenant Commander Leslie signaled his pilots to arm their thousand-pound bombs as they approached fifteen thousand feet altitude. They preserved radio silence by passing the word via hand signals. Bombing Three's SBD-3s had electric arming switches to simplify the method of making their bombs "hot." When Leslie flipped his arming switch, his Dauntless unexpectedly lurched upward. Far below his Wildcat, Jimmy Thach glimpsed a strange splash to starboard as Leslie's bomb geysered into the ocean.[62]

Lefty Holmberg could see that the skipper was irate, making wild gestures with his hands and cursing his luck. Leslie realized that some-one had mixed up the wiring between the arming and release circuits so that arming the bombs actually released them. Leslie banged on the side of his SBD, his standard method of attracting the attention of Bill Galla-gher in his rear seat. He wondered aloud whether they would have time to land back aboard and quickly load another bomb. Gallagher, an old hand who had joined the Navy in the 1930s, had a healthy distrust of brass. He remarked to Leslie that they would probably be kept on the ship. Leslie replied, "We don't want that," so on they flew.[63]

The skipper's ire was further raised when another bomb exploded far below the circling VB-3 planes. A squadron mate signaled to Charlie Lane that his bomb was gone. Lane was so mad he didn't even acknowl-edge. "I was stunned, angry, bitterly disappointed, felt cheated and was frustrated at suddenly becoming powerless just as the moment of oppor-tunity to hit the Japs a real blow approached," Lane said. Then Bud Merrill felt a sudden jump after arming his bomb, though he did not re-alize what had happened. The rear gunner in a nearby SBD signaled via Morse code to Merrill's radioman, Dallas Bergeron, that their bomb had dropped. "Bergeron said something to me about our bomb, but I couldn't quite get the full impact of what he was saying," said Merrill. The shock-ing truth soon hit home, however.[64]

Leslie angrily broke radio silence to warn his other pilots. Bombing Three now faced an attack on the Japanese fleet with one-quarter of its power wasted. "How pitiful it might have been had the whole squadron lost their bombs!" said Syd Bottomley.[65]

Yorktown's group was the only one of the three carrier air groups to properly form on June 4. Lem Massey's TBDs flew at fifteen hundred feet, just below a scattered cloud formation, with two F4Fs cruising above them at twenty-five hundred feet. The other four Wildcats

Morning Carrier Strike Group
Yorktown's Bombing Three (VB-3): June 4, 1942

FIRST DIVISION		
PLANE	**PILOT**	**REAR SEAT GUNNER**
3-B-1	Lt. Cdr. Maxwell Franklin Leslie[1, 2]	ARM1c William Earl Gallagher[1, 2]
3-B-2	Lt. (jg) Paul Algodte Holmberg[1]	AMM2c George Albert LaPlant[1]
3-B-3	Ens. Paul Wahl Schlegel[3]	ARM3c Jack Alvin Shropshire[3]
3-B-4	Ens. Robert Keith Campbell[3]	AMM1c Horace Henry Craig[3]
3-B-5	Ens. Alden Wilbur Hanson[3]	ARM3c Joseph Vernon Godfrey[3]
3-B-6	Ens. Robert Haines Benson[3]	ARM3c Frederick Paul Bergeron[3]
SECOND DIVISION		
PLANE	**PILOT**	**REAR SEAT GUNNER**
3-B-7	Lt. (jg) Gordon Alvin Sherwood[3]	ARM2c Harman Donald Bennett[3]
3-B-8	Ens. Roy Maurice Isaman[2, 3]	ARM3c Sidney Kay Weaver[2, 3]
3-B-9	Ens. Phillip Walker Cobb[3]	ARM2c Clarence Eugene Zimmershead[3]

3-B-10	Lt. Harold Sydney Bottomley Jr.[3]	AMM2c David Frederick Johnson Jr.[3]
3-B-11	Ens. Charles Smith Lane[2,3]	ARM2c Jack Charles Henning[2,3]
3-B-12	Ens. John Clarence Butler[3]	ARM3c David Donald Berg[3]

THIRD DIVISION

PLANE	PILOT	REAR SEAT GUNNER
3-B-13	Lt. DeWitt Wood Shumway[3]	ARM1c Ray Edgar Coons[3]
3-B-14	Ens. Robert Martin Elder[3]	RM3c Leslie Alan Till[3]
3-B-15	Ens. Bunyan Randolph Cooner[3]	AOM2c Clifton R. Bassett[3]
3-B-16	Lt. (jg) Osborne Beeman Wiseman[3]	ARM3c Grant Ulysses Dawn[3]
3-B-17	Ens. Milford Austin Merrill[2,3]	ARM3c Dallas Joseph Bergeron[2,3]

Torpedo Three (VT-3): 12 TBDs under Lt. Cdr. Lance Edward Massey

Fighting Three (VF-3): 6 F4Fs under Lt. Cdr. John Smith Thach

[1]Ditched following June 4, 1942, morning strike.
[2]Lost bomb en route to fleet.
[3]Landed on *Enterprise* following morning strike.

deployed at five thousand feet, while Bombing Three leveled off at six-teen thousand feet. *Yorktown*'s aviators made the only successful rendez-vous and would ultimately fly the most direct route to the Japanese carriers.[66]

Wade McClusky's *Enterprise* Air Group was already well divided. His SBDs had been ordered to proceed southwest without their fighter escorts or with Gene Lindsey's Torpedo Six. Lindsey kept his TBDs low, cruising at two thousand feet on a heading of 240 degrees. They made their approach to the enemy force without fighter cover, as Lieutenant Jim Gray's VF-6 Wildcats had taken off ahead of the Devastators. Gray's F4Fs were unable to find McClusky's dive-bombers, but eventually spot-ted a torpedo squadron ahead—although it would prove to be *Hornet*'s VT-8.

McClusky's pilots had wasted considerable fuel while circling their task force, and more than 130 miles from their ship, they had spotted nothing. McClusky was down to thirty-two SBDs with the departure of Rodey Rodenburg's troubled plane, and now the engine of Tony Schnei-der's aircraft was beginning to run rough. Schneider persisted in hold-ing his formation with Bombing Six even as his Dauntless rapidly burned through its fuel. He was flying toward the back of the *Enter-prise* formation, attempting to track navigational information on his plotting board. Tony wanted to make sure he had a fighting chance of getting back home if he became separated.

Mike Micheel tried his best to conserve fuel during the long flight with-out pumping his throttle. He marveled at how well his section leader, Norm West, kept proper formation by weaving his SBD back and forth.

Dick Jaccard and Bill Pittman hung tight to the CEAG, although they were beginning to wonder if they would have enough fuel to make it home. McClusky was leading them all over the vast Pacific in search of a Japanese fleet based solely on Army Air Force intelligence. *The Air Force must have given us bum information*, Pittman thought. *They will certainly hear from us on our return to Pearl!* He found it impossible to actually navigate or record flight changes in his log while still flying tight on the CEAG. "Nervousness was creeping up on us," said Pittman. "I could see Dick Jaccard in number three position also wondering when, or if, the 'old man' was going to turn back."[67]

McClusky frequently scanned the horizon with his binoculars. Visibility was good, but there was no sight of Japanese carriers at the estimated point of contact, around 0920. *The sea is empty*, McClusky thought. *Not a Jap vessel in sight.* A hurried review of his navigation convinced him that he had not erred. What was wrong?[68]

Don Hoff, riding rear seat for Jim Dexter, was dismayed at the lack of ships. For as far

U.S. Navy

Lieutenant Commander Wade McClusky.

as he could see there was nothing, absolutely nothing, only an immense stretch of ocean. McClusky checked his charts and allowed a maximum rate of advance for the enemy surface ships of twenty-five knots. He felt that the Japanese force could not have already passed by, if they were truly approaching Midway. Surely they had to be to starboard, to the west or maybe the north. He had no knowledge that Gene Lindsey's TBDs had taken their own course, and had no inkling of where the *Hornet* and *Yorktown* air groups were.[69]

McClusky decided to continue on a 240-degree heading for another thirty-five miles. He would then turn northwest in the precise reverse of the original Japanese course. McClusky knew that the SBDs' climb to altitude with heavy bomb loads had eaten considerable fuel. The CEAG made another quick calculation and decided that his men would stay on course 315 degrees until 1000. At that point, he would have to lead them back northeastward toward *Enterprise*, and terminate the hunt.[70]

Ed Anderson was shivering. The Bombing Six gunner had donned cold-weather gear for the long flight at high altitude, but he had neglected to put on his winter flying boots. His feet were numb. Shortly into the high-altitude flight, Anderson had another problem: Nature was calling. "It was getting colder and I was getting desperate," he said. He was bundled up in a parachute, life jacket, a zippered leather flying coat, a zippered flying suit, and trousers. *I'm supposed to be watching out for Jap fighters, but a guy can only stand so much*, he thought. *To hell with the Japs!*[71]

Anderson quickly unzipped his flight gear, took care of business, and buckled back into his rear compartment with much relief. An hour and a half into the flight, he and pilot Lew Hopkins ran out of their oxygen supply. The oxygen deprivation began to play on them. "Every move became an effort and it was hard to stay awake," Anderson wrote in his diary. He called up to check on Ensign Hopkins to make sure he was still alert. He said that he was feeling okay, but Anderson was left with a new fear: What if his young pilot dozed off while they were flying formation?

The long flight and dwindling fuel played hell on the younger pilots' nerves. Other than himself, skipper Earl Gallaher of Scouting Six could count only Dick Dickinson, Reid Stone, Norm West, Charlie Ware, Mac McCarthy, and Dusty Kleiss as his air combat veterans. Gallaher had eleven pilots in his squadron who had never experienced combat. Nine were airborne with him for this strike. How would they do?

Dick Dickinson, leading VS-6's second division, knew that fuel would become an issue at their high flight speeds. The SBDs were using about ninety-five percent power from the time they reached any altitude whatsoever. *We are using a lot of our gasoline*, Dickinson felt. Gunner Don Hoff knew that their bomb load added to the fuel problem. *It is gonna be close*, he thought.[72]

Jack Waldron's Sioux instincts and his inherent conviction that the Sea Hag was heading on the wrong bearing both worked in his favor on June 4 in finding Admiral Nagumo's carrier force. While Waldron's course did not take him directly to the Kido Butai, his scouting line efforts worked for Torpedo Eight, with their VF-6 *Enterprise* Wildcats in tow. Shortly after 0915, VT-8 had the smoke of enemy ships within view, and Lieutenant Commander Waldron could soon make out three Japanese carriers.[73]

Waldron took his fifteen Devastators down to the wave tops shortly before 0930 and prepared to attack the nearest carrier, which proved to be *Soryu*. Almost immediately they were set upon by more than two dozen Zero fighters from the Japanese CAP. Bombing Eight radioman

LeRoy "Lee" Quillen could hear the chatter of Torpedo Eight as Waldron led his TBDs in. "Watch those fighters!" As the Zeros began tearing into the VT-8 planes, Quillon heard Waldron call to his rear seat man, "How am I doing, Dobbs?"[74]

One by one, the outclassed TBDs were hammered by the superior Zeros. Quillen and others heard the tragedy played out on the radio. "My two wingmen are going in the water," Waldron finally announced. Moments later, Waldron was gone, too. Fighters and fierce AA fire destroyed the first fourteen torpedo planes, leaving only Tex Gay still inbound against *Soryu*. He managed to drop his torpedo from eight hundred yards out before the Zeros shot his Devastator into the ocean as well. His radioman was killed, but Gay survived the crash and remained afloat in the ocean, the sole survivor of his brave squadron. Torpedo Eight had lost fifteen of fifteen TBDs, as well as twenty-nine of thirty airmen. *Soryu* remained untouched. Only after the battle, Gay would learn that another six planes of Torpedo Eight had launched an attack against the Japanese carriers. Flying from Midway Atoll in newer TBF Avenger torpedo bombers, the shore-based contingent of VT-8 suffered a similar slaughter. Only one Avenger and two of eighteen aviators made it back to Midway alive.

Jim Gray's VF-6 fighters, high above the Japanese fleet, missed the action entirely. About the time that the last VT-8 planes were hitting the water, another American torpedo squadron was moving in. Lieutenant Commander Gene Lindsey spotted smoke thirty miles to the northwest just after 0930 and swung his *Enterprise* VT-6 planes to the right to investigate. Torpedo Eight's attack had forced Admiral Nagumo's carriers to reverse course out of the wind. This delayed their ability to respot the flight decks with strike planes that were being serviced on the hangar decks. This hiatus was further extended as Lindsey's Torpedo Six approached.

Japanese lookouts spotted the next wave of American attackers coming in at 0938, low on the water and making about a hundred knots. The carriers were now forced to conduct fighter operations to combat the U.S. Devastators instead of working to launch more strike groups. Lindsey's pilots split into two divisions, and chased Japanese warships making thirty knots. It made for a long, slow approach to launch their torpedoes.

With no fighter cover, Torpedo Six was subjected to the same cruel fate that Torpedo Eight had just endured. Lindsey and his second division leader, Arthur Ely, were soon shot down and killed. The Zeros began picking off the other Devastators one by one.[75]

Jim Murray of Bombing Six heard a Torpedo Six pilot calling desperately for Gray's VF-6 to come down and help them. Three of Lindsey's seven planes of the first division were lost before they could launch against the twisting *Kaga*. Lieutenant (j.g.) Robert Laub, leading the last section of this division, was too busy lining up on the carrier to notice his squadron mates going down in flames. His gunner, ARM1c William C. Humphrey, managed to shoot down one of the attacking Zeros. Laub dropped his torpedo inside a thousand yards and banked away with only light damage to his Devastator. Laub's wingman, Irvin McPherson, recovered from his attack and joined up with Ensign Ed Heck, Lindsey's surviving wingman. Heck managed to chase off one fighter that moved in on McPherson as the two zipped by the Japanese escort ships.[76]

Only two Devastators of Torpedo Six's second division survived to launch their torpedoes toward *Kaga*'s starboard side. They were T-11, piloted by machinist Stephen Smith, and T-8, piloted by Smith's *Enterprise* roommate, machinist Albert Walter Winchell. Smith watched Lieutenant Pablo Riley exchange gunfire until Riley's TBD lost the fight. Smith's plane was hit by bullets on four or five passes by the Zeros as he bored in. He could hear his rear gunner, Sea1c Wilfred N. McCoy, start shooting. Then their plane was hit again. Slugs ripped Smith's right-wing gas tank, causing gasoline to spew. Two bullets thumped into the back of his armored seat. "I wanted to shrink up a little," he said. "One burst hit over my shoulder and into the instrument panel, breaking my compass." *Kaga* was making a left turn as Smith finally dropped his torpedo and made a skidding turn to his right ahead of the flattop.[77]

Walt Winchell was the fifth VT-6 pilot to make a torpedo drop on the carrier, but his T-8's fuel tanks were riddled from passes made by as many as five Zeros. His rear gunner, twenty-three-year-old ARM3c Douglas Marvin Cossitt, chased off two of the fighters with his shooting before Winchell turned his crippled TBD back toward the American fleet. En route home, Winchell's fuel ran out and he put his battered T-8 in the drink. Their Devastator sank from sight in forty seconds, but both aviators managed to scramble aboard their life raft with a small amount of rations, their first-aid kit, and both parachutes.[78]

Cossitt had received minor shrapnel wounds in the legs. He and Winchell made a sea anchor of their parachutes and laid to, trying to decide what their next move should be. But their only option was to stay alive. The two men endured seventeen days of drifting in the ocean, surviving on their meager rations, captured rainwater, and an albatross they managed to kill. Doug Cossitt kept his sanity by scribbling in a little diary with a fountain pen that had survived his brief swim in the ocean. Finally, on June 21, some 360 miles from Midway, a badly sunburned Cossitt looked up into the sky as he heard the engines of the Midway-based PBY flying boat of Lieutenant (j.g.) John E. White coming down to effect their rescue. The VT-6 survivors were the last downed American aviators from the Battle of Midway to be picked up. "Walt and I matched nickels to see who would keep the original of the log and he won," Cossitt said.

Kaga had survived the attack by Torpedo Six without damage, and Gene Lindsey's squadron had paid the sacrifice of ten downed Devastators. Thus, of twenty-nine *Hornet* and *Enterprise* carrier-based Devastators to take on the Japanese carriers on June 4, only four had any real chance of making it home. Seven different Navy, Marine, and Army air attacks had been made on the Japanese at this point, none with success.

Torpedo Eight and Torpedo Six had kept the Japanese carriers maneuvering for about forty minutes. Their sacrifices ensured that no strike planes were hauled topside from the Kido Butai's hangars. Nagumo's flattops had run northwest for a full twenty minutes as VT-6 bored in. Once the aerial assaults ceased, it would take the Japanese about forty-five minutes to fully spot their flight decks to begin launching attacks on the U.S. fleet. The question was whether the incessant American strikers would ever allow such a break.[79]

Wade McClusky still had no sign of the Japanese fleet by 0935. Reaching the end of the extra thirty-five miles he had opted to fly on past his original 155 miles, he swung to starboard on the reverse of Nagumo's reported path. He was unknowingly only fifty miles due south of his target. It was a fateful turn that would change the course of the world's greatest carrier battle.[80]

McClusky led *Enterprise*'s SBDs northwest for twenty minutes in another leg of a methodical box search. After an additional five minutes, he would be forced to turn northeast. If the carriers were still not in sight, it would be time to head for home. Tony Schneider in Bombing Six watched his fuel gauge dip toward empty as the *Enterprise* Air Group made its final leg.

Tony realized that his air group was now committed to the search. There was no time to go back, refuel, and set out again. Their own flight decks might be destroyed during that wasted time. His mind was racing. *What do we do now? Are we going to turn around and go back to the* Enterprise? *Or do we stick with it, even if it costs us the whole air group?*[81]

Earl Gallaher, leading Scouting Six, was concerned. "I began to worry for fear we had in some way missed them. In addition to wondering whether we would find the Japanese force, I was beginning to wonder if our fuel would hold out long enough to make an attack and get home."[82]

Good fortune shined at 0955. McClusky suddenly spotted a lone ship below, steaming at high speed, crossing his path at almost a right angle. He believed it was an enemy cruiser on a liaison mission between the carriers and the Midway invasion force. It was actually the destroyer *Arashi*, which had attacked an American submarine and was now headed for the carrier force.

From Ensign Dexter's 6-S-18, Don Hoff looked down at the tiny ship far below. He noted that *Arashi* was not zigzagging, but moving at flank speed. He could see the water boiling up white behind the racing vessel.[83]

McClusky eyed his compass and noted that the warship was heading northeast. He swung his formation around on this new heading and decided to move in the direction *Arashi* was pointing.

Dick Best, leading Bombing Six, failed to notice *Arashi*. At the moment he was taxed with other troubles. His wingman, Bud Kroeger, had just sent a signal across via his rear seat man, Gail Halterman, to Best's gunner, Jim Murray. Kroeger had run out of oxygen, and Best did not want to lose anybody for this important mission. So he took off his oxygen mask and held it up to Kroeger. Best then hung his mask over the throttle and started descending gently to get down to fifteen thousand feet.[84]

Bombing Six eased its altitude lower, and finally the aviators could breathe without the use of their oxygen masks. Best was about a half mile ahead of group commander McClusky, who gradually caught back up with VB-6 and took the lead. McClusky's decision paid off ten minutes after he decided to follow the Japanese destroyer. Almost straight ahead, just a few degrees to starboard, was a break in the blue curve of the Pacific below. McClusky realized he was looking at the white wakes of the carrier striking force. The time was 1002.

Earl Howell, riding in the rear cockpit of Mac McCarthy's dive-bomber, looked down at the ships on the horizon. "Do you think we're home?" he asked.[85]

McCarthy took a long look at the Japanese vessels coming into view and replied, "No, that's not home."

Finally, after eighty minutes in the air, Aviation Radioman Third Class Lloyd Childers could see it. A column of smoke was visible to the northwest as machinist Harry Lee Corl's rear gunner peered off to his right. It was 1003, only fifteen minutes since Torpedo Three had rendez-voused with *Yorktown*'s bombers and fighters.

Childers signaled skipper Lem Massey, flying in the lead section off Corl's wing. Massey brought his squadron around to a heading of 345 degrees to approach the Japanese fleet. Max Leslie and Jimmy Thach noticed the course change and followed Massey's lead. From their higher altitude, the Wildcat and Dauntless pilots could not see what Massey had spotted, but Leslie assumed it was the enemy. The pilots of VT-3, how-ever, could clearly see the smoke of ships some twenty miles distant. Five minutes later, ARM1c Bill Gallagher spotted white wakes ahead and called them to his skipper's attention. Leslie saw them at almost the same moment, some thirty to thirty-five miles ahead, but he never saw any smoke.[86]

Massey led his twelve TBDs up to twenty-six hundred feet to accumu-late more speed for their attack approaches. The heavy cruiser *Chikuma* fired her first salvo of eight-inch shells at 1010 as the Devastators were about fourteen miles from the nearest carrier. Leslie tried to raise Massey on the radio, but to no avail. *Yorktown*'s torpedo squadron headed in solo to attack the Japanese—whose ships were still maneuvering as the VT-6 survivors staggered away from the battlefield. *Yorktown*'s strikers would have to brave the presence of some forty-two Zeros, including six that were just taking off.[87]

As the new American planes approached, most of the Zeros broke off their pursuit of Torpedo Six's survivors, preferring to use their ammunition on Devastators that still lugged torpedoes that could threaten their flight decks. Jimmy Thach's fighters were suddenly fighting for their lives, and one of his pilots was shot down. Massey pressed on northward to take on the fourth carrier in his view. This was *Hiryu*, operating several miles north of the main body of ships.[88]

Thach's Wildcats were heavily engaged by 1020. Both Massey and Leslie were approaching the Kido Butai and would select different targets. It took some fifteen minutes for the lumbering Devastators to cue up for their final runs in against *Hiryu*. The Japanese combat air patrol, drawn away from the main carrier force, worked over Fighting Three and Torpedo Three. By 1035, Massey's TBD crews were paying the same price that VT-8 and VT-6 had so recently paid. Lloyd Childers heard his pilot, Harry Corl, shout, "Look at the skipper!"

Chief Aviation Pilot Bill Esders was flying on Massey's wing when, all at once, he saw the skipper's plane erupt into a big ball of flame. Massey stood up in his open cockpit, with one foot on the stub wing and the other on the seat, as his TBD dropped toward the water 250 feet below. The skipper did not have the altitude to survive the jump from his flaming wreck. With Massey dead, Esders took the lead of VT-3's first division as Zeros continued to slash through the *Yorktown* Devastators.[89]

"We aren't going to make it," muttered Harry Corl behind his pilot controls. His birthday-boy gunner, Lloyd Childers, responded, "Let's get the hell out of here!" Corl dropped his torpedo earlier than normal and maneuvered radically to fight through slashing fighters and AA fire. The Zeros scored hits on Corl's 3-T-3, and two bullets tore into Childers's left thigh. The lead was hot but, strangely, he felt little pain.[90]

Childers continued to fire at his attackers, and then another bullet hit his right leg just above the ankle. He let out a loud grunt. His third wound hurt like hell, feeling as though someone had bashed his shin with a baseball bat. He knew his right leg was broken badly, but he continued to shoot at every attacking fighter. The Zeros made dozens of firing runs until Childers exhausted his ammunition. He finally resorted to his .45-caliber pistol, firing only when a Zero came deadly close. "Then a miracle occurred," he said. "The Zeros left us."[91]

Bill Esders continued his approach on *Hiryu* around 1040. His TBD was hit and his gunner, ARM2c Robert Boyd "Mike" Brazier, was painfully wounded. Only four planes of Lieutenant Pat Hart's second division remained. Esders saw all four make their drops and flash past *Hiryu*'s bow. He saw all four crash within moments, apparently taken down by AA gunfire. Esders made his own torpedo drop from about eight hundred yards out and passed over the Japanese destroyer screen. Zeros picked up Esders and made firing runs on him for the next twenty miles. When the last Zero finally turned away, the Japanese pilot appeared to execute a half salute, perhaps in respect to Bill Esders's maneuvers to escape. At that moment, Esders felt like he had just defeated the entire Japanese fighter force.[92]

Corl rejoined Esders and together they headed for *Yorktown*. *Hiryu*'s skipper skillfully evaded the VT-3 torpedoes that ran true, escaping any damage. Lem Massey's other ten Devastators were gone. Only one other pilot of Torpedo Three managed to bail out of his flaming torpedo bomber and survive. Gunner Benjamin Dodson rode their TBD into the ocean to his death, but Ensign Wesley Frank Osmus—his face and hands painfully burned—was still alive. Osmus managed to inflate his Mae West and remained bobbing in the ocean near *Hiryu* and the Japanese fleet as the American dive-bombers moved in.[93]

Max Leslie led Bombing Three down to 14,500 feet. He found himself over the northeastern portion of Nagumo's carrier striking force and could see three flattops heading northeast. The most fascinating of the three prime targets was a carrier with a large red sun painted forward on her flight deck, which was packed with aircraft. Leslie maneuvered his squadron into the sun. Gunner Bill Gallagher announced that the carrier was turning to starboard into the wind to begin launching planes.[94]

Leslie's continued attempts to raise Lem Massey were fruitless. By this time, the air was filled with radio messages. Leslie could hear that

Torpedo Three was beginning its runs on a carrier and that they were under heavy attack by Japanese fighters.[95]

Leslie knew that his time was running out—the element of surprise would be lost forever if he paused much longer. A Japanese carrier flight deck, loaded with aircraft, lay vulnerable below, and the Zeros had yet to make their presence known. Leslie's efforts to raise Wally Short's scouts had gone without answer, as he was still unaware that VS-5 had not been launched. It was now or never.

Of the 151 strike planes launched from *Hornet*, *Enterprise*, and *Yorktown* on June 4 to attack Nagumo's carriers, 101 planes had been either shot down or had failed to inflict any damage on the Kido Butai. One of Wade McClusky's dive-bombers had been forced to turn back with a faulty engine, leaving only forty-nine Dauntlesses from two carriers to change the course of the battle—and four of them had already lost their payloads.

During the early morning hours, Midway-based aviators had gone in four separate groups to attack the Japanese carriers, but all were without success. These strikers had included sixteen Marine SBDs under Major Lofton "Joe" Henderson and eleven SB2U Vindicator dive-bombers led by Major Benjamin W. Norris. Henderson and half of his Dauntless crews failed to return from this mission, and their target carrier *Hiryu* suffered no damage. They were followed by three carrier-based torpedo squadrons—Torpedo Eight, Torpedo Six, and Torpedo Three, all of whom paid the ultimate price in their attacks on Nagumo's fleet.

Lieutenant Earl Gallaher was still hoping to make his mark on the enemy fleet to settle old scores. He would never forget the sacrifices of the three American torpedo squadrons. "We had no fighter opposition whatsoever," he said of his approach to the carrier fleet. The path to glory had been paved by the fallen, and Gallaher felt that the brave Devastator airmen all deserved the Medal of Honor. The Zeros were equally busy attacking *Yorktown* torpedo bombers at low altitude as Gallaher and company approached. The fighters were also excitedly mixing it up with Jimmy Thatch's Wildcats, the first carrier-launched fighters to engage them this day.[96]

The Imperial Japanese Navy's gunners and fighter pilots had concentrated their best efforts on wiping out the persistent waves of American strikers, which had prevented the Japanese carriers from spotting their decks with their own strike group. *Kaga, Akagi, Soryu,* and *Hiryu* had been maneuvering out of the wind to dodge the Devastator attacks since about 0920. At 1020, Massey's Torpedo Three was still driving home its futile assault.

Yet this hour-long delay in respotting the Kido Butai's flight decks with strike planes had been costly. The stage had thus been set perfectly for the three Dauntless squadrons from *Yorktown* and *Enterprise.*

TEN

Five Minutes of Glory

Ensign Bill Pittman had been concentrating on flying wing on Wade McClusky when he noticed the CEAG gesturing. Looking out, Pittman could see many types of ships—at first just wakes on the surface some thirty-five miles away. Soon he saw the distinctive shape of aircraft carriers steaming in a southerly formation. For Pittman and the other rookie SBD pilots of the *Enterprise* Air Group, the trying hours of the hunt had come to an end. It was now time to attack.[1]

"Adkins, there they are," Pittman called back to his gunner. Floyd Adkins had joined Scouting Six in January 1940, and he felt the squadron was like his second home. He looked over his right shoulder to where his pilot was pointing and counted approximately twenty Japanese ships.[2]

Tony Schneider of Bombing Six was at first relieved. *We've made it back to our fleet, and just in time!* Schneider's engine sputtered; his last fuel tank ran dry as he spotted the ships far below. But he quickly realized it was not the U.S. carrier fleet. Division leader Joe Penland watched his wingman's prop windmill to a halt. Schneider nosed over for a gentle power glide toward the wave tops.[3]

Tony switched through each of his fuel tanks in desperation, managing to keep his SBD aloft a few more minutes by sucking up the last of the fumes from each tank. *My mission has changed,* he thought. *I can't make an attack without gas. My mission now is to make a safe water landing and hope for the best.*

Schneider jettisoned his thousand-pound bomb and yelled back to Glenn Holden to throw his twin .30-caliber machine guns overboard. He turned his Dauntless away from the Japanese fleet toward the direction he believed Midway to be. His final glance toward the enemy carriers was rewarding, as Tony saw explosions in the distance. The last of his fumes were gone now. His prop locked up again and his dive-bomber became a powerless glider. Tony used full flaps and pushed on the stick to level his plane's nose into the waves. His 6-B-8 bounced once off the Pacific surface and then slammed hard into the ocean, coming to an abrupt halt.[4]

Gunner Holden had not followed his pilot's orders. He had merely hooked his twin machine guns into place instead of jettisoning them, and then turned to face forward for the impact. "His decision cost him," said Schneider. The heavy guns slammed into the back of Holden's head as their Dauntless skidded into the ocean, smashing his face into the front of his rear cockpit and knocking the man unconscious. Tony moved quickly to release himself from his straps and parachute in the front cockpit. He jumped out on the starboard wing in his haste to escape their sinking aircraft.

Tony gathered his senses quickly and moved to the port wing to retrieve the two-man life raft from its compartment. He worked fast, inflating the raft and then holding on to one of its cords to keep from losing it. He inflated his own Mae West and then reached into the rear cockpit to pull the toggles on Holden's vest. His gunner was out cold and bleeding heavily as Tony unbuckled him and shoved him out of his rear seat. He climbed into the raft and wrestled his senseless radioman in as well.

He watched the weight of the heavy Wright Cyclone engine pull their SBD's nose under the water. Holden lay moaning in the bottom of the raft as their three-ton Dauntless bubbled under the waves and sank to a resting place nearly three miles below the Pacific surface. Schneider hoped that *Enterprise*'s dive-bombers had plastered the Kido Butai. He had seen explosions in that direction before he crash-landed, and felt a certain pride that his friends had likely exacted some revenge on their enemy. Tony was equally "chagrined that I had not managed my fuel better and was unable to add my weight to the attack."[5]

. . .

Wade McClusky was now left with thirty-one Dauntlesses to carry out an attack. As he examined the Japanese ships through his binoculars, the CEAG saw that the carriers were dispersed in a circular formation. Each flattop was maneuvering independently in the formation's center, as if dodging a torpedo attack. McClusky could plainly see two carriers. A third was out toward the east and a fourth was up north. Two battleships and various cruisers and destroyers were stacked close to the carriers. An outer warship ring, about twelve to fifteen miles from the carriers, appeared to be cruisers or destroyers.[6]

McClusky broke radio silence to inform *Enterprise* of his find. "Figuring that possibly the *Hornet* group commander would make the same decision that I had, it seemed best to concentrate my two squadrons on two carriers," McClusky said. Any greater division of the bomb load his squadrons had might spread out the damage, but he firmly believed it would not sink or completely put out of action more than two carriers.[7]

Dick Dickinson, leading the second division of Scouting Six, took in the sight below. He saw fighter planes on the deck of each carrier, and also noticed that the flight decks were undamaged, in perfect condition to launch aircraft. He called back to his gunner, Joe DeLuca, to keep a sharp eye out for enemy fighters.[8]

Dickinson correctly believed the northernmost carrier to be *Hiryu*, and he identified one of the closer flattops to be her sister carrier, *Soryu*. He was correct in noting that the *Hiryu* and *Soryu* were smaller carriers, while the forty-two-thousand-ton *Kaga* and *Akagi* were more prominent. He believed that McClusky had singled out *Kaga* for his target.[9]

For Scouting Six, it was retribution time. Their war had started suddenly and violently over Pearl Harbor six months earlier. Scouting Six had lost many good pilots and gunners since that day. As fate would have it, most of the *Enterprise* dive-bombers were lining up on the mighty *Kaga*. On December 7, her Zeros had destroyed the Dauntless of Scouting Six's Johnny Vogt over Pearl Harbor, thus inflicting the first wartime casualties for *Enterprise*. It was payback time for *Kaga* now.

The *Enterprise* SBDs approached the Japanese carriers and formed into diving positions, easing down from their higher altitude. John Snowden, rear gunner for Dusty Kleiss, had been on oxygen for about two hours during the group's high-altitude flying. "For almost any reason, I was glad to be going down," he said.[10]

Kleiss noted the enemy fleet's longitude and latitude on his plotting board, and recorded the time and his altitude. He next ordered Snowden to change radio coils to the YE-ZB, and he logged the Morse code signal showing the exact course back to *Enterprise*. Kleiss then manually armed his five-hundred-pound bomb and his two hundred-pound wing bombs, not trusting the electric arming button.[11]

Wade McClusky opted to attack the two nearest carriers in his line of approach. He broke radio silence with, "Earl, you take the carrier on the left, and Best, you take the carrier on the right. Earl, you follow me down."[12]

McClusky's instructions never made it to Best, who was thousands of feet below the CEAG. The Bombing Six skipper was either flying in the blind spot of McClusky's transmitting zone or he had opened up on his own radio at the same moment. In any event, Best sent a broadcast to VB-6 to attack the nearest carrier. There was never a question for Best regarding which carrier McClusky would attack. *It's clear to me what he's going to do,* he thought. *Navy doctrine for dive-bombing or horizontal bombing says that the leading element of the attack group attacks the far target; the trailing element attacks the near target. This way you go in simultaneously. All get the same degree of surprise.*[13]

Such doctrine was apparently unknown to *Enterprise*'s new air group commander, whose background was that of a fighter pilot. Seeing a beautiful carrier target below, he was thrilled with the lack of enemy fighters or even AA fire at this point. The fact that McClusky would do anything but follow Navy doctrine never crossed Lieutenant Best's mind.

Just as Dick Best never heard McClusky's direction to take the carrier on the right, Best's own transmission, "CAG Six, I'm attacking according to doctrine," was likewise never received by McClusky. Best turned toward the nearest target, *Kaga,* and signaled his other divisions out to his right and left.[14]

One remarkable fact stood out to McClusky as he approached the diving point: Not a single Japanese fighter plane was there to molest his dive-bombers. At 1022, the lieutenant commander abruptly pushed his stick and rudder and drew a bead on the rectangular enemy flight deck nearly four miles below. Behind the CAG section, Earl Gallaher had time to observe the two other carriers in the near vicinity. *None of the three has suffered any apparent damage*, he thought.[15]

Bill Pittman was startled by his leader's sudden descent. He assumed that since he was to take pictures, McClusky would remain and be last to dive. To his astonishment, the CEAG dived first. Scared, nervous, and a little uncertain of himself, Pittman was late in pushing over. Number three pilot Dick Jaccard promptly took his place and followed McClusky down. In his own nervousness, Jaccard accidentally pushed the selector lever marked "W" and extended his landing gear instead of his flaps. "It was funny to see Dick push over and let his wheels down instead of opening his dive flaps," said Pittman.[16]

Pittman remembered to flip the switch to turn on his camera, but never thought of the equipment again. The camera apparently recorded nothing but horizon and sky as he went down in his dive. Behind the lead trio, Earl Gallaher and the rest of Scouting Six pushed over as well.

As he nosed in, McClusky had a grand view of his carrier target. He believed that her flight deck was filled with dozens of planes and she was steaming upwind, preparing to launch them. In reality, only some CAP fighters were warming up on deck. McClusky was halfway down before the Japanese spotted his Dauntless. Some scattered AA fire finally rose toward him, but it was too late. He released at eighteen hundred feet and pulled in his flaps to recover as low as he dared. McClusky's bomb landed in the ocean barely ten yards from the carrier's bridge. Pittman and Jaccard also achieved only near misses that exploded close enough to throw water onto *Kaga*'s deck but left her undamaged.[17]

Floyd Adkins's twin .30-caliber gun mount came loose from its rack in the rear cockpit during Pittman's dive. His older-model mount fit into the gun ring, fastened by a nut that screwed onto the mount. "The nut had either been left off on installation or came off in flight!" said Adkins. He quickly unfastened his regular seat belt so that he could stand up, while keeping his gunner's belt fastened. Adkins—a man of slight build—wrestled mightily with the heavy guns against the intense g-forces asserted by their descent.[18]

He tried jamming the gun back into its mount but the slipstream was too strong. He couldn't do it. About that time, Adkins looked up and saw a Japanese fighter getting ready to make a run on his plane. *Christ, this is all we need!* he thought. Picking up the mike, he told Pittman, "We have a fighter on our tail! You'd better take evasive action. He's getting ready to fire and my guns are all screwed up!"[19]

Pittman pulled out of his dive low on the water, passing between two escorting warships that were putting up heavy fire. Adkins managed to hold the 175-pound guns steady enough to fire at the Zero as they recovered. He believed the Japanese pilot looked like he would break to his right after he completed his firing run on their SBD. Adkins stood up and rested the guns on the right side of the fuselage, his left side. Sure enough, the Zero broke to his right. He immediately opened fire. "I must have hit him, because he crashed into the ocean in flames," Adkins said.[20]

Later, upon landing, Adkins struggled to lift the heavy guns, but could not. Earl Gallaher wrote him up for a promotion and the Distinguished Flying Cross. The Zero attack had damaged Pittman's 6-S-8, including one 20mm hit that blew a soccer ball–size hole in his nearly empty starboard inboard fuel tank. "[Adkins] was a great gunner and radioman and I was fortunate to have him as my partner," Pittman later said. In the heat of combat, however, the young pilot felt he would never get out of range and was unaware that his aircraft had sustained damage.[21]

Wade McClusky leveled off at masthead height after dropping his bomb. He was well through the screen of warships before he noted any bursting shells creeping up from behind. McClusky kept his throttle practically pushed through the instrument panel as he jinked left and right through the gunfire to escape.[22]

Fourth down on *Kaga* was Scouting Six skipper Earl Gallaher. Normal dive-bombing doctrine called for the pilots to dive vertical at ninety degrees and then ease back to a seventy-degree angle in order to safely toggle their bombs. In this case, Gallaher's initial dive ended up at an angle exceeding vertical. "The dive was steeper than I would have liked it to be, but was steady enough that I knew my bomb would hit," he said. Gallaher released at low altitude and had to pull out sharply to avoid the waves. He had the pleasure of looking back to see his five-hundred-pound bomb crash into the tightly packed planes waiting to launch. From the rear seat Tom Merritt howled, "That was a beaut, Cap'n!" Back on

December 7, Gallaher had seen the destruction of the battleship *Arizona*, the first vessel he had served upon after graduation from the academy. Through his brain flashed the satisfying thought, *Arizona, I remember you!*[23]

Gallaher's bomb hit *Kaga*'s flight deck aft near the third aircraft elevator, detonating in the crew spaces adjacent to the hangar deck and setting the compartments ablaze. *Kaga*'s woes were only beginning, but her antiaircraft gunners quickly attained some vengeance in downing one of the American dive-bombers.[24]

Reid Stone, fifth in dive order, missed to port with his bomb. Following him was John Roberts, who had sworn that he would score a hit even if he had to take it aboard. Squadron mate Rodey Rodenburg remembered that Roberts "often mentioned he would dive down the stack of a Jap carrier if he ever had the chance. We all believe he kept his word." Roberts's Dauntless was damaged by flak and, although he managed to release his bomb, his 6-S-3 was seen to slam into the water several hundred yards to starboard of *Kaga*. He and AOM1c Thurman Swindell died instantly.[25]

Three planes behind Gallaher was Dusty Kleiss. He decided to aim for the undamaged forward portion of the deck, making the big red circle on the flight deck his aiming point. "You don't aim where it is," he explained. "You aim where it is going to be." As he prepared to drop, he noted flames fifty feet high from Gallaher's hit. Kleiss released his big bomb and then dropped another five hundred feet before toggling his pair of hundred-pound wing bombs. To ensure a hit, he pulled out of his dive at a mere one thousand feet—a nine-g pullout that barely missed hitting the ocean. Kleiss looked back and saw an explosion bursting out on the big red circle.[26]

The antiaircraft fire was intense. Kleiss's gunner, Johnny Snowden, could see tracers streaking past their plane as he faced astern. His SBD was hit several times, but remained airworthy. He and Kleiss were attacked by a fighter as they pulled away from *Kaga*. Snowden attacked with his guns to chase away the Zero. "We remained low on the water," he remembered, "dodging through minor units of the fleet." After pulling away, the young gunner was struck with a wave of relief. *It's warm and sunny, our airplane is apparently all in one piece, and we've come through it alive.*[27]

Kleiss's bomb was devastating—it smashed through the forward elevator into its well and detonated in the fighter stowage spaces below. The concussion from the blast blew out all of *Kaga*'s bridge windows. Captain Jisaku Okada and his helmsman lost visibility to steer their carrier due to the ensuing heavy smoke, so the captain ordered emergency steering to shift to the engine spaces.[28]

The remaining Dauntlesses screamed down, releasing on the carrier as she began to turn to starboard. But it was too late for *Kaga*. Eighth to dive was Jim Dexter, who narrowly avoided colliding with the wild mix of planes jockeying to pounce on *Kaga*. He ended up in a much steeper dive than was customary. "Rather than angling down in a seventy-degree dive, he ended up over on his back, so he was over ninety degrees," said his rear gunner, Don Hoff.[29]

Hoff was pinned to the back of his seat as the angle exceeded vertical and his ammunition belts began to fall out of his rear cockpit. "They started to come out of the can like a big old snake," he said. "I couldn't do anything with the guns because you didn't want to have a fouled-around ammunition belt hanging out the back of the plane while you're diving." Dexter made his drop and pulled up sharply as Hoff struggled to retrieve his ammunition belts. Scouting Six aviators credited Dexter with landing his bomb beside a refueling cart parked in front of *Kaga*'s island. Yet more recent analysis of Scouting Six's pounding of *Kaga* indicates that Dexter's bomb more likely struck the carrier's bridge structure. Captain Okada and four of his senior officers were killed by the terrible blast that literally shredded *Kaga*'s command center.[30]

Dexter made a sharp turn to port as he roared away from *Kaga* in order to avoid a Japanese cruiser in his path. As he retired low on the water, Hoff found a new threat in their path. "Suddenly there were these big columns of water that were exploding and coming up in front of us," Hoff said. The warships fired into the water near the retiring SBDs to throw up deadly waterspouts that could knock the planes down. Dexter weaved and jinked his Dauntless violently to avoid each spout. A collision with one of these water plumes would be like flying into a concrete wall. "About that time, one of those shells hit in the water right below us and it exploded," said Hoff. "It lifted us right straight up in the air about forty or fifty feet."[31]

Dick Dickinson was still stunned by the gift lying below him. He had dreamed of catching Japanese carriers. But he had never imagined a situation like this, where he could prepare for his dive without a trace of fighter opposition. As the skipper's division nosed into its dives, Dickinson kicked his rudders back and forth, creating a ducklike twitching of his SBD's tail to signal his division to attack.[32]

He was the ninth pilot from *Enterprise*'s strike group to dive on *Kaga*. In peacetime, Dickinson had been accustomed to releasing at around twenty-seven hundred feet. Now that it really mattered, his squadron was making their drops at lower altitudes of sixteen hundred to eighteen hundred feet—this to help ensure "that the brand-new boys [could] obtain hits." Ahead, he saw the carrier's flight deck splinter from the first two bomb hits. "The target was utterly satisfying," Dickinson said. "This was the absolute."[33]

As his altimeter wound down rapidly, Dickinson kept the pipper at the middle of his optical sight to point his plane. As he was almost at the dropping point, he saw Dexter's bomb hit right behind where he was aiming—the center of the red disk forward. Dickinson saw the deck rippling, curling back in all directions, exposing a great section of the hangar below. He then released his own five-hundred-pound load and pulled out. Dickinson immediately kicked his rudder and put his plane into a stall in order to see the effects of his beautiful dive. He was certain that his big bomb hit right abreast of the island and that his smaller wing bombs struck in a group of parked planes.[34]

Dickinson felt, and his fellow pilots later agreed, that he made the best dive he had ever attempted. As he pulled away from *Kaga*, he spotted three Japanese fighters below him and to his right. In his excitement in trying to close his diving flaps, he grabbed the wrong handle and dropped his landing flaps. One of the three Zeros was seen to climb rapidly astern of his SBD. Radioman Joe DeLuca opened up with his machine gun when the Japanese came within seven hundred yards. Then the Zero made a steep turn to his left. As he was turning, DeLuca fired his guns again. And then the Zero was gone.[35]

Mac McCarthy, following Dickinson in dive order, noted his target carrier's island structure to starboard, one Zero just behind the forward elevator, and only a few other aircraft spotted aft. McCarthy made a good dive, but judged his bomb a near miss.[36]

Dick Best had deployed his squadron for attack just as Gallaher's VS-6 prepared to dive. He noted that each section and division was correctly spaced—each SBD no more than 150 feet apart. Second section leader Bill Roberts was amazed by two sights. First, he had never seen so many ships in one group before. Second, his skipper had suddenly fishtailed his Dauntless to signal their division to string out in a column formation.[37]

From a column formation, we can dive independently without worrying about colliding with one another. On the other hand, a column makes us more vulnerable to fighter attacks.

After these thoughts raced through Roberts's mind, they were replaced by another. *I have never known Dick Best to make a bad decision.*[38]

Roberts soon realized his skipper was correct. There were no Zeros at their altitude. Therefore, the concentrated firepower advantage of their tightly bunched rear gunners would not be needed. Best's lead section was almost over his target carrier *Kaga* when he pushed his nose over to go into his vertical dive. Bombing Six's skipper had just split open his dive flaps when he was suddenly shocked by a mass of blue-gray streaks plunging vertically in front of him. "Here came McClusky with Gallaher from Scouting Six pouring neutral, belting right in front of me," he said. "They had jumped my target!"[39]

Gunner Jim Murray felt that the three-plane CAG section narrowly missed VB-6's first division as they dived. "Only a blur was visible as the diving SBDs blanked out our forward view," he said. This caused Best to scramble out of the way before his section became victims of a large midair collision.[40]

Twelfth to dive on *Kaga* was Norm West. His second section of Dickinson's second division included two other pilots who were making their first combat dives. Wingman Mike Micheel had set the arming switches on his bombs as he noted West salute him, signaling to dive. Just before nosing over, Micheel saluted flight school buddy John Lough just off his starboard wing.[41]

They dived lengthwise along the target. "How nice it was to have a big red dot in the center of the flight deck for an aiming point!" Micheel said. During his dive, he saw two fires burning on the carrier, one forward and one on the starboard quarter. He could also see aircraft on deck and sailors scurrying about. A barrage of ack-ack had been bursting in his vicinity, but now red tracers were zipping past his cockpit from smaller-caliber weapons. *Those guys are shooting at me!* Micheel thought as the combat suddenly became more personal.[42]

"Three thousand feet!" John Dance called from his rear seat. Micheel waited a second longer before yanking the bomb release and pulling out of his dive to the right. He had no time to look back to see the result of his attack, for Micheel quickly realized that his Dauntless was acting sluggishly to his controls. In his excitement, he had failed to release his two hundred-pound wing bombs. Micheel spotted a cruiser cutting directly across his path below and corrected his error by releasing both small bombs as he passed the ship broadside. He was sure that he missed his target, as he was jinking so much trying to avoid AA fire. Micheel never saw an enemy fighter.[43]

On the tail of the West/Micheel/Lough section was Charlie Ware with ensigns Frank O'Flaherty and Jim Shelton. The situation over the Japanese carrier was horribly confused. Two-thirds of Bombing Six carried out their original plans and joined suit with Scouting Six in diving on *Kaga*. Lieutenant Joe Penland, leading Bombing Six's second division, delayed his attack momentarily.

Penland knew that his VB-6 planes packed a more lethal punch with thousand-pound bombs, as opposed to the five-hundred-pounders being dropped by the scouts. He observed several misses on *Kaga*, and decided to lead his division down. He considered Dick Best to be the best dive-bomber pilot in the fleet and was certain his men would take care of *Akagi*. Penland noted one or more hits on the carrier from planes ahead of him. He made a good dive and felt confident that he added another direct hit. His gunner, Harold Heard, excitedly agreed that they had scored. Penland viewed heavy flames on the flight deck of *Kaga* as he looked back during retirement.[44]

Lew Hopkins was the fourth to dive from Penland's division. He put the crosshairs of his gunsight on *Kaga*'s deck and kept the carrier in his sights the whole way down. Ed Anderson in the rear seat could see that the carrier had already been hit. "You couldn't see aft of the island structure because of the black smoke pouring out of it," he said. Anderson called out the altitude down to twenty-five hundred feet. At that instant, he hollered, "Twenty-five hundred and Zero coming from the right!"[45]

Hopkins released his thousand-pound bomb, then immediately turned into the Zero in a defensive maneuver while retiring low on the water. Anderson found himself glued to his seat by the heavy g-forces during the pullout. Hopkins did not have the opportunity to look back to determine the outcome of their bomb drop. His primary focus was escaping the pursuing Zero and clearing the Japanese task force.

"Let's get the hell out of here!" Anderson implored his pilot.

"What do you think I'm trying to do?" Hopkins snapped.

John Van Buren and wingman Norm Vandivier followed Penland's division. Ensign George Goldsmith, third in Van Buren's division, peered down at Kaga. He saw hits and near hits with almost every drop. As James Patterson called off the altitude during their plunge, the rear gunner found the antiaircraft fire to be of little consequence. His larger concern was in keeping a heads-up for fighters.[46]

Goldsmith observed Kaga to be in a hard turn. He forced his bomber into a corkscrew spin as he followed the flattop all the way down. Patterson was used to Goldsmith releasing their bomb at about twenty-two hundred feet during dive-bombing practice, but now he watched the altimeter spin past two thousand feet. Finally, he howled, "Fifteen hundred feet!" and Goldsmith released their bomb and pulled out hard. Their Dauntless was pulling so many g's that Patterson could not even raise his hands up to his guns to strafe a destroyer that flashed past his plane during their recovery. "He had been the world's worst dive-bomber pilot during the practice hops I'd flown with him previously," said Patterson. "But that day Ensign Goldsmith earned every dime invested in him as he put our bomb right through the flight deck, just aft of amidships."[47]

Second to last to dive on Kaga was Andy Anderson. His rear gunner, Stuart Mason, could see two carriers ablaze from the bow back to the stern as they pulled out. He could see another squadron in the distance attacking a third carrier, which suddenly erupted with a direct bomb hit.[48]

Kaga was doomed. When the U.S. planes came roaring in, her

hangar deck crews had been busy loading strike aircraft with bombs and torpedoes to make another attack against the Americans, and her planes were fully fueled. The bomb blasts mowed down scores of mechanics, plane handlers, armorers, and damage-control men while also destroying the fire mains. Water was unavailable now to fight the flames that raged everywhere. More than eighty thousand pounds of explosives were scattered throughout the hangar deck in addition to the thousands of gallons of aviation fuel in the parked aircraft and in the shredded fuel lines. It was just a matter of time before the roaring fires in *Kaga*'s hangar would touch off a tremendous explosion.[49]

Dick Best quickly recovered from his shock. McClusky and VS-6 had flashed past him down onto *Kaga*, so he closed his dive flaps. Wingmen Bud Kroeger and Fred Weber hung tight to their skipper as he proceeded at full throttle toward the next carrier, *Akagi*. Best was pleased that his SBDs were still encountering neither AA fire nor fighters. Some twelve to fifteen miles distant, he could see a third carrier, *Hiryu*.

Best found the math was not in his favor now. Lieutenants Penland and Van Buren had taken their divisions down on *Kaga* in the confusion, leaving VB-6's skipper with only three SBDs to disable one of Japan's largest aircraft carriers. At the moment, he believed he still had all five planes of his first division and would not find out until much later that he had actually lost his second section.[50]

Best led his wingmen up to fourteen thousand feet. He opened his flaps as they approached *Akagi* downwind from slightly abaft her port beam. With dive flaps fully employed, his airspeed during descent would be around 240 knots. The carrier still appeared to be steaming blissfully along into the wind without a hint of danger, preparing to launch aircraft. There was no time to question his good fortune. He radioed to his remaining pilots, "Don't let this carrier escape!"[51]

Many years later, Best learned that his second section had become mixed-up in the confusion over *Kaga*. Bill Roberts and his wingman, Pete Halsey, missed their skipper's shift and they ended up piling onto *Kaga* with the tail-end VB-6 division of Joe Penland. Roberts was certain as he went into his dive that his target carrier's island structure was to port because of how unusual this seemed to him in comparison to American carriers. He felt that his bomb was a near miss off *Kaga*'s starboard bow. Rear gunner Bill Steinman snapped photos of their target, which Roberts said were "later confiscated by Commander Murr Arnold." Roberts saw when the water-damaged film was developed "in the centers of several frames there were images of the three burning carriers."[52]

Commander Takahisa Amagai, the air officer on *Kaga*, stated in 1945 that there were "four hits on the *Kaga*. The first bomb hit the forward elevator. The second bomb went through the deck at the starboard side of the after elevator. The third bomb went through the deck on the port side abreast of the island. The fourth bomb hit the port side aft." Amagai also stated that *Kaga* had some thirty loaded and fueled aircraft on her hangar deck, while other planes were still spotted on deck for launch.[53]

Kaga's bridge crew accurately assessed the four hits and five misses from the first nine *Enterprise* dive-bombers to attack the carrier before the bridge was evacuated and they quit logging the attacks. At least several thousand-pounders also ripped *Kaga* after the first four hits made by Gallaher, Kleiss, Dexter, and Dickinson.

Lieutenant Best wasted no time in attacking *Akagi*. His section pushed over about 1025, just minutes after Wade McClusky had abruptly plunged down on *Kaga*. The Japanese—whose estimates of how many dive-bombers hit each of their ships this day would prove to be very accurate—counted only three American dive-bombers that attacked *Akagi*.[54]

Jim Murray, facing aft behind his twin .30s, was well aware that Bud Kroeger and Fred Weber were the only VB-6 pilots still clinging to the skipper's tail. He felt his 6-B-1 slow down, so Murray stowed his guns and faced forward as his SBD went into its dive.[55]

Dick Best was determined not to miss as he looked at what he believed to be the carrier's island structure to the starboard side of the flight deck. *Akagi*'s island was actually to port, which would eventually lead to much confusion in who attacked which carrier. Years later, when presented with a model of the *Akagi* that he could stand above as if dive-bombing the ship, he was shown that what he had believed to be her island structure was actually *Akagi*'s large, downward-facing starboard-side stack structure.[56]

At six thousand feet, Murray began calling off the altitude over the intercom in descending thousand-foot increments. All the while, he could see shells passing over and beyond their port wing. At thirty-five hundred feet, Best put his sights just forward of *Akagi*'s bridge and saw a Zero run through on the deck. He thought to himself, *Best, if you're a real hero, when you've dropped your bomb you'll aileron around and shoot that son of a bitch down.*[57]

At two thousand feet—their normal release point—Murray began excitedly calling off the altitude in one-hundred-foot intervals.

"Nineteen hundred! Eighteen hundred!"

Best plunged close to fifteen hundred feet before Murray felt the skipper toggle their big bomb free. Best's number two wingman, Bud Kroeger, wondered whether the skipper would ever pull out, and finally released his own bomb first while Best was still in his bombsight ahead of him. Bombing Six's skipper had ditched his thoughts of attacking the just-launched Zero. Instead, he opted to watch the results of his own drop. Murray resumed his aft-facing position as their 6-B-1 started to pull out of its dive. He saw Kroeger's bomb splash in the sea alongside the Japanese carrier just as Best flipped B-1 on its side. Best and Murray both watched as their bomb hit dead center in the forward group of planes.[58]

"The first bomb hit near the forward elevator and the bridge, amidships," Best said. "I had the whole vision laid out twelve hundred feet below me," during pull-out.[59]

Kroeger's first bomb hit the ocean just yards to port and slightly forward of *Akagi*'s island structure. The explosion sent a geyser of water towering high over the bridge, drenching everyone there with seawater. Best's bomb—a thousand-pounder with a one-one-hundredth-second-delay fuse that allowed the weapon to penetrate a flight deck before exploding—created havoc on *Akagi*'s hangar deck. As Best hauled clear of *Akagi*, he believed that he saw Weber's bomb explode beside the lead fighter of a half dozen that were preparing to launch back on the fantail. The resulting explosions from the armed and fueled aircraft were tremendous. "*Akagi* didn't get a gun firing before the first three bombs hit," said Best.[60]

Although Weber's bomb appeared to some on *Akagi* to have hit the after portion of the flight deck, Japanese cameraman Makishima Teiuchi was standing on the flight deck with his camera. He said the third thousand-pounder dropped by VB-6 almost grazed the deck's edge before landing in the water alongside the stern. The upward force of its blast bent the edge of the flight deck upward. The concussion also damaged *Akagi*'s rudder such that when she attempted a starboard turn moments later it locked in position and forced the carrier into an eternal thirty-degree circle. After moments of helpless circling, *Akagi*'s crew was forced to kill her engines.[61]

The effects of Dick Best's solitary direct hit were far more devastating, exploding among eighteen Kate torpedo planes on the hangar deck. Fires spread quickly to other ordnance lying on the racks along the bulkhead. Internal explosions would continue to eat up the once-proud flagship for hours as her crew fought to save the doomed vessel.[62]

Lieutenant Best headed out of the immediate area, noting smoke and flames from one of the other carriers. He realized that another SBD squadron had wrecked another carrier at the same time he was making his attack.

I n the same five-minute span that Scouting Six and Bombing Six were wreaking havoc with the Kido Butai, *Yorktown*'s Bombing Three also made its presence known to Admiral Nagumo's carrier force.

Max Leslie glanced at his instrument panel clock. It showed 1023 as he looked over at his wingmen, Lefty Holmberg and Ensign Paul Schlegel, to check their spacing. Leslie was still unaware that Wally Short's Bombing Five had not been launched behind his group. He had attempted to direct VB-5 to attack the smaller carrier to the west, but heard nothing in reply. Leslie figured he had done all he could to carry out the attack as planned. It was time to dive.[63]

Leslie patted the top of his head to signal, "I've got the lead," and rolled into his dive at 1025—just as Dick Best was pushing over on *Akagi*. Leslie's rear gunner, Bill Gallagher, noticed a Zero closing on their tail as they prepared to push over. He quickly cleared his twin .30s and trained his sights on the incoming fighter. Gallagher was so intent on aiming his fire that he did not observe his bullets hitting his target. But when he looked up again, the Zero was on fire and circling down.[64]

Dave Shumway, leading Bombing Three's third division, thought the

Japanese formation below appeared scattered. *Soryu* had just turned to starboard at 1024 to begin launching fighters. Lookouts spotted the first SBDs of Leslie and Holmberg plunging down, and the order was passed to commence firing on them. *Soryu* immediately began swinging back to port as her 25mm gun mounts blazed to life.[65]

Having earlier accidentally jettisoned his bomb, Leslie dived anyway from fourteen thousand feet. He opened up with his .50-caliber guns, hoping to suppress antiaircraft fire for his following pilots. He believed his target to be the carrier *Kaga*, with a starboard-side superstructure, which fit the latest model he had seen of that carrier. He fired for six thousand feet, aiming at the carrier's bridge, until his guns jammed. "This was the climax of a sad moment for me, because I thought I was in a perfect dive," he said. When he finally pulled out, he could not see damage to the other two carriers in the area.[66]

Leslie flew from aft to bow over *Soryu*, allowing Bill Gallagher ample time to rake the carrier's side with his twin .30s. As he faced rearward, he had the satisfaction of seeing Bombing Three's first bomb, dropped by the number two pilot, hit amidships.

Lefty Holmberg rode Leslie's tail all the way down. Once the skipper had cleared the way, Holmberg finally had a good view of *Soryu*. He centered the crosshairs of his telescopic sight on the big red meatball painted on the flight deck. The flashes from guns firing along the edges of the flight deck reminded him of a birthday cake with lighted candles.[67]

Holmberg heard shrapnel clattering off his SBD like a handful of rocks thrown against a tin roof. Once gunner George LaPlant hollered, "Twenty-five hundred," from the backseat, Holmberg held his SBD steady and pushed the electric bomb-release button on the top of his stick. Just to make sure, he held his dive further as he tugged on the manual release. His Dauntless pulled out level just as his thousand-pound bomb smashed through *Soryu*'s painted red disk. LaPlant shouted that it was a hit. Max Leslie looked back in time to see his wingman's bomb create a terrific explosion on the flight deck.[68]

Holmberg glanced over his shoulder with satisfaction, but only for a split second. Shell splashes thrown up by ships' gunfire forced him to maneuver his Dauntless quickly. Getting back home would be no walk in the park, but Holmberg was pleased. *Even if none of us make it back to the* Yorktown, *we have accomplished our mission.*[69]

Holmberg's bomb exploded at the forward starboard edge of the carrier's number one elevator, blowing *Soryu*'s executive officer, Commander Hisashi Ohara, across the bridge and burning him badly. The number one antiaircraft gun forward of the island structure was demolished, and great damage was inflicted below the flight deck.[70]

As Oley Hanson prepared to dive, his gunner, Joe Godfrey, noticed a Zero that passed his tail so close he felt he could have spit in the pilot's eye. Godfrey found his plane's dive was much steeper than usual and lower in duration than what he had been accustomed to. Hanson saw that Paul Schlegel and Bob Campbell ahead of him both missed with their bombs. Hanson then released at twenty-five hundred feet. Looking back upon pullout, he watched several bombs hit the flight deck, creating a blazing inferno.[71]

Hanson's SBD retired low on the water on a course directly between two Japanese warships. "It seemed they were shooting every gun they had at us," said Godfrey. "Fortunately, they were rather close abeam of each other, and we were so close to the water that they couldn't get their guns to bear on us and were, as a result, shooting the hell out of each other."[72]

Sixth to dive on *Soryu* was Ensign Bob Benson, a twenty-two-year-old graduate of San Francisco Junior College and son of a Marine major. His rear gunner was eighteen-year-old ARM3c Fred Bergeron from Texas. Like Earl Gallaher of Scouting Six, Bergeron had been ready to get revenge since he had first seen the smoldering wreckage of the battleship *Arizona* one week after the Japanese attack on Pearl Harbor.[73]

Bergeron's hopes of quickly fulfilling this wish had been dashed a month later, when his carrier *Saratoga* was hit by a torpedo. He had been shooting the breeze on the flight deck at the time with three other young men who also hailed from the Texas Gulf Coast town of Freeport. Among them was his older brother Dallas Bergeron, with whom he had enlisted in the Navy in December 1940. Dallas and Fred had both qualified for radio school, graduated, and were assigned together to Bombing Three. *Saratoga*'s torpedo damage had sidelined their war effort for several

months. Now the siblings were both plunging down on Japanese warships in their respective rear cockpits.[74]

Fred Bergeron kept a sharp vigil astern of his Dauntless as Benson
fishtailed in for his dive on *Soryu*. Black bursts of antiaircraft fire were
peppering the sky around their plane. Bergeron suddenly felt something
strike the back of his head. *Oh, my God, they got me!*[75]

He reached back and found a pair of goggles and helmet in his hand.
They had ripped loose as his pilot glanced over into their slipstream.
Bergeron realized he was not wounded and proceeded to call out the altitude as Benson plunged down on *Soryu*. Benson released at twenty-five
hundred feet and pulled out low on the water. His gunner was uncertain
whether their bomb hit home due to flames and smoke obscuring the
Japanese flight deck beneath him. Benson effected a rendezvous with
other VB-3 planes after clearing the enemy fleet and called for Bergeron
to pass up his helmet for the return flight.

Several fighter planes were on *Soryu*'s flight deck as Lefty Holmberg's bomb exploded. The SBDs following Holmberg added more direct
hits and close near misses. Ensign Roy Isaman, flying in Gordon Sherwood's second division, felt that no one wavered in his attack, whether
he carried a bomb or not. Isaman, diving without a bomb, was "impressed by the unqualified courage exhibited by all."[76]

Ensign Phil Cobb was ninth to dive. He saw chunks of flight deck
and aircraft thrown into the air as he plummeted below three thousand
feet. *If I make it back to my own ship,* he thought, *this is one carrier we
won't have to worry about for the rest of the battle.*[77]

Lieutenant Syd Bottomley was scared to death as he prepared to dive
on *Soryu*. He was leading VB-3's second section of the second division.
At high altitude during his final approach, he was also freezing. He felt
cold, compounded by shivers of dread and anticipation, that ran up and
down his spine and made his teeth chatter.[78]

Bottomley saw Holmberg's bomb explosion flip a Japanese airplane
like a matchstick. Bottomley pulled the controls back into his gut as he
passed through three thousand feet. Then he closed the dive brakes and
jammed on full throttle as he pulled out low on the water. *Let's get the
hell out of here!* he thought as he banked his SBD toward open water.
AMM2c David Johnson shouted into the intercom, "We got her!"

Bottomley, unable to resist sneaking a look back at *Soryu*, saw his target enveloped in flames as bombs exploded among parked aircraft.[79]

By the time the bombless eleventh Dauntless of Ensign Charlie Lane had pulled out of its dive, the carrier was belching smoke and flames. Lane fired his fixed guns all the way down, sighting through the crosshairs while Jack Henning blazed away in the rear seat with his twin .30s on pullout. Dave Shumway noted the progress of the two VB-3 divisions ahead of his own. The pilots ahead of him each dived from the north along the fore and aft lines of *Soryu*. Shumway clearly saw Lefty Holmberg's damaging hit and believed that his squadron landed four more direct hits and three very near misses.[80]

The second big bomb to strike *Soryu* landed in the middle of her flight deck. It penetrated deeply into the lower hangar, rupturing steam pipes in her boiler spaces. The third VB-3 bomb to land hit the after section of the flight deck dead center, between the second and third aircraft elevators, and detonated in the upper hangar. It exploded among Type 97 Kate torpedo bombers, destroying them and engulfing the rear of the hangar in fire.[81]

Bob Elder could see that *Soryu* was a wreck. The carrier was burning furiously as his third division of Bombing Three approached. He saw at least three direct hits and decided that his bomb would be better served against one of the carrier's screening warships. He shifted to the destroyer *Isokaze*, operating off *Soryu*'s bow, and Ensign Randy Cooner followed him down. Elder and Cooner managed only near misses on the agile destroyer before pulling free of the carrier group.[82]

Lieutenant Ozzie Wiseman and Ensign Johnny Butler also switched targets, deciding to take on one of the battleships. Bombing Three's action report would credit the duo with landing one direct hit on her stern and one near miss, although Japanese records do not bear out a hit. Dave Shumway, diving thirteenth, stayed in line on *Soryu*, hoping to finish off the carrier. He was later credited with making the fourth direct hit.[83]

Ensign Bud Merrill was frustrated. Here was his big chance to finally lay a bomb on an enemy flight deck, yet he had no payload to deliver. A graduate of the civilian pilot training program while attending Long Beach Junior College in California, he was one of Bombing Three's more seasoned pilots. Much of his experience had come while serving as a loaner pilot with *Enterprise*'s Scouting Six after *Saratoga* had been torpedoed in January. Merrill had participated in the Wake and Marcus Island strikes. Now, as he brought up the rear of Bombing Three's attack, he saw Dave Shumway's bomb explode ahead of him. Merrill longed to claim his own hit as he dived his bombless SBD through the hailstorm of flak toward *Soryu*, but he could use only his forward guns to create damage.[84]

As Max Leslie made for the rendezvous point, he proudly noted his target carrier burning furiously. He felt that out of the nine pilots who had dropped their thousand-pound bombs on *Soryu*, four had scored direct hits, three had exploded close aboard the port beam, and two near-missed to starboard, wrecking the carrier. He had often described the accuracy of dive-bombing to others as "trying to hit a fast-moving Florida cockroach with a marble from eye height. It was clearly evident that the squadron had been remarkably accurate against that cockroach."[85]

The *Yorktown* pilots correctly believed their target had a starboard-side island, thus eliminating *Akagi* as the carrier they hit. Leslie would forever believe that Bombing Three had struck *Kaga*, although he had clearly seen a starboard-side island structure. Junior pilot Bob Elder came away with a clear vision of having seen a plane blown over VB-3's target carrier's starboard side, ahead of the island.[86]

Aerial opposition had been low. One Zero attacked the VB-3 SBDs during their dives, and a floatplane made a pass on Roy Isaman as he was low on the water. Isaman's gunner, Sidney Weaver, had no intentions of being its victim, however. He had been forced into the ocean just four days after the Pearl Harbor attack when his VB-3 Dauntless experienced engine failure. Weaver had been most impressed with skipper Max Leslie as he and his pilot bobbed in their life raft awaiting rescue from a destroyer. Leslie had circled overhead for two and a half hours until he was certain of their recovery.

Weaver trusted Lieutenant Commander Leslie to lead his squadron to safety again this day. The Japanese floatplane bearing in on his tail now was just a minor distraction. Weaver opened up with his Browning machine guns and put enough lead in the air to make the Japanese pilot turn tail. All seventeen of Leslie's Dauntlesses had escaped during their attacks.

Leslie orbited at the rendezvous for some time, circling around in search of his pilots. Bill Gallagher in the rear seat became nervous about fighters. He called up, "Skipper, maybe we'd better leave here." At length, only Ensign Oley Hanson managed to join him. The other VB-3 planes had withdrawn to the northeast, merging in three-plane sections before setting course for home.[87]

Leslie and Hanson banked around. Leslie, ignoring the gunfire from a nearby Japanese destroyer, saw two more carriers burning and exploding about twelve miles to the west. The American dive-bombers had certainly made their mark.

Thirty-nine bombs had been dropped on three carriers in less than five minutes, resulting in at least eleven direct hits and many close near misses. In the two years prior to America's entry into World War II, the U.S. Navy had put its dive-bombers through rigorous attack exercises to improve the pilots' skills. Dive-bombing was now considered the primary strike weapon of the carriers, and the Navy's effort to perfect this doctrine paid big dividends on June 4 at Midway.[88]

Twenty eight SBDs had made dives on *Kaga*, landing as many as seven direct hits—a success rate that may have been as high as twenty-five percent. Dick Best's three dive-bombers all scored either direct hits or damaging near misses on *Akagi*. *Yorktown*'s Bombing Three, with only fourteen of seventeen planes still carrying bombs, was equally effective. Four Dauntless pilots attacked other warships, leaving only nine bomb-toting SBDs to attack *Soryu*. No fewer than one-third of them landed direct hits. The hit ratio on *Kaga* and *Soryu* of between twenty-five and thirty-three percent was perfectly consistent with what *Enterprise*'s Bombing Six had achieved prewar in October 1940. The unit's peacetime bombing drill had involved dropping water-filled practice bombs on a target sled towed by a destroyer. The fact that the Dauntless squadrons at Midway had achieved equal scores while under Zero attacks and anti-aircraft fire was directly attributable to the stable performance of their rugged dive-bombers and the skill of the pilots.[89]

Akagi, *Kaga*, and *Soryu* were mortally damaged. *Akagi* had suffered 267 fatalities but would remain stubbornly afloat until Japanese destroyers scuttled her with torpedoes early the following morning. *Kaga* had suffered 811 men killed and was also finished off by two torpedoes from one of her escorting destroyers on the afternoon of June 4. *Soryu* suffered 711 of 1,103 crewmen lost, and she too was scuttled.[90]

Only *Hiryu*, off to the north, had escaped damage from the U.S. Dauntless dive-bombers during Midway's glorious minutes.

ELEVEN

The Deadly Flights Home

The Dauntless aviators had wrecked three enemy flattops in a five-minute span, and now, as they raced back to their own carriers, they could only hope that the Japanese aviators had not played equal hell in their absence.

Max Leslie's Bombing Three had an easier escape than any of the other units that attacked Nagumo's Kido Butai. Leslie was unaware of any Japanese planes following him as he flew toward *Yorktown*. Some sources would later claim that another strike from *Hiryu* followed VB-3 toward home, but postwar analysis would show that *Hiryu*'s strike did not launch until nearly 1100—a full half hour after Bombing Three pushed over.[1]

Lefty Holmberg led the procession back toward *Yorktown*. In his excitement, he began pulling ahead at a fast clip. Lieutenant Syd Bottomley opened up on the radio and snapped at him, "Dammit, slow down!"[2]

Holmberg had reason to hurry. Fluid was spilling into his cockpit from shrapnel damage he had incurred during his dive. Oil splattered on his goggles and around the cockpit, causing him concern that a broken oil line would soon cause his engine to seize up. He was elated at getting a bomb hit, but felt like a football player who breaks his leg scoring the winning touchdown in a big game. He called back to George LaPlant to assess the damage. LaPlant guessed that it must be hydraulic fluid, as their oil pressure was remaining steady.[3]

Ensign Bob Elder spotted a Japanese floatplane after completing his dive and momentarily began a pursuit to attack, but his better sense took over with one sobering realization: *I don't know the way home.* Elder turned about and chased after his squadron mates, who were retiring to the northeastward. Bud Merrill, flying tail-end Charlie with Dave Shumway's third division, was unable to locate any *Yorktown* aviators. He found comfort in a small group of *Enterprise* SBDs making their return flight. *Any port in a storm!* he thought.[4]

Bill Esders and Harry Corl were the only Torpedo Three pilots to survive the slashing Zeros and deadly AA fire from the *Hiryu*. Corl's engine was spewing oil badly, and his throttle functioned only at the cruising speed of 2,100 rpm. Mike Brazier in Esders's rear seat was critically wounded. Corl's gunner, Lloyd Childers, had also been hit several times by Japanese bullets. In spite of his wounds, Childers had fired twice at Zeros with his .45 Colt pistol after his .30-caliber machine gun froze up. It would be a trying flight home for both TBD pilots as they hoped to haul their wounded radiomen to safety.

Unknown to these four VT-3 survivors, one more of their own was still alive. Ensign Wesley Osmus was spotted bobbing in the ocean that afternoon by the Japanese destroyer *Arashi*. The destroyer lowered a boat and brought the American swimmer aboard. At first he was treated well, yet his captors felt less gracious when Commander Watanabe Yasumasa brought *Arashi* within sight of the three blazing, wrecked carriers. He had his prisoner interrogated and managed to extract the composition of Task Forces 16 and 17, including the names of the three U.S. carriers. Yasumasa then ordered the VT-3 pilot's disposal. Osmus was thrown over *Arashi*'s stern, but he managed to hang on to a chain railing. A crewman struck him in the neck with a fire ax, and his body plunged into the ocean.[5]

Enterprise's SBDs did not have an easy departure from the Kido Butai. It was a 175-mile return flight the aviators would never forget.

Dusty Kleiss of Scouting Six had escaped one Zero already. He circled wide around the carrier task force after his drop, but found another fighter coming in to make a pass. Gunner Johnny Snowden managed to chase it off. Kleiss cleared the fleet and tried to join a section of newer

VS-6 pilots. "They thought I was a Jap, poured on the soup, and pulled away," he said. Kleiss decided the protection wasn't worth the waste of gas, so he throttled back to a hundred knots and chugged toward Midway.[6]

Scouting Six skipper Earl Gallaher was joined by Reid Stone during his retirement from *Kaga*. One Zero made a halfhearted firing pass on their SBDs but gave up because of how low to the water they were flying. Gallaher then saw heavy black bursts of AA fire ahead, followed by splashes in the water. He realized he was heading directly for a destroyer, and executed a radical ninety-degree turn to port to dodge the hailstorm.[7]

Wade McClusky was contemplating the most direct route home. As he looked over his navigation, he suddenly heard a stream of tracer bullets chopping the water around his plane. Chocalousek in the rear cockpit alertly opened fire on the Zeros that had closed on them. One of the fighters overshot McClusky's SBD as it pulled out of a high-speed dive. Another Zero was about a thousand feet above, to the left and astern, about to make another attack run.[8]

McClusky, a former fighter pilot, knew just what to do. He remained about twenty feet above the water until the Zero was committed to his firing run, then wrapped his Dauntless in a steep turn to port to allow Chocalousek to open fire again. A five-minute chase ensued. First one Zero attacked from the right, then the second from the left. As each Mitsubishi made its approach, McClusky maneuvered his bomber like a fighter plane to put Chocalousek in firing position.[9]

A burst from one of the Zeros riddled the port side of the Dauntless, and bullets ripped into McClusky. *The left side of my cockpit is shattered. My left shoulder feels like it has been hit with a sledgehammer. This must be the end. Surely we are goners.*[10]

McClusky, his wounds throbbing, heard nothing but the noise of his own engine for several seconds. He grabbed the inner phone and yelled to Chocalousek, but heard no answer. The pain in his left shoulder and arm was intense, but he finally managed to turn around. There sat Chocalousek, facing aft with his guns at the ready, and unharmed. "He had shot down one of the Zeros—probably the one that had got the big burst in on us—and the other decided to call it quits," McClusky remembered. He climbed to a thousand feet and set course for *Enterprise*. The Zeros had put three large 20mm holes and more than fifty bullets through his fuselage and wings.

Bill Pittman, McClusky's wingman, escaped the Japanese screen with a 20mm shell through his starboard fuel tank. Gunner Floyd Adkins was still clinging to his broken .30-caliber twin mount. They headed east in retirement, uncertain of which direction their task force lay. Adkins did not help his pilot's stress by describing their plane's damage over the intercom. "There's a hole at the right wing root big enough to put my leg through," he announced. Fortunately, this tank had been depleted of fuel, and the Dauntless flew stubbornly on. Pittman soon spotted some SBDs ahead. He slipped into position on skipper Gallaher and his wingman, Reid Stone. Ensign Dick Jaccard joined the little formation during their return, followed sometime later by the arrival of Jim Dexter.[11]

Dexter had dodged the heavy AA fire with violent maneuvers as he cleared the Japanese fleet. Gunner Don Hoff spotted a Zero low on the water crossing behind his aircraft. The fighter began a wide sweeping turn to attack the Dauntless from the rear. Fear gripped young Hoff. He waited until the Zero was just coming out of its turn before he opened up. He felt certain that his .30-calibers struck home. The Zero flipped its wing and dropped out of sight below Dexter's SBD. Hoff was not concerned whether he had made the kill or not. *All that matters is that I scared him away*, he thought. *That's all I wanted.*[12]

Dick Best recovered from his dive on *Akagi* with wingman Fred Weber on his tail. He spotted several TBDs retiring about a mile ahead of him and decided to join them. A pair of Zeros suddenly flashed past the SBDs, apparently intent on hitting the Torpedo Three survivors. *Too much unfavorable attention*, Best thought. He opted to move out of their way. Jim Murray in his rear seat found another Zero closing in on them from behind. He feared hitting his own vertical stabilizer and rudder, but Murray was able to rake the Zero's starboard wing with his Browning. To his relief, the fighter fell off out of sight.[13]

As Ensign Weber straggled behind as much as six hundred yards during the encounter, a Nakajima E8N2 Type 95 floatplane attacked him, making two firing passes. This fighter, operating from one of the Japanese battleships, was less nimble than the dreaded Zeros, and Weber was able to escape. He quickly closed formation on Lieutenant Best's

6-B-1 and later swore to his skipper back on board ship he would never be caught straggling again.[14]

Jim Murray saw a Japanese floatplane approaching his Dauntless, closing to within firing range as they retired from the Japanese force. A few bursts from his twin .30s sent the enemy aircraft on its way. *I'll bet he finds a few bullet holes when he returns to his cruiser*, thought Murray. As they cleared the area, Best and Weber were joined by Bud Kroeger in 6-B-2, who flashed the "okay" sign to Murray. The trio had survived and claimed three hits on *Akagi* for the only three planes to attack her. *What a bombing feat!* Murray thought.[15]

Departing, Best caught sight of *Soryu* being smothered by bombs from Max Leslie's VB-3 unit. "Best bombing I ever saw," he said. "They were hitting from stem to stern, a mass of smoke and flame." Best's section was lucky to escape the wrath of the Japanese CAP, but many of their shipmates were less fortunate.

Lieutenant Dickinson came under heavy fire from a Japanese destroyer during his pullout, but the shells were bursting a thousand yards ahead. He glanced at his airspeed indicator. He realized he was making only ninety-five knots, since he had accidentally dropped his landing gear instead of closing his dive flaps after pullout. Dickinson frantically pulled up and then dived down toward the water to spoil their aim. He also did some grabbing at handles to correct his landing-flaps problem. "Some of our people who were still around told me later it seemed as if I were demonstrating my Douglas dive-bomber," he said. "Landing flaps were opening; diving flaps were opening; my wheels were up and down; and my activity was like a three-ring circus."[16]

By the time Dickinson sorted out all of his controls, another Zero had passed to his right and drew slowly ahead toward another group of SBDs. He moved in behind and triggered about forty rounds from his twin .50s, two armor-piercing bullets for each visible tracer. The fighter fell off on its port wing and spun into the water.[17]

Dickinson proudly noted three carriers burning fiercely and exploding as he moved away. He witnessed an enormous orange-black explosion on his own target *Kaga* that he estimated to be twelve hundred feet above the water. *Kaga* appeared to erupt from her middle in a ball of fire that mushroomed up through the lower clouds as aviation fuel exploded. The fireball, also witnessed by Dusty Kleiss, came just moments after the first *Enterprise* bomb hits. This was followed by six more powerful blasts.[18]

Dickinson's thoughts immediately turned to his dire fuel situation. The only planes he could see ahead of him were streaking away. *I can't afford the gasoline to go wide-open trying to catch up with them. My inboard tanks each register thirty gallons. If we have to go no more than 150 or 175 miles on the return flight, sixty gallons ought to be enough, if I am careful. It might not get me aboard but it will get me back.*

After Lieutenant Joe Penland pulled out from diving on *Kaga*, ARM2c Harold Heard informed him that their dive flaps were still open. Penland cranked his flaps closed, and his airspeed fell off enough to allow a Zero to slide in behind him. He pushed his throttle forward but found three Zeros locked onto his tail. They had blasted his 6-B-7 and punctured its fuel tanks by the time he reached the safety of a cloud formation.[19]

Penland emerged from the cloud bank spewing gasoline into his slip-stream. He was relieved to see a friendly SBD moving to catch up with him. It was John Van Buren, leader of VB-6's third division, who slid up alongside with his 6-B-13. Van Buren signaled that he would remain with Penland, whose fuel was being rapidly depleted.

He made it only thirty miles away. Penland's engine coughed and sputtered as his tanks ran dry, and he began his descent toward the ocean. He turned into the wind to ease his landing and noted that Van Buren flashed past him as he was about a hundred feet over the water. Van Buren gave a final wave before disappearing, leaving Penland and Heard to scramble out of their rapidly sinking SBD and into their life raft.

Mac McCarthy was on his own. He had become separated from his division leader when Lieutenant Dickinson lost airspeed while trying to retract his landing

Ensign Mac McCarthy.

U.S. Navy

gear. McCarthy found it was impossible to stay behind him without stalling his own SBD. He gave up efforts to slow down when gunner Earl Howell suddenly called out from the rear cockpit. "Mr. McCarthy, there's a Zero climbing onto our tail!"[20]

McCarthy dived for the deck with the Zero well placed on his tail. Howell alertly called out the Zero's position and urged his pilot to bank to port. There was a chattering burst of Browning .30-caliber machine-gun fire from the rear seat and Howell yelled, "I think I got him." Howell would later receive credit for two kills plus an assist during VS-6's return flight. McCarthy caught a fleeting glimpse of the Zero erupting in flames and dropping toward the ocean surface. He felt a brief sense of relief. His first brush with Zeros at Pearl Harbor had not turned out so well. It had cost him his aircraft, the life of his rear gunner, and a broken leg.[21]

McCarthy sought the company of other SBDs for mutual firepower. He came upon Charlie Ware, who was grouping with Carl Peiffer and Jim Shelton. McCarthy, next in experience and seniority behind Ware, slid into the little group with two other VS-6 pilots, ensigns Frank O'Flaherty and Johnny Lough. Ware had drilled division defensive tactics into his VS-6 pilots, valuable skills he had learned early in the war from Lieutenant Commander Bill Burch while serving under him in VS-5. McCarthy's trio had just taken station above Ware's section when more Zeros buzzed in to attack.[22]

Twelve .30-caliber free gun mounts were able to bear on each fighter that came within range. McCarthy thought the tracer display was very impressive as well as effective. The Zeros made singular attacks, failing to press home their runs in groups. Ware dropped his SBD formation close to the water in order to deny the Zeros the chance to recover under their unprotected bellies. He wisely cut the speed of his group to 115 knots, or about 133 miles per hour, in order to conserve their scant fuel supplies. From an altitude of ten thousand feet, the Japanese fighters could plunge in at speeds exceeding three hundred miles per hour.[23]

McCarthy realized that few of his companions had enough fuel to survive this flight. *We are not all going to make it back to the carrier we came from*, he thought. Charlie Ware had chosen to comply with the original directions to retire toward Midway, and he led his little formation away from the blazing carriers. The Zero activity tapered off after about eight miles of action, and Ware's group was able to begin their return leg toward *Enterprise*. The six SBDs gradually climbed to twelve hundred feet and adjusted their advance to save fuel. McCarthy experimented a little further with the mixture by selecting a control setting just ahead of "idle cutoff."[24]

Mac began carefully sweating out the details necessary for making it home. He had already been airborne more than four hours. *If I can just keep my engine from crapping out, I might be able to squeeze out another twenty gallons of fuel. That pocket fuel will be above my division's average.* McCarthy figured he just might get his old war-weary SBD back after all. His calculations were interrupted as he caught sight of Lieutenant Ware's lead three planes suddenly diving toward the water.[25]

He followed and quickly spotted the reason for Ware's action— another group of Japanese aircraft were on their tails and climbing from two thousand feet altitude. The formation was the attack group from *Hiryu* that was destined to assault *Yorktown*. From this group, another Zero contingent appeared red-hot to fight, according to McCarthy.[26]

Ware snugged up his SBDs to again allow the rear gunners to bunch their firepower. McCarthy and his companions resumed defensive tactics, sliding and weaving as tracers laced the sky about them. Within five minutes, Frank O'Flaherty's Dauntless was exhausted of fuel and he headed for the water. His fuel tanks had been pierced during the earlier Zero battle. To his right, McCarthy watched his wingman ditch, noting that O'Flaherty's propeller blades bent over the cowl as his SBD hit the ocean. From his rear seat, Earl Howell reported that O'Flaherty and Gaido escaped their Dauntless and scrambled safely into their rubber raft.[27]

U.S. Navy

Ensign Frank O'Flaherty.

Ware brilliantly led his remaining five SBDs through the long encounter with the Zeros without further loss. In hindsight, Ensign McCarthy felt that Ware did one of the most remarkable

Douglas SBD Dauntless dive bombers of Scouting Six (VS-6) soar above USS *Enterprise* on October 27, 1941. On the morning of December 7, 6-S-14 (*top*) was flown by Ensign Edward Deacon as the *Enterprise*'s SBDs were attacked by Japanese aircraft while approaching Pearl Harbor. Below Deacon's SBD is 6-S-7, flown by Lieutenant (j.g.) Dale Hilton with rear gunner RM2c Jack Leaming.

Lieutenant Commander Howard Leyland "Brigham" Young, the Enterprise Air Group Commander (CEAG). Young led his Dauntless aviators into Pearl Harbor on the morning of the surprise Japanese attack.

The tail wreckage of Ensign Mac McCarthy's SBD photographed weeks after the Pearl Harbor attack. The VS-6 pilot suffered a broken leg after bailing out of his burning plane.

Aboard the Japanese carrier *Akagi*, a Mitsubishi A6M "Zero" fighter of the second strike group warms up for takeoff on December 7. Aichi D3A1 "Val" dive bombers are seen in the background.

Pearl Harbor is under attack as *Enterprise* SBDs make their landing approaches. The battleship *California* is slowly sinking near Ford Island while other U.S. ships burn in the background.

Lieutenant Dick Dickinson (*left*) of Scouting Six received his second Navy Cross in three days for sinking the Japanese submarine *I-70*. In a photo taken on May 12, 1941, *I-70* (*above*) is seen after a collision with a sister submarine.

Lieutenant (j.g.) John Van Buren in the VB-6 ready room, just before the Marshall Islands strike on February 1, 1942. Behind him (*left*) is Ensign Bucky Walters, who later disappeared in May during a scouting mission. Van Buren was lost at sea after ditching at Midway.

Bomb-armed *Enterprise* SBDs launch to attack Japanese installations in the Marshalls, America's first offensive carrier strike. Note the hundred-pound bombs under each wing.

Enterprise flight deck crews quickly reload returning SBDs with five-hundred-pound bombs as the Marshalls strikes continue.

A U.S. cruiser floatplane from Task Force 8 flies above Wotje Island on February 1 after the SBD strike. Note the ships anchored offshore.

This SBD was sheared in half on the carrier deck by a Japanese kamikaze bomber, which was fired upon by VS-6's Bruno Peter Gaido from the rear seat of the Dauntless. Admiral Halsey promoted Gaido on the spot for his bravery.

Moisture-laden air creates halo rings around the propeller of an SBD taking off for Wake Island on February 24. Perry Teaff of VS-6 crashed overboard due to this effect, injuring him and killing his gunner.

Pilots gather in the Big E's Torpedo Six ready room in early 1942: (*front, left to right*) Ensign Irvin McPherson, Lieutenant Art Ely, and Ensign Severin Rombach; (*middle, left to right*) Ensign Edward Heck, Lieutenant (j.g.) Lloyd Thomas, and Lieutenant Donald White; (*rear, at far left*) Ensign Glenn Hodges and two unidentified pilots. Many of these men would be lost at Midway.

Smoke rises from Wake Island on February 24 during the *Enterprise* air strikes as a Torpedo Six Devastator flies over.

Flight operations often included tense moments, as evidenced by this SBD of Bombing Six, which caught an arresting wire and slid into *Enterprise*'s port catwalk while landing in early 1942.

Dauntless bombers pack *Enterprise*'s forward flight deck, preparing for a strike in March. Note the coverings being removed from the cockpits and tail surfaces.

Admiral Bill Halsey (*right*) stands with his chief of staff, Captain Miles Browning (*left*), aboard *Enterprise*. Halsey, a qualified naval aviator, was popular with his men, while Browning was despised by many SBD pilots.

Lieutenant Colonel Jimmy Doolittle's Army B-25 bombers are spotted on the flight deck of the new carrier *Hornet* as she heads for Tokyo in April.

Lieutenant (j.g.) Ozzie Wiseman of Bombing Three drops a beanbag message on the deck of *Enterprise* on May 18. The message reported that Japanese vessels had been sighted as the Doolittle force approaches Tokyo.

Lieutenant Commander Wade McClusky, the new Commander, *Enterprise* Air Group, receives a Distinguished Flying Cross from Admiral Chester Nimitz on the Big E's flight deck at Pearl Harbor on May 27, just before Midway. At far right is mess attendant Doris Miller, awarded the Navy Cross for his heroism on December 7. To Miller's right are Lieutenant (j.g.) Cleo Dobson and Lieutenant (j.g.) Dusty Kleiss, both Scouting Six pilots also being decorated.

A Fighting Six Wildcat lifts off from *Enterprise*'s flight deck on the morning of June 4 at Midway. More F4Fs and SBDs are spotted aft.

The Japanese carrier *Kaga*, viewed here in 1939, was the target for VS-6 pilots on June 4. Built in 1926, she had a starboard side island structure and displaced 42,500 tons when fully loaded.

Hornet's Air Group prepares to launch on June 4 at Midway. Spotted forward are Commander Pat Mitchell's Wildcat fighters. The first SBD in the center of the flight deck, with a five-hundred-pound bomb underneath, is manned by Ensign Clayton Fisher of VB-8. Fisher was wingman this day for Commander Stan Ring.

The Japanese carrier *Soryu*, viewed in 1938, was attacked by *Yorktown*'s Bombing Three on June 4. Commissioned in 1937, she had a starboard side island structure like *Kaga* and, fully loaded, displaced 19,500 tons.

Ensign George Goldsmith's shot-up 6-B-15 from *Enterprise*, with Jim Patterson in the rear seat, just after landing on *Yorktown* at about 1150 on June 4.

Patterson climbs from his rear seat as his SBD is pushed forward.

Tall, lanky RM2c Oral "Slim" Moore looks on as his pilot, Ensign Doug Carter, points to friendly-fire damage their Dauntless suffered over Midway on June 4.

Ten SBDs of Scouting Five were launched from *Yorktown* after 1130 to locate the carrier *Hiryu*. Ensign Leif Larsen is seen here warming up his 5-B-17.

Yorktown blazes after taking three direct bomb hits, forcing returning pilots to seek out refuge on *Enterprise*.

Yorktown's crew abandons ship as destroyers stand by to pick them up.

Unable to land on the badly damaged *Yorktown*, Lieutenant (j.g.) Paul Holmberg ditches near the cruiser *Astoria*. He and his gunner, George LaPlant, were picked up by the cruiser.

Moments later, Lieutenant Commander Max Leslie also ditches near *Astoria*.

Astoria's motor whaleboat heads over to retrieve Leslie and rear gunner Bill Gallagher. Near the base of *Astoria*'s crane, Holmberg and LaPlant watch their skipper's rescue.

Eleven VB-8 Dauntlesses returned just as *Hornet* prepared to launch her strike against *Hiryu*. In this photo, a Bombing Eight pilot lands well off center, narrowly missing the LSO's head. Three other planes are seen at top, waiting to land.

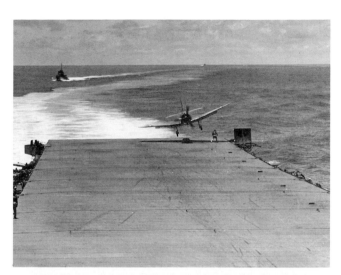

The carrier *Hiryu* is seen under attack by Air Force B-17s from Midway. Note bomb splashes far to her starboard side. Eager Air Force pilots would quickly claim credit for sinking Japanese carriers in spite of their failed efforts.

U.S. Air Force

Bombing Three's AOM2c Clifton Bassett is carried across *Enterprise*'s flight deck in a stretcher after suffering a serious shrapnel wound in his right knee during the *Hiryu* attack. His pilot, Ensign Randy Cooner, is walking directly behind the group.

Hiryu lies dead in the water, burning heavily from the bomb damage caused by *Enterprise* strike group. Note the extensive damage and open pit where her forward aircraft elevator has been blown away.

Another view of the mortally wounded *Hiryu*, photographed late on June 4.

The Japanese destroyer *Tanikaze* managed to evade more than forty bombs dropped on her by American Dauntless pilots on June 5.

Mikuma burns below as a pair of Scouting Eight SBDs from *Hornet* prepare to dive during their second strike of June 6.

Mikuma ablaze from numerous bomb hits.

Mikuma is dead in the water as destroyer *Asashio* or *Arashio* stands by to rescue crewmen. This photograph was taken by John Tereskerz, who was looking back past the tail of his VS-8 SBD.

Mikuma's remains—note her drooping gun barrels and the wreckage of her forward guns.

Four Bombing Six gunners who survived Midway pose on board *Enterprise*, August 1942: (*from left*) ARM2c Harold Heard, AMM1c William Steinman, ARM2c Stuart Mason, and AMM2c Herman Caruthers.

Dusty Kleiss of Scouting Six kisses his new bride, Jean, upon receiving his Navy Cross in 1942. They married just weeks after America's victory at Midway.

Bombing Six skipper Dick Best (*left*) is reunited with his rear gunner, Jim Murray, in 1983 at a Midway convention.

jobs of flying under all combat problems known during the first six months of World War II. He had led his squadron mates through multiple Zero attacks while conserving their fuel as best as the situation allowed.[28]

Once the Zeros departed, McCarthy felt that it was anybody's best guess as to where the Big E might be. Still, his own calculations went against the course that Lieutenant Ware was determined to fly. *Charlie is heading too far north. By my best guess, he's twenty-five degrees off course.* McCarthy simply could not maintain his position in good faith. He throttled up beside Ware's lead SBD to confer.[29]

Radio silence was a strict order, so McCarthy gestured his intentions with hand motions. He pointed in the direction that he felt Point Option would be found and held up two fingers to indicate that Ware should turn at least twenty degrees.

Ware only waved his hand straight ahead. *We're going straight.*

McCarthy repeated his hand-signal appeal in hopes of convincing his flight leader of the better option. Ware acknowledged his junior pilot's intentions with a hand-to-the-head break-off signal. The meaning was clear. *You're on your own, Ensign. Good luck. Kiss off.*

With that, Charlie Ware continued on his course with Shelton and Lough in tow. McCarthy veered onto his own course and but found that his wingman, Carl Peiffer, had plans of his own. Peiffer decided he had a better intuition on the course, so he broke to starboard on another fifteen- to twenty-degree course differential. Ware's three planes and Peiffer became mere specks in the distance within fifteen minutes. Young Mac and his gunner were on their own.[30]

Their eight comrades would never be seen again.

Peiffer, Ware, Lough, and Shelton all took courses that led them only to empty ocean. At some point, they were all forced to ditch and take their chances on the open seas in their life rafts. Neither these four pilots nor their gunners—ARM3c Frederick Jeck, ARM1c Bill Stambaugh, RM3c Lou "Speed" Hansen, and RM3c Dave Craig—had the good fortune to be recovered by friendly search planes in the days that followed.

Dusty Kleiss and his gunner, John Snowden, proceeded toward home. About forty miles from Midway, Kleiss climbed to pick up the homing signal. He suddenly spotted a Japanese fighter ahead, poking out of the clouds and heading directly toward him. He prepared to open fire, but the Zero changed course into a cloud bank when still one mile out. Dusty changed course to the right, and headed after him. In the cloud formation, however, the opponents lost each other, and Kleiss finally turned back toward Midway.[31]

Bombing Six was also hounded during its retirement. The last section to attack *Kaga* had been that of Lieutenant (j.g.) Bill Roberts and Ensign Pete Halsey. They were jumped by Zeros before they could catch another group of retiring SBDs in the distance, and Halsey's fuel tanks were perforated.[32]

The pair soon caught up to Ensign Norm Vandivier. He had retired low on the water, but turned in to each attacker to allow rear gunner Lee Keaney a chance to open fire. Roberts, technically the senior pilot of the trio, was content to have himself and Halsey fall in behind Vandivier because of the deep respect he had for Vandivier's flying ability. Moments later a fourth SBD was spotted coming up from their starboard, and Vandivier turned the group to allow it to catch up.[33]

It was 6-B-15, piloted by George Goldsmith. His rear gunner, Jim Patterson, saw his best friend in VB-6, Keaney, still seated at his guns in the rear of Vandivier's SBD. The little group was almost immediately jumped by a group of Japanese fighters. They were flying right down on the water, and the Japanese made many passes on them. From his cockpit, Goldsmith could see the bullets hitting the water ahead of him. Other rounds quickly began finding their mark, however.[34]

Goldsmith's Dauntless was already riddled. Fighters had been waiting for his plane as he pulled out of his dive on *Kaga*. As he joined with Vandivier, Goldsmith's bomber was ripped by both 7.7mm and 20mm fire. He felt the Zeros had so much speed on his little group that they flew circles around the Americans. "We were pulled into tight formation. They would climb above us, dive, make their firing run, go on past and underneath us," said Goldsmith. "Then they would pull up in front of us in a sheer zoom."[35]

His SBD was shot to pieces. "We just had to sit there and take it," Goldsmith said. His tail was chewed up, and the elevator trim tab was shot completely away. He wound up flying by holding the stick with both hands to keep the nose down. Another 20mm round punched a fist-size hole through Goldsmith's right inboard fuel tank, but the self-sealing tank functioned as advertised. In addition, his right wing and after cockpit were holed, and his radio and ZB homing equipment were destroyed.

Goldsmith estimated that the Zeros made about six passes against his group of planes. Another bullet made a direct hit on gunner Jim Patterson's twin-mount Browning machine gun, striking the bolt mechanism. Patterson opened his safety belt, stood up, and leaned out to fix his mount. At this inopportune moment, another Zero unleashed a torrent of 7.7mm fire toward Goldsmith's SBD. Patterson was winged in the arm and in his hip by three bullets. He fastened his lap belt again. Although his wounds stung badly, he found that he could at least return fire with only one shot at a time. The last Zero finally pulled up on the port side, very close to his dive-bomber. Patterson felt the Zero was out of ammo, for the pilot just stared at him for a few seconds, and then broke away.[36]

Two more Bombing Six Dauntlesses—those of Andy Anderson and Ensign Bert Varian—joined Vandivier's group just as the Zeros hit. On its first firing pass on Anderson's SBD, one of the Zeros ripped bullets into the rear cockpit, damaging the radio, destroying the interphone, and shredding fabric. Some of the enemy's ammunition was incendiary type, and Anderson considered himself lucky indeed that none went through his fuel tanks. The explosions sent shrapnel ripping through the flesh of gunner Stuart Mason, who began bleeding severely.[37]

"My goggles were covered with blood and I couldn't see, so I had to take them off," he said. "Then my eyes filled with blood." He had been hit in the face and legs with shrapnel. Nonetheless, Mason doggedly fought back against his opponents. He burned through a hundred-round can of .30-caliber ammunition and then swiftly loaded the next. Mason finished another ammo can, tossed the empties over the side of his cockpit, and loaded one after another.[38]

The Zeros took their toll on Anderson's wingmates in the heated dogfight. Varian's 6-B-18 had its fuel tanks punctured, as did Pete Halsey's 6-B-6, which began sputtering as his fuel ran dry shortly before the Zeros departed. Halsey announced over the radio that he was making a forced landing. Anderson and Varian continued on with their crippled SBDs, while Vandivier, Goldsmith, and Roberts circled once to watch the ensign make a perfect, powerless water landing. Halsey and his gunner, RM3c Jay Jenkins, were last seen climbing into their rubber raft.[39]

Andy Anderson's Dauntless hung on in spite of the damage it had suffered. Radioman Mason was shooting from ammunition cans seven and eight—a separate can for each .30-caliber gun—by the time their battered dive-bomber escaped the nest of Zeros.[40]

Mason, bloodied and dazed, now found that his plane was all alone. He realized later that he was in a slight state of shock from serious blood loss. His radio gear was badly shot up, and their plane's intercom was not functioning. Andy Anderson finally got his attention by giving his control stick a good shake and then passing back a note asking whether Mason could get their ZB direction finder working. His pilot also passed him his dirty windshield rag to use to wipe off his face, a little event Mason later found to be quite amusing. At the time, however, he was more than happy to use the dirty rag to blot some of the heavy bleeding from his face.[41]

There were other light moments in the deadly scrap. AMM1c Bill Steinman called his pilot, Bill Roberts, on the interphone in the heat of the shooting, saying that he'd been badly hit. Roberts tried to talk to his radioman, but received no reply. *He must be dead*, he thought. Soon after the Zeros departed, Steinman got back on the intercom, chipper as could be.[42]

"Say, Mr. Roberts, wouldn't you like me to take a picture of number fifteen there with all the holes in it?" Steinman asked.

It was like hearing a voice from the grave, Roberts thought. He glanced over to wingman Goldsmith's 6-B-15, and found it to be amazingly shot up. Roberts advised Steinman to snap away with his camera, which he did.

Steinman's wound had not been as deadly as Roberts thought. One of the Zero's bullets had ricocheted through the rear cockpit, finally passing through Steinman's lower lip. The spent piece of warm lead literally came to rest in his mouth. "The bleeding of his lip and his confusion caused him at first to think he was badly hurt," Roberts said. "Luckily, he wasn't at all." Their plane had taken eight bullets but sustained no heavy damage. Steinman was able to maintain his composure to use their SBD's Zed Baker to home in on the Big E for the return flight.[43]

Norm Vandivier continued his retirement in company with Goldsmith and Roberts. They were soon joined by John Van Buren, who had recently lost Joe Penland to a water landing. Van Buren took the lead of the quartet, with Vandivier on his wing and Goldsmith forming up on Roberts. The four VB-6 pilots, free of the deadly Zeros, began climbing slowly in the direction of the Big E.

*H*ornet's luckless fighters and dive-bombers escaped the wrath of the Japanese Zeros but still lost many planes en route home. Pat Mitchell's ten Wildcats approached Task Force 16 shortly after 1000, but began running out of fuel before they could find a flight deck on which to land. Singly and in groups, all ten *Hornet* strike group F4Fs were forced to ditch in the ocean by 1045.

The *Hornet* SBDs had better luck in preserving their planes. They were picked up by *Hornet*'s radar around 1100, and their carrier quickly cleared her decks of CAP fighters in order to land the fuel-starved Dauntlesses. CHAG Stan Ring was first to land on *Hornet*, followed by sixteen of Walt Rodee's Scouting Eight SBDs and Bombing Eight's Clay Fisher of the CHAG section.

Rodee had relied on his YE-ZB homing equipment for VS-8, which took him right back to the carrier. Ensign Fisher trailed Scouting Eight back to *Hornet* and was the first from his unit to land. He made his way to the squadron ready room, and was greeted by the stay-behind junior pilots of VB-8. Ensign Frank Christofferson, quite upset, exclaimed, "Fisher, you're the only one who's returned from our squadron. None of the fighter or torpedo pilots have gotten back yet."[44]

Lieutenant Gus Widhelm made it on board but was sick at the losses his air group had suffered. Commander Ring immediately retired to his cabin, leaving Walt Rodee to report alone to the bridge on what had gone wrong. The only other planes of *Hornet*'s strike group to appear around 1145 were Lieutenant Abbie Tucker of VB-8 and his two wingmen, Gus Bebas and Don Adams. Four planes from Bombing Eight had returned, but another fourteen dive-bombers were absent. Tucker could offer little explanation of their whereabouts. Fortunately for Captain Pete Mitscher, *Hornet* soon received word from Midway around 1200 that eleven SBDs had landed safely.[45]

Troy Guillory faced a sudden crisis around 1030. He was flying the dud VB-8 Dauntless that a senior pilot had refused to fly. The reduction gear in his engine came apart and his propeller flew off with a big bang. Guillory's SBD, still some 150 miles from Midway, plunged for the waves, where he made a good water landing. He and ARM2c Billy Cotrell scrambled into their life raft without injury and waited out the day. John Lynch, Guillory's section leader, watched his wingman go in and waited to see that he was safe. Lynch carefully noted the position to help effect a rescue if possible.[46]

Lieutenant Commander Ruff Johnson had a plan. He made contact with a retiring PBY patrol plane and learned the course to Midway, so he decided to take his thirteen remaining SBDs there to refuel. Their fuel situation was critical. As Bombing Eight approached the atoll, Ensign Tom Wood was the next to go down, his tanks empty. That morning, he had boasted to his squadron mates that he would personally sink the flagship *Akagi. I know I'll have to eat my words,* he thought as he put his Dauntless in the drink near Midway. Ensign Jim Riner watched his fellow pilot go down and circled around long enough to see Wood and his gunner, ARM3c George Martz, climb into their rubber raft.[47]

Johnson realized his planes lacked the proper identification as they approached Midway. Lieutenant Moe Vose recalled that it was an even-numbered day and that the identification procedure was to make left turns and dip their left wing twice. He fully expected the Marine gunners to fire at his bombers even with the proper signal. In order to show that his aircraft were friendly, Johnson ordered his pilots to jettison their bombs off the reef. Vose found this only increased the friendly fire from shore. He realized the bomb explosions gave them the impression that they were Japanese planes trying to blast a channel through the coral reef.[48]

Midway sounded the air raid alarm at 1115 as the *Hornet* bombs exploded in the water, and its gunners immediately opened fire. Three VB-8 SBDs were hit before they could be properly identified by the Marines. John Lynch's Dauntless was struck by shrapnel behind the cockpit. Bullets clattered off the canopy right behind the head of ARM2c Slim Moore in Ensign Doug Carter's rear seat. "A piece of shrapnel took out our hydraulic gear, something very important," said Moore. "Doug had the wheels down, so we were able to land."[49]

A third Bombing Eight Dauntless was unable to reach the airstrip. Ensign Forrester "Joe" Auman exhausted his gas and was forced to ditch in Midway's lagoon. *PT-28* was dispatched at 1141 to effect the rescue of Auman and his gunner, ARM3c Samuel McLean. Eleven VB-8 planes did manage to land on Midway in order to refuel and head back to *Hornet* as soon as possible.[50]

Ensign Ken White was the last of his tail-end VB-8 division to land after three of his comrades had ditched. He went straight in, low on gas, without attempting to dodge any flak. White's gunner, ARM3c Lee Quillen, talked with a B-17 crew and learned that Torpedo Eight had found the Japanese carriers and pressed home their attacks. Quillen surveyed his surroundings on Midway, and saw hangars and gasoline tanks still burning from the Japanese strike.[51]

Moe Vose found some of the local command was relieved by the presence of U.S. carrier aircraft only a short while after the Japanese had pounded their installations. John Lynch quickly alerted the air/sea rescue group as to the position where Troy Guillory had gone in. Lynch then ran into two old friends, now Marine aviators. When Lynch asked one of his buddies for a drink of water, he was handed a canteen filled with straight bourbon.[52]

Ensign Roy Gee watched as ground crews worked to refuel their planes. The Marines used gasoline drums, since their fuel trucks had been disabled by the attack. *Hornet*'s air group was effectively out of the carrier battle on June 4, badly scattered and half of its number in the ocean.[53]

Ensign Mike Micheel of VS-6 was unsure of the way home. He cleared the Japanese task force without being attacked but found no other SBDs waiting at the squadron's rendezvous spot. Micheel took a guess as to the course back to the Big E and departed. He was low on fuel and all alone, and was "starting to pucker."[54]

Minutes later, John Dance called out from the backseat. Two dive-bombers were coming up on their starboard quarter. They zoomed by in front of Micheel's SBD and he recognized them as Tom Ramsay and Lew Hopkins of VB-6. *I'll tag along with them*, he thought. *Three together is better than being alone.* Ramsay's group was moving faster than Micheel wanted to go in order to preserve fuel, but he applied just enough throttle to keep them within eyesight in the distance. *They look like they know where they're going.*

Lew Hopkins had encountered a Zero that closed on his port beam shortly after he had pulled out of his dive. Rear gunner Ed Anderson did not see the fighter until it started zooming away. Hopkins was jinking and weaving about, and once Anderson swung his guns around to line up on the fighter, it was gone. Hopkins then went to work on his plotting board to figure out just where in the hell he was. He caught up to Ramsay and moments later they were joined by Ensign Gene Greene, also of Bombing Six. Hopkins spent the balance of his flight closely monitoring his low-fuel situation. He, Ramsay, and Green throttled back to a slower speed to maximize their distance toward the task force.[55]

The *Enterprise* SBDs still airborne were widely scattered. One of the larger clusters was that of Bombing Six's Van Buren, Vandivier, Roberts, and Goldsmith. Ten minutes after the Zeros had finally left them, Vandivier signaled that he was heading down, his riddled plane finally out of fuel. Jim Patterson in George Goldsmith's rear seat felt a great sense of loss as he watched one of his best friends, Lee Keaney, go into the ocean with Vandivier's 6-B-14. *It is a very helpless feeling not to be able to do anything for them,* Goldsmith thought as he circled above Vandivier's crew manning their life raft.[56]

Five minutes later, Van Buren dropped out of formation. He glided down toward the ocean and made an effective splash landing. Radioman Patterson watched as Van Buren and his gunner, ARM1c Harry Nelson, climbed out of their sinking Dauntless and manned their life raft. Patterson's pilot did not opt to circle over this second downed crew. *We can do nothing to help and gas is critical,* thought Goldsmith. He was blindly following Bill Roberts, as his own plane's radio and antenna post had been shot out of commission. Goldsmith learned through an exchange of hand signals that Roberts's radio and homing device were also not working.[57]

The Bombing Six section of Andy Anderson and Bert Varian was also struggling toward home. Varian's damaged fuel tanks ran dry about fifty miles northeast of the Japanese fleet. He signaled Anderson that he was making a water landing. Anderson saw Varian land but did not have the fuel to loiter and check his condition. Varian and his gunner, ARM3c Charles Young, were seen to climb into their life raft.[58]

Mac McCarthy was still hoping to make it home. He had opted to leave his VS-6 squadron mates, and climbed to thirty-five hundred feet to turn on his YE-ZB very high-frequency homing beacon. His two outboard fuel tanks were exhausted and he was working on the remnants of his two smaller inboard tanks. McCarthy and Howell discussed their situation and agreed that removing excess weight was most important for conserving fuel. Howell shot his remaining .30-caliber ammunition and tossed the spent cans overboard while his pilot emptied his two forward .50-caliber guns. *At this point, it's been five hours since we launched, and a lot can happen to home base in that time in a carrier duel*, thought McCarthy.[59]

McCarthy then asked Howell to try tuning their YE-ZB in to the *Yorktown* frequency. Howell announced in minutes that he had *Yorktown* loud and clear. *What a radioman I have on board*, McCarthy thought. He then lowered his altitude and made a beeline for *Yorktown*. Spotting a TBD floating in the water to his left as he approached Task Force 17, he flew over the downed Devastator crew, waggling his wings before heading for the nearest destroyer. About halfway to the tin can, McCarthy's luck—and his remaining fuel—finally gave out.[60]

His engine quit with only 150 feet of altitude. McCarthy dropped his plane's nose, leveled off above the wave tops, and waited for the impact. But his plane was too light for an easy landing. His tanks were dry, all extra weight having been emptied en route home, so McCarthy struggled to put his SBD in the drink. He flared his plane to try to mush softly into the water, but he found that it would not sink down. His engine quit with a final sputter, and his dive-bomber then dropped like a rock. In his excitement, McCarthy allowed one of his wings to drop. As it caught a wave top, his Dauntless cartwheeled—wingtop to wingtip—and plowed into the ocean.

The force of the crash slammed McCarthy into his control panel. Salt water flooding his cockpit brought him back to his senses. His face was spewing blood from deep lacerations and a broken nose. He knew he had only seconds before his Dauntless would bubble under the waves and drag him to the bottom of the Pacific. He heard Howell yelling from the wing, "Mac, you're hurt!"[61]

Howell extracted their life raft as water filled the cockpit. McCarthy's facial injuries would require some work. His broken nose would leave him with two badly blackened eyes, and the gashes in his face would require seventeen stitches. The pair managed to clamber aboard their life raft with both of their parachutes. They jettisoned one parachute, found the oars, and McCarthy tied a scarf around his forehead to keep the blood out of his eyes. They began paddling "Indian fashion" before McCarthy thought to use the Very signal pistol he had salvaged. It fired as designed, and he watched in awe as the beautiful red star shot skyward.[62]

Commander Arnold True's destroyer *Hammann* moved in. His sailors were throwing lines to Howell and McCarthy's life raft within five minutes. Once McCarthy was stitched and bandaged, he hurried to check on the recovery of the downed TBD crew he had spotted. It was that of Chief Bill Esders and radioman Mike Brazier of *Yorktown*'s Torpedo Three. Esders had successfully ditched his Devastator around 1305, but young Brazier soon bled to death while in their life raft.

His last two hours of life had been truly heroic. Brazier had been hit at least seven times with 7.7mm ammo and twice with 20mm explosive projectiles. "As if the small-caliber wounds were not enough, the 20mms exploded, blowing away all the flesh on his legs between the knees and ankles," said Esders. "However, despite his enormous wounds, Mike somehow managed to change the coils in the radio receiver and helped me steer closer to the task force, where we ditched."[63]

Esders was nearly killed when a *Hiryu* plane circled to make a strafing run on his raft. Fortunately, Lieutenant (j.g.) Art Brassfield of VF-3 arrived in time to shoot down the Japanese plane. Guided in by circling SBDs, *Hammann* hauled aboard Chief Esders and Brazier. McCarthy thought that Brazier was still alive, in a rigid state of shock on the wardroom table. He soon learned, however, that the gallant VT-3 gunner had already expired from his terrible wounds.[64]

McCarthy and Howell spent the remainder of the day on *Hammann*, helping to tend to other wounded men who were pulled from the sea. Howell found friends in the CPO quarters, while his pilot took Commander True's invitation to rest in the skipper's cabin. They both found comfort in their sleep but would be troubled later to learn of their good fortune. Of the six SBDs that had retired together from the carrier strike, they were the only VS-6 crew to survive. Ware, Shelton, O'Flaherty, Peiffer, and Lough had all been lost with their gunners.[65]

The *Enterprise* SBDs dropped into the Pacific at an alarming rate between the Japanese task force and their own fleet. Some very nearly made it home.

Radioman Ed Anderson of Bombing Six knew it would be close. His pilot, Lew Hopkins, was wisely conserving their precious fuel as they kept company with VB-6 squadron mates Gene Greene and Tom Ramsay. During the return, Anderson hand-signaled back and forth with RM3c Sammy Muntean, a young man of Portuguese ancestry who had attained flight status back in April at the same time. From Greene's rear seat, Muntean kept Anderson apprised of their fuel status.

Muntean signaled to Anderson that they were making an ocean landing near the task force. Their fuel was gone. Anderson watched Ensign Greene peel off and head for the water. He followed him all the way down and saw their blue-gray SBD make a splash landing. Both men were seen to climb into their yellow rubber life raft. "There wasn't anything we could do but continue on," Anderson said. "They were never recovered. That's just the way it was."

Hopkins climbed to higher altitude to help determine whether he was on the proper heading. Anderson worked intently in the rear seat with his head down, tuning the little ZB black box. After much careful tuning, he finally announced that he had the proper heading.

Ensign Ramsay made it even closer to *Enterprise*. He and Hopkins had just spotted their own fleet about twenty miles away when Ramsay's rear gunner, AMM2c Sherman Duncan, signaled his buddy Ed Anderson that they were out of gas at that moment. Ramsay's engine gasped and died. He made a forced landing some fifteen miles short of home base. Hopkins and Anderson watched both Ramsay and Duncan climb safely into their life raft. Their own fuel situation was so dire, however, that they could do nothing but press on.

Dick Dickinson of Scouting Six also nearly made it back to *Enterprise*. His starboard tank ran dry when the gauge still read seventeen gallons. *I felt as if the devil had just stolen seventeen gallons from me,*

Dickinson thought. He switched to his port tank and warned DeLuca to prepare for a water landing. Minutes later, he was surprised to see Norm West coming up on his tail rapidly. West took formation on his XO and the pair soon sighted their own fleet, fifty miles away.[66]

Twenty miles short of the task force, Dickinson's engine began to miss as the last of its fuel was consumed. He called for a ship to pick him up, but there was no acknowledgment. On his second call, he received a reply as West kept close watch on him. Dick's fuel gauge was stuck on zero, so he nursed his sputtering Dauntless toward a destroyer that was tailing the fleet. He and DeLuca braced themselves for the crash. Their SBD went into the drink at eighty miles per hour, the force of the impact throwing Dickinson's cheek into the bombsight. DeLuca was facing forward for the landing, and the brunt tore the frame holding his twin machine guns. The aviators climbed out onto either wing and tried to haul out their rubber boat. Dickinson saw the destroyer coming and shouted to DeLuca to jump clear to avoid being pulled down by the Dauntless's tail section. Their plane sank nose-first in less than forty-five seconds.[67]

"I'm glad we're back," the gunner said. "Just enough gasoline."

"Gasoline! DeLuca, I *prayed* that plane back the last twenty miles."

The destroyer *Phelps* approached and cut her engines. Dickinson told DeLuca not to inflate the raft but to swim to the destroyer now stopped in the water. Two life rings landed near the aviators and they were hauled to the side to crawl up a cargo net. "This was just like getting home," said Dickinson. "She was my old ship. I had lived in her for much of the two years and four months before I went to Pensacola to learn how to fly."[68]

Phelps's doctor bandaged a cut below Dickinson's black eye and tended to his cut lip. The tin can sent a message to *Enterprise* that the two Scouting Six aviators had been picked up. Her transmission that Dickinson had a "slightly scarred face" was received as "scared face." He thought, *Even so, that was close to the truth.*[69]

Of the thirty-three *Enterprise* SBDs launched against the Japanese carriers, sixteen planes failed to return. Tony Schneider of VB-6 had been the first to go into the drink prior to the attacks on *Kaga* and *Akagi*. Seven others from his squadron—Halsey, Penland, Greene, Ramsay, Van Buren, Vandivier, and Varian—had also gone down. From Scouting Six, another eight crews—those of Dickinson, J. Q. Roberts, McCarthy,

Peiffer, Lough, Ware, O'Flaherty, and Shelton—never arrived back. More SBDs might have returned except for a discrepancy in the position of Point Option. *Enterprise* was sixty miles from the briefed coordinates, and even with the aid of the new ZB homing beacon, some pilots did not have enough fuel to make it.

All seventeen of Max Leslie's VB-3 pilots found their way home. Around 1130, they had reached the vicinity of Task Force 17 and were hoping to land. *Yorktown* instead signaled the SBDs to circle while she first brought on board her fuel-starved fighter planes.

Yorktown's bombers had more fuel because they had been launched about an hour and a half after those of *Enterprise*. Lieutenant Commander Leslie's dive-bombers orbited above TF-17 as their carrier cleared her deck. Ten Dauntlesses of Scouting Five were being prepared to scout in pairs to the north and northwest for the enemy carriers. Admiral Fletcher, still lacking knowledge of the morning strike's results, was eager to find the remaining flattops. He had *Yorktown* turn into the wind at 1133 to begin launching the scouts.[70]

Scouting Five's searchers were sent in pairs: Ensign Ben Preston and Lieutenant Johnny Neilsen, Lieutenant Sam Adams and Lieutenant (j.g.) Rockey Dickson, Lieutenant (j.g.) Bill Christie and Lieutenant (j.g.) Hank McDowell, Lieutenant (j.g.) Dave Berry and Lieutenant (j.g.) Duke Berger, and Lieutenant (j.g.) Carl Horenburger with Lieutenant Wally Short. Each plane, armed with a thousand-pound bomb, was sent to search two hundred miles from the ship in sectors ranging from 280 degrees to 020 degrees. Seven armed SBDs of VS-5 remained on the hangar deck for further use as *Yorktown* began landing the returning morning strike. John Bridgers was among those of the reserve strike group. He and his fellow pilots had taxied their planes onto the elevators, parked them on the hangar deck, and then retired to the ready room to wait.[71]

Leslie's VB-3 strikers continued to circle above as *Yorktown* sent out her searchers and then launched and recovered Wildcats from her combat air patrols. Finally, at 1150, her flight deck was opened for business for the Dauntless crews. The first two SBDs to approach the landing circle were not from *Yorktown* but were instead two VB-6 pilots who had happened upon their sister ship while searching for *Enterprise*.

They were Bill Roberts and George Goldsmith. Both were desperately low on fuel. Their return flight had been tense. Jim Patterson had been unable to call the ship or even talk to other planes due to his shot-up radio gear.[72]

Roberts flew past *Yorktown*'s starboard side with his hook down and blipped his throttle to request a forced landing. Yet Goldsmith landed first, running out of gas in the arresting gear. Gunner Jim Patterson looked in his pilot's cockpit after landing and noticed a chunk of metal missing out of the center of his right rudder pedal—obviously knocked away by a direct hit. "I think I was sitting on my feet while they were shooting at us," the uninjured Goldsmith said to Patterson.[73]

Roberts made it on deck with only four gallons of fuel remaining. It was his hundred and eightieth carrier landing, and his would be the last SBD to ever land on the *Yorktown* flight deck. Roberts proceeded to the bridge to make a report to the air command while Goldsmith headed below, helping Patterson to sick bay to have the minor bullet wounds to his arm and rear end tended to. Scouting Five's Tex Conatser noted that rear seat man Bill Steinman had been injured by a bullet. "His lip was bleeding, but he said it didn't hurt much," Conatser said.[74]

Goldsmith stuck around sick bay long enough to make sure that his squadron's two wounded enlisted men were given proper attention. Before the ensign departed, Roberts's gunner, Steinman, handed the officer the spent slug that had come to rest in his mouth. Goldsmith would carry the souvenir from their brush with Japanese Zeros for many years.[75]

Next into the landing pattern on *Yorktown* behind Roberts and Goldsmith were four of Jimmy Thach's VF-3 fighters. Skipper Thach landed first and raced up to flag plot to offer Admiral Fletcher his first assessment of the success of the morning carrier strike. Thach stated that three carriers were burning furiously and were out of commission, while a fourth's condition and location were unknown to him.[76]

Two more of Thach's Wildcats landed in the meantime. The fourth, piloted by machinist Tom F. Cheek, came in with its tail high, missed the cables, and flipped over on its back. Deck crews struggled to hoist the inverted fighter onto dollies and cart it below to the hangar deck. Flight operations were temporarily put on hold and Max Leslie's SBDs were told to continue circling.

. . .

Several miles away, the deck crews of *Enterprise* were also busy pull-ing in fuel-starved morning strike planes. Lieutenant Dick Best of Bombing Six was among the first. His section of *Enterprise* strikers ar-rived in his carrier's landing pattern around 1145. Best was followed down by his wingmen Bud Kroeger and Fred Weber. Best taxied his 6-B-1 forward and his plane was lowered by the number one elevator. On the hangar deck, the lieutenant ordered Jim Murray to stay with their plane while he headed straight for the bridge to report to Admiral Spru-ance.[77]

Meanwhile, Murray exchanged his used .30-caliber ammunition cans for new ones. Maintenance crew swarmed over his Dauntless, refueling and arming it with another thousand-pound bomb. Murray was swamped by ship and air group personnel who wanted to know the results of their attack on the carriers. Their excitement dampened as he related how the Big E's torpedo planes were decimated by the Zeros. He told them it would be lucky if any returned.[78]

Best was intercepted by Miles Browning upon reaching the flag bridge. He told the staff officer that three Japanese carriers were aflame, while a fourth remained untouched. Best informed Browning that he desired to be immediately refueled and sent back out to attack. Air group commander Wade McClusky appeared before the conversation was com-plete, ready to give his own report.[79]

McClusky had found no carrier at Point Option during his return. Climbing to four thousand feet to use his ZB homing device, he had bro-ken radio silence to call Task Force 16's communications officer, Lieu-tenant Commander Leonard "Ham" Dow. "Ham, have you changed Point Option?" he asked. Dow's reply was only, "Wait." Moments later, he offered McClusky a new Point Option that was sixty miles from the previous location.[80]

McClusky homed in at five thousand feet and dropped into the land-ing circle of the first carrier he saw. He was in his downwind leg when he realized it was *Yorktown.* He wanted to report to the admiral, so he pulled up and headed for *Enterprise.* His fuel gauge was flicking danger-ously around the five-gallon mark as he bore in on the Big E some five miles away. Another SBD was in the landing circle and he was given a wave-off. McClusky thumbed his nose good-naturedly at the LSO and came on in anyhow. His battered SBD made it on board with three gallons of fuel remaining at 1150. He had been in the air almost five hours.[81]

McClusky was rushing to the bridge ladder to report to Admiral Spruance when *Enterprise*'s XO, Commander Tom Jeter, noticed McClusky's bloody flight suit and cut the CEAG short: "My God, Mac, you've been shot!" McClusky was rushed to sick bay to treat five shrapnel splinters in his left arm and shoulder. His part in the Battle of Midway was over.[82]

Next to land around noon was Earl Gallaher and his scout group of Reid Stone, Bill Pittman, Dick Jaccard, and Jim Dexter. They were followed by squadron mates Dusty Kleiss, Norm West, and Mike Micheel. "Each of us had fewer than ten gallons remaining of the original three hundred and ten," said Kleiss. Three ordnancemen rushed under his Dauntless before he could climb out. They held up the three arming wires that proved that Kleiss's bombs were armed to detonate when they were released over *Kaga*. "They immediately made those wires into the shape of an aircraft, and with a sharp end, bent them so that they could be easily attached to a uniform like a medal," Kleiss said. "They gave one to each person who had put bombs, gasoline, or other services on my airplane. Of course, John Snowden and I also got one."[83]

Ensign Micheel's eighteenth carrier landing was a good one. En route home, he had seen the Bombing Six planes of Joe Penland and Tom Ramsay go into the drink and witnessed their crews climbing into life rafts. Micheel told John Dance to meet him in the ready room while he headed for the bridge to report their position from his plotting board. Before going below, Dance noted that their SBD had but four gallons of fuel remaining.[84]

The last *Enterprise* SBDs from her morning strike group to land made it into the groove around 1210. They were Lew Hopkins and Andy Anderson of Bombing Six. Anderson was unable to land on *Yorktown*, and doubted he had the fuel to reach his own flight deck. Hopkins was the only pilot of his division to touch down on the Big E. Radioman Ed Anderson attributed their safe return to Hopkins's wise fuel consumption. "We got back with just a cupful of fuel," he said. Only five planes from VB-6 had returned.[85]

Ed Anderson was distraught over his squadron's losses. Sammy Muntean, Sherman Duncan, Harold Heard, Jay Jenkins, Glenn Holden, Harry Nelson, Lee Keaney, and Charles Young did not come back. Some he had witnessed in their life rafts. Others he had heard over the radio as they went into the Pacific. He knew that Bill Steinman and Jim Patterson had been in planes that survived the Zero attacks, but neither of their SBDs had returned to *Enterprise*. Many of Scouting Six's enlisted men were gone, too, including Anderson's good buddy Dave Craig. "I only hope that the majority of the men will be picked up by the patrol planes from Midway," he wrote in his diary.[86]

Radioman Stuart Mason was in great pain and slight shock. Shrapnel wounds had ripped open his legs and face, yet he had remained calm enough to get their ZB equipment functioning during their return flight. His pilot, Andy Anderson, made his approach, and then proceeded to make a recognition turn to indicate his plane's friendly status. To his chagrin, the carrier's nervous gunners opened fire, forcing him to turn away and make another recognition run.[87]

Anderson was given a wave-off by the LSO on his second approach. He made a tight 360-degree turn, and then flew past the carrier's island structure, giving the command staff the emergency landing signal— indicated by choppy increases and decreases of his throttle. This time, *Enterprise* turned right into the wind and accepted his battered Dauntless. He was the last of the *Enterprise* air group to land. Anderson considered himself to be "a very lucky young man."[88]

His rear cockpit and tail section were bloodstained, Mason's flight gear soaked. Their aircraft was a shambles, with machine-gun and 20mm holes all over and no fabric left on the elevators. A pharmacist's mate helped Mason from his SBD and took him to a dressing station. Surgeons pulled shrapnel from his face and legs and grounded him from further action. It was of little consequence to him, as his Dauntless was deemed a wreck.[89]

Seaman First Class Eugene Braun, an untested VB-6 gunner not assigned to the morning strike, was shocked by the appearance of his buddy Mason, who returned with blood covering his face. "He said, 'By God, I get a Purple Heart for this!'" recalled Braun.[90]

The cost was staggering for the *Enterprise* SBD airmen on June 4. Of the sixty-four Dauntless aviators who had reached the Japanese fleet, exactly half of them had been shot down or were forced to ditch their bombers. Five of those who had survived their water landings were injured to varying degrees. Of the thirty-two men who made it back to *Enterprise* or *Yorktown*, four had been wounded by bullets or shrapnel. The *Enterprise* staff was at the moment unaware that Roberts and Goldsmith of Bombing Six had managed to land on *Yorktown*.

The surviving Devastators of Torpedo Six were last to reach the landing pattern of *Enterprise* from her carrier strike force. Ten TBDs had been shot down or forced to ditch, but four VT-6 pilots landed on *Enterprise* shortly after 1215: Lieutenant (j.g.) Bob Laub, Ensign Irvin McPherson, Ensign Ed Heck, and Machinist Stephen Smith.

McPherson and Heck had to fight their way through friendly fire from jittery task force gunners as they closed in on their carrier. Their TBD took a few slugs through the wings but was otherwise undamaged. Smith's TBF, sporting a "Scat Cat" logo he had painted on it, was also fired on by a task force destroyer. As he approached *Enterprise*, he was challenged with a signal light. Smith responded by making a tight right turn, the prearranged signal to indicate that he was a friendly plane, to which he received the okay to land.

As Smith entered the landing pattern about ten minutes ahead of his surviving comrades, a Wildcat pilot from his own carrier's VF-6 attacked his plane. The F4F came in with all guns blazing, but had started firing too soon; all the slugs fortunately passed astern. "But it sure didn't help my morale!" said Smith. When he landed, his TBD was so badly shot up that the deck crews considered tossing it overboard. Jim Murray recalled that Smith climbed out of his crippled Devastator "with fire in his eyes and a .45 on his hip."[91]

Smith was "old Navy." He had joined as an enlisted man and started his pilot training in 1927. Constant service had prevented him from seeing his wife and three kids for fourteen months. Now most of his squadron mates had been lost, he had made the return flight in a tattered plane with most of its instruments destroyed, and his own forces had nearly taken him down twice. He removed a handful of spent slugs from the seat of Scat Cat, which sported sixty-eight bullet holes.[92]

Smith reported to the bridge to alert the command staff on Torpedo

Six's attack, then stormed down to the fighter squadron ready room, fit to be tied. He confronted VF-6 skipper Jim Gray in an exchange that became so tense he had to be restrained by other pilots and squadron mates who had followed him. Smith told the fighter pilots exactly what he and the rest of the torpedo squadron thought of them, and invited any one of them outside. "Nobody said a word, so I left," he said. Gunner Ron Graetz of Torpedo Six learned that Smitty had pulled out his .45 and laid it up on the podium in Fighting Six's ready room. He then announced, "One of you sons of bitches made a firing run on me, and if I ever find out who he is, I'm going to shoot the son of a bitch!"[93]

TWELVE

The Japanese Strike Back

Max Leslie was eager to make his poststrike report to Admiral Fletcher. He could only hope that his fuel would outlast the time it was taking to clear Tom Cheek's inverted fighter from *Yorktown's* flight deck.

Leslie had no inkling of a bigger problem that was beginning to develop. *Yorktown's* radar had picked up an unidentified flight of aircraft, closing from thirty-two miles out. The orbiting Wildcat CAPs were vectored out to intercept what proved to be a Japanese air strike that had been launched from *Hiryu* to cripple the American carriers.

Admiral Nagumo's carrier fleet had moved quickly to strike back at the U.S. flattops. Just twenty minutes after his flagship *Akagi* was wrecked, Nagumo had transferred his command staff to the light cruiser *Nagara.* *Hiryu's* air group had assembled two dozen strike planes on her flight deck a half hour after McClusky and Leslie's SBDs had departed. She dispatched eighteen Type 99 Val dive-bombers with six Zero escorts, all led by Lieutenant Michio Kobayashi. En route to the American task force, Lieutenant Yasuhiro Shigematsu's Zeros had tangled with Charlie Ware's Scouting Six planes. Two of the Japanese fighters had been crippled enough to turn back. As the noon hour approached, Kobayashi's Vals were closing in on *Yorktown's* Task Force 17. *Hiryu*, in the meantime, readied a second strike group of Kate torpedo planes to follow up on what the first strikers could accomplish.

Lieutenant Commander Leslie was settling into the groove. He was making a good approach when *Yorktown*'s command staff made the call to shut down operations again. Kobayashi's dive-bombers were expected at any moment, thus necessitating full task force defense against aerial attack. As 3-B-1 dropped low with its hook extended and wheel lowered, LSO Norwood "Soupy" Campbell waved his paddles frantically at Leslie to abort his landing.

The skipper's wingman, Lefty Holmberg, unaware of the looming Japanese strike, was baffled by the LSO's rebuff. *The skipper is an expert pilot. And he is in a good approach position to land. What's wrong?* Holmberg hurriedly took over his spot but was also given a frantic wave-off by Lieutenant Campbell. The reason soon became apparent. "Get clear!" *Yorktown* radioed. "We're being attacked!"[1]

Holmberg turned out of the landing circle just as *Yorktown*'s antiaircraft batteries began firing. His SBD was jarred by flak bursts as he joined Leslie in speeding away from the formation. To add to his problems, Holmberg noticed that one of his wheels, which had been lowered for landing, failed to retract due to his shot-up hydraulic system.[2]

Bud Merrill was also preparing to land when the warning was announced. The antiaircraft batteries started firing as he hurriedly cleared the scene. In the ensuing aerial fights over Task Force 17, several of the SBDs Merrill joined with were engaged by VF-6 Wildcats that came in with guns blazing. One Wildcat pilot turned away only after Syd Bottomley yelled, "Can't you see these stars?" Ensign Charlie Lane heard Bottomley holler at an *Enterprise* fighter, "Knock it off, you bastard! This is us down here!"[3]

Oley Hanson spotted a Japanese plane coming in for an overhead run against an SBD. A Grumman Wildcat was close on its tail, and the F4F pilot quickly hammered the Japanese aircraft into the ocean. Ensign Bob Elder dived for the wave tops between the warships, as friendly gunfire erupted on both sides of him. "I went straight down the center with all hell breaking loose," he said.[4]

In contrast to the Coral Sea carrier battle one month prior, the Dauntless was not intentionally deployed to intercept enemy strike planes at Midway. The allotment of fighter planes had been increased and the F4F pilots tore into the *Hiryu* group as it moved in on *Yorktown*. Task force gunners helped account for other planes, but at least seven Val dive-bombers made it in to drop their bombs on *Yorktown* at 1210. One Val was hit by AA fire and exploded into three pieces, although his bomb tumbled free and exploded on contact with *Yorktown*'s flight deck, blowing a twelve-foot hole in the surface.

Scouting Five's seven operable SBDs were on the hangar deck, and the explosion sent shrapnel ripping through them. One Dauntless was fully fueled and carrying a thousand-pound bomb, but an alert hangar deck officer quickly extinguished the blaze with the sprinkler system. Below deck, Tex Conatser and his remaining VS-5 pilots had retired to their ready room. He was standing at the chalkboard, writing out the afternoon schedule, when the first bomb hit about thirty-five feet aft of Scouting Five's ready room. The blast knocked Conatser flat on his butt, and threw other pilots from their chairs. The lights went out, and the ready room filled with smoke. Squadron yeoman Bud Neister, manning the battle phones in the room, told the aviators to cover their mouths with handkerchiefs and to lie down on the deck.[5]

A second Val bomber, similarly blasted apart, managed to land its load close enough to *Yorktown*'s stern to send bomb splinters ripping into the carrier. Another 250-kilogram armor-piercing bomb ripped through the flight deck and exploded deep enough in the ship to disrupt *Yorktown*'s engineering spaces. A third bomb fell through the forward elevator, created additional damage, and sparked serious fires. The three direct hits caused extensive damage to *Yorktown*, knocked her dead in the water, and filled the ship with black smoke and raging fires.

Conatser and his junior pilots abandoned their smoke-filled ready room once the attack was over and headed for the flight deck. They passed through a casualty station en route, climbing over dead and injured men, as well as severed body parts. Ensign John Bridgers made his way to the hangar deck to check on his SBD, finding it parked directly below the spot where a bomb had exploded on the flight deck. "All the fabric on the control sections of rudder, ailerons, and horizontal stabilizers had been shredded," he said. He realized his chance to take part in the historic Battle of Midway was very likely relegated to a sideline role.[6]

Jim Patterson of Bombing Six was confronted by a *Yorktown* officer, his face dirty, and wearing a partially burned life jacket. The man was obviously in a state of shock. "You led them here!" the officer screamed upon finding that Patterson was in the last SBD from the strike group to land. He tried to hit Patterson but Ensign Goldsmith managed to pull the shocked officer away from his gunner.[7]

Enterprise and *Hornet*, about twenty miles away, were untouched, and they were able to land the rest of their aircraft. Bombing Three was ordered to land aboard *Enterprise* to await developments. Another straggler from *Yorktown*'s carrier strike was the VF-3 Wildcat piloted by Ensign Daniel C. Sheedy, who came in with one wheel collapsed. Sheedy, wounded in the ankle and shoulder, skidded his plane to the right as he landed on *Hornet*, and his one good set of landing gear collapsed. The F4F's forward machine guns erupted in automatic fire when the wingtip slapped the deck. Twenty sailors were wounded and five men were killed, including the son of an admiral.[8]

Lieutenant George Ellenburg of Bombing Eight, still grounded from flying, had gone topside to watch the aerial dogfights with his binoculars when he was caught in Sheedy's machine-gun fire. Clay Fisher was shocked moments later when an enlisted man from the squadron rushed into the VB-8 ready room carrying a pair of bloody binoculars, saying, "Lieutenant Ellenburg has just been killed!" Fisher was relieved, however, to see Ellenburg stride through the door, holding a compress against his forehead with blood streaming down his face and onto his shirt. Ellenburg's nonlethal lacerations had been caused by metal fragments from the island structure when it was hit by bullets.[9]

Dave Shumway and VB-3 saw that *Yorktown* was too damaged for landings. They shifted to *Enterprise*, and the first to land on her were Paul Schlegel and Ozzie Wiseman, at 1237 and 1238. During the next half hour, the *Enterprise* LSO brought on board thirteen more SBDs of Bombing Three, as well as six Wildcats from VF-3.

Bob Elder watched from above as *Enterprise*'s flight deck was quickly jammed with refugee aircraft crowding back toward the crash barriers. The carrier's elevators were in the process of moving planes down below as Elder approached, but LSO Robin Lindsey skillfully coached the VB-3 ensign down onto the first arresting cable.[10]

Max Leslie and Lefty Holmberg sighted the Devastator of Chief Bill Esders bobbing in the Pacific below as they approached Task Force 17.

Holmberg dropped a float light to mark the downed TBD, and the destroyer *Hammann* effected their rescue.[11]

Meanwhile, Leslie and Holmberg headed for *Enterprise.* Earl Gallaher in the rear of Leslie's plane spotted another ditched aircraft about ten miles away, likely Mac McCarthy's SBD. The two bombers circled the downed crew while a destroyer was called to pick up the aviators. Leslie dropped a beanbag on the forecastle of the nearest destroyer regarding the survivors in the water, then relocated the downed plane and flew back over *Hammann.* This time Gallagher sent a searchlight message to the destroyermen to help direct them to the downed VS-6 crew.[12]

Leslie and Holmberg circled the boat until *Hammann* had brought the men aboard; then the pilots headed for the Big E again, dangerously low on fuel. Holmberg had leaned out his engine in order to save gas, but his situation was becoming critical. They opted to ditch beside nearby cruiser *Astoria,* the same ship that had signaled, "Good luck and a safe return," to them five hours before.[13]

Leslie directed Holmberg to land first. His fuel was lower and one of his wheels was already extended. Holmberg ditched his 3-B-2 right alongside *Astoria* at 1342. The sudden impact slammed his head into the instrument panel, narrowly missing the telescopic bombsight. Gunner George LaPlant retrieved their rubber raft and inflated it on the port wing. Holmberg stepped out onto the wing in ankle-deep water and joined LaPlant in their raft. The Dauntless sank within moments— followed by their raft. Holmberg assumed the rubber boat had been punctured by Japanese AA fire.[14]

Holmberg was still wearing his leather jacket and .45-caliber pistol as he treaded water for several minutes. The number two motor whaleboat from *Astoria* chugged over and quickly retrieved him and LaPlant. Two minutes later, Max Leslie set his B-1 down in the ocean alongside *Astoria* at 1348. Gallagher felt that Leslie's water landing was perfect, as good as any seaplane could do. As he scrambled out of his rear compartment, he noted that his skipper was still seated in the cockpit, apparently slumped over his controls. Gallagher, assuming that Leslie had been knocked out, reached in and grabbed his shoulder. He was surprised to find the squadron commander fully alert, methodically going through the process of flicking every button on the instrument panel to the off position before clearing his sinking plane.[15]

Leslie, Holmberg, and their gunners would remain on board *Astoria* until June 12, thereby turning over effective command of VB-3 at Midway to Dave Shumway. The last surviving plane of *Yorktown*'s carrier strike was the TBD of machinist Harry Corl. He also ran out of fuel and ditched near Task Force 16. His gunner, Lloyd Childers, was dazed from blood loss from his three bullet wounds when their 3-T-3 hit the ocean. His pilot grabbed his Mae West and helped him escape their sinking TBD.[16]

A whaleboat from the destroyer *Monaghan* quickly rescued Corl and Childers from the ocean. As Childers was pulled into the boat, a doctor forced ingested seawater from his stomach. On board *Monaghan*, he was placed on the wardroom table to receive plasma and attention for his bullet wounds. The doctor told VT-3's sole surviving radioman later that he would have been dead in another thirty minutes without medical help.[17]

Lieutenant Earl Gallaher tried to comfort his VS-6 pilots during their poststrike briefing. "The boys who came back felt badly about the empty seats in the ready room, but we all knew that we had made the Japanese pay dearly for them," he said.[18]

Mike Micheel found the mood to be bittersweet. The men were energized by the damage they had inflicted on the Japanese carriers. His roommate, Bill Pittman, talked excitedly about how his gunner, Adkins, had shot down a fighter while holding up a broken machine gun. Yet there was also great tension over those who did not make it back. Four ACTG new boys were missing, plus J. Q. Roberts, who had gone through basic training at St. Louis with Micheel. Even three of the old guys had failed to return.

Gallaher and Lieutenant Patriarca, the acting flight officer, went over the plans for a follow-up strike. "I want to go," Micheel announced. "I don't want to stay on the ship." He assumed that the most experienced pilots would go first, but Patriarca explained, "If your airplane is flying, you go."

Fine with me, Micheel thought.

Dave Shumway, acting commander of *Yorktown*'s VB-3, had fifteen planes of his squadron for a follow-up strike. He found the Big E's ready rooms crammed with the ragtag remnants of VB-6 and VS-6. He and nine of his pilots had previously served on board *Enterprise* during the Doolittle Raid, so the ship was quite familiar to them. It was even more of a homecoming for Bud Merrill, Oley Hanson, and Bob Campbell—who had also flown as part of Scouting Six as loaner pilots for the Wake and Marcus Island strikes.

Charlie Lane, bombless on the first strike, hoped for another chance. Shumway's new acting XO, Syd Bottomley, grabbed a peanut-butter sandwich brought in by the stewards to feed the hungry pilots. "I will always remember how dry my mouth was after all that excitement," said Bottomley, "and how I tried to swallow that peanut butter in pain!"[19]

Joe Godfrey and other rear gunners felt the carrier strike had been their baptism under fire. "I remember how eager we all had been before takeoff on that first combat mission," Godfrey said. He had found that the "serious business" of war quickly molded boys into men "in a matter of about three hours." Don Hoff felt a deep sense of loss for his Scouting Six comrades he had gone to radio school with. In the heat of the moment, however, he realized there was nothing he could do about it. *We have to carry on*, Hoff thought. *We still have a job to do out here.*[20]

Jim Murray was not with the radiomen who had gathered in the radio shack to wait for word on their next mission. He remained with his skipper's SBD on the hangar deck, and begged sandwiches and coffee from willing shipmates who were eager to hear more about the damage inflicted upon the Japanese carriers. He encountered VB-6 radioman Ed Anderson while in the hangar. Anderson related their successful attack on *Kaga* and their fight with the Zeros en route home. Murray, after hearing of the losses they suffered, silently hoped that some of their downed fellow airmen would be recovered from the Pacific by search-and-rescue efforts.[21]

Oley Hanson noted that many of his comrades were grumbling about the various personal effects they had lost aboard *Yorktown*. The only things he regretted losing were the diaries he had written during various combats. "I couldn't complain too loudly, because it was supposed to be against the rules to have any kind of diary that might conceivably fall into the hands of the Japanese," Hanson said.[22]

The Japanese were sending out their own follow-up strike from the undamaged *Hiryu* as the American aviators prepared to attack again. Reports from Nagumo's scout planes indicated that the Americans had three carriers. By 1300, further confirmation was reported to *Hiryu's* command staff from the interrogations of captured Torpedo Three pilot Wesley Osmus, who had revealed the *Enterprise*, *Yorktown*, and *Hornet* by name while under torture. The second strike group launched from *Hiryu* at 1331, consisting of ten Kate torpedo planes under Lieutenant Joichi Tomonaga and six Zero fighters under Lieutenant Shigeru Mori.[23]

Yorktown's damage-control crews fought hard during the two hours following her bomb wreckage and finally managed to get her back under way. By 1430 she was making fifteen knots, but the cruiser *Pensacola's* radar had already picked up *Hiryu's* inbound strike group. The American carriers scrambled to launch additional Wildcat fighters to intercept this latest threat, but there was insufficient time to launch any of their SBDs.

The bombing attack had destroyed many of *Yorktown's* remaining Dauntlesses on the hangar deck. Lieutenant Tex Conatser found that only his SBD and one other were flyable. He consulted with Air Officer Murr Arnold, asking that he and John Bridgers—whom he considered one of his choice pupils—be allowed to launch. Arnold, however, replied that their launch was impractical at the moment.[24]

The CAP accounted for some of the *Hiryu* strikers, but at least six of the Kates made it in close enough to effect good torpedo drops. Captain Buckmaster, with his carrier struggling to make nineteen knots, was unable to dodge all of them, and two torpedoes slammed into *Yorktown's* port side around 1444. *Yorktown's* rudder was jammed, and her power was knocked out once again, plunging the ship into darkness.

The torpedo explosions were violent. Tex Conatser, Ray Miligi, and Bill Roberts had gone down to rest in Conatser's stateroom, since their ready room was out of service. "When the first torpedo hit, it raised me a foot off my bunk," said Conatser. "It knocked Ray Miligi onto the deck and roughed up Bill Roberts, too." Another pilot, John Bridgers, had heard that many of the men wounded or killed during the earlier bombing attack had been standing upright. Now he and others in a compartment near the island structure lay prone on the deck to avoid shrapnel. Bridgers was lifted more than a foot off the deck when one of the torpedoes exploded. *I now know what a torpedo hit feels like*, he thought.[25]

Ensign Bob Gibson, another VS-5 rookie pilot, had ridden out the bombing attack in the ready room, then retired to officers' country to rest while the firefighters did their work. As fires were raging, the damage-control men started throwing mattresses overboard to avoid further blazes. Gibson, still wearing his Mae West life jacket, was stretched out on his mattressless bunk when the torpedoes hit. "They shook the ship radically, like a baby rattle," he said. As the lights went out and smoke filled his stateroom, Gibson tried to leap from his bunk. His Mae West, however, became hopelessly tangled in the coil springs, leaving him feeling like Don Quixote fighting the windmill as he tried to wrestle free from the springs.[26]

Yorktown orphan pilot George Goldsmith had gone to the hangar deck to inspect his aircraft following the bombing attack. Amazed at the jolt created by the exploding torpedoes, Goldsmith felt the hits shake the ship like a cat shaking a rat.[27]

The ship's list increased dramatically, and Captain Buckmaster feared that his carrier might capsize. He ordered the engine rooms secured and directed the men to come topside and don their life jackets. Flight operations from CV-5 were over for the dozens of VS-5, VB-3, and VB-6 Dauntless aircrews on board, who were now contemplating their chances of survival.

Lieutenant Sam Adams of Scouting Five helped avenge his ship's wounds by finding the source of her suffering. Wally Short's search group, launched at 1130, had flown out three hundred miles with five-hundred-pound bombs. Contact was made at almost the same moment that *Yorktown* collected two torpedo hits from *Hiryu*'s strike group.

Luck seemed to be with Adams and his wingman, Lieutenant Rockey Dickson. Adams had received good news that morning in the form of a dispatch from home announcing that his wife had just delivered a baby.

"The news really set him up," said fellow VS-5 pilot Dave Berry, an academy classmate of Adams's.[28]

Lieutenant Adams had seen nothing until about halfway back toward home; then suddenly he spotted the white wakes of ships on the ocean surface below and led Dickson down for a closer look. Adams made out ten ships, all heading north. He had ARM1c Joe Karrol carefully send out the contact report in dots and dashes to reach the fleet. Fifteen minutes after his first sighting, he radioed a contact report: "One CV, two BB, three CA, four DD, thirty-one-fifteen north, one seventy-nine-oh-five west, course 000, speed fifteen." *Hiryu* at this time was only 110 miles northwest of *Yorktown*.[29]

Adams ordered his radioman to send the same report by code key, but Karrol was occupied. "Just a minute, Mr. Adams," he called. "I have a Zero back here to take care of first."[30]

Adams, considered by many of his peers to be the best pilot of VS-5, calmly set up his plane in order to give Karrol a clean shot at their opponent. Karrol and Dickson's gunner, ARM2c Joseph Lynch, poured lead into the Zero and believed that they sent it down in flames. Only then did Sam Adams continue to send his contact report via keying. Adams and Dickson carefully monitored *Hiryu*'s force for another half hour before turning for home with just enough fuel to make it.

Admiral Fletcher had transferred his flag to the cruiser *Astoria* once *Yorktown* had first gone dead in the water after her bomb damage. Captain Buckmaster now found his carrier dead in the water once again from her two torpedo hits, vulnerable to further enemy attacks, and in danger of rolling over from her heavy list. At 1455, he passed the word, "Abandon ship," in order to prevent more loss of lives.

More than two dozen Dauntless airmen, pilots, and gunners still on board *Yorktown* were now caught in the abandon-ship process. From Bombing Three, this included a handful of rear gunners and the two junior pilots who had not been assigned to the morning strike—ensigns Jack Rugen and Raymond Reynolds. Tex Conatser, with his ten remaining VS-5 pilots (Bridgers, Miligi, Jerry Richey, Spike Conzett, Richard Wolfe, Ray Kline, Leif Larsen, Blackie Ammen, Bob Gibson, and Larry Comer), and the two *Enterprise* refugee crews (Roberts, Goldsmith, and their gunners) proceeded to the hangar deck. They removed some of the rubber rafts from the SBDs and prepared to go over the side. Conatser, wary of burning his hands while sliding down the lines, made sure he found a knotted line before proceeding toward the ocean below. He dropped their plane's life raft to his gunner and then climbed down.[31]

Conatser found that many of the men in the water were without life jackets, although plenty had been available. He and his gunner, who were wearing their Mae Wests, turned their rafts over to four swimmers without jackets. Conatser bobbed in the ocean for several minutes and then was pulled aboard another raft with men from his squadron. His group was brought on board the destroyer *Balch* within an hour.

Still on board *Yorktown*, John Bridgers was trying to decide when he would follow his comrades into the water. He retrieved his Mae West life jacket from the ready room and stood topside on the flight deck watching the abandon-ship process, secretly hoping someone would change his mind about the whole affair. Captain Buckmaster, making an inspection tour, ordered the young ensign overboard. The captain was less than pleased when he encountered Bridgers again moments later. "Son, I thought I told you to get off this ship," Buckmaster said. "Now get moving!"[32]

Bridgers climbed down a line into the ocean. He helped tow an injured sailor to a life raft crowded with mess attendants and a British officer, Commander Michael B. Laing—who had been on the carrier as an observer. Bridgers tried swimming toward a distant destroyer, but his clothing and shoes slowed his progress. Sometime later, the exhausted aviator—having ditched his size-fourteen AA footwear—was finally hauled on board another destroyer.[33]

Radioman John Iacovazzi of Scouting Five swam to the destroyer *Benson*. "Being that I had a flight suit on and a firearm with no identification, they must have thought I was an officer," said Iacovazzi, "so I got to take a shower right away." Ensign Bob Gibson forgot to lock his feet as he slid down a line toward the water and burned his hands in the process. Then he was unable to swim away from the carrier due to waves that kept forcing him back against the hull. Gibson tried diving underwater to swim past the oily surface, but was continually carried back.

Commander Murr Arnold finally helped haul the exhausted pilot onto a life raft, where they were picked up by the destroyer *Balch*.[34]

Bill Roberts from *Enterprise*'s VB-6 searched his SBD on the hangar deck before abandoning ship, retrieving his life raft and camera. He then met up with a *Yorktown* sailor who proposed that they share the two-man rubber raft. The sailor went down a line first and Roberts tossed the raft down. He lost his grip fifteen feet above the ocean and fell, still wearing his leather flight jacket and carrying his .45 pistol and camera. Roberts struggled to the surface, only to find that the *Yorktown* sailor and his SBD's raft were not to be seen. He swam to a nearby life raft, happy to be wearing his Mae West, and hung on until he was rescued.[35]

George Goldsmith and gunner Jim Patterson also retrieved the two-man raft from their VB-6 Dauntless. They moved to the fantail, pulled the inflation toggle, tossed it into the sea below, and prepared to jump after it. "As it hit the water, it shriveled up into nothingness," said Patterson. They realized the raft had been shot full of holes during the fighter attacks. Goldsmith was forced to paddle through the oily water wearing his Mae West. When Patterson climbed down a line and dropped into the ocean, he was met immediately by a large steward's mate, who cried out, "Don't leave me, boss! I can't swim!" Patterson offered a quick course on dog-paddling to the frantic young man and they set off, with the steward's mate paddling with one hand and gripping Patterson's shoulder with the other. Both men were rescued by a boat from the destroyer *Balch*.[36]

The four VB-6 airmen from the Big E and the remaining *Yorktown* Dauntless aviators were all retrieved from the water by Task Force 17 screening vessels. Goldsmith, exhausted from a long time in the water, fell asleep in the officers' wardroom under a table where *Balch* doctors were tending to the wounded.[37]

THIRTEEN
The Flying Dragon Strike

In the Bombing Six ready room on *Enterprise*, miles from his own crippled carrier *Yorktown*, Ensign Oley Hanson worked out the navigation on his plotting board. Scouting reports were filtering in about an undamaged fourth Japanese carrier, and Hanson was eager to get in another attack on the Kido Butai. Fifteen of Bombing Three's seventeen Dauntlesses had landed on *Enterprise* after *Yorktown* was bombed and were thus available for follow-up strikes. Hanson hoped the two missing crews, those of skipper Max Leslie and Lefty Holmberg, had made it on board *Yorktown*.[1]

Chief of Staff Miles Browning pushed for a quick second strike against the Japanese carriers, but Admiral Spruance waited for more definitive news. Once the location report from Sam Adams was in hand, he waited no more. Dive-bombers were readied on *Enterprise*'s deck, but the staff decided that fighter escorts could not be spared. Spruance also prudently held back his three flyable TBDs after the morning's staggering torpedo squadron losses. Hitting the *Hiryu* would depend solely upon the Dauntless boys.

"Pilots, man your planes!" The annoucement came on *Enterprise* shortly after 1500. Eleven SBDs were armed with thousand-pound bombs and the rest with five-hundred-pound general-purpose bombs. It would be a mixed bag of strikers. Max Leslie of VB-3 was stuck on board the cruiser *Astoria*. *Enterprise* air group commander Wade McClusky was wounded and in sick bay. Lieutenant Earl Gallaher, skipper of VS-6, was given the nod to lead the strike group. He held seniority over Dick Best and Dave Shumway, who were academy classmates just behind Gallaher in tenure.

There was no lack of volunteers to fly against the Japanese carriers. Ensign Don Ely, a junior pilot of VB-6, sat in the ready room through the morning's action with his plotting board in hand, ready to man an aircraft on the next mission. He was pleased to discover that Fred Weber thought the other pilots should have a chance. Ely was disappointed to find, however, that skipper Best wanted his most experienced pilots, and slated Weber to attack the *Hiryu*. Ely had lost his roommate, Bert Varian, in the morning strike, and now he was destined to once again sit on the bench.[2]

Dick Best's 6-B-1 had been hauled back to the flight deck. Jim Murray, who had remained faithfully with his plane, rode it up the elevator topside, where it was spotted aft of Scouting Six's ready planes. At the moment, the Bombing Six SBDs of Best, Bud Kroeger, and Fred Weber were ready to go. Shumway's Bombing Three had fourteen of fifteen planes ready for action. Only Bob Elder of VB-3 would not be making this strike. To round out Shumway's group to three even divisions of five planes, Best loaned out Ensign Stephen Hogan of Bombing Six. Hogan would fly 6-B-12, the Dauntless flown during the morning by Lew Hopkins, who remained on board ship for this strike.

Lieutenant Best became frustrated in the confusion that ensued. He fully expected another three SBDs to round out his VB-6 division. The secondary strike roster, in fact, called for Lloyd Smith's 6-B-4, Harvey Lanham's 6-B-10, and Arthur Rausch's 6-B-17 to be spotted along with Best's section. In similar fashion, the secondary strike roster also called for Pat Patriarca's 6-S-13 and Eldor Rodenburg's 6-S-9 to join Scouting Six for this mission. All five of these SBDs were gassed and armed, waiting on *Enterprise*'s hangar deck to be lifted to the flight deck.

Gallaher and Best were counting on these extra bombers to boost their striking power. In the rush to launch the strike group, however, there was a foul-up in the operations order being passed to the hangar deck crews. The list that reached the officer in charge did not include any of these five SBDs. Pilots like Rodenburg were briefed on the strike and made their way to the flight deck to discover their mounts were missing. They proceeded to the hangar deck, and found their Dauntlesses armed and ready, with their gunners waiting to be hoisted topside. Once again, young Lew Jones was assigned with Rausch to a carrier strike but they were prevented from departing. "I certainly wanted to go!" Jones said.[3]

Lieutenant Patriarca, a Pearl Harbor survivor eager for vengeance, argued his case with the hangar deck officer. By the time the snafu was unsnarled, the strike force was already launching. Mike Micheel, after seeing *Yorktown* get hit, wanted off the ship if more attacks were coming. He said his customary preflight prayer before he and John Dance prepared to set off again.[4]

Enterprise turned into the wind, and at 1525, she launched eight Wildcats for CAP duty, followed by the twenty-five SBDs under Earl Gallaher. Almost immediately, two of his planes began malfunctioning. Norm West of Scouting Six developed engine problems and had to make a forced landing shortly after takeoff. Stephen Hogan soon began to worry that he might have to return as well. Gene Braun, his equally battle-untested rear seat man, was concerned when their dive-bomber's engine began acting up shortly after they were airborne. *Holy mackerel, if we can't keep up with the formation, we're dead*, he thought. Braun immediately reached for the wobble pump, the hand-operated fluid pressure pump used to prime the engine. "But then it hit me hard. Hogan was already using it to full capacity." Hogan managed to keep his engine running and held formation with Lieutenant Shumway's VB-3 first division of Bombing Three.[5]

The two dozen remaining SBDs climbed to thirteen thousand feet for the ninety-minute flight. Don Hoff felt a sense of purpose as he checked over his guns in the rear seat of Jim Dexter's SBD. The orphaned *Yorktown* aviators were now mixed with their *Enterprise* brothers, and together they had a mission of vengeance. *We are bound and determined*, thought Hoff. *We know what that baby—the fourth Jap carrier—did to* Yorktown. *We are going to pay her back!*[6]

The launching snafu on *Enterprise* was minor in comparison to the strike that departed from *Hornet*. Walt Rodee's Scouting Eight had been spotted on the flight deck for launch by 1456, yet moments before *Enterprise*

Afternoon Strike on *Hiryu*
Enterprise Group: June 4, 1942

SCOUTING SIX (VS-6) FIRST DIVISION

PLANE	PILOT	REAR SEAT GUNNER
6-S-1	Lt. Wilmer Earl Gallaher	ACRM Thomas Edward Merritt
6-S-2	Ens. Reid Wentworth Stone	RM1c William Hart Bergin
6-S-11	Ens. Richard Alonzo Jaccard	RM3c Porter William Pixley
6-S-7	Lt. (jg) Norman Jack Kleiss	ARM3c John Warren Snowden
6-S-16	Lt. (jg) John Norman West*	ARM2c Albert R. Stitzelberger*
6-S-17	Ens. Vernon Larsen Micheel	RM3c John Dewey Dance
6-S-18	Ens. James Campbell Dexter	RM3c Donald Laurence Hoff

BOMBING SIX (VB-6) SECOND DIVISION

PLANE	PILOT	REAR SEAT GUNNER
6-B-1	Lt. Richard Halsey Best	ACRM James Francis Murray

(continued)

Afternoon Strike on *Hiryu*
Enterprise Group: June 4, 1942 (cont.)

BOMBING SIX (VB-6) SECOND DIVISION

PLANE	PILOT	REAR SEAT GUNNER
6-B-2	Lt. (jg) Edwin John Kroeger	RM3c Gail Wayne Halterman
6-B-3	Ens. Frederick Thomas Weber**	AOM3c Ernest Leonard Hilbert**

BOMBING THREE (VB-3) STRIKE FORCE

PLANE	PILOT	REAR SEAT GUNNER
3-B-13	Lt. DeWitt Wood Shumway	ARM1c Ray Edgar Coons
3-B-15	Ens. Bunyan Randolph Cooner	AOM2c Clifton R. Bassett
3-B-3	Ens. Paul Wahl Schlegel	ARM3c Jack Alvin Shropshire
3-B-16	Lt. (jg) Osborne Beeman Wiseman**	ARM3c Grant Ulysses Dawn**
3-B-17	Ens. Milford Austin Merrill	ARM3c Dallas Joseph Bergeron
6-B-12	Ens. Stephen Clement Hogan Jr.***	Sea1c Eugene K. Braun
3-B-7	Lt. (jg) Gordon Alvin Sherwood	ARM2c Harman Donald Bennett

3-B-8	Ens. Roy Maurice Isaman	ARM3c Sidney Kay Weaver
3-B-9	Ens. Phillip Walker Cobb	AMM2c Clarence E. Zimmershead
3-B-10	Lt. Harold Sydney Bottomley Jr.	AMM2c David Frederick Johnson
3-B-11	Ens. Charles Smith Lane	ARM2c Jack Charles Henning
3-B-12	Ens. John Clarence Butler**	ARM3c David Donald Berg**
3-B-4	Ens. Robert Keith Campbell	AMM1c Horace Henry Craig
3-B-5	Ens. Alden Wilbur Hanson	ARM3c Joseph Vernon Godfrey
3-B-6	Ens. Robert Haines Benson	ARM3c Frederick Paul Bergeron

*Aborted and returned to *Enterprise*.
**Lost in action on *Hiryu* strike.
***Bombing Six crew that flew with Bombing Three (VB-3).

launched her strike, Ruff Johnson's eleven VB-8 Dauntlesses returned from Midway. Captain Mitscher proceeded to land his returning aviators by clearing *Hornet*'s flight deck. Many of Rodee's senior air crews rode their SBDs down to the hangar deck to make room for landing operations.

Despite the delay, there was much celebrating as Johnson's SBDs returned. Slim Moore was happy to find his buddy Dick Woodson had survived the morning flight with VS-8, but was stunned that their other close friend, Ronnie Fisher, was among the fifteen TBD crews missing from Torpedo Eight. As his plane captain helped him unstrap from his parachute, he said, "Slim, the torpedo bombers are all overdue."[7]

"All of them?" Moore asked in disbelief.

"Yes, every one of them."

The three gunners from Denver had become a close bunch on board *Hornet*. "Ronnie was the unlucky one of our group," recalled Moore. "He had joined the ship before Dick and I, and he had been our inspiration."

Pilot Roy Gee was similarly shocked. He went to VB-8's ready room after landing with the Midway group, and learned that no planes from Torpedo Eight or Fighting Eight from the morning strike had returned. He paused in the wardroom to look at the empty chairs normally filled by his friends. "It was a sorrowful sight," Gee said.[8]

Gee had only moments to reflect. An announcement was suddenly made for all bomber pilots to report to their ready rooms. There the pilots were informed that they would be launched immediately to attack the undamaged Japanese carrier, and that no fighters would be escorting this long-range mission. Around 1540, the SBD crews were called to man their planes. *This could be VB-8's first exposure to real combat*, Gee hoped.[9]

Scouting Eight's senior pilots—Walt Rodee, Gus Widhelm, Ray Davis, and others—were among those whose planes were pulled to the hangar deck to land VB-8. Now the flight deck crews swiftly pushed the remnants of the strike group aft into takeoff position. Senior VB-8 pilots Johnson, Moe Vose, and Abbie Tucker similarly were stuck on board ship in the swift launch that ensued.

Lieutenant (j.g.) Fred Bates ended up as the senior pilot of seven Bombing Eight crews launched around 1600. With him were three junior ensigns and only three pilots from the morning carrier strike—Clay Fisher, Ken White, and Roy Gee. Five of the nine VS-8 crews launched had not been a part of the morning "flight to nowhere." The senior pilot of the sixteen *Hornet* SBDs launched well behind the *Enterprise* group was VS-8's Lieutenant Edgar Stebbins.

Dark-haired and slight, with an odd gap between his two front teeth, Ed Stebbins had left Southern Methodist University in Dallas to fly for the Navy. His *Hornet* bunch was about half an hour behind the *Enterprise* group. Mitscher signaled Stebbins to take charge of the *Hornet* SBDs and proceed on the assigned mission, placing him in his first command role.[10]

Lieutenant Edgar Stebbins.

U.S. Navy

Stebbins lost two SBDs en route. Lieutenant Griff Sexton and Ensign Phil Rusk of Scouting Eight were forced to turn back, leaving fourteen aircrews for the attack.

Yorktown's Bombing Three was already operating in full harmony with Dick Best and Earl Gallaher's SBD squadrons. Eight more Dauntless crews of Scouting Five, returning from snooping out the *Hiryu* force, would join the *Enterprise* air group.

The team of Lieutenant Johnny Neilsen and Ensign Ben Preston shot up a Japanese scout floatplane—a Nakajima E8N "Dave" from the battleship *Haruna*—during their return. When they reached Point Option, they did not find their home carrier *Yorktown* but did spot downed American fliers drifting in a yellow raft. They attempted to direct the cruiser *Portland* to make a rescue but had to move on due to low fuel. En route toward *Enterprise*, Neilsen spotted VF-3 pilot Willie Woollen standing in his rubber boat, waving skyward toward his SBD. This time Neilsen was able to guide the destroyer *Benham* properly toward Woollen's position and help effect his rescue.[11]

Neilsen finally took the cut and caught a wire with only a few gallons of gas remaining. He reported to air plot officer Bert Hardin about the two aviators in the raft where Point Option should have been. His and other reports of downed aviators' positions were collected to report to CinCPac in order to help direct PBYs from Midway to search for the crews. Captain Miles Browning, however, would not authorize this important transmission to be sent.[12]

Other returning VS-5 searchers were able to locate *Yorktown*, but

Afternoon Strike on *Hiryu*
Hornet Group: June 4, 1942

SCOUTING EIGHT (VS-8) STRIKE FORCE (9)

PILOT	REAR SEAT GUNNER
Lt. Edgar Erwin Stebbins	ARM2c Ervin R. Hillhouse
Lt. Ben Moore Jr.	ARM2c Richard C. McEwen
Lt. (jg) Albert Harold Wood	ARM2c Richard Thomas Woodson
Lt. (jg) Ivan Lee Swope	ARM2c Harmon L. Brendle
Ens. Helmuth Ernest Hoerner	ARM3c David T. Manus
Ens. Harold H. White	ARM3c John Stephen Urban
Ens. William E. Woodman	ARM2c Gerald S. McAffe
Lt. Orman Griffith Sexton III*	ARM2c William L. Payne
Ens. Philip James Rusk*	ARM2c John H. Honeycutt

BOMBING EIGHT (VB-8) STRIKE FORCE (7)

PILOT	REAR SEAT GUNNER
Lt. (jg) Fred Leeson Bates	ARM1c Clyde S. Montensen
Ens. Henry John Nickerson	ARM1c Elmer Edwin Jackson
Ens. Roy Philip Gee	ARM1c Donald L. Canfield

Ens. Kenneth Broughton White	ARM3c Leroy Quillen
Ens. Robert Pershing Friesz	ARM1c Clarence C. Kiley
Ens. James Clark Barrett	ARM3c William H. Berthold
Ens. Clayton Evan Fisher	ARM3c George E. Ferguson

*Aborted mission and returned to *Hornet*.

they were stunned by the sight of their own listing, abandoned carrier. "When I took off, the *Yorktown* was the fightingest ship in the Navy," said Dave Berry. "And when I got back, it was dead in the water."[13]

Scouting Five skipper Wally Short and wingman Carl Horenburger followed an oil slick in to *Yorktown*. Short moved on to *Enterprise* to land. Horenburger's fuel situation was serious enough that he decided to make a wheels-up landing in the water near the cruiser *Astoria*. "Just as we slowed and started to flare out I took one last look aft and the *Enterprise* was frantically signaling, 'PC, PC, PC,'" radioman Lynn Forshee said. He knew that "Prep Charlie" meant for his plane to prepare to land. "We didn't know it at the time, but she had lost so many planes that she needed every one she could get," said Forshee. Horenburger pulled back up, banked left, and swung into the *Enterprise* landing pattern.

We don't have the fuel to make another go-around, thought Forshee. *The pressure is really on Mr. Horenburger*. Forshee's fingers were crossed as his pilot caught the second cable, and the engine died as he throttled forward to start up the deck. Horenburger and Forshee were sent to sick bay for a calming shot of whiskey. Forshee was then led down to an enlisted bunk area, where he crawled into an open bunk. Just before drifting off, he noted the name stenciled on his mattress cover: "Red Durawa." Gregory Durawa, one of those killed from Torpedo Six, was another young man with whom Forshee had attended radio school in San Diego.[14]

Eight VS-5 searchers landed on *Enterprise*, where they would help supplement the morning's losses from Bombing Six and Scouting Six. All ten of Short's scouts returned safely, although the last two pilots—Lieutenant (j.g.) Bill Christie and Lieutenant (j.g.) Hank McDowell—landed on *Hornet*.

"A fouled deck and our extreme shortage of fuel forced us aboard the *Hornet*," Christie said. McDowell and Christie, due to their experience, were integrated into Scouting Eight for the remainder of the battle.[15]

Earl Gallaher peered ahead through his windshield and smiled.

Six hours earlier, he had planted a direct bomb on the carrier *Kaga*—one of the flattops that had launched the strike planes that destroyed his beloved battleship *Arizona* at Pearl Harbor. Up ahead, Gallaher could see the three burning carriers the Dauntlesses had hit during the morning strike as he approached again. By 1645, just less than an hour after takeoff, he spotted the undamaged *Hiryu* some thirty miles ahead from his vantage point at thirteen thousand feet.

Nothing could be more satisfying than hitting two enemy carriers in one day. *Here is our chance to get that fourth carrier and to repay the call her planes made on the* Yorktown, Gallaher thought.[16]

Despite his eagerness, he felt it unlikely that the Americans could catch an enemy off guard twice in one day. Gallaher led his sections into a climbing port turn, working his way around to the other side of the Japanese formation to make his approach from the sun and downwind. *A downwind dive is usually more accurate and can be made steeper, which makes it more difficult for the antiaircraft gunners*, he felt. Gallaher expected the Zero CAP to slice into them at any moment as they climbed to nineteen thousand feet.[17]

Weather conditions were ideal: excellent visibility, unlimited ceiling, low scattered clouds at twenty-five hundred feet, and a smooth sea. The SBDs reached attack altitude of nineteen thousand feet, just south of the carrier. *Hiryu*, known in Japanese as "Flying Dragon," had five Vals, four Kates, and a *Soryu* Aichi reconnaissance plane spotted on her deck. A mixed group of twelve Zeros from *Soryu*, *Kaga*, and *Akagi* were on station above *Hiryu*, while another two *Akagi* Zeros were aloft in the general vicinity.[18]

Lieutenant Gallaher looked over his shoulder to check the dispositions for the final time. Everyone was tucked in and stepped down by threes and sixes. He nosed down toward the pushover point, away from the sun, and made his dispersal order. *Enterprise* planes would dive on *Hiryu*, while *Yorktown*'s Bombing Three was to head for the nearer of two battleships. Gallaher then pulled up and over his wingman to dive. One of his pilots suddenly broadcast a warning: "Enemy fighters attacking from the rear!"[19]

It was 1701 as Gallaher plunged at seventy degrees, lined up on the flight deck below as Zeros began slashing into his squadron. The leading Zero overtook the Scouting Six skipper—within spitting distance—and nearly collided with him. The Japanese on *Hiryu* below suddenly became aware of their danger as the sunlight flashed off the polished SBD canopies. Her skipper, Captain Kaku Tomeo, turned hard to starboard to evade. At the beginning of his dive, Gallaher was feeling confident. *A hit is in the bag!* Yet, as Gallaher saw *Hiryu* turn, he tried to toss his bomb ahead of his target by pulling up sharply as he released. His bomb missed the mark and he hurt his already injured back—strained during his morning attack—further in the process.[20]

Reid Stone also missed. Dusty Kleiss, diving fourth, felt that Dick Jaccard ahead of him landed a direct hit on *Hiryu*'s forward elevator. Kleiss noted *Hiryu*'s sharp turn, and aimed his bomb toward where the carrier's progress would take her. "I don't know where mine landed, because of the flames from the bomb hit ahead of me," Kleiss admitted to his diary that night.[21]

Mike Micheel, diving fifth, saw *Hiryu* maneuvering radically, making his aim more difficult than his earlier effort against *Kaga*. He was nearly vertical, hanging in his shoulder straps with his rear lifting out of his seat bottom. John Dance called off the altitude during their plunge, and then Micheel threw his SBD into a bit of a skid to starboard to stay on target. He saw no need to try to watch the results after pulling his bomb release. *If you skid, you miss.* Jim Dexter, next in line, later informed Micheel that his bomb had exploded just off the carrier's starboard bow.[22]

Although some of Scouting Six's aviators believed that Jaccard had hit her, others thought that *Hiryu* still showed no signs of damage. Dave Shumway wisely decided to shift targets back to the carrier instead of diving on his assigned battleship. He swung his fourteen Bombing Three planes around to strike. *Hiryu*'s turn and thick flak had thrown off VS-6, but Shumway sized up his target well as he came in. The Zeros had time to swarm in on the SBDs, and six VB-3 planes were attacked while in their dives.[23]

The AA fire was brutal. Shumway was forced to release at four thousand feet. Those following him released closer to two thousand feet, but their first drops were all misses. Shumway's SBD was hit repeatedly by flak. He feinted toward the ocean as if his plane were crippled, then pulled out at the last instant and took shelter in a nearby cloud layer. His decision to shift Bombing Three from the battleship to the carrier gave the Americans better odds of disabling the last Japanese flight deck. In so doing, however, Shumway's Naval Academy classmate Dick Best was cut off for the second time this day.[24]

Best was slightly behind Gallaher's lead VS-6 division, preparing to push over. He too found that the ships' AA fire was intense. *Everybody is firing. Everybody is madder than hell*, he thought. Best knew the Japanese were furious with their earlier carrier losses, but he believed that some ships were firing so low at retiring American dive-bombers they must be holing their own ships in the frenzy.[25]

Shumway, Cooner, Schlegel, Wiseman, Merrill, and Hogan all dived on *Hiryu* ahead of Best. Bud Merrill found the confusion over the Flying Dragon to be complete. Three divisions from three different squadrons converged from different directions. "One guy said later that if that had happened during training in Pensacola, the flight instructors would have torn our heads off," said Merrill.[26]

Hiryu's flight deck appeared to Merrill from great altitude to be about one to two inches long. As he started down, however, her size grew in a hurry. At eighteen hundred feet, he toggled his bomb into the smoke and flames erupting from the flight deck.

Shumway, Cooner, and Merrill were all attacked by Zeros during their dives. Steve Hogan of Bombing Six was flying tail-end Charlie with Shumway's first division. His rear gunner, Gene Braun, felt the whole world would explode as the sky erupted with black bursts of AA fire and swirling Zero fighters. He opened up with his Browning as Hogan pulled out. Braun noted with satisfaction that Ensign Hogan's bomb was a direct hit.[27]

Dick Best was right on Hogan's heels. He was thirteenth to dive on *Hiryu* as he led Kroeger and Weber down into the middle of Bombing Three's divisions. Best had avoided another midair collision by pulling his planes up and out as his division was once again cut off by other eager dive-bomber pilots. "Man-made confusion struck Bombing Six again," said gunner Jim Murray.[28]

Best's planes became scattered momentarily, and Fred Weber fell astern. Weber, often warned by his skipper about the dangers of straggling, was once again in a bad situation. This time, however, it was no fault of his own. He had checked his dive to avoid stalling as Shumway's VB-3 planes cut off the VB-6 group. Jim Murray saw that a lurking Zero immediately took advantage of the situation and raked Weber's plane with 7.7mm bullets. Murray

U.S. Navy

Ensign Fred Weber.

felt the Zero must have hit gunner Ernest Hilbert, as he saw no return fire. Murray motioned for Weber to close in on Best and Kroeger to take advantage of their mutual firepower.[29]

The Zero approached again, this time firing his 20mm cannon. Murray saw the flames from the Zero's muzzle flash and opened up with his own rear guns, even though his adversary was still out of range. He was still firing as 6-B-1 pushed over into its dive on *Hiryu*, leaving him and his twin .30s dangling. Murray tried to steady himself by grabbing the equipment rack with his right hand. As he flailed for his unsecured guns with his left hand, he caught his index and middle fingers between the mount and its securing ring. Yet he had no time to worry about the dripping blood from his gashed fingers as he swung sidesaddle in his seat. In this position, he could not read the altitudes for his skipper, so Best had to watch the altimeter himself.[30]

Another fighter flashed in as 6-B-1 was diving. Murray saw the Zero pass over their tail without firing. Best dived straight down *Hiryu*'s flight deck from bow to stern and released his thousand-pounder. Murray saw the flash of their bomb through the smoke as it struck amidships forward of the island. Richard Halsey Best is believed to be the first American pilot to successfully bomb two Japanese carriers in one day.[31]

The results of Bud Kroeger's drop could not be determined. Diving next, Fred Weber paid the price for being forced out of position. The Zero that blasted his 6-B-2 caused damage from which the young pilot could not recover. "He never pulled out of his dive and at twenty degrees went into the ocean," Best said. Weber and radioman Hilbert perished in the crash.[32]

Behind Best's section, Bombing Three still had two divisions with bombs to release on *Hiryu*. Lieutenant (j.g.) Gordon Sherwood led the second division of Roy Isaman, Phil Cobb, Syd Bottomley, Charlie Lane, and Johnny Butler. As they approached the pushover point, Ensign Lane heard someone yell, "Fighters coming ahead!"[33]

Ensign Oley Hanson of Shumway's VB-3 division was caught lagging behind in the strike formation and ended up mixed in the fray of sections diving on *Hiryu*. Instead of being tail-end Charlie for his division, he ended up behind Best's section. "Just as I pushed over in my dive, I heard Johnny Butler say that he was being attacked by fighters," Hanson said. He saw several near misses on the carrier as he dived and was very unhappy to find that his own load was another close miss. His disgust was washed away by the sight of three bombs that quickly ripped *Hiryu*'s deck. "It was a beautiful sight," Hanson said. He saw that the Flying Dragon was turned into a mass of flames.[34]

Charlie Lane's last vision of Johnny Butler was a momentary wave just as they prepared to roll into their dive. "He was supposed to follow me down," remembered Lane. "He wanted to be a fighter pilot." Butler never got the chance, as the Zeros followed him into his dive approach. Murray in Best's rear seat saw the numerals "12" on the bottom of the wings of Butler's 3-B-12. A Zero poured lead into the SBD, and Murray saw Butler's

U.S. Navy

Ensign John Butler.

bomb fall free, likely jettisoned as his electrical release was shot away. Butler and his gunner, ARM3c David Berg, were killed as their Dauntless slammed into the Pacific.[35]

The Zeros gave equal focus to the other diving Bombing Three planes. Gordon Sherwood found that fighters in echelon made sweeping scissors back and forth across his tail. "At the top of my dive a Zero pulled up from the tail of the preceding plane and dove at me," he said. Two planes behind Sherwood, Phil Cobb was amazed at the tenacity of one Zero that stuck with him during his dive on *Hiryu*. "He pulled up and made a second run while I was in the same dive," he said. Cobb pulled out of his dive and found himself in the center of the enemy task force with Japanese battleships firing main batteries at him. He tried to rendezvous with another SBD as he cleared the AA fire, but the dive-bomber's rear seat man was so spooked by Zeros that he briefly opened fire on Cobb's approaching plane.[36]

Another Zero made an overhead pass on Syd Bottomley's SBD as he prepared to dive. He opened his dive flaps, slowing his plane and causing the fighter to overshoot him. The Zero then pulled up and spoiled the aim of two other Zeros waiting to make runs on Bottomley's bomber. At seven thousand feet, another fighter appeared and made steep shooting runs against his SBD. Bottomley felt that the aggressive Japanese fighter looked like a falling leaf. His rear seat man, AMM2c David Johnson, used his twin .30s to drive off their attacker. Bottomley released five hundred feet lower than he had during his morning strike on *Soryu*. This time he thought, *I know I can't miss!* Johnson in his rear seat confirmed another direct hit for them.[37]

It was impossible to accurately assess the hits and misses of each pilot. The tail end of Scouting Six was piled on nearly simultaneously by Shumway's Bombing Three group and Best's Bombing Six section. What is certain is that *Hiryu* was slammed in rapid succession by four thousand-pound bombs, all on the forward third of her flight deck. Nineteen Zero fighters parked in the forward hangar deck added to the devastation aboard *Hiryu* as fires began raging through her forward section.[38]

The final two VB-3 pilots in line, Bob Campbell and Bob Benson, saw that *Hiryu* was hit hard and switched back to the battleship *Haruna*. They scored only near misses. Fred Bergeron, rear gunner for

Benson, found that the battleship had a whole lot more firepower than what he had experienced during his morning dive on *Soryu*. He returned the favor by unleashing his .30-caliber against the massive warship as Benson pulled out of his dive. "I wasn't trying to kill anybody," Bergeron said. "I was just shooting at where the firing was coming from, trying to protect ourselves."

I t was a shoot-out to escape the *Hiryu* task force. The mixed bag of *Enterprise/Yorktown* SBDs were jumped by at least a dozen fighters after their pullouts. They believed them to be both Zeros and Messerschmitt 109s, a mistaken identity. From Shumway's first division, Ozzie Wiseman was last seen being chased by Zeros after making his bomb drop. Neither he nor his radioman, ARM2c Grant Dawn, were seen again.

Dusty Kleiss of VS-6 was also attacked following his pullout. Johnny Snowden in his rear seat put out a heavy barrage of machine-gun fire that set the Japanese fighter's engine to smoking. The enemy pilot gave up the fight but was soon replaced by a second one. Kleiss poured on full throttle and did not let the fighter gain any ground on his SBD. Kleiss joined up with several other Dauntlesses for the return flight.[39]

Oley Hanson cleared *Hiryu*'s immediate area, and heard Joe Godfrey open up with his rear guns. He quickly jinked left and right before diving for the water. Hanson saw a long string of machine-gun bullets hitting the water to his left and decided to seek safety. He tightened up on two other SBDs, and the mutual firepower of their tail gunners was enough to convince the Zero pilot to break away.[40]

Dave Shumway was pursued by a Zero that stayed with him through much of his retirement. Several 20mm shells tore through his plane's right wing, damaging the right dive and landing flaps, as well as his right elevator and stabilizer. His right main gas tank was holed and fuel began streaming out. Another shell exploded in the SBD's baggage compartment, throwing shrapnel into Shumway's rear gunner, ARM1c Ray Coons. Some of the Zero's 7.7mm slugs holed the plane's nose section and fuselage as well. Despite the extensive harm to his plane, Shumway doggedly fought his 3-B-13 all the way back to *Enterprise*.

Gordon Sherwood was chased for eight minutes but managed to escape damage. Bud Merrill was less fortunate. His rear gunner, Dallas

Bergeron, became fully engaged with two Zeros. Merrill, who had flown a bombless SBD in his morning dive on *Soryu*, had successfully delivered his load against *Hiryu*. Now his Dauntless and Bergeron paid the price for that delivery. Small-caliber fire ripped through their SBD before it was rocked by a pair of 20mm shells that struck just aft of Bergeron's rear cockpit. Explosions frayed the plane's control cables and sent shards of shrapnel slicing through Bergeron's compartment. One piece of hot metal lodged in the young Texan's left leg and another in his right ankle. Merrill applied full throttle and dived into a cloud bank, where he was able to shake off his pursuer.

Ensign Randy Cooner came under hot fire from a trio of Zeros. A 20mm shell ripped into his rear cockpit and exploded in the radio transmitter. His gunner, AOM2c Clifton Bassett, was seriously wounded in the right knee. Another 20mm shell hit at the base of their SBD's fin, exploding in the baggage compartment and shredding their life raft. Cooner suffered a slight leg wound from fragments of his own plane in the explosion. Although weak from blood loss, Bassett stayed with his twin .30-caliber guns and shot up a Japanese seaplane that moved in to attack their Dauntless after the Zeros departed.

Earl Gallaher was chased throughout his dive by a Zero, which roared past so close as he pulled out that Gallaher could almost reach out and touch its belly. Gallaher soon collected five other SBDs and used a low-speed, low-altitude retirement. "This time we made no effort to deceive the Japs and headed straight for our task force," he said.[41]

Four American bombs had landed ahead of *Hiryu*'s island structure, leaving her forward elevator jammed up against the bridge. Dusty Kleiss observed the flight deck flipped backward like a taco. The forward third of *Hiryu*'s deck was a blazing pit of fire. The strike that mortally wounded this fourth Japanese carrier of the day cost the Americans three Dauntlesses and six lives.[42]

For six survivors of the attack on Pearl Harbor flying among Gallaher's and Best's squadrons, the mortal wounding of the *Hiryu* was sweet revenge. Fred Weber, a seventh veteran of December 7, perished in his attack. Leaving the carrier behind, blazing in the Pacific, the ragged formation of Bombing Six, Scouting Six, and Bombing Three triumphantly turned for their shared home—the flight deck of USS *Enterprise*.

. . .

Roughly twenty minutes after the *Enterprise* group completed its dives on the enemy carrier, Ed Stebbins arrived overhead with his sixteen *Hornet* SBDs at 1730. Roy Gee was happy that his predecessors had cleared the upper altitudes of Zeros, leaving Bombing Eight with an unopposed approach. He saw that *Hiryu* was "completely on fire."[43]

Stebbins directed his group toward other suitable target ships. He led VS-8 toward an escorting cruiser and signaled Fred Bates that VB-8 should attack the heavy cruiser *Tone*. Bates led his squadron down from out of the sun from fifteen thousand feet and landed his bomb fifty feet off the starboard bow. His wingman, Ensign Henry Nickerson, dropped his bomb one hundred feet astern. Gee was credited with a hit on *Tone*'s stern as he dodged the orange balls of ack-ack popping up at him. He proudly thought, *Bombing Eight has lost its combat virginity.*[44]

Ensigns Ken White and Robert Friesz of VB-8's second section both missed, but Ensign Clark Barrett claimed a hit on her starboard quarter. Japanese records, however, show that the *Hornet* strike achieved nothing better than near misses. Clay Fisher, the last of his squadron to dive on *Tone*, pressed the electrical bomb release switch at low altitude. Nothing happened. His bomb was hung up. Fisher nearly blacked out from the heavy g-forces as he frantically pulled back on the stick to recover from his dive. He crossed three hundred feet over the fantail of a Japanese destroyer as all of its guns blasted away at him. Shrapnel splashed like huge raindrops in the water below his plane. His SBD's tremendous acceleration allowed Fisher to safely clear the AA fire, and he finally shook off his hung bomb with the manual release.[45]

Fisher and Gee were surprised to see clusters of explosions erupting in the water near the cruiser during their dives. They would later learn that a group of Midway-based B-17s had made a high-level bombing run at the same time as *Hornet*'s SBDs were attacking. The exuberant Army pilots claimed one hit and two near misses, and a destroyer as sunk. A second wave of B-17s also attacked, claiming more hits on the carrier and her escort ships. Yet postwar analysis would show that the Army bombers had hit nothing.[46]

. . .

Dick Best continued to the west for ten to fifteen miles after hitting *Hiryu*. He did not want any Zeros to come back at him when he was all alone. Swinging out to the south to give them a wide berth, he spotted smoke columns on the horizon. He dropped down for a closer look and was rewarded with a satisfying sight. *There are the three carriers we hit this morning, and they're all still burning!* Bombing Six's skipper hung around only briefly to soak up the scene—the fine results of his lifetime of training.[47]

Best escaped Japanese fighters during his return to *Enterprise*, only to be jumped by eager American CAP Wildcats who mistook him for the enemy. "We were at least ten miles out when the Wildcats closed on our tail," Jim Murray said. "I recognized the fighters as F4Fs and hoped they would recognize us." Best opened up on his radio and convinced the friendly fighters that his plane belonged where it was. "I had to call them off savagely," he said.[48]

Mike Micheel of Scouting Six watched his navigation like a hawk during his return flight, still wary of his narrow return to *Enterprise* from the morning strike. Earl Gallaher noticed an eerie sight as his SBDs approached the U.S. task force. There sat poor *Yorktown* with only a guardian destroyer—as though waiting for the planes above to make their report. "She reminded me of a ghost ship," said Gallaher.[49]

Best flew close by *Yorktown*, allowing his radioman to get a good look at the abandoned carrier. Murray had served on CV-5 for nearly three years while a member of her Torpedo Squadron Five. "This brought tears to my eyes, seeing my old home in such shape," he said.[50]

At 1820, *Enterprise* began recovering some of her CAP fighters. Behind them came the first of the twenty-one SBDs to return from the *Hiryu* strike. Sunset was approaching as the last of the planes came aboard after more than three hours in the air. Gallaher landed with only about a gallon of fuel remaining and a badly wrenched back. "The pain was so severe that I couldn't reach down to put my hook down," he said. He turned the lead over to Reid Stone and flew around trying to lower his hook while the others landed. Gallaher did not dare touch down without his hook because of the terrible barrier crash he would endure. He knew that a water landing was out of the question. *I probably will not be able to get out of the plane.*[51]

Finally reaching the hook handle in desperation, he almost passed out from the pain. He made an admittedly shaky landing and had to be helped out of his Dauntless by the flight surgeon, Lieutenant (j.g.) David P. Hightower, and two corpsmen. His back ached so badly he could hardly move. Gallaher was grounded, and he knew that it was the end of the battle for him.[52]

The *Enterprise* strike group returned with the exception of Bombing Six's Fred Weber and two pilots of VB-3. Charlie Lane made it down after having exhausted his starboard fuel tanks. He was spent, having flown ten and a half hours that day and eight hours the preceding day. Randy Cooner's gunner, Clifton Bassett, was lifted from his bullet-riddled plane by corpsmen, placed on a stretcher, and hustled toward sick bay, where his right leg wound could receive proper attention.[53]

Gunner Fred Bergeron was concerned for his brother. The SBD that Dallas Bergeron had flown in had not returned. The Texas teenager spent anxious moments wondering whether he had lost his older sibling. "It was thought that everybody that was coming back was there," he said. Finally, Bud Merrill's battered Dauntless appeared on the horizon and the Big E turned into the wind to recover it. Deck crews swarmed over the plane as Fred counted numerous bullet holes in his brother's dive-bomber.[54]

Dallas was unable to climb out of the rear cockpit. His flight suit was splattered with blood from bullets that had lodged in his left leg and right ankle. He was lifted out and taken below to have the slugs surgically removed, although some shards of shrapnel would remain in his legs for the remainder of his life. Fred busied himself that evening with

Courtesy of Fred Bergeron

Dallas Bergeron (*left*) with his brother, Fred, receiving the Distinguished Flying Cross for their action at Midway.

gathering razors, toothpaste, soap, and other personal supplies for himself, his brother, and another of their wounded VB-3 comrades, Clifton Bassett. "All of our possessions were on the *Yorktown*," said Fred. "It was pretty bad knowing you didn't have anything left except the clothes on your back." He delivered the grooming supplies to sick bay, where Dallas was lying in the bunk beside Bassett.

The trio of Bombing Three gunners found comfort in the fact that they had survived two bombing attacks that helped sink four Japanese carriers. "It had been a very hair-raising day," Fred said. Three of VB-3's Dauntlesses—those of Shumway, Merrill, and Cooner—were deemed inoperable for further combat.

Dick Best was the last of the afternoon strike group to return. He did not reach *Enterprise* until 1834 due to his lengthy detour to view the other three blazing Japanese carriers. At first, Jim Murray could not understand the peculiar looks from some of the flight deck crew. He soon learned that their plane had been reported shot down over *Hiryu* by some of the first strikers to return. Murray was further surprised as he climbed out of his rear cockpit to hear Lieutenant Best say, "I may need some help." [55]

A flight deck crewman joined Murray in helping Best to the deck. After his pilot was guided down to sick bay, Murray was left wondering what was wrong. He climbed back into 6-B-1's rear cockpit and sat for several minutes, reflecting on the day's events. He finally headed below to the chiefs' mess for dinner, stopping by sick bay to receive his "medicinal" shot of hundred-proof bourbon. [56]

Chief Murray was in such a daze that he had even forgotten to have the medical staff look at his lacerated left hand, pinched in his gun mount during the *Hiryu* attack. He reached the CPO mess for dinner and ate in silence. "It was a weird feeling sitting there eating, having the chiefs and cooks look at you as if you were a ghost," he said. They respected his silence, however, and only nodded at him. Murray, unable to muster any words, could only nod in return. [57]

Hornet began landing the fourteen SBDs of Ed Stebbins's strike group at 1857. Seven Dauntless squadrons had attacked the Japanese fleet during the day, including one Marine bunch from Midway. Some thirty-five SBDs and about forty aviators had been lost. The three carrier fighter squadrons had lost nineteen Wildcats and five pilots, while thirty-seven of the slow TBD torpedo planes had gone down on June 4. As for the Japanese air groups, many of their planes had been shot down in aerial combat, and others were forced to ditch. Those who made it back on board their ships would ultimately go down with their carriers.[58]

It had been a decisive day of retribution for the Dauntless airmen. In a matter of hours, they had completely wrecked four IJN flattops that had participated in the Pearl Harbor assault six months prior. Some 2,181 Japanese sailors perished with the loss of *Akagi*, *Kaga*, *Soryu*, and *Hiryu*—a death toll that almost equaled the number of Americans killed on December 7.

The afternoon of June 4 did not end gloriously for the downed Scouting Six crew of Ensign Frank O'Flaherty and his gunner, Bruno Gaido. Around 1630, the cruiser *Nagara* spotted a life raft in the water and ordered the destroyer *Makigumo* to investigate. The destroyer duly effected the rescue of the *Enterprise* SBD crew under orders to interrogate the Americans "to ascertain the enemy's situation and then dispose of them suitably."[59]

Makigumo's surgeon treated various wounds on O'Flaherty and Gaido and the crew shared cigarettes with the Americans. During their subsequent interrogations, Lieutenant Ryuhichi Katsumata threatened the aviators with a sword when they refused to answer questions. The VS-6 duo gave up no details of importance about the American carrier forces, but did offer creative information about Midway's defenses that proved to be fairly accurate.[60]

Commander Isamu Fujita decided he had extracted all he could from the American aviators. A call for executioners found no willing volunteers following the battle of Midway, as *Makigumo* was headed toward the Aleutian Islands. Some were even promised the borrowed cigarette lighter of Ensign O'Flaherty (a single man), which had been inscribed, "To My Matchless Husband." Late at night, O'Flaherty and Gaido were taken on deck, blindfolded, weighed down with five-gallon kerosene cans filled with water, and thrown overboard. *Makigumo*'s navigation officer, Shigeo Hirayama, later stated that the Scouting Six aviators showed no sign of fear as they were tossed to their deaths.[61]

Dusty Kleiss would long mourn the loss of squadron mate Bruno Peter Gaido, who had been promoted on the spot by Admiral Halsey on February 1 for shooting down a kamikaze. They had met when the pilot was making his first carrier qualification landings. Gaido volunteered to join in his rear seat for the landings. "I'm supposed to have only sandbags," Kleiss had protested. "You got wings, ain'tcha?" Gaido retorted as he replaced the sandbags with his stout frame. "Peter Gaido was the bravest man I ever met," Dusty said.[62]

Ensign Tom Wood of *Hornet*'s VB-8 and gunner George Martz were still paddling as evening approached, having managed to cover more than a dozen miles in toward Midway in their rubber raft. They had gone into the water when their SBD ran out of fuel following the long morning mission. They reached the reef opposite Sand and Eastern islands around dusk, but found that they were still miles from solid ground. To complicate matters, the reef they had to cross with their rubber boat was occupied by a massive bull sea lion.[63]

Luckily, Wood and Martz still had their shoes. They waded to the reef carrying the rubber boat. The sea lion, ignoring their shouts, refused to move from the one easy high point where they planned to cross the reef. Both men were very tired, wet, and hungry. "Finally, I went up to him, kicked him in the rear, and the huge creature flopped into the water after several kicks," said Wood. The airmen removed their clothes to put on the reef to protect their rubber boat. "Meanwhile, the sea lion bull was swimming around and around the reef raising all kinds of hell," Wood said. "I still laugh when I think of the picture of two bare-assed people sitting on the rock and the bull circling and barking like the devil."

The Bombing Eight aviators managed to dodge the sea lion and paddle the remaining way into Midway Island. The last leg of their voyage was not without incident, however, as they spotted a huge shark following their raft. The shark was still trailing them when they approached the dock. Wood was greatly relieved to spot a small personnel boat chugging out to pick them up. He stood up and fired six shots at the shark with his .45-caliber pistol. When the boat approached them, a Marine was standing in the bow manning a .50-caliber mounted machine gun that was trained on them. "Neither he nor I could ever figure why he didn't blow us out of the water when I started shooting," Wood said. "Needless to say, personnel on the island were very trigger-happy on 4 June and it was quite dark."[64]

Martz and Wood reported in to Colonel Ira Kimes of the Marine Corps and offered their services to help with the personnel losses on Midway, since their own bombing squadron had long since flown back to *Hornet*. Kimes greeted Ensign Wood with a "welcome aboard" before handing him a bottle of Old Crow whiskey.[65]

Wood's squadron mate Ensign Troy Guillory was more fortunate. He was discovered at sea by a Midway PBY from Patrol Squadron 23, piloted by Lieutenant (j.g.) Harold W. Lowe. Guillory nearly shot the PBY with his Very pistol when it appeared Lowe was going to leave the SBD crew in the water after circling several times. The VB-8 aviators had spent some seven and a half hours in their life raft when they were discovered around 1930.[66]

Lowe was eager to get his PBY back into the air as quickly as possible due to Japanese forces in the area. When he noticed Guillory struggling to pull his rubber raft into his flying boat, Lowe impatiently snapped, "Turn that damned thing loose!" Guillory shot right back with, "This damned raft got me this far. I'm not about to let it go!" Lowe's PBY returned to Midway with Guillory and Billy Cotrell safely aboard, and Guillory slept in a foxhole for much of the night.

The *Hornet, Enterprise*, and orphaned *Yorktown* SBD aircrews were exhausted by day's end. Aboard the Big E, Wally Short's fliers moved into the nearly vacated Torpedo Six quarters for the night, and the *Enterprise* and *Yorktown* pilots relived their day's successes over evening chow. A cheer rang out when a dispatch was read over the PA system from CinCPac congratulating them on sinking four carriers in one day.[67]

On *Hornet*, Bombing Eight gunner Slim Moore listened to the scuttlebutt in the radio shack regarding the fate of Torpedo Eight's aviators. *They all had Mae Wests and life rafts. Maybe some of them are alive in the ocean.*[68]

Slim, hurting for his best friend, Ronnie Fisher, wandered around like a lost soul that evening. *I don't think I'm ever going to see Ronnie again*, he thought. *They say those guys might be out there, but I don't believe anybody survived an attack like that.*

Moore eventually drifted up to the VT-8 pilots' ready room. The door was open, so he strolled in. As he gazed about the empty briefing room, his eyes settled on the large chalkboard at the front of the compartment. He focused on what he believed must have been skipper Jack Waldron's last message to his fallen Torpedo Eight pilots. Printed in large yellow chalk letters was a single command:

ATTACK!

On *Enterprise*, Charlie Lane of Bombing Three was worn-out. Assigned the room of one of Torpedo Six's lost pilots, Lane first noticed the man's family pictures and a Bible on his desk as he entered the stateroom. Lane realized he would never see his own keepsakes—a 1940 Clemson graduation ring and his Hamilton watch, left aboard *Yorktown* that day in case he never came back. The shot of brandy from the *Enterprise* medics helped him forget about these things and drift off to sleep.[69]

Gunner John Snowden of VS-6 felt a twinge of depression while he lay among the empty bunks. He had lost many good friends in the morning battle over the carriers, and retired with a profound sense of personal loss.[70]

Snowden's pilot, Dusty Kleiss, having made two carrier attacks, was relieved to finally get some rest. He noted in his diary, "I took a slug of whiskey and turned in."[71]

FOURTEEN

"The Little Devil Was Most Difficult to Hit"

Tony Schneider and Glenn Holden were all alone in the Pacific. The Japanese fleet passed from their area on the afternoon of June 4, and the Bombing Six aviators took stock of their situation.

To Tony, Holden's head looked like a football. It was lacerated and swollen both front and back. Holden's first concern upon regaining his senses was that he had failed to retrieve any rations from their plane. Tony assured him that he had gathered all that he could into their little yellow life raft. He had retained his .45-caliber service revolver, and both men were wearing their Mae West life preservers. The emergency items on their raft included: a raft repair kit, smoke grenades, a fluorescent-dye sea marker, a sea anchor to help steer their raft, a safety knife, a signal mirror, a Very pistol with signal flares, a book on survival at sea, and K-rations. Tony found that they had a quart of water per person in addition to small cans of pemmican, a fat-and-protein survival ration made largely of mixed dried meats and fruits.

Schneider had resolved to abstain from drinking any of his water or touching the canned rations for as long as his body would hold out. Holden, on the other hand, drank a considerable portion of his water right away. "I'm sure he needed his," said Tony. "He had a bad rap on the head." The pair simply sat squeezed into their rubber boat with each man's knees near the other man's face. Tony saw no need in trying to row. The nearest land was beyond what he considered to be a realistic chance of making it. *I know that a lot of other guys probably had to go into the drink out of gas*, he thought. *Search planes will be out looking for us.* Late in the afternoon, they heard the distant hum of engines. When several Army B-17s passed over at high altitude Tony tried to attract their attention with his soggy Very pistol charges but failed.[1]

The air grew colder as the afternoon sun dipped below the horizon. Holden's head wounds still throbbed but his mental faculties had returned. Tony avoided using any of his water during the night, knowing that they could be in for a long ordeal. The air warmed quickly again as the sun rose on June 5. In order to protect them from extreme exposure, Tony rigged a sun cover over their raft from the silk parachute he had thought to haul on board with them.

The silence of bobbing in the Pacific swells was broken at one point by the distant hum of an engine. Tony gazed skyward and finally made out a seaplane in the distance. Using the little signal mirror, he tried to catch the attention of the flight crew, yet his hopes were dashed when it gradually moved closer to their position. Its silhouette was not that of an American search plane, but likely a single-engine Japanese seaplane that had been catapulted from a cruiser or battleship to scour the area for Americans as the Japanese fleet retired from the area.[2]

I don't think we have any single-engine seaplanes out there at Midway. It must be a Jap. If he sees us, this might be the end for us, Tony thought. He had heard stories of Japanese planes strafing survivors in the water. He told Holden they had no choice but to dive overboard and put their heads under the water if the floatplane made a strafing run.

Fortunately, the Japanese plane continued on without giving any indication that its crews had spotted the two Americans adrift on the ocean below. The midday sun grew quite uncomfortable as the hours whittled away slowly. All they could do was continue to wait and pray that the next aircraft to come over the horizon would be American.

Fatigue set in during the afternoon. Holden and Schneider finally drifted off to sleep, still sitting upright in the raft. Tony woke up suddenly when water splashed his face. He was startled to see four large dorsal fins cutting the surface and large tails slapping the water. *Sharks!*

Tony knew there were likely even more of the deadly creatures schooling around that he could not see. Several brushed against the raft and he worried that one of the sharks might puncture their rubber vessel.

Tony estimated the sharks to be about eight feet in length. He was still carrying his pistol that he took on all missions. One of the more aggressive sharks came up beside their raft with his head halfway out of the water. "He was so close I could have touched him," Tony said. Instead, he pushed his .45-caliber close to the shark's face and squeezed off a round right between his eyes. The shark thrashed backward violently and created a huge geyser of water. The others scattered with the gun blast, and peace returned to their lonely vigil. It did take Holden several minutes to recover from his rude awakening.

There's no reason to panic, Tony thought as he settled back down to wait for rescue. *I'm here and I know they'll be out looking for me. At least I know we've got a chance.*

Admiral Spruance safeguarded his SBDs during the morning of June 5, holding them back for expected follow-up strikes once other capital warships of the Japanese fleet were located. Admiral Yamamoto approved orders early that morning to cancel the occupation of Midway, and his landing forces turned back to the west. Fog and rain during the early morning hours further reinforced Spruance's desire to hold back on his carrier planes. He would wait for land-based searchers to solidly locate the Japanese first.

Ten PBY search planes departed from Midway on patrols at 0415, followed fifteen minutes later by eight B-17s still operating from the atoll. Troy Guillory of Bombing Eight was awakened in his foxhole at 0200. A Marine informed him that Captain Cyril T. Simard, the island commander, wanted to see him in the operations center. Simard needed Navy pilots to fly with his Army B-17s to assist in identifying friendly versus enemy ships.[3]

Guillory climbed aboard the B-17 of Captain Donald Ridings. In addition, ensigns Joe Auman and Tom Wood of VB-8—the latter having rowed ashore the previous evening—hitched a ride in the B-17 flown by Lieutenant Colonel Brooke E. Allen to assist with spotting. The Army aircraft were in search of a Japanese force reported by the U.S. submarine *Tambor* during the night. In stalking these ships, *Tambor* was spotted and caused the warships to maneuver to avoid her. The heavy cruiser *Mikuma* turned into the path of her sister cruiser *Mogami*. In the ensuing collision, *Mogami*'s bow was buckled back, and ruptured fuel tanks from the cruisers left a telltale oil wake.[4]

The B-17s failed to find these ships, but a PBY radioed a contact report at 0630 of two "battleships" trailing oil. Six Marine SBDs and six SB2Us from Midway attacked *Mogami* and *Mikuma*. They scored only near misses, and lost one plane in the process. At 0830, Brooke Allen's B-17s found the damaged cruisers about 130 miles west of Midway and dropped five hundred-pound bombs from high altitude. When the antiaircraft fire became heavy toward his bomber, Troy Guillory squatted behind the pilot's seat, which he assumed was protected by armor plating. "On the way home, I learned that this was not armor plate, but a cabin fuselage fuel tank which I was taking shelter behind," he said.[5]

Other early Midway planes continued to send in contact reports that reached Admiral Spruance's carrier group. At 0800, a PBY reported two battleships and one carrier afire, with three cruisers in company. It was *Hiryu*, abandoned during the night and drifting. She sank around 0900 that morning, unknown to either the Americans or the Japanese, and created a great deal of confusion throughout the day.[6]

Task force destroyers transferred all of their *Yorktown* survivors to the cruiser *Portland* during the morning hours. *Hammann* likewise sent over the SBD crew of Ensign Mac McCarthy, gunner Earl Howell, and VT-3's Chief Bill Esders. PBYs from Midway picked up other carrier aviators from the water during the day, including Ensign George Gay, VT-8's only survivor of the carrier-based portion of that squadron.

Dick Dickinson and gunner Joe DeLuca of VS-6 had ridden out the remainder of June 4 on *Phelps*. The next morning, their destroyer investigated a report of a rubber boat in the water near the task group. They found Bombing Six's Joe Penland and his gunner, Harold Heard.

During the previous afternoon, Heard had counted five different PBYs, but none had spotted him and his pilot in their little yellow raft. Paddling through the night, they sighted their task force after daybreak on June 5. They climbed up *Phelps*'s cargo net, where Dickinson greeted his friend. He saw that Penland was sunburned and that his face was swollen. He also had lacerations surrounding a blackened eye.[7]

In spite of these discomforts, Penland and his gunner could count themselves among the more fortunate downed crews at Midway. Penland felt in hindsight that his squadron's high loss of planes on June 4 did not slight the success of their mission in destroying Japanese warships. "We had the satisfaction of feeling that we had used our planes to good advantage," he said.[8]

The ragged collection of Dauntless aircrews on *Enterprise* was reorganized during the morning of June 5. Eight Scouting Five pilots were merged with the remnants of Earl Gallaher's Scouting Six to unofficially create "Scouting 65." A second makeshift squadron, "Bombing 63," was organized with the surviving SBDs of Bombing Three and Bombing Six. Lieutenant Dave Shumway had become senior aviator in command of VB-63, as Bombing Six skipper Dick Best was out of action as of that morning. Reporting to sick bay throwing up blood, Best was diagnosed with miliary tuberculosis and would spend thirty-two months in naval hospitals as he struggled to recover. He believed his ailment had been triggered by breathing in caustic soda powder from his oxygen container during his flight to attack *Akagi*. His naval career was finished after Midway, but he had left his mark. In one day, Best had made dives on two carriers, scored two hits, and had the satisfaction of knowing that both targets sank. *I had my day*, Best thought. *I finished on the big one.*[9]

Meanwhile, Miles Browning was creating another controversy. He drew up an attack plan during the early afternoon of June 5 in order to get the carrier's dive-bombers back into the pursuit of Japanese shipping. *Enterprise* and *Hornet* had launched only Wildcat CAP flights throughout the morning hours, but Browning now wanted SBDs loaded with thousand-pound bombs to launch around 1400, at a range of 275 miles, to investigate the early morning reports of the burning *Hiryu*.[10]

Admiral Spruance approved the plan, but the mission did not go over well with the Dauntless squadron commanders on board *Enterprise*. Dave Shumway was outraged. His SBDs did not have the distance to make such a long flight with thousand-pound bombs and return to the carriers. Shumway met with Wally Short, the VS-5 skipper, and they sought the advice of the wounded air group commander, Wade McClusky. Short and McClusky gathered injured VS-6 skipper Earl Gallaher and headed for the flag bridge with *Enterprise*'s skipper, Captain George Murray, to confront Browning.[11]

McClusky ended up in a shouting match with Browning, arguing that the chief of staff had never flown a fully fueled, heavily armored dive-bomber with a thousand-pound bomb on a mission of that range. McClusky recommended the mission be delayed for one hour and that the bombs be changed to five-hundred-pounders. Spruance finally put an end to the shouting by stating to McClusky, "I will do what you pilots want." Browning promptly stomped off to his stateroom to pout over his crushed plans.[12]

The revised plan was blinkered over to *Hornet*, and in the meantime the carrier groups continued to narrow the range that the SBDs would be forced to fly. On *Enterprise*, the deck crews worked feverishly to replace the thousand-pound bomb loads with smaller five-hundred-pounders as crews on *Hornet* began arming their planes. Task Force 16 turned into the wind at 1500 for flight operations. Twelve minutes later, the order was passed on to *Hornet* to begin launching. The only contingent immediately ready to go was a group of twelve SBDs, all loaded with five-hundred-pound bombs.

The Sea Hag, Stan Ring, had a three-plane section, along with nine more Bombing Eight planes under Lieutenant Commander Ruff Johnson. Ring grouped his dozen strikers and departed immediately. In the meantime, the *Hornet* plane handlers labored to ready a second deckload of SBDs. This group included fifteen SBDs of VS-8 under Lieutenant Commander Walt Rodee, most also carrying the lighter five-hundred-pound bomb load. Scouting Eight's seven-plane second division under Lieutenant Gus Widhelm, however, still sported the thousand-pound bombs in spite of Spruance's orders to change them out. Neither Hornet strike included Wildcat escorts due to the extreme length of the missions.

Rodee and Widhelm were accompanied by only one VS-5 refugee pilot, Bill Christie. His companion, Hank McDowell, was off flying status for the day due to a minor ailment that prevented him from sitting down comfortably. Christie, based on his experience, had been made a division leader and McDowell a section leader within Scouting Eight. From Bombing Eight, Lieutenant (j.g.) Fred Bates would lead the remaining five SBDs of his squadron out at the tail of VS-8's two divisions.

Strike on *Tanikaze*
Hornet Group: June 5, 1942

BOMBING EIGHT (VB-8) FIRST STRIKE GROUP (11 SBDS)

PILOT	REAR SEAT GUNNER
Lt. Cdr. Robert Ruffin Johnson	ACRM Joseph G. McCoy
Ens. Philip Farnsworth Grant	ARM2c Robert H. Rider
Ens. William Douglas Carter	ARM2c Oral Lester Moore
Lt. James Everett Vose Jr.	ARM2c Joseph Yewonishon
Lt. John Joseph Lynch	ARM1c Wilbur L. Woods
Ens. Roy Philip Gee	ARM1c Donald L. Canfield
Lt. Alfred Bland Tucker III	ARM1c Champ T. Stuart
Ens. Gus George Bebas	RM3c Alfred W. Ringressy Jr.
Ens. Don Dee Adams	ARM2c John B. Broughton Jr.

CHAG SECTION

PILOT	REAR SEAT GUNNER
Cdr. Stanhope Cotton Ring	ARM2c Arthur M. Parker
Ens. Clayton Evan Fisher	ARM3c George E. Ferguson
Ens. Benjamin Tappan Jr.	ARM3c Earnest Ray Johnston

SCOUTING EIGHT (VS-8), SECOND STRIKE GROUP (16 SBDS)	
PILOT	**REAR SEAT GUNNER**
Lt. Cdr. Walter Fred Rodee	ACRM John Lenzy Clanton
Ens. Paul Edmond Tepas	ARM3c Moley J. Boutwell
Lt. (jg) William Francis Christie (VS-5)	ARM1c Alvin Arthur Sobel
Lt. Ray Davis*	ARM1c Ralph Phillips
Lt. Laurens Adin Whitney	ARM2c Angus D. Gilles
Lt. (jg) Jimmy McMillan Forbes	ARM3c Ronald H. Arenth
Lt. Ben Moore Jr.	ARM2c Richard Cusack McEwen
Ens. Stanley Robert Holm	ARM2c James H. Black Jr.
SECOND DIVISION, VS-8	
PILOT	**REAR SEAT GUNNER**
Lt. William Joseph Widhelm	ARM1c George D. Stokely
Lt. (jg) Donald Kirkpatrick Jr.	ARM2c Richard Thomas Woodson
Ens. Don "T" Griswold	ARM1c Kenneth Cecil Bunch
Ens. Helmuth Ernest Hoerner	ARM3c David T. Manus
Lt. Edgar Erwin Stebbins	ARM2c Ervin R. Hillhouse

(continued)

Strike on *Tanikaze* *Hornet* Group: June 5, 1942 (cont.)	
SECOND DIVISION, VS-8	
PILOT	**REAR SEAT GUNNER**
Ens. Philip James Rusk	ARM2c John H. Honeycutt
Ens. Harold White	ARM3c John Stephen Urban
Ens. Augustus Appleby Devoe	ARM3c John Louis Tereskerz
BOMBING EIGHT (VB-8) SECOND STRIKE GROUP (5 SBDS)	
PILOT	**REAR SEAT GUNNER**
Lt. (jg) Fred Leeson Bates	ARM1c Clyde S. Montensen
Ens. James Austin Riner Jr.	ARM2c Floyd Dell Kilmer
Ens. Arthur Caldwell Cason Jr.	ARM3c Alfred D. Wells
Ens. Frank E. Christofferson	ARM2c Barkley V. Poorman
Ens. Joe Wiley King	ARM3c Thomas M. Walsh

*Ditched and recovered following strike. VS-8 composition per Mark E. Horan research.

Hornet's second deckload was airborne by 1543, and Rodee led the flight in a climb toward eighteen thousand feet as they tailed the Sea Hag's leading formation by some distance.[13]

The well-blended *Enterprise* strike group began its departure at 1530. Dick Best, Wade McClusky, and Max Leslie were out of action, so the senior SBD commander heading up this mission became Dave Shumway.

Earl Gallaher was also grounded with his back injury, and his 6-S-1 was assigned to rookie pilot Ensign Clarence Vammen. Gallaher felt that Vammen was elated by his chance to fly, as he had been the only pilot of his squadron to not participate in the previous day's carrier strikes.[14]

Ensign Phil Cobb of VB-3, in his urgency to depart for this mission, neglected to bring some of the most basic necessities. "We had no helmets and no chart boards to do our DR navigation," he said. For his dead reckoning, he would have to keep track of headings, times, and other crucial data with simple pencil and paper.[15]

The planes and crews were sorted out as best as possible under the circumstances. Andy Anderson of VB-6, whose gunner, Stuart Mason, had been wounded on June 4, picked up Walter Chocalousek from the CEAG's rear seat—whose pilot had been shot the previous day. Lew Hopkins was back in his familiar 6-B-12, which had been used by Stephen Hogan for the previous afternoon's *Hiryu* strike. Eldor Rodenburg, again flying the cranky 6-S-9, was relieved that his SBD was in good operation this day.

Bob Benson's 3-B-6 never made it off the flight deck. His gunner, Fred Bergeron, had taken his position in the rear seat as the pilot tried to rev up their engine. When that failed, Benson asked Bergeron to perform a function called "flashing the field." Bergeron explained: "You climb out on the wing, take some butterfly nuts off a box, and stick your finger on a relay. I flashed the field, but that sucker wouldn't start." Benson's SBD was thus scratched from the June 5 mission.[16]

Shumway departed with thirty-two dive-bombers. He had ten crews from his own VB-3, seven VS-5 crews, nine from VS-6, and a half dozen more from VB-6. The flight remained at low altitude until approximately one hundred miles from the anticipated enemy position. Bombing Three began climbing for altitude and Shumway reached the expected position at 2000. The enemy was nowhere in sight, so he spent the next twenty minutes searching to the southwest.

Stan Ring's *Hornet* group flew at eighteen thousand feet, well ahead of the *Enterprise* group. After about an hour, Roy Gee noticed five B-17s, apparently returning to Midway. Forty-five minutes later, Ring spotted what he believed to be a Japanese light cruiser. It was the two-thousand-ton destroyer *Tanikaze*, heading south after having conducted a search to

Strike on *Tanikaze*
Enterprise Group: June 5, 1942

SCOUTING FIVE (VS-5) DIVISION

PLANE	PILOT	REAR SEAT GUNNER
5-B-2	Lt. Wallace Clark Short	ACRM John W. Trott
5-B-13	Lt. (jg) Carl Herman Horenburger	ARM3c Lynn Raymond Forshee
AGC	Lt. (jg) David Render Berry	ARM2c Earnest Alwyn Clegg
5-B-15	Lt. Sam Adams*	ARM1c Joseph John Karrol*
5-B-11	Lt. Harlan Rockey Dickson	ARM2c Joseph Michael Lynch Jr.
5-B-4	Lt. John Ludwig Neilsen	ACRM Walter Dean Straub
5-B-1	Lt. (jg) Nels Luther Alvin Berger	ACRM Otto Russell Phelps

SCOUTING SIX (VS-6) DIVISION

PLANE	PILOT	REAR SEAT GUNNER
6-S-13	Lt. (jg) Frank Anthony Patriarca	ACRM Jack Richard Badgley
6-S-16	Ens. William Robinson Pittman	AMM2c Floyd Delbert Adkins

6-S-11	Ens. Richard Alonzo Jaccard	RM3c Porter William Pixley
6-S-7	Lt. (jg) Norman Jack Kleiss	ARM3c John Warren Snowden
6-S-9	Ens. Eldor Ernst Rodenburg	Sea2c Thomas James Bruce
6-S-18	Ens. James Campbell Dexter	RM3c Donald Laurence Hoff
6-S-2	Ens. Reid Wentworth Stone	RM1c William Hart Bergin
6-S-17	Ens. Vernon Larsen Micheel	RM3c John Dewey Dance
6-S-1	Ens. Clarence Earl Vammen Jr.**	AMM2c Milton Wayne Clark**

BOMBING THREE (VB-3) STRIKE FORCE		
PLANE	**PILOT**	**REAR SEAT GUNNER**
3-B-3	Lt. DeWitt Wood Shumway	ARM1c Ray Edgar Coons
3-B-14	Ens. Robert Martin Elder	RM3c Leslie Alan Till
3-B-6	Ens. Paul Wahl Schlegel	ARM3c Jack Alvin Shropshire
3-B-4	Ens. Robert Keith Campbell	AMM1c Horace Henry Craig
3-B-5	Ens. Alden Wilbur Hanson	ARM3c Joseph Vernon Godfrey

(continued)

Strike on *Tanikaze*
Enterprise Group: June 5, 1942 (cont.)

SECOND DIVISION, VB-3

PLANE	PILOT	REAR SEAT GUNNER
3-B-7	Lt. (jg) Gordon Alvin Sherwood	ARM2c Harman Donald Bennett
3-B-8	Ens. Roy Maurice Isaman	ARM3c Sidney Kay Weaver
3-B-9	Ens. Phillip Walker Cobb	AMM2c Clarence E. Zimmershead
3-B-10	Lt. Harold Sydney Bottomley Jr.	AMM2c David Frederick Johnson
3-B-11	Ens. Charles Smith Lane	ARM2c Jack Charles Henning

BOMBING SIX (VB-6) DIVISION

PLANE	PILOT	REAR SEAT GUNNER
6-B-4	Lt. Lloyd Addison Smith	AMM2c Herman Hull Caruthers
6-B-2	Lt. (jg) Edwin John Kroeger	RM3c Gail Wayne Halterman
6-B-12	Ens. Lewis Alexander Hopkins	RM3c Edward Rutledge Anderson
6-B-10	Lt. Harvey Peter Lanham	ARM1c Edward Joseph Garaudy

6-B-1	Lt. (jg) Edward Lee Anderson	ARM1c Walter George Chocalousek
6-B-17	Ens. Arthur Leo Rausch	AOM3c Harold Llewellyn Jones

*Lost in action on *Tanikaze* strike.
**Returned to *Hornet*.
VS-5 composition is per the research of Mark E. Horan.

see whether the carrier *Hiryu* was still afloat. Ring led his flight out to 315 miles in search of bigger prey. "We passed it by to locate the damaged carrier, but to no avail," said Gee. Ring, unable to find any other ships, led his men back toward the "cruiser" and ordered an attack at 1810. The Bombing Eight group used the available clouds for cover to mask their approach on the lone warship. Gee watched the tin can begin to increase speed and send up AA fire as the *Hornet* SBDs formed to attack.[17]

Commander Ring was unable to deliver his five-hundred-pound bomb. He tried pressing a button he believed to be the bomb release but nothing happened. The other ten VB-8 pilots following him were successful in unleashing their ordnance on the wildly twisting *Tanikaze*. Ruff Johnson and his wingmen, Phil Grant and Doug Carter, all missed wide. Slim Moore, rear gunner for Doug Carter, was amazed by "the darnedest ship maneuvering I ever saw," as the Japanese skipper managed to dodge bomb after bomb."[18]

Moe Vose, leading the second section of the first division, also missed wide with his five-hundred-pounder. John Lynch felt the *Tanikaze* skipper was doing a corkscrew to throw off their aim. It worked. Lynch's bomb landed a hundred feet off *Tanikaze*'s port-side astern. Roy Gee followed through with a drop that landed about a hundred feet astern. Lieutenant Abbie Tucker, leading VB-8's second division, was closest to the mark: His bomb hit the water only about twenty-five feet directly ahead of the destroyer. Gus Bebas planted his bomb about a hundred feet off *Tanikaze*'s port quarter, followed by Don Adams with another close miss astern.[19]

Clay Fisher ended up as tail-end Charlie of the *Hornet*'s strike group. He saw bombs exploding ahead of him, making large circular patterns in the water. He changed his aim twice, but underestimated her speed. Fisher's five-hundred-pound bomb landed about a hundred feet astern of *Tanikaze*.[20]

Commander Ring's Dauntlesses had delivered ten of eleven bombs but failed to score a hit on the highly maneuverable destroyer. "The dive-bombing attack was a fizzle," Ring said. *Tanikaze*'s skipper, Commander Motoi Katsumi, impressed the Americans with his adept ship handling while traveling at well over thirty knots. He relied heavily upon the skills of a twenty-year-old signalman named Masashi Shibata, who called out course changes as he watched each plane coming down. "I climbed out of a window hatch of the bridge and leaned my body back so I could see the sky," Shibata said. "As each dive-bomber approached, I shouted, 'Enemy bomber right,' or, 'Bomber left.'" Skipper Katsumi shouted maneuvering commands based upon the position of each incoming SBD.[21]

The second half of *Hornet*'s strike group did not even have the satisfaction of scoring misses on *Tanikaze*. Walt Rodee's sixteen VS-8 bombers and five VB-8 planes searched for any Japanese ships until 1720. He was forced to turn back, as the seven VS-8 Dauntlesses that had carried thousand-pound bombs consumed fuel at a much higher rate. Rodee set course for home, empty-handed again. Admiral Spruance was irate to find when Scouting Eight returned that they had gone out against his orders toting thousand-pound bombs.

Unaware that *Hiryu* now lay at the bottom of the ocean floor, Dave Shumway still hoped to find a crippled Japanese carrier. He deployed planes from Wally Short's VS-5 and Pat Patriarca's VS-6 in a scouting line abreast to extend his search area during his outbound flight with the *Enterprise* group. The group had flown out 265 miles by 1730 without a sighting, so Lieutenant Shumway changed his course twice during the next half hour in hopes of improving his luck.[22]

At 1810, he picked up Stan Ring's transmission to attack the lone cruiser, and Shumway recalled the VS-5 and VS-6 planes. He had the wily *Tanikaze* in sight within minutes, and the *Enterprise* group deployed for attack. The afternoon sun was dipping lower toward the ocean's surface. Commander Katsumi and his able lookout Masashi Shibata once again employed their tactic of spotting and dodging the incoming American dive-bombers.

Rodey Rodenburg watched *Tanikaze* twisting like a snake below him. For him, this would be his first combat dive of the war. Shumway pushed over first with ten VB-3 pilots in tow. The destroyer sported six 5.5-inch guns and proved that her gun crews were quite capable, in spite of the long odds against them.[23]

Oley Hanson chose his own course. Flying the tail end of Shumway's division, he did not follow directly, but instead dived from abeam in hopes of making a head-on run at *Tanikaze*. He made a corkscrew dive and released his ordnance at two thousand feet. Hanson pulled back hard on the stick to avoid hitting the ocean and saw with disgust that his bomb, like the four others before him, was a miss.[24]

Lieutenant (j.g.) Gordon Sherwood's second division of Bombing Three did no better. Next to dive were the six VB-6 planes under Lieutenant Lloyd Smith, and their bombs also fell harmlessly into the sea. "Hitting a destroyer is not easy," said one of Smith's wingmen, Lew Hopkins. Even with a much larger carrier, bombing dives typically yielded a small number of hits. Hopkins found that reducing the size of the target vessel and adding speed and maneuverability further reduced the odds for his fellow pilots. His radioman, Ed Anderson, saw plenty of small-caliber fire zinging up past their tail section throughout the attack. To Charlie Lane, *Tanikaze* looked like a speedboat, throwing out a long white wake in zigzags and circles. He could see tracers flashing past his SBD that appeared to be getting closer. "I kicked my rudder and threw my bomb; I don't know where," Lane said.[25]

Lieutenant Patriarca was seventeenth to dive on *Tanikaze*. Dusty Kleiss was third from Patriarca's VS-6 contingent to make the plunge. "The little devil fired everything he had at us, put on full speed, zigzagging nicely, and was most difficult to hit," Kleiss wrote in his diary.[26]

Wally Short's Scouting Five refugees brought up the rear. Lieutenant (j.g.) Dave Berry had flown wing on Lieutenant Sam Adams during seven previous dive-bombing attacks. Now Berry found himself leading his senior officer down on *Tanikaze*. One of the flak bursts connected with the SBD of Adams and brought him down. The loss of Adams—a Coral Sea veteran who had located *Hiryu* the previous afternoon—hit home hard with Dave Berry. *For the first time, I really hate those little yellow bastards.*[27]

The popular Lieutenant Adams and his veteran gunner, Joe Karrol, would be mourned by many SBD aircrews. The remaining thirty-one *Enterprise* Dauntless crews headed home without having scored a single direct hit.

Tanikaze's ordeal was not yet complete. The scouting flight of seven B-17s found the destroyer on their return to Midway and attacked shortly after the carrier bombers had moved on. Troy Guillory and Tom Wood, observing aboard different aircraft, watched as six of the B-17s made high-level runs on *Tanikaze*, dropping twenty-three bombs. The optimistic Air Force pilots claimed three hits and four near misses. Yet Wood was realistic in assessing from Lieutenant Colonel Sweeney's B-17. "Although right in the center of the pattern, there were no direct hits," he said. According to signalman Shibata, *Tanikaze* suffered leaks from two near misses and six gunners killed by bomb fragments that swept through the number two gun. In return, Shibata said "the gunnery crew of turret number three hit a dive-bomber [that of Adams], and it fell into the sea."[28]

The luckless attack on *Tanikaze* had been frustrating, yet even greater despair faced the *Hornet* and *Enterprise* bombers. They were taxed with long flights back to their task force with low fuel and the daunting prospect of having to land on board after dark—a challenge many of the young pilots had never faced.

Lew Jones, gunner for Arthur Rausch of VB-6, had the only workable ZB homing device in Lloyd Smith's division. He navigated through this direction finder and led his small group back to the ship. "We had three planes with us that probably would have been lost otherwise," said Jones. As fuel became critical during the return flight, Rausch advised Jones to stand by for a possible ditching.[29]

Stan Ring's VB-8 bunch did not fly in formation on their return but instead opted to form a long line. "Group doctrine had called for individual return rather than complete rendezvous," Ring said. In the absence of air opposition, such a maneuver was deemed necessary to conserve fuel.[30]

Ruff Johnson struggled home on the two different signals being picked up by his plane's YE-ZB device. When he had drained his tanks, with only his reserve left, Johnson called Chief McCoy.[31]

"Can you swim?" he asked.

"Negative," McCoy said from the rear cockpit.

"You'd better get out your survival book and learn quickly," the skipper warned him as their situation began to look more dire.

Radioman Dick Woodson found his YE/ZB signal was good enough to help guide his VS-8 pilot, Don Kirkpatrick, back to *Hornet*. When Clay Fisher approached the American task force, his gunner, George Ferguson, announced that he was receiving both a weak signal from *Hornet* and a strong one from *Enterprise*. Fisher opted for his own carrier's signal and arrived over Task Force 16 shortly after sunset. Ben Tappan, flying wing on Gus Widhelm, credited VS-8 flight officer Ray Davis with figuring out a way to bracket the different homing signals to guide Scouting Eight back to *Hornet*.[32]

The darkened flight deck posed a real safety challenge for the *Hornet* fliers as well as the men standing by on deck to assist with the returning planes. Ruff Johnson finally opened up on the radio, calling to "Pete from Ruff," a prearranged code for distress directed toward Captain Pete Mitscher of *Hornet*. Mitscher obliged by turning on two signal searchlights to help direct the approaching SBDs into the landing circle.[33]

Fisher was the first into the landing circle, and was relieved to see *Hornet*'s small flush deck lights come on during his approach. Ruff Johnson dropped directly into the groove for a perfect landing. He did not have enough fuel to even taxi out of the arresting gear.[34]

The leading VB-8 plane captain eagerly jumped upon Johnson's wing. In his excitement to see the skipper return, he blurted, "Captain, you son of a bitch, are we glad to see you! Oh, I beg your pardon."

There were fewer deckhands excited to see the return of the Sea Hag. Ring had been joined by Ensign Ken White for the return flight. As the CHAG lowered his landing gear, White frantically signaled to him that only one of his wheels had extended. Ring assumed that a shell fragment from the AA fire had damaged his hydraulic lines. He managed, after a bit of violent maneuvering, to properly extend both wheels.[35]

Forty-year-old Commander Ring landed on *Hornet* after 4.3 hours aloft, and complained to his plane captain that his bomb failed to release when he tried pressing the button on his throttle handle. Roy Gee and other SBD pilots on the flight deck who heard of this comment were astounded. They knew that the throttle handle button was used to transmit voice radio messages. "Commander Ring could have easily dropped his bomb by using the emergency release, but he didn't even know it existed, let alone the handle's location," Gee said. "I lost all my respect for CHAG." Wingman Clay Fisher was ordered up to Ring's cabin that evening to provide instructions to the air group commander on how to properly release his bomb in the future. Fisher entered CHAG's cabin nervously and went through the procedure before being dismissed. In spite of his worries over what might happen, Fisher never received any repercussions from Ring—who likely realized that the ensign's lesson had been ordered by one of his senior squadron mates.[36]

Admiral Spruance showed his concern for his aviators—and his desire not to lose the last of his dive-bombers—by allowing the carriers to switch on their landing lights. This obviously posed a large threat from lurking Japanese submarines, but *Enterprise* turned on her sidelights at 1933, followed minutes later by her thirty-six-inch searchlights.[37]

Don Adams of Bombing Eight was riding on fumes. He had resigned himself to ditching while his engine still had power. Before he could do so, John Broughton in his rear seat spotted a light, and Adams was able to locate *Hornet*. His SBD literally exhausted its fuel as Adams's tail hook engaged the arresting gear wire. John Lynch, in contrast, had no problem with his first night carrier landing and made it on board with sufficient fuel. Ensign Paul Tepas of VS-8 was quite relieved when he finally found *Hornet*. He used the rear lights on the carrier to guide him into the groove for landing.[38]

Bombing Three's SBDs all returned undamaged. Oley Hanson had become separated from his group during the return flight. He utilized slow speed on his return to conserve fuel, and opted not to tell gunner Joe Godfrey how low their gauges were reading. *There's no use in disturbing him*, Hanson thought. Godfrey, however, was wise to their situation. He had started taking an inventory of the survival gear he planned to gather in the event they were forced to ditch. Hanson fortunately got aboard on his first pass in the darkness. "As he cut the power, the engine froze solid," Godfrey said.[39]

Charlie Lane of VB-3, approaching the groove on *Enterprise*, kept a hand on the tank selector to be sure every drop of gas was used and that his emergency was saved for landing. Ray Davis of VS-8 ran out of fuel in the landing pattern just 150 yards from *Enterprise*'s stern. His SBD hit the ocean with his tail hook and wheels still down and flipped. It was a hell of a struggle for the two aviators to escape their inverted plane. Davis and gunner Ralph Phillips did not bother with using their life raft, as a screening vessel was rapidly approaching. The destroyer *Aylwin* picked them up within five minutes. "That was all of the battle for us," said Davis.[40]

Rodey Rodenburg was making only his fourteenth carrier landing at sea in wartime conditions. More seriously, this was the first time he was forced to land on a carrier in the dark. Five other VS-6 rookies—Dick Jaccard, Mike Micheel, Bill Pittman, Jim Dexter, and Clarence Vammen— were also facing their first night landings. It was a true test of LSO Robin Lindsey's abilities. Vammen was returning from his first combat strike, having been designated the lone stay-behind of VS-6 the previous day.[41]

Ensign Pittman admitted to Floyd Adkins as he neared *Enterprise* that he had never made a night carrier landing. "That really made me feel great!" said Adkins. "My job prior to landing was to check with Mr. Pittman that the landing gear, flaps, and tail hook were down. I asked him *a little louder* that night." Adkins was comforted to find that Pittman made the best landing of his life.[42]

Scouting Six skipper Earl Gallaher, grounded with a badly wrenched back, stood on the Big E's open bridge and mentally tried to guide his rookies in. He had paced the deck with increasing anxiety during the hours his men were gone, in spite of Dr. Hightower's orders to be on bed rest.[43]

Andy Anderson of Bombing Six was not concerned. He had qualified for such an operation by making six night landings in the three months preceding the Pearl Harbor attack. Harvey Lanham made it back on *Enterprise*'s deck with only a few "teacups" of fuel remaining, per his twenty-one-year-old rear gunner, ARM1c Ed Garaudy.[44]

Lew Hopkins and Arthur Rausch had each made more than twenty daytime carrier landings, but none at night. Hopkins was concentrating, but found it was not too different from trapping his plane in the daylight. He carefully watched Robin Lindsey's lighted paddles, adjusted his plane accordingly as he came into the groove, and safely caught a wire.[45]

Ensign Vammen was also attempting his first night landing on *Hornet*. One of his fellow Pensacola training pilots, Ensign Fred Mears of VT-8, recalled that Vammen's landing was the only sloppy one of those coming in. As Mears watched, Vammen approached without lights on his plane. He gunned the motor at the cut instead of chopping it, hit the barrier, and cut his forehead in the crash.[46]

In the darkness, a number of *Hornet* pilots missed their own flight deck. Roy Gee of Bombing Eight formed up on Moe Vose during the return flight. "By the time we approached the task force, darkness had enveloped the ships," Gee said. Suddenly the lights below came on and he fell in behind Vose for his first night landing. He successfully caught the third wire, waited for his tail hook to be cleared, and then revved forward to clear the landing area. Gee and gunner Don Canfield climbed down from their SBD and proceeded to their ready rooms.[47]

Gee felt uncomfortable with the surrounding bulkheads and passageways as he went through the hatch and down the ladder. Somehow they looked strangely unfamiliar to him—and for good reason. Entering what he thought was VB-8's ready room aboard *Hornet*, Gee discovered that he had landed on its sister ship *Enterprise*.

He was not alone. Four other lost *Hornet* pilots soon made their way into the groove on *Enterprise*. Lieutenant Lindsey was expecting as many as thirty-two dive-bombers to be coming back from the strike. After landing most of the strikers, Lindsey turned to his assistant LSO, Cleo Dobson of VS-6, and asked how many more they had to go to make a complete group. "I'll be damned if I know," said Dobson. "We've got more than we are supposed to have already."[48]

Enterprise also landed Vose and Doug Carter of VB-8, plus Laurens Whitney and Jim Forbes of VS-8. As Vose climbed out of his SBD, he encountered a crew chief who he knew served on *Enterprise*. "What the hell are you doing on *Hornet*?" he asked. The burst of laughter around him quickly informed Bombing Eight's flight officer that he had landed on the wrong ship.[49]

The weary Dauntless aviators headed to their ready rooms for the customary debriefings. The galley crew had ham and eggs waiting, and many seized the offer of a shot of medicinal brandy from sick bay to calm their nerves. The *Hornet* and *Enterprise* LSOs had performed admirably, bringing sixty-three of the returning SBDs down safely in the darkness.

Many of the pilots were discouraged with the results of their late-day mission. Dusty Kleiss's diary entry for the *Tanikaze* attack likely summed up the feelings of most aviators on *Enterprise*: "This flight not worth the gas, bombs, and loss of a plane."[50]

FIFTEEN
"I Wish I Had Just One More Bomb"

Tony Schneider was beginning to doubt that he would ever be rescued. He and his gunner spent a second long, cold night drifting in the swells of the Pacific in their little life raft. Glenn Holden's lacerated head was bruised and swollen. The hunger pains gnawing at Tony's midsection were beginning to make him think of opening the canned pemmican. At least the sharks had not returned. The morning sun on June 6 brought warmth to their third day adrift, and Tony held on to his hope. "I heard the engines of planes going out to search that morning," he said. "I looked and looked but I just couldn't see them."[1]

He hoped the Midway PBY would return later along the same route. The winds had picked up a bit by midday, and the swells were increasing. Sometime after noon, Schneider and Holden heard the distant sounds of engines again. The PBY that had passed them in the morning was on his way back to Midway, and now he flew closer to their raft. The Bombing Six aviators stuck their oars into their bright white parachute and held it aloft like a giant flag.

This time they were in luck. The pilot of the big Catalina seaplane was Lieutenant (j.g.) August A. "Al" Barthes from Biloxi, Mississippi. The VP-23 patrol crew spotted the white parachute on the ocean below and dropped down low to investigate. Barthes had his crew toss a smoke bomb to mark their spot and to judge the wind direction. Then he circled, landed into the wind, and taxied toward the downed aviators. Tony noted that the American flying boat crew had guns trained on them. "They didn't know whether I was a friend or not," he said.

Barthes and his crew stowed their guns once they realized they had found American aviators. Tony was badly dehydrated. He had still been holding off on drinking his single container of water. In spite of his dire thirst, his first desire was to cure his nicotine fit. He had no matches on his raft, and the salt water had ruined his lighter. "Camel used to have a line in their advertising: 'I'd walk a mile for a Camel,'" Tony recalled. At the moment, he could only think: *I'd row a mile for a Camel! If I could have picked up that smoke bomb with the little flame coming out of it, I'd have lit one of my cigarettes!*

Holden and Schneider maneuvered their raft beside one of the PBY's side blisters and were helped inside, where they were offered something to drink for the first time in some fifty-two hours. Lieutenant Barthes lifted back off for Midway with two very appreciative *Enterprise* airmen. They were the second-to-last survivors of Bombing Six to be rescued of those who were part of the Midway carrier strikes.

Roy Gee of VB-8 woke around 0500 on *Enterprise*. He hopped out of the bunk, washed up a little, and slipped into his flight suit. He then hurried to the wardroom for breakfast, where he encountered an atmosphere similar to the one in *Hornet*'s wardroom the previous morning: Many missing pilots would never again sit in the empty chairs.[2]

Task Force 16 held a westward course during the night. By 0500, it was more than 350 miles northwest of Midway. Admiral Spruance, hoping to further pound the retiring Japanese fleet, ordered *Enterprise*'s air group to launch a search. Sixteen SBDs departed at dawn, including the five *Hornet* refugees who had landed after dark. They were to search a western semicircle out to two hundred miles before returning. About an hour into their flight, the mixed *Enterprise/Yorktown/Hornet* pilots made contact.

Ensign Gee spotted two capital warships with two escorting destroyers on a southwesterly course. Remaining safely out of AA range, he dictated a message for Don Canfield to transmit to Task Force 16. Canfield, however, failed to get a confirmation that their transmission had been received. Gee decided to hurry back to the task force to make his report.[3]

One of Gee's squadron mates, Doug Carter, did manage to get off a contact report. Radioman Slim Moore attempted to report in code at 0645 that the search teams had found a battleship, a cruiser, and three destroyers steaming due west at ten knots. Moore's garbled transmission, however, was misunderstood to report one carrier and five destroyers roughly 128 miles southwest of Task Force 16. Admiral Spruance directed Curtiss SOC floatplanes from the cruisers *New Orleans* and *Minneapolis* to clarify this report.[4]

Roy Gee arrived over *Enterprise* at 0730 and dropped a beanbag message with more accurate information. His report of two cruisers and two destroyers placed the enemy ships about 133 miles away from TF-16. Spruance was thus left believing he was dealing with two enemy ship groups. Gee was recovered by *Hornet* at 0815 and reported to Captain Mitscher on the bridge. Afterward, he was informed upon returning to his own VB-8 ready room that he would not be flying any more that day. Lieutenant (j.g.) Jimmy Forbes of Scouting Eight was also recovered by *Hornet*, but Lieutenant Whitney of VS-8 and Lieutenant Vose of VB-8 landed on *Enterprise* again.

Pete Mitscher's *Hornet*, not involved in the morning search efforts, was first to launch a strike group beginning at 0757. Commander Stan Ring in the CHAG Dauntless led the procession, along with eleven SBDs of Bombing Eight under Lieutenant Abbie Tucker, fourteen SBDs of Scouting Eight under Lieutenant Gus Widhelm, and eight escorting VF-8 Wildcats led by Lieutenant Warren W. Ford.

In his VS-8 pilot briefing, Widhelm declared, "I'm going to drive my bomb right down the smokestack of the biggest cruiser we find."[5]

Widhelm's VS-8 group included two orphans. Bill Christie of Scouting Five had been fully integrated, but Clarence Vammen of VB-6 was under orders to return to his own *Enterprise* following the attack. Eight of the *Hornet* SBDs carried five-hundred-pound bombs, while the rest toted the more potent thousand-pounders. The Sea Hag took the lead, and began a slow climb toward fifteen thousand feet.[6]

Enterprise recovered her morning strike group shortly after the *Hornet* group's departure. After Gee's corrected report was blinkered to Admiral Spruance, *Enterprise* radioed Commander Ring at 0850: "Target may be battleship instead of carrier. Attack!"[7]

Morning Strike on *Mikuma, Mogami*
Hornet First Group: June 6, 1942

BOMBING EIGHT (VB-8) DIVISION (12 SBDS WITH CHAG)

PILOT	REAR SEAT GUNNER
Lt. Alfred Bland Tucker III	ARM1c Champ T. Stuart
Ens. Frank E. Christofferson	ARM2c Barkley V. Poorman
Ens. Don Dee Adams	ARM2c John B. Broughton Jr.
Lt. John Joseph Lynch	ARM1c Wilbur L. Woods
Ens. Arthur Caldwell Cason Jr.	ARM3c Alfred D. Wells
Ens. Clayton Evan Fisher	ARM3c George E. Ferguson
Lt. (jg) Fred Leeson Bates	ARM1c Clyde S. Montensen
Ens. Joe Wiley King	ARM3c Thomas M. Walsh

SECOND DIVISION

PILOT	REAR SEAT GUNNER
Lt. Cdr. Robert Ruffin Johnson	ACRM Joseph G. McCoy
Ens. Philip Farnsworth Grant	ARM2c Robert H. Rider
Ens. James Austin Riner Jr.	ARM2c Floyd Dell Kilmer

(continued)

Morning Strike on *Mikuma, Mogami* *Hornet* First Group: June 6, 1942 (cont.)	
CHAG PLANE	
PILOT	**REAR SEAT GUNNER**
Cdr. Stanhope Cotton Ring	ARM2c Arthur M. Parker
SCOUTING EIGHT (VS-8) DIVISION (14 SBDS)	
PILOT	**REAR SEAT GUNNER**
Lt. William John Widhelm	ARM1c George D. Stokely
Ens. Donald Kirkpatrick	ARM2c Richard Thomas Woodson
Ens. Don "T" Griswold*	ARM1c Kenneth Cecil Bunch*
Lt. (jg) William Francis Christie (VS-5)	ARM1c Alvin Arthur Sobel
Lt. (jg) Ralph B. Hovind	ARM3c Charles B. Lufburrow
Ens. Helmuth Ernest Hoerner	ARM3c David T. Manus
Lt. (jg) Ivan Lee Swope	ARM2c Harmon L. Brendle
Ens. Paul Edmond Tepas	ARM3c Moley J. Boutwell

SECOND DIVISION	
PILOT	**REAR SEAT GUNNER**
Lt. Edgar Erwin Stebbins	ARM2c Ervin R. Hillhouse
Ens. Philip James Rusk	ARM2c John H. Honeycutt
Ens. Benjamin Tappan Jr.	ARM3c Earnest Ray Johnston
Lt. Ben Moore Jr.	ARM2c Richard Cusack McEwen
Ens. Stanley Robert Holm	ARM2c James H. Black Jr.
Ens. Clarence Earl Vammen Jr.* (VS-6)	AMM1c Milton Wayne Clark*
Fighting Eight (VF-8): 8 F4Fs under Lt. Warren W. Ford	

*Shot down and killed.
Scouting Eight composition compiled by Mark E. Horan.

The confusing contact reports mentioning a possible carrier and a second Japanese warship force were straightened out in due time. The *Hornet* strike group was actually facing only one nearby force of ships, the cruisers *Mogami* and *Mikuma* and their escorting destroyers *Arashio* and *Asashio*. *Mikuma* had been mistakenly reported as a battleship, since her sister ship *Mogami* appeared smaller due to her crumpled bow from her collison the previous day.[8]

The SOC search planes from *New Orleans* monitored the four enemy warships and helped guide Ring's strike group into the target area. Ruff Johnson of VB-8 spotted the *Mikuma* and *Mogami* force at 0930. The flight doctrine of the day was to use "first name" calls to contact other squadron and division leaders. Johnson thus called over the voice radio, "Stanhope from Robert, enemy below on port bow."[9]

Ring, uncertain that this force truly included a battleship, flew several miles beyond the vessels in search of another group of warships. When he decided that this group was his target, the CHAG circled his *Hornet* formation around to make a second approach out of the sun. They commenced their attack at 0950, with VS-8 pushing over on *Mogami*.[10]

Scouting Eight's long wait to draw blood finally came to an end. Gus Widhelm's pilots witnessed him follow through on his promise of making a hit, as his load landed squarely amidships just behind the smokestack. His bomb exploded on *Mogami*'s aircraft deck, sparking fires in the torpedo room. Lieutenant Ben Moore's big bomb smashed through the roof of turret number five, killing its crew. Bill Christie had plenty of time to pick a target before making his dive through intense AA fire. He felt that his bomb made a direct hit amidships. *Mogami*'s crew had fortunately jettisoned their torpedoes following their June 5 collision with *Mikuma*, and the crew was able to contain the resulting fires within an hour.[11]

The antiaircraft fire was heavy over the Japanese warships, despite efforts made by Lieutenant Warren Ford's fighters to strafe their decks. The Japanese gunners hit several *Hornet* dive-bombers and brought down two from Widhelm's group. Ensign Don Griswold's 8-S-12 was struck, trailed heavy smoke, and was seen to splash down into the ocean. He and his radioman/gunner, ARM1c Kenneth Bunch, were both killed. Clay Fisher had heard Griswold tell another squadron pilot he had a premonition he was going to die on that flight. Another shell hit Vammen's 6-S-1, which had been flown by Earl Gallaher on the June 4 carrier strikes. Vammen's dive-bomber disintegrated instantly, killing him and his veteran gunner, AMM1c Milton Clark.[12]

Ensign Lefty Hoerner from Ilion, New York, was among the Scouting Eight pilots making their first combat attack. As he plunged down on *Mogami*, he realized in his excitement that he had forgotten to employ his wing flaps to slow his descent. Hoerner hastily reached for the lever but grabbed the wrong one, lowering his wheels. He overshot the cruiser and suddenly found himself approaching one of her escorting destroyers. This time he found the bomb release and made his drop. "I went back to the ship feeling pretty bad," Hoerner said. "I was sure I was going to catch hell." His squadron mates, however, were all complimentary of Hoerner's result, as they told him how his bomb had exploded squarely on the afterdeck of a destroyer. Japanese reports would confirm that *Asashio* was struck squarely in the stern by a five-hundred-pound bomb during the *Hornet* Air Group's first strike.[13]

Ray Johnston called off the altitude during Ben Tappan's dive on *Mogami*, and saw his pilot land "a paint scraper" on the cruiser's port bow. Abbie Tucker's ten VB-8 planes concentrated on *Mikuma*. Ensign Phil Grant, in the excitement of the moment, accidentally dropped his bomb before diving, leaving only nine planes with payloads. Lieutenant Tucker missed *Mikuma*'s starboard bow by no more than fifty feet, while his wingman, Frank Christofferson, missed by a wider mark. Tucker's other wingman, Don Adams, attacked a screening destroyer and was credited with a direct hit with his five-hundred-pound bomb.[14]

John Lynch's section also attacked *Mikuma*. He, Arthur Cason, and Clay Fisher achieved nothing better than near misses. The next three pilots—Fred Bates, Joe King, and skipper Ruff Johnson—managed two more paint scrapers. Ensign Jim Riner, the last of VB-8 still toting a bomb, completed *Hornet*'s attack by landing his ordnance within seventy-five feet of the heavy cruiser's starboard bow.

Hornet's strikers had finally made their mark at Midway, plastering both heavy cruisers and damaging the destroyer *Asashio* with direct hits. "In executing our dive-bombing attack, everyone did much better than he had the day before, when buck fever probably had us," said Ring.[15]

The CHAG detoured about twenty-five miles to the southward on the way back to *Hornet* to look for other ships. They began landing on *Hornet* at 1035, having lost only two of their number. Captain Mitscher had his deck crews begin to immediately refuel and rearm the SBDs for a follow-up strike. "When I returned aboard after about three hours flying, it developed that the radio in my plane was not functioning properly," said Ring. "*Hornet* had not received my report of attacking the enemy; nor had I received their dispatches requesting information as to the latitude and longitude of the group attacked. Captain Mitscher decided, therefore, that I should not accompany the final attack group which was being readied for takeoff."[16]

Hornet's aviators had finally delivered a sting to their enemy, and now those in *Enterprise*'s ragtag squadrons were eager to get in their licks as well. Admiral Spruance ordered off an *Enterprise* strike group at

Afternoon Strike on *Mikuma, Mogami*
Enterprise Group: June 6, 1942

SCOUTING FIVE (VS-5) DIVISION

PLANE	PILOT	REAR SEAT GUNNER
6-S-7	Lt. Wallace Clark Short Jr.	ACRM John W. Trott
6-S-8	Lt. Harlan Rockey Dickson	ARM2c Joseph Michael Lynch
6-S-9	Ens. Carl Herman Horenburger	ARM3c Lynn Raymond Forshee
6-S-10	Lt. John Ludwig Neilsen	ACRM Walter Dean Straub
6-S-11	Lt. (jg) Nels Luther Alvin Berger	ACRM Otis Albert Phelps
6-S-12	Lt. (jg) David Render Berry	ARM2c Earnest Alwyn Clegg
6-S-15	Ens. Benjamin Gifford Preston	ARM1c Harold R. Cowden

SCOUTING SIX (VS-6) DIVISION

PLANE	PILOT	REAR SEAT GUNNER
6-S-16	Lt. (jg) Frank Anthony Patriarca	ACRM Jack Richard Badgley
6-S-2	Ens. Reid Wentworth Stone	RM1c William Hart Bergin
6-S-11	Ens. Richard Alonzo Jaccard	RM3c Porter William Pixley

6-S-7	Lt. (jg) Norman Jack Kleiss	ARM3c John Warren Snowden
6-S-17	Ens. Vernon Larsen Micheel	RM3c John Dewey Dance
6-S-18	Ens. James Campbell Dexter	RM3c Donald Laurence Hoff
6-S-9	Ens. Eldor Ernst Rodenburg*	Sea2c Thomas James Bruce*

BOMBING THREE (VB-3) STRIKE FORCE

PLANE	PILOT	REAR SEAT GUNNER
3-B-3	Lt. DeWitt Wood Shumway	ARM1c Ray Edgar Coons
3-B-14	Ens. Robert Martin Elder	ARM3c Leslie Alan Till
3-B-6	Ens. Milford Austin Merrill	ARM3c Jack Alvin Shropshire
3-B-4	Ens. Robert Keith Campbell	ARM3c Frederick Paul Bergeron
3-B-5	Ens. Alden Wilbur Hanson	ARM3c Joseph Vernon Godfrey

SECOND DIVISION, VB-3

PLANE	PILOT	REAR SEAT GUNNER
3-B-7	Lt. (jg) Gordon Alvin Sherwood	ARM2c Harman Donald Bennett
3-B-8	Ens. Roy Maurice Isaman	ARM3c Sidney Kay Weaver

(continued)

Afternoon Strike on *Mikuma*, *Mogami*
Enterprise Group: June 6, 1942 (cont.)

SECOND DIVISION, VB-3

PLANE	PILOT	REAR SEAT GUNNER
3-B-9	Ens. Bunyan Randolph Cooner	ARM2c Clarence E. Zimmershead
3-B-10	Lt. Harold Sydney Bottomley Jr.	AMM2c David Frederick Johnson
6-B-10	Ens. Charles Smith Lane	ARM2c Jack Charles Henning

BOMBING SIX (VB-6) DIVISION

PLANE	PILOT	REAR SEAT GUNNER
6-B-1	Lt. Lloyd Addison Smith	AMM2c Herman Hull Caruthers
6-B-16	Lt. (jg) Edward Lee Anderson	ARM1c Walter George Chocalousek
6-B-2	Ens. Don Lelo Ely	AOM3c Harold Llewellyn Jones
6-B-10	Lt. Harvey Peter Lanham	ARM1c Edward Joseph Garaudy
6-B-17	Ens. Harry Warren Liffner	AMM3c Milo L. Kimberlin

VB-8	Lt. James Everett Vose Jr.	ARM2c Joseph Yewonishon
VS-8	Lt. Laurens Adin Whitney	ARM2c Angus D. Gilles
Fighting Six (VF-6): 12 F4Fs under Lt. James Seton Gray Jr.		
Torpedo Six (VT-6): 3 TBDs under Lt. (jg) Robert Edward Laub		

*Forced to abort mission.

1045, just minutes after *Hornet*'s first strike group had returned to Task Force 16.

Lieutenant Wally Short of VS-5 would lead the strike as the senior uninjured aviator on *Enterprise*. He had thirty-two dive-bombers available from a mix of six squadrons. Short would also lead a division of seven VS-5 *Yorktown* crews, while Lieutenant Frank Patriarca would lead a second division of his eight remaining VS-6 SBDs. Lieutenant Dave Shumway had two five-plane divisions of Bombing Three. Bombing Six's exec, Lieutenant Lloyd Smith, had five planes loaded with thousand-pound bombs, as were most of the other SBDs. Finally, the two remaining *Hornet* orphans—Moe Vose and Laurens Whitney—were launched, with orders to return to their own ship after the strike.

Ed Garaudy, gunner for Harvey Lanham, became a reluctant volunteer to photograph this mission. The ship's intelligence officer went from plane to plane before takeoff, trying to get someone to take an aerial camera to get some pictures. "I agreed to take it with the stipulation that it would go over the side if we were attacked by fighters," Garaudy said.[17]

Bob Benson of Bombing Three had flown the morning search in his 3-B-6. When word came that another strike group was being launched, Bud Merrill took over his aircraft, flying with Jack Shropshire as a replacement gunner for his own wounded Dallas Bergeron. Benson went below for lunch, but his gunner, Fred Bergeron, was detained by Bob Campbell.[18]

Campbell's regular gunner, Horace Craig, had fallen ill and was scratched from the regular rotation. Campbell, hoping to grab a quick replacement radioman, was waving freshly made ham sandwiches. "I'll give you these if you'll fly with me," he propositioned Fred Bergeron.

"I don't think your wife knows what kind of man you are, enticing a nineteen-year-old kid to go on a dangerous mission with you for a ham sandwich," Bergeron chided. Truth be told, he preferred the real ham sandwich over the SPAM he would have received in the mess hall. "He wouldn't even have had to offer that, because I had had a lot of fun flying with him."

Norm West's finicky VS-6 bomber was unable to launch, leaving Short with thirty-one SBDs airborne. Rodey Rodenburg was once again robbed of bombing Japanese warships on this flight, just as he had been on June 4. As he reached fourteen thousand feet while climbing outbound from *Enterprise*, Rodenburg heard gunner Thomas Bruce groaning. He realized that his plane's oxygen system had failed and that Bruce had passed out as the plane reached high altitude. He quickly dropped his altitude and aborted his flight.[19]

This time the *Enterprise* bombers were accompanied by twelve Wildcat fighters led by Lieutenant Jim Gray. Admiral Spruance decided at the last minute to also include his surviving Devastators of VT-6 on the attack. The admiral held a hasty conference with CEAG Wade McClusky and the senior surviving Torpedo Six pilot, Lieutenant (j.g.) Bob Laub. "I am not going to lose another torpedo plane if I can help it," Spruance told Laub. If any accurate antiaircraft fire was encountered, VT-6 was to turn around and bring their torpedoes back home. Laub launched in company with two wingmen, Chief Aviation Pilot Harry Mueller and Ensign Jamie S. Morris. Laub had grounded the squadron's other June 4 survivors, as he had ample volunteers for this mission.[20]

Lieutenant Short received orders via radio at 1057 to seek out and destroy a battleship suspected to be forty miles farther beyond the *Mikuma* and *Mogami* force. He led his SBDs up to 22,500 feet while making gentle S-turns to allow Bob Laub's TBDs to catch up. Ensign Carl Horenburger, one of Short's VS-5 wingmen, struggled to reach high altitude with his thousand-pound bomb load. Gunner Lynn Forshee recalled during the outbound flight that another rear seat man with a small voice was chattering to his pilot, oblivious to the fact that he was not using the

ICS intercom but was instead broadcasting his every word. "Someone finally went on the air and told him to shut up," Forshee said.[21]

By noon, Johnny Neilsen of VS-5 spotted two large oil slicks trailing from the damaged Japanese ships. The visibility was perfect from seventeen thousand feet. The thin, white, feathery lines of the enemy warships' wakes were perfect guides for the SBD crews. Neilsen saw that much of the cruisers' antiaircraft fire was bursting a quarter mile behind their SBDs. He noted wingmen Dave Berry and Rockey Dickson tight on his wings and then glanced at his oxygen gauge. His pressure was running down. As he waited to attack, the pressure kept dropping, and he found it difficult to breathe.[22]

Wally Short led his flight thirty miles beyond the cruiser in search of the mysterious battleship. He found nothing but empty ocean, and then turned to head back to attack the *Mogami* and *Mikuma* group. Johnny Neilsen's oxygen supply was finally exhausted and he began to feel lightheaded. He motioned to Dickson to stay with him, and dived down to ten thousand feet, where there was enough oxygen to breathe without a mask.[23]

Pat Patriarca, leading VS-6, was ready to dive. His planes had been circling overhead while the Japanese peppered away at them with AA. On board *Enterprise*, Spruance's staff listened impatiently to the radio chatter between the little groups of dive-bombers, fighters, and torpedo planes. Jim Gray of VF-6, believing that one of the two heavy cruisers was a battleship, radioed, "Let's go! The BB is in the rear of the formation."[24]

Enterprise bluntly radioed Short at 1235: "Expedite attack and return."

Dave Shumway finally called, "Wally, this is Dave. I'll take the cruiser to the northeast."[25]

"We'll take the other one," Short replied. "Where is the rest of our attack group?"

"We are right behind you; get going!" called back Lloyd Smith.[26]

"Smith from Wally. What the hell are you doing over here?" Short was under the impression that Smith's VB-6 should be following Shumway's VB-3 group down on the other cruiser.

Short finally radioed that he was pushing over on the rear cruiser, *Mikuma*. He became impatient as he entered his dive with some VS-6 pilots who were not following quickly enough. "Our objective is rear ship," Short called. "Step on it! Are we going to attack or not?" As VB-3's Charlie Lane remembered, "Finally, after much cussing over the air, our attack began."[27]

Short was first to dive. Torpedo Six pilot Jamie Morris believed that Short made a perfect drop for a direct hit. Two planes back, Carl Horenburger rolled to the left and plunged into his dive on *Mikuma*. Gunner Lynn Forshee, bracing himself for the pain in his ears from the pullout, saw their bomb land right behind the stack amidships, and told Horenburger they had made a good one.[28]

Johnny Neilsen witnessed Rockey Dickson's bomb appear to drop right down the cruiser's stack and blow it over the side. Dusty Kleiss, fourth of Patriarca's VS-6 pilots to dive, was equally certain that he landed his bomb right near the stack. He felt that his squadron's five planes scored three direct hits on the cruiser. One of the VS-6 pilots attacked a destroyer and managed a near miss within fifty feet.[29]

Some individual pilots opted to dive on the less damaged "light cruiser," actually *Mogami*. Shumway circled Bombing Three while the two scouting squadrons and VB-6 made their dives. "I saw four hits on the big cruiser and she turned into a flaming, burning hulk," said Al Hanson of VB-3. Short felt that his Scouting Five alone tagged *Mikuma* with five hits and two close misses.[30]

Lloyd Smith's VB-6 division pushed over with its two orphaned *Hornet* SBDs in company. Don Ely, who had been deprived of making the attacks on the previous two days, was eager for the kill. "Conditions were ideal for this attack," Ely said. "All my flight training resulted into one shot, and it'd better be good."[31]

Gunner Lew Jones, normally assigned to Arthur Rausch, had been tapped to fly with Ely on this strike. They dived from sixteen thousand feet. At thirty-five hundred feet, Jones yelled, "Mark!" Ely then dropped and pulled out as Jones shouted, "Get right down on the water!" His rookie pilot responded by flying a mere fifty feet above the ocean to avoid AA fire from the two destroyers. Jones looked back and saw Ely's bomb hit near the fantail of the ship. Ely was consumed after that with dodging the waterspouts from exploding shells for the next mile.[32]

Gunner Ed Garaudy could feel the flak rocking his SBD. As Lanham made his dive on *Mogami*, Garaudy could see that the cruiser had been hit badly at the stern, and that some personnel were going over the side. Ill prepared as a photographer, he dutifully snapped pictures of the damaged Japanese cruisers in hopes that the image quality would please the intelligence gang.[33]

Lieutenant Shumway pushed over with VB-3 to join the pounding of *Mikuma*. Replacement gunner Fred Bergeron used his twin .30s to shoot up the heavy cruiser as Bob Campbell pulled out of his dive. Right behind Campbell, Ensign Hanson felt that his own bomb was a direct hit amidships. Gordon Sherwood followed with his second division of VB-3. Flying the tail-end Charlie spot, Charlie Lane saw intense flak coming toward his plane. He yanked back hard on the stick after his drop with both hands and thought, *I'll never make it*. As he roared out low on the water, Lane blurted into his radio, "That scared hell out of me. I thought we weren't going to pull out!"[34]

Lane's gunner, Jack Henning, thought that the pilot landed their bomb squarely on the cruiser's fantail. Shumway estimated that Bombing Three added another four direct hits and five near misses to the score. Only one of his ten pilots, Roy Isaman, did not dive on *Mikuma*. The other cruiser, *Mogami*, appeared undamaged to him, so Isaman braved the heavy AA fire alone and was seen by other aviators to score a direct hit aft.[35]

Mogami was hit by two bombs that caused medium damage, while at least five bombs from Wally Short's collective squadrons struck the luckless *Mikuma*. Two loads tore through her port after engine room, while two others ripped into her starboard forward engine room. Another big bomb exploded atop *Mikuma*'s number three turret, sending shrapnel tearing through her bridge structure and killing her skipper, Captain Shakao Sakiyama. Heavily damaged, *Mikuma* lost power and drifted to a halt. Her executive officer passed the word to abandon ship, and the destroyer *Arashio* moved in to help remove survivors.[36]

Back on board the Task Force 16 ships, cheers erupted as excited radio transmissions from the pilots crackled over the loudspeakers in a frenzy of shouts. "Look at that son of a bitch burn!" . . . "Hit the son of a bitch again!" . . . "Your bomb really hit them on the fantail. Boy, that's swell!" . . . "These Japs are as easy as shooting ducks in a rain bar-rel. . . ." "Gee, I wish I had just one more bomb. . . ." "Tojo, you son of a bitch, send out the rest and we'll get those, too!"[37]

Bob Elder soaked in the scene of the dive-bombers' handiwork before departing. *Mikuma* and *Mogami* had absorbed tremendous damage, with superstructures battered and guns drooping in the water. Dusty Kleiss from VS-6 later wrote, "Our target [was] a complete mass of wreckage, dead in the water and burning from stem to stern." To Moe Vose of VB-8, flying with the *Enterprise* group, the cruiser pounding "was a good day's work."[38]

Adhering to Admiral Spruance's orders, Bob Laub kept his VT-6 Devastators out of harm's way due to the heavy AA fire. "We only got close enough to draw a little antiaircraft fire once in a while but not close enough that they could hit us," said Ron Graetz, rear gunner for CAP Harry Mueller. "We just sat there and watched those SBDs pound the hell out of them. When we turned to head back to the ship, that cruiser looked like a big bathtub full of junk."

Hornet had already started launching a second attack group at 1330 as *Enterprise*'s jubilant aviators made their way back to Task Force 16. This group comprised twenty-four Dauntlesses, all that were flyable with two exceptions: The Sea Hag SBD was grounded due to faulty radio gear, and Ensign Stan Holm's VS-8 Dauntless had sustained AA fire damage during the morning strike. Three of the recently returned *Hornet* dive-bombers that had made the morning scout mission from *Enterprise* helped to round out the afternoon strike.

Scouting Five's Bill Christie and six VS-8 pilots would be making their second attack of the day. Ben Tappan and four others of Scouting Eight were given a rest to let some of their squadron mates—Jimmy Forbes, Bill Woodman, Al Wood, and Harold White—fly the second strike. "There were just not enough planes left in our squadron to go around, so we rotated the aircrews," said Tappan's gunner, Ray Johnston.

Walt Rodee—who had missed the morning strike—took command, heading a dozen VS-8 planes and another dozen VB-8 SBDs under Lieu-tenant Abbie Tucker. Eight Bombing Eight crews from the morning strike group were joined by four fresh aircrews. All were loaded with thousand-pound bombs. Rodee's flight departed at 1345, although one plane was

Afternoon Strike on *Mikuma, Mogami*
Hornet Afternoon Group: June 6, 1942

BOMBING EIGHT (VB-8) DIVISION (12 SBDS)

PILOT	REAR SEAT GUNNER
Lt. Alfred Bland Tucker III	ARM1c Champ T. Stuart
Ens. Don Dee Adams	ARM2c John B. Broughton Jr.
Ens. Joe Wiley King	ARM3c Thomas M. Walsh
Lt. John Joseph Lynch	ARM1c Wilbur L. Woods
Ens. Clayton Evan Fisher	ARM3c George E. Ferguson
Ens. Henry John Nickerson	ARM1c Elmer Edwin Jackson

SECOND DIVISION, VB-8

PILOT	REAR SEAT GUNNER
Lt. (jg) Fred Leeson Bates	ARM1c Clyde S. Montensen
Ens. James Clark Barrett	ARM3c William H. Berthold
Ens. Gus George Bebas	RM3c Alfred W. Ringressy Jr.
Ens. Frank E. Christofferson	ARM2c Barkley V. Poorman
Ens. Robert Pershing Friesz	ARM1c Clarence C. Kiley
Ens. James Austin Riner Jr.	ARM2c Floyd Dell Kilmer

(continued)

Afternoon Strike on *Mikuma, Mogami*
Hornet Afternoon Group: June 6, 1942 (cont.)

SCOUTING EIGHT (VS-8) DIVISION (13 SBDS; ONE ABORTED)

PILOT	REAR SEAT GUNNER
Lt. Cdr. Walter Fred Rodee	ACRM John Lenzy Clanton
Ens. Paul Edmond Tepas	ARM3c Moley J. Boutwell
Lt. Ben Moore Jr.	ARM2c Richard Cusack McEwen
Lt. (jg) William Francis Christie (VS-5)	ARM1c Alvin Arthur Sobel
Lt. (jg) Henry Martin McDowell (VS-5)	ARM2c Eugene Clay Strickland
Lt. (jg) Jimmy McMillan Forbes	ARM3c Ronald H. Arenth

SECOND DIVISION, VS-8

PILOT	REAR SEAT GUNNER
Lt. William John Widhelm	ARM1c George D. Stokely
Lt. (jg) Ralph B. Hovind	ARM3c Charles B. Lufburrow
Lt. (jg) Albert Harold Wood	ARM3c John Louis Tereskerz
Ens. Hellmuth Ernest Hoerner	ARM3c David T. Manus
Lt. Edgar Erwin Stebbins	ARM2c Ervin R. Hillhouse

Ens. Harold White	ARM3c John Stephen Urban
Ens. William E. Woodman	ARM2c Gerald S. McAffe

Scouting Eight composition is courtesy of the research of Mark E. Horan.

forced to abort the mission with engine problems. The distance to *Mikuma* and *Mogami*'s force had been narrowed to only ninety miles. With good visibility, Air Group Eight soon had both their carrier force visible far astern and the smoke from the Japanese ships ahead in the distance.[39]

Don Kirkpatrick, whose SBD had suffered minor AA damage during *Hornet*'s morning strike, remained in VS-8's ready room. His gunner, Dick Woodson, mentioned to a buddy how it had hurt to wear a helmet for so long in the air. "What's all that blood?" his friend asked. Woodson took his helmet off, got some pliers, and pulled a half-inch piece of shrapnel from under his left ear. The young gunner never reported the injury, knowing that there was another flight to be made that he did not want to miss.[40]

Enterprise's force appeared overhead shortly after the departure of *Hornet*'s strike group. At 1415, the Big E's aircraft were recovered with the exception of three planes. Two, piloted by Moe Vose and Laurens Whitney, landed back on their own *Hornet*. Lloyd Smith, the XO of Bombing Six, spent nearly an hour flying around before he was able to land. Only one gear leg of his landing gear would let down due to AA fire that had damaged his hydraulic system. Once Smith finally got the second wheel down, *Enterprise* had respotted her flight deck, forcing him to seek refuge on *Hornet*.[41]

Hornet's strike group was eager for more action. Her pilots had listened to the lively commentary over the radio from the mixed *Enterprise/ Yorktown* strike group. Ralph Hovind of VS-8 heard one of Bombing Three's pilots joyfully singing a popular song of the day, "Someone's Rocking My Dreamboat," in the midst of attack.[42]

Rodee's SBDs struck at *Mikuma* and *Mogami* around 1445, attacking both cruisers and their two accompanying destroyers. *Mikuma* was dead in the water, her crew in the process of abandoning ship. Fire had cooked off some of her remaining torpedoes, ripping apart her upper works shortly before the third wave of American SBDs arrived. Hundreds of sailors were still trapped on *Mikuma* as *Hornet*'s new strike pushed over. Hundreds more bobbed helplessly in the ocean as the Japanese destroyers tried to fight back.[43]

Rodee toggled his big bomb toward *Mikuma* and a destroyer along-side her, and then strafed the other destroyer with 20mm fire. Bill Christie, making his second cruiser attack of the day, judged that his bomb struck *Mogami*'s after section. "Two bombing runs, two hits," Christie said. For him, it felt good and made up for missing out on the carriers two days prior. His squadron mate, Hank McDowell, claimed a direct hit on *Mikuma* while making his first attack at Midway.[44]

Ensign Harold White was credited with landing a direct hit with his thousand-pound bomb. Gus Widhelm of VS-8 dived on a destroyer and ran the length of the ship, spraying it with bullets. He turned and repeated the process as George Stokely in his rear seat joined in the shooting. The destroyer's AA fire finally damaged Widhelm's Dauntless during their third pass. He shouted to Stokely to prepare for a water landing as their engine sputtered, but he found his rear seat man to be fully engaged in shooting up Japanese shipping.[45]

John Tereskerz, flying as gunner for Lieutenant (j.g.) Al Wood, had orders to photograph the strike. Carrying a K-20 Fairchild aerial camera, which was manually operated by pulling the trigger to make a photo and cocking the right handle forward to wind the film, Tereskerz snapped pictures of the burning cruisers in the distance as Wood pulled out of his dive and flew away. He was surprised months later to see some of the photographs he had taken on June 6 printed in an issue of *Life* magazine about Midway.[46]

Abbie Tucker led his first section of Bombing Eight down on *Mikuma*. He and Don Adams missed, but Joe King made a direct hit on *Mikuma*'s starboard bow, just inside the waterway. John Lynch, unhappy with his poor bombing of *Tanikaze* the previous day, allowed his sight to be fully filled with *Mikuma* before making his drop. This time he scored a solid hit. Many of VB-8's other pilots opted to attack *Mogami*, which they still believed to be a "light cruiser" due to her crumpled bow. Henry Nickerson was seen to make a hit on the stern of *Mogami*, while Fred Bates and Clark Barrett missed fifty feet astern.[47]

Next in was Gus Bebas, a twenty-eight-year-old Chicagoan making his third Midway flight, who landed a paint scraper on the starboard quarter of *Mogami*. Frank Christofferson followed with a miss, and Robert Friesz made a direct hit on her forecastle, port side near the waterway. Two of the remaining pilots took on the Japanese destroyers. Jim Riner landed his big bomb fifty feet from *Asashio*. Clay Fisher saw more than two hundred survivors bobbing in the water as VB-8 prepared to dive. He selected *Arashio*, which was in a shallow turn and increasing its speed.[48]

He made an easy glide bombing run and dropped from about fifteen hundred feet. Gunner George Ferguson shouted that their bomb was a direct hit on her stern. Fisher's thousand-pounder actually landed close astern of *Arashio*, causing considerable damage and killing thirty-seven survivors clustered on her stern.

Yet both *Arashio* and *Asashio* would survive their damage from the three SBD attacks. They limped off to the west with the battered *Mogami*, which was still under way. *Mogami* had taken one more thousand-pound bomb, while *Mikuma* was plastered with as many as six additional big bomb explosions. Some 240 *Mikuma* survivors were rescued before the other three Japanese ships struggled toward Wake Island. More than 650 of *Mikuma*'s officers and men had perished due to the dive-bombing attacks.

When *Hornet*'s air group returned, Bill Christie and Hank McDowell were eager to rejoin Wally Short and their other squadron mates flying off *Enterprise*. To his disappointment, Christie was told that he could do more good on *Hornet*, so that was that. Gus Widhelm managed to land his battle-damaged SBD safely, then made his way to the bridge to report to Captain Marc Mitscher. The pilot was eager to make another strike against the cruisers, but Mitscher waved him off. "Gus, you're intoxicated with battle," he said.[49]

In all, 112 sorties were flown against *Mikuma* and *Mogami*, of which eighty-one were by SBDs. They claimed twenty bomb hits on the two cruisers in exchange for one SBD shot down. *Mogami* took five bombs and barely limped back to Truk. She would be out of action for two years. Her sister, *Mikuma*, was decimated. When she finally rolled over on her port side and sank after dark on June 6, she was the first Japanese cruiser to be lost in the Pacific War.[50]

Johnny Neilsen, last of the mixed *Enterprise* group to land, was told to report to Admiral Spruance when he reached the ready room. He found Dave Shumway and Wally Short already in conversation with the admiral and his chief of staff, Captain Miles Browning. Neilsen insisted that his target was a heavy cruiser, although Shumway had reported the larger cruiser as a battleship.[51]

The staff was not pleased that *Enterprise*'s strike had failed to return with any telltale photos of the ships they had attacked. When Harvey Lanham had landed, one of the intelligence officers ran up to his SBD and grabbed the aerial camera from rear gunner Ed Garaudy. "I found out later that the film was blank," Garaudy said. "Apparently the lens had fogged over at high altitude!"[52]

Spruance decided to end the debate by sending a VS-6 photo plane to document the Japanese ships and their damage. Assistant LSO Cleo Dobson took off at 1553 in company with Bud Kroeger. In Dobson's rear seat was chief photographer J. A. Mihalovic, while Kroeger carried movie cameraman Al Brick from Movietown News to film the cruiser.

Dobson found *Mikuma* "in a very bad condition." Bodies littered the deck as he flew within a hundred feet. He estimated as many as five hundred Japanese sailors were in the water as he swept in low for Chief Mihalovic to snap photos of the devastated heavy cruiser. Dobson had been ordered to strafe the cruisers after taking his pictures. "[The sailors] were waving at me and I just couldn't do it!" he told squadron mate Dusty Kleiss back on board ship. In his diary that night, Dobson wrote, "After flying over those poor devils in the water I was chicken-hearted and couldn't make myself open up on them."[53]

Dobson's efforts to approach *Mogami* and her destroyers for photos was met by AA fire, so he gave up on that effort. He and Kroeger finally turned back for home, and within two hours of this photo flight, *Mikuma* would roll over and sink. The two *Enterprise* SBDs landed at 1907, and Spruance called them up to the bridge. The admiral wanted to finally determine whether the air groups had indeed hit a battleship. Dobson was asked what kind of ship the larger one was. "Sir, I don't know, but it was a hell of a big one," he said.

Spruance was further irritated that Dobson had not taken his ship identification cards aloft with him, yet Chief Mihalovic saved the group from further trouble by announcing that he had snapped some fantastic photos. Once his images were developed in the *Enterprise* photo lab that night, the scenes of destruction on board *Mikuma* left no doubt that the Americans had pounded a *Mogami*-class cruiser and not a battleship.[54]

While the third Task Force 16 flight had been airborne, the Japanese submarine *I-168* had slipped up on the battle-damaged *Yorktown* and fired torpedoes. The destroyer *Hammann*, alongside the carrier, was broken in two and she sank almost immediately with a heavy loss of life. The damage control crews on *Yorktown* were evacuated once again.

Enterprise changed course to the northwest to rendezvous with the fleet oilers the following morning. The pursuit was over, and the Battle of Midway was thus effectively ended. The Big E's aviators gulped down coffee and sandwiches while congratulating one another on another successful strike. That night, Scouting Five gunner Lynn Forshee went to work making squadron insignia patches for his fellow fliers.[55]

The bombing squadrons were a mess at the end of the day. In Bombing Six, Dick Best was permanently sidelined with his illness. His only veteran pilots still on board were Bud Kroeger, Harvey Lanham, Andy Anderson, and Arthur Rausch. The only four other pilots available for any further action—Lew Hopkins, Steve Hogan, Don Ely, and Harry Liffner—each had less than two months of experience with the squadron.

On *Hornet*, Clay Fisher found it depressing to eat in the wardroom with all the empty chairs around the Torpedo Eight and Fighting Eight tables. "After having flown all five of the attack missions launched from the *Hornet* and logging seventeen combat hours, I was emotionally drained and physically tired," Fisher said.[56]

Dusty Kleiss wrote a letter to his girlfriend, Jean, back in California before he turned in. "I'm okay but am tired to the dickens," he scribbled. Kleiss, of course, could not relate what had happened at Midway, but he offered her a hint. "I've had more than my share of luck and Tojo is most unhappy about it all."[57]

Some of the airmen had a good grasp of just what they had accomplished at Midway. "I believe that the Jap losses were so great," Ed Anderson confided in his diary, "that this will be a turning point in our favor for a final victory."[58]

EPILOGUE

It was Sunday, June 7—six months to the day after Pearl Harbor had been bombed—and the Battle of Midway was finished. Shortly before 0700, the battered carrier *Yorktown* finally rolled over and sank in about three thousand fathoms of water.

Admiral Spruance's task force turned eastward to link up with the fleet tankers. During the refueling process, the destroyer *Phelps* sent Dick Dickinson and Joe DeLuca of Scouting Six and Joe Penland and Harold Heard from Bombing Six over to a tanker in bosun's chairs. Other destroyers came alongside the tanker and deposited their collected airmen. Dickinson was pleased to meet up with Lieutenant Ray Davis from *Hornet*, whom he had known for years. That afternoon, *Enterprise* came alongside to fuel, and the tanker prepared to send the Big E's pilots back over.

From the tanker, Dickinson spotted Ensign Bill Pittman standing on *Enterprise*. Well out of shouting distance, Dickinson used hand signals to run through his squadron's eighteen planes, holding up fingers to see which SBDs had survived the battle. Pittman answered a surviving plane's number with a nod. When they were finished, Dickinson was sick at heart. "This was my first knowledge of the price our squadron had paid for its share in the victory," he said. Pittman had nodded only eight times. Dickinson soon spotted an officer of Bombing Six who had

U.S. Navy

Ensign John Lough.

observed the little pantomime. He wearily held up four fingers, then turned his back.[1]

The return voyage to Pearl Harbor was sobering. Personal effects of those lost in action were gathered to be shipped home to their families. Mike Micheel of Scouting Six took the time to write a letter to the family of Johnny Lough, his best friend on *Enterprise*. Some of the SBD crews had been pulled from the water, but Micheel held little hope for Lough, who had been downed by Zeros on June 4.[2]

Nearly 110 U.S. carrier aircraft were lost to all causes during the Midway battle, or about half of what had departed Pearl Harbor. Scouting Six and Bombing Six had suffered the heaviest losses in terms of planes and personnel during the Japanese carrier strike on June 4. Most of the downed crews suffered a cruel fate adrift on the ocean; only the SBD crews of Dickinson, Penland, McCarthy, and Schneider were rescued by PBYs and destroyers over the first couple of days. One more VB-6 crew amazingly survived a grueling ordeal in the ocean before they were rescued. Ensign Tom Ramsay and his gunner, AMM2c Sherman Duncan, drifted in their life raft for a week before a Midway PBY found them on June 12. They were badly sunburned and malnourished, but alive. Ramsay—who had delivered dairy products for the Borden company after graduating from Mississippi A&M—climbed up to the cockpit to thank the pilot and was stunned. It was Lieutenant (j.g.) Al Barthes (who had also rescued Tony Schneider), a man he had not seen since the two had attended high school together in Biloxi, Mississippi.[3]

Tony Schneider and Glenn Holden had been kept on Midway for a day to recover from their experience. Medics declared them healthy enough to travel and they were taken back to Pearl Harbor in a big Consolidated flying boat. Schneider was hospitalized for observation and his roommate was Ensign George Gay, the sole survivor of the carrier-based portion of Torpedo Eight.

One-third of America's carrier power present for the Battle of Midway was sunk, while the Japanese lost one hundred percent of its Kido Butai. The U.S. lost half of its carrier planes in the battle, while four air groups of Japanese aircraft were destroyed. By sinking four carriers, the U.S. Navy's SBD squadrons had deprived Japan of forty-seven percent of its first-line carrier tonnage. It was the ultimate payback for the *Enterprise* crews who had been ravaged on December 7.[4]

Replacement aircraft arrived just too late to partake in the Battle of Midway. The carrier *Saratoga* reached Pearl Harbor on June 6 after a four-month hiatus to repair her torpedo damage, and raced for Midway the following day with 107 aircraft, including forty-five dive-bombers. The *Enterprise* and *Yorktown* squadrons were down to half strength when the spare Dauntlesses reached Admiral Spruance on June 8.[5]

Jim Murray took note of some of the Midway SBDs that were slated to go to combat virgin *Saratoga* as replacements. The maintenance crews had a field day. They painted "all kinds of signs and sayings on the planes, showing the *Sara* what bullet holes looked like," he said.[6]

The triumphant U.S. carrier task forces steamed back into Pearl Harbor on June 13, preceded by a massive fly-in of their aircraft. Stuart Mason, wounded in the face and legs on June 4 over the Japanese carriers, was back in the rear seat with Andy Anderson as their air group flew into Kaneohe Air Station. "As each plane taxied up to the line, two Marines would give the crew two cans of beer," said Mason. "One SBD wasn't able to get the gear down and landed wheels up. Two Marines ran out on the runway with two cans of beer for the crew."[7]

Mason and his fellow aviators found a grand celebration awaiting them at the Kaneohe Air Station, including a Navy band. Bombing Six was a much-depleted unit upon its return. Since their war began six months earlier on December 7, 1941, the squadron had lost seven of its pilots. Only seven original VB-6 rear gunners remained: Jim Murray, Ed Garaudy, Mason, Herman Caruthers, Harold Heard, Bill Steinman, and Gail Halterman. Four of their peers had been transferred during the previous months (one wounded) and nine others had been killed in service. Scouting Six had paid even more dearly during the first six months of the

Pacific War. A stunning fifty percent—nineteen out of thirty-eight—of the pilots flying missions during this period were killed, wounded, or captured by the enemy. Fourteen out of thirty VS-6 gunners flying combat missions during this period were similarly killed, wounded, or captured.[8]

Bombing Six's Lieutenant Harvey Lanham would never forget "the hordes of Navy yard workers and others who lined the shores at Pearl Harbor and cheered our return after the battle."[9]

Others saw their homecoming in a different light. Jim Murray remained on board ship, since his pilot, Dick Best, was in sick bay. As the Big E passed close to the USAAF air base at Hickam Field while negotiating the channel at Pearl Harbor, he heard Army personnel mockingly shouting, "Where was the Navy?" Murray heard other "derogatory, often obscene comments. We were dumbfounded by this exhibition—a far cry from the flag-waving and cheering by these same men who greeted the Big E on her return from the Marshalls raid in February," he said.[10]

The answer to this peculiar behavior did not take the pilots long to decipher once ashore. They found that the Air Force pilots who had flown the B-17s from Midway had already been largely credited with smashing the Japanese fleet. "The Honolulu newspapers told the story," Murray said. "The Army held an awards ceremony at Hickam Field June 12, taking upon itself responsibility for the victory at Midway."[11]

The truth would eventually be found that the Air Force planes had hit absolutely nothing in three days of bombing. All hits had actually been made by Dauntless dive-bombers. The news greatly disturbed Murray. Once he was free to disembark *Enterprise*, he checked into the Royal Hawaiian Hotel and wandered across the street to the Wagon Wheel Restaurant and Bar for dinner and a nightcap.[12]

A group of Army Air Corps noncommissioned officers bragged loudly as Murray listened in about their heroics at Midway and the commendations they had already been given. Finally he had heard enough, and he explained exactly what the Navy dive-bomber crews had done at Midway. "There's not even evidence that B-17 bombs landed close enough to splash water on the Japs, let alone damage them!" he said. Murray wisely finished his meal and retreated back to the Pink Palace before his words had time to stir a good fistfight.

Things did not end so peacefully for a group of Scouting Six pilots in the dining room of the Royal Hawaiian. The loud boastings from a table of nearby Army pilots claiming to have won the battle at Midway soon became too much for them to bear. Ensigns Dick Jaccard, Bill Pittman, and others found themselves in a brawl that took the shore patrol some twenty minutes to subdue.[13]

The Dauntless aviators made the most of their liberty upon reaching Pearl Harbor. "The gang went wild," Dusty Kleiss wrote in his diary. "Seems as though a big Saturday night is in the offing." Scouting Five's Lynn Forshee joined a group of enlisted men in hitting the bars and awoke the next morning to find a new souvenir of his former ship emblazoned on his arm. "I decided to be sociable and had a drink, then blotto— I awoke next morning in the hotel with my arm in a bandage," he said. He assumed he must have gotten in a bar fight that he could not recall. Forshee removed his bandages and found a rather large tattoo of a skull with a flying helmet and the words U.S.S. YORKTOWN. "I discovered later that these friends, and I use the term loosely, had slipped me a Mickey," he said.[14]

George Goldsmith, who had been forced to abandon ship after landing on *Yorktown* on June 4, made his way back on board *Enterprise* at Pearl Harbor. He found to his surprise that his Bombing Six squadron mates had packed up all of his personal gear for shipment back to his parents. "I was very fortunate in being able to call my mother after first arrival," he recalled. "Of course, the call was carefully censored and all I could really say was, 'No matter what you hear, I am okay.'" Goldsmith found out later that his phone call was preceded by a telegram from the Navy Department to his parents by about four hours. The telegram had simply stated that Ensign Goldsmith was "missing in action" following engagement with the enemy.[15]

Ensign Fred Mears, a junior pilot of *Hornet*'s Torpedo Eight who had not flown at Midway, was reunited with many of his flight school buddies while on liberty on Oahu. He heard countless stories of the dive-bombing attacks from Dick Jaccard, Jim Dexter, Bill Pittman, and Jerry Richey. Mears also encountered Tom Durkin of Scouting Six, who was freshly returned from fourteen days at sea after his SBD had gone down in late May.[16]

Dusty Kleiss made his way back stateside to begin training new dive-bomber pilots. He had been gone longer than the twelve months he had expected, but he wasted no time in starting his new life. Detached from *Enterprise* on June 22, he headed for San Francisco on a transport ship, where he took the first train to Los Angeles to reunite with his beautiful fiancée, Jean Mochon, who met him at the station. Jean and Dusty piled into a car with her sister and brother-in-law and immediately headed to Las Vegas. There, the Kleisses were married on July 3—just weeks after the battle of Midway. It was the beginning of sixty-four wonderful years of marriage that would produce five children for the couple.

Seven of Kleiss's fellow Scouting Six pilots had been lost at Midway. All had ships named after them, and the six who had been lost on the June 4 carrier strike all received the Navy Cross posthumously. Lieutenant Charlie Ware, who had brilliantly guided his Scouting Six division through two Zero attacks, disappeared en route home at Midway. On April 12, 1945, his mother christened the destroyer *Charles R. Ware* (DD-865) in his honor. Four other warships were launched during the war in honor of Ware's four fellow missing VS-6 aviators: USS *Lough* (DE-586) for John Lough, USS *O'Flaherty* (DE-340) for Frank O'Flaherty, USS *Shelton* (DE-407) for Jim Shelton, and USS *Peiffer* (DE-588) for Carl Peiffer.[17]

Wade McClusky and sixteen men from VS-6 received the Navy Cross (some posthumously). Three other pilots received the Distinguished Flying Cross. Bombing Six pilots were awarded sixteen Navy Crosses for Midway (six posthumously) and three Distinguished Flying Crosses. Bombing Six's radiomen-gunners received seventeen DFCs (six posthumously) and three Air Medals. Four destroyer escorts were later named for VB-6 personnel killed at Midway: *Frederick T. Weber* (DE-675), *Norman F. Vandivier* (DE-540), *Bertram S. Varian Jr.* (DE-798), and *Ernest L. Hilbert* (DE-742).[18]

The Navy honored other lost Dauntless crews from the first six months of the Pacific War with ships in their names. Destroyer escorts served during the war that were the namesakes of William C. Miller and Walter M. Willis, two VS-6 aviators killed at Pearl Harbor. In 1943, another destroyer escort was converted to a high-speed transport—USS

Hopping (APD-51)—named in honor of VS-6's late skipper, Hal Hopping. Two other VS-6 aviators killed on February 1 were also honored with destroyer escorts: USS *Fogg* (DE-57) for Ensign Carl Fogg and USS *Dennis* (DE-405) for his gunner, Otis Lee Dennis.

Earl Gallaher, skipper of Scouting Six, found that the most difficult part of his job after Midway was writing letters to the families of the men he had lost. "It was the one thing I hated more than anything else," he said. To Zena Ware, mother of his late division leader Charlie Ware, Gallaher wrote that he was "very proud indeed to have commanded such a fine bunch of men." Offering some consolation to Mrs. Ware, he told her that Charlie went out in a "blaze of glory" during his action at Midway. Gallaher was approached sometime later in Pensacola by the former girlfriend of Ware. She was still distraught, not wanting to believe that her future husband was truly gone. "It was awfully hard to talk to people like that," Gallaher felt.[19]

Bombing Six skipper Dick Best—sidelined late on June 4 with tuberculosis that would eventually force his medical retirement—had landed bomb hits on two Japanese carriers that day. After Best passed away in 2001, a serious effort was made to recommend him posthumously for the Congressional Medal of Honor. Spearheaded by Admiral Thomas H. Moorer, a former chief of naval operations and Chairman of the Joint Chiefs of Staff, and Vice Admiral Bill Houser, a former deputy CNO for Air Warfare, this movement to further honor Best was not fulfilled.

Best's gunner, Jim Murray, was transferred along with Walter Chocalousek to Carrier Aircraft Service Unit One (CASU-1) at NAS Ford Island upon his return from Midway. Murray was rightfully proud of the fact that his Bombing Six was the only U.S. carrier squadron that participated in the destruction of all three first-line Japanese carriers in the decisive battle. The only Midway veterans to remain with the reorganized Bombing Six that would later serve at Guadalcanal in 1942 were ensigns Don Ely and Harry Liffner. The reconstituted VB-6 would, however, include many of the veteran gunners who had helped earn the victory at Midway: Ed Anderson, Gene Braun, Herman Caruthers, Sherman Duncan, Ed Garaudy, Gail Halterman, Harold Heard, Lew Jones, Milo Kimberlin, Stuart Mason, Jim Patterson, and Glenn Holden.[20]

Ed Anderson completed another tour of duty on *Enterprise* at Gua-

dalcanal and began dating his future wife upon his return stateside. He
flew as a gunner with an escort squadron, VC-40, for most of 1943 into
early 1944. Approached a number of times to go through flight training
to become a pilot, he declined on account of an old injury. During high
school basketball, he had suffered an impaired retina and was fearful
that if the Navy found out it could jeopardize his ability to continue serving as an aerial gunner. Ed was honorably discharged from the Navy in
September 1945. He began his civilian life in California as a claims ad-
justor and raised two daughters with his wife. In November 2001, he was
inducted into the Enlisted Combat Air Crew Roll of Honor during a
ceremony aboard *Yorktown*'s Naval & Maritime Museum at Patriots
Point, South Carolina. He was not presented with the many Air Medals
and Distinguished Flying Crosses that he had earned during the war because of a mix-up in his personnel files. This was finally rectified in a
2007 ceremony at the U.S. Naval and Marine Corps Reserve Center in
Alameda before his proud family. Anderson's love for the ocean never
ceased, and upon his death in April 2013, his family scattered his ashes
in San Francisco Bay.

Gunner Don Hoff, awarded the Distinguished Flying Cross for his
valor at Midway, served on *Saratoga* late in 1942 into the next year. In
June 1943, he went stateside to flight school with VS-6 buddy Johnny
Snowden. In the end, he opted to remain an enlisted man while radio-
men/gunner comrades like Snowden, Joe DeLuca, Stuart Mason, Joe
Godfrey, Jim Patterson, and Earl Howell became commissioned officers.
After leaving the Navy, Hoff worked three years as a draftsman and
twenty-three years for the Fresno County Sheriff's Office before settling
into the relaxed life of a retired square-dance caller.[21]

After the war, Jim Murray became a commissioned officer, retiring
as a lieutenant commander in November 1957 after thirty years of
service. In civilian life, he spent another decade working for the Ryan
Aeronautical Company before retiring in Imperial Beach, California.

Murray felt that certain individuals and even the devastated torpedo
squadrons received the lion's share of the praise for helping the U.S. Navy
achieve its stunning victory over Japan at Midway. Yet he believed that
there were many "unsung heroes" among the Dauntless squadrons, par-

ticularly those who gave their lives in the missions against the IJN's flat-tops.[22]

The naval aviators who achieved the great payback at Midway received at first only lukewarm praise. At Pearl Harbor they found that CinCPac's public relations office had allowed the Army Air Corps to release their version of the Battle of Midway to the media before the carriers even returned to port. The B-17 crews reveled in their celebrity for days as the heroes of the grand carrier conflict.[23]

The Navy fliers, in contrast to the Army Air Corps' award ceremony held on June 12 at Hickam Field, had to wait until September 1942. Then the media injustice was reversed as Admiral Nimitz himself presented awards to many Dauntless veterans on the flight deck of *Enterprise*. Murray considered it a further discrepancy that *Hornet*'s Torpedo Squadron Eight was the only Navy carrier squadron to be awarded the Presidential Unit Citation for its heroism at Midway. Torpedo Eight had lost fifteen of fifteen Devastators and twenty-nine of thirty aviators while inflicting no damage on Japanese shipping. *Yorktown*'s Torpedo Three and *Enterprise*'s Torpedo Six, which suffered losses nearly as traumatic, received no such award. Murray, for one, wondered why the Dauntless squadrons were passed over for the PUC award. His Bombing Six had participated in the destruction of three Japanese flattops and a heavy cruiser. "In achieving this heroic deed, Bombing Six suffered the loss of eleven aircraft and twelve aircrewmen," Murray said.[24]

Many of the *Yorktown* rear seat gunners were also given awards for their valor at Midway. Bombing Three's brothers Dallas and Fred Bergeron each received a Distinguished Flying Cross, and the elder Bergeron was later pinned with a Purple Heart for his bullet wounds sustained on June 4. News of the victory at Midway was kept under tight wrap for some time, so the men could not share explicit details of their involvement. Fred Bergeron sent a brief cable back home, saying simply, "Dallas has been injured and is doing well. Don't worry. Tell all hello." His intended reassurance fell far from bestowing the comfort he had hoped. The next wire dispatch from his mother firmly demanded, "Dallas injured? How? Where?"[25]

All of Max Leslie's Bombing Three pilots who flew on June 4 received the Navy Cross, several posthumously. Wally Short's Scouting (Bombing) Five pilots earned nine Navy Crosses. From *Hornet*'s air group, DFCs went to five Bombing Eight pilots and eight gunners. Another five VB-8 gunners would be pinned with the Air Medal. From Scouting Eight, four pilots received the Navy Cross and nine pilots earned the Distinguished Flying Cross. Scouting Eight gunners received an additional four DFCs and three Air Medals.

The SBD pilots and their rear gunners were heroes all. Unfortunately, many of them would later be lost in combat or operational accidents as the long war played out. Among the SBD pilots active during the first six months of the Pacific War and at Midway who later died during World War II were Dave Berry, Leonard Check, Larry Comer, Randy Cooner, Jim Dexter, Rockey Dickson, Phil Grant, Dick Jaccard, Paul Tepas, Abbie Tucker, and Harold White.

On the positive side of the tally sheet, two early 1942 Dauntless heroes shot down during enemy action finally made their way back home from prisoner-of-war camps in Japan. Dale Hilton and radioman Jack Leaming, lost from *Enterprise*'s Scouting Six during the March 1942 Marcus strike, survived three and a half years of slave labor, malnutrition, beatings, and various forms of abuse as they were moved through different POW camps during the war. After the atomic bombs were dropped and Japan surrendered, Hilton and Leaming finally made it on board one of the hospital ships in Tokyo Bay for medical evaluation. The officer of the deck told the newly freed Americans that they had their choice of entrées for their first real meal in years. "Most of us chose filet mignon," said Leaming, who later retired to Las Vegas.[26]

Junior dive-bomber pilots from the first six months of war who later commanded SBD squadrons during World War II were Gus Widhelm, Dave Shumway, Ray Davis, and Moe Vose. A number of the early 1942 SBD pilots also went on to command squadrons of the newer Helldiver carrier bomber during the war. Among them were Vose, Dave Berry, Tony Schneider, Harvey Lanham, Andy Anderson, Lloyd Smith, and Jack Blitch. From Scouting Six, Cleo Dobson completed the war in command of a fighter squadron, VF-86, aboard the new *Wasp* (CV-18).

Those brave pilots who flew the Douglas Dauntless in the early Pacific actions went on to lengthy Navy careers in many cases. Twenty-one of them retired as rear admirals: Bob Armstrong, Bill Burch, Clarence Dickinson, Bob Dixon, Earl Gallaher, Bill Guest, Herbert Hoerner, Bill Hollingsworth, Paul Holmberg, Lew Hopkins, Roy Isaman, Ruff Johnson, Harvey Lanham, Max Leslie, John Lynch, Wade McClusky, Bill Roberts, Walt Rodee, Wally Short, Curt Smiley, and Howard Young. Five of the SBD pilots retired as vice admirals: Pete Aurand, Turner Caldwell, Edgar Cruise, Stan Ring, and Ralph Weymouth. Two—Ralph Cousins and Don Felt—fleeted all the way up to full admiral during their careers.

The Battle of Midway was the most decisive naval victory for the United States during World War II, and it was decided by carrier aviators flying the Douglas SBD Dauntless. The war was still young, and four more major carrier battles would be fought in the Pacific, three of which also included SBD dive-bombers. Dauntless alumni from the first six months of the Pacific War participated in each of those clashes. Yet the prospect for an American victory in World War II was achieved by the carrier aviators who took the fight to the Japanese during those first six months. By June 1942, the advance of the Japanese war machine had been checked at times, and was forcibly thrown back at Midway.

Many forces had contributed to the early efforts during America's desperate hours—including surface sailors, the Submarine Force, Marines, Army soldiers, and Air Force crews. The U.S. Navy's fighter pilots had developed into a lean fighting team, while the Navy's torpedo bomber crews paid dearly in human lives for the victories that were earned. But there is no denying the brave spirit of the determined young men who flew the Navy's latest carrier dive-bombers into action during the first six months of the Pacific War. They had provided that determining extra edge that was the Dauntless factor.

My only regret with this tribute to the Dauntless airmen of early 1942 is in not starting my research sooner. Many of the radiomen/gunners I had the privilege of interviewing are now in their late nineties. Willard "Rocky" Glidewell of Yorktown's Scouting Five is a hundred years of age as of early 2013. With the passing of Bombing Eight's Clay Fisher in January 2012, only two Dauntless pilots who flew at Midway are still living as I complete this tribute to their services: Austin "Bud" Merrill of *Yorktown*'s Bombing Three and Jack "Dusty" Kleiss of *Enterprise*'s Scouting Six.

Texas resident Kleiss recently pondered why the good Lord had blessed him with such strength and endurance. He reflected on the "many brave souls who gave everything for our wonderful country and who gave unbelievable strength when needed." He considered himself fortunate to have had the best aviation instructors, to have had the best rear seat gunner in 1942, and to have been kept safe throughout the battle of Midway.[27]

The ninety-six-year-old, retired in San Antonio, was as sharp-minded in late 2012 as he was seventy years before at Midway. "The only thing I can presume is that He has not yet found me worthy to reach all those other saints above us," Kleiss said.

He is one of the Dauntless heroes who helped hold the line in the Pacific during six trying months, and who helped change the course of World War II for America on one unforgettable day of retribution near Midway. "Without the SBDs, we would certainly have lost the Battle of Midway," Kleiss stated to me in the fall of 2012. "No question about it. If we had lost the Battle of Midway, there would probably be a lot of Japanese and German being spoken in the United States and in London."

APPENDIX

Decorations Awarded to USS *Enterprise* Dauntless Airmen for Action from December 7, 1941–June 6, 1942

KEY	
MOH	Congressional Medal of Honor
NC	Navy Cross
DFC	Distinguished Flying Cross
AM	Air Medal
GS	Gold Star, in lieu of second or third award of same
LC	Navy Letter of Commendation

Bombing Squadron Six (VB-6) Commendations	
NAME, RANK/RATE	**COMMENDATIONS**
Anderson, Lt. Edward Lee	NC, AM
Anderson, ARM2c Edward Rutledge	DFC

(continued)

Bombing Squadron Six (VB-6) Commendations (cont.)	
NAME, RANK/RATE	**COMMENDATIONS**
Arnold, Sea2c George H.	AM
Best, Lt. Richard Halsey	NC, DFC, LC
Blitch, Lt. (jg) John Devereux	DFC
Braun, Sea1c Eugene K.	DFC
Brost, RM3c Allen James	AM
Caruthers, AMM2c Herman Hull	AM
Check, Lt. (jg) Leonard Joseph	AM
Chocalousek, ACRM Walter George	DFC
Doherty, Ens. John Joseph	DFC, LC
Duncan, AMM2c Sherman Lee	DFC
Ely, Ens. Don Lelo	DFC
Garaudy, ARM1c Edward Joseph	AM
Goldsmith, Ens. George Hale	NC
Greene, Ens. Eugene Allen	NC
Halsey, Ens. Delbert Wayne	NC, AM
Halterman, ARM2c Gail Wayne	DFC
Heard, ARM2c Harold Francis	DFC
Hilbert, AOM3c Ernest Leonard	DFC

Bombing Squadron Six (VB-6) Commendations	
NAME, RANK/RATE	**COMMENDATIONS**
Hogan, Ens. Stephen Clement Jr.	NC
Holcomb, Ens. Keith Haven	AM
Holden, ARM2c Glen Lester	DFC
Hollingsworth, Lt. Cdr. William Right	NC, LC
Hopkins, Ens. Lewis Alexander	NC
Jenkins, RM3c Jay William	DFC
Jones, AOM3c Harold Llewellyn	AM
Keaney, Sea1c Lee Edward John	DFC
Kimberlin, AMM3c Milo L.	AM
Kroeger, Lt. (jg) Edwin John	NC, DFC
Lanham, Lt. Harvey Peter	DFC, AM
Mason, ARM2c Stuart James Jr.	DFC
McCauley, Lt. (jg) James Wickersham	DFC
McClusky, Lt. Cdr. Clarence Wade	NC, DFC
Muntean, RM3c Samuel Andrew	DFC
Murray, ACRM James Francis	DFC, AM
Nelson, ARM1c Harry William Jr.	DFC

(continued)

Bombing Squadron Six (VB-6) Commendations (cont.)	
NAME, RANK/RATE	**COMMENDATIONS**
Patterson, ARM3c James William Jr.	DFC
Penland, Lt. Joe Robert	NC, AM
Ramsay, Ens. Thomas Wesley	NC
Rausch, Ens. Arthur Leo	DFC
Roberts, Lt. (jg) Wilbur Edison	NC, AM
Schneider, Ens. Tony Frederic	NC, AM
Smith, Lt. Lloyd Addison	DFC, AM
Steinman, AMM1c William Burr	DFC
Van Buren, Lt. (jg) John James	NC, DFC
Vandivier, Lt. (jg) Norman Francis	NC, AM
Varian, Ens. Bertram Stetson Jr.	NC
Walters, Ens. Clifford Raymond	AM
Weber, Ens. Frederick Thomas	NC, AM
Young, ARM3c Charles Robert	DFC
Young, Cdr. Howard Leyland	DFC

Scouting Squadron Six (VS-6) Commendations	
NAME, RANK/RATE	**COMMENDATIONS**
Adkins, AMM2c Floyd Delbert	DFC
Badgley, ACRM Jack Richard	AM
Bergin, RM1c William Hart	DFC
Bruce, Sea2c Thomas James	DFC
Clark, AMM2c Milton Wayne	AM
Craig, RM3c David Bruce	DFC
Dance, RM2c John Dewey	DFC
Deacon, Lt. (jg) Edward Thorpe	AM, LC
DeLuca, RM1c Joseph Ferdinand	DFC
Dexter, Ens. James Campbell	NC
Dickinson, Lt. Clarence Earle	NC, GS (2), AM
Dobson, Ens. Cleo John	DFC
Donnell, Ens. Earl Roe Jr.	AM
Fogg, Lt. (jg) Carleton Thayer	AM
Gaido, AMM1c Bruno Peter	DFC, LC
Gallaher, Lt. Wilmer Earl	NC, LC
Hansen, RM2c Louis Dale	DFC
Hoff, RM3c Donald Laurence	DFC

(continued)

Scouting Squadron Six (VS-6) Commendations (cont.)	
NAME, RANK/RATE	**COMMENDATIONS**
Hopping, Lt. Cdr. Hallsted Lubeck	LC
Howell, ARM2c Earl Edward	DFC
Jaccard, Ens. Richard Alonzo	NC
Jeck, RM3c Frederick Charles	DFC
Kleiss, Lt. (jg) Norman Jack	NC, DFC
Lough, Ens. John Cady	NC
McCarthy, Ens. John Reginald	NC
Merritt, ACRM Thomas Edward	DFC
Micheel, Ens. Vernon Larsen	NC
Miller, ARM1c William Cicero	LC
O'Flaherty, Ens. Frank Woodrow	NC
Patriarca, Lt. Frank Anthony	DFC, AM
Peiffer, Ens. Carl David	NC
Pittman, Ens. William Robinson	NC
Pixley, ARM3c Porter William	DFC
Rodenburg, Ens. Eldor Ernst	DFC
Roberts, Ens. John Quincy	NC
Rutherford, Lt. Reginald	AM

Scouting Squadron Six (VS-6) Commendations	
NAME, RANK/RATE	**COMMENDATIONS**
Seid, Ens. Daniel	AM
Shelton, Ens. James Arnold	NC
Snowden, RM2c John Warren	DFC
Stone, Ens. Reid Wenworth	NC, AM
Swindell, AOM1c Thurman Randolph	DFC
Teaff, Lt. (jg) Perry Lee	NC
Troemel, Lt. (jg) Benjamin Henry	AM
Vammen, Ens. Clarence Earl Jr.	DFC
Ware, Lt. Charles Rollins	NC
West, Lt. (jg) John Norman	NC, AM
West, Ens. William Price	LC

USS *Yorktown* (CV-5) SBD Commendations Bombing Squadron Three (VB-3) Bombing Squadron Five (VB-5) Scouting Squadron Five (VS-5)		
NAME, RANK/RATE	**SQUADRON(S)**	**COMMENDATIONS**
Adams, Lt. Samuel	VB-5, VS-5	NC, GS (2)
Ammen, Ens. John N., Jr.	VB-5	NC

(continued)

USS *Yorktown* (CV-5) SBD Commendations Bombing Squadron Three (VB-3) Bombing Squadron Five (VB-5) Scouting Squadron Five (VS-5) (cont.)		
NAME, RANK/RATE	**SQUADRON(S)**	**COMMENDATIONS**
Bassett, AOM2c Clifton R.	VB-3	DFC
Bennett, ARM2c Donald Harmon	VB-3	DFC
NAME, RANK/RATE	**SQUADRON(S)**	**COMMENDATIONS**
Benson, Ens. Robert Haines	VB-3	NC
Berg, ARM3c David Donald	VB-3	DFC
Bergeron, ARM3c Dallas Joseph	VB-3	DFC
Bergeron, ARM3c Frederick Paul	VB-3	DFC
Berry, Lt. (jg) David Render	VB-5	NC, GS (2)
Bottomley, Lt. Harold Sydney, Jr.	VB-3	NC
Butler, Ens. John Clarence	VB-3	NC
Campbell, Lt. (jg) Robert Keith	VB-3	NC, AM
Christie, Lt. (jg) William Francis	VB-5, VS-5	NC, GS

USS *Yorktown* (CV-5) SBD Commendations Bombing Squadron Three (VB-3) Bombing Squadron Five (VB-5) Scouting Squadron Five (VS-5)		
NAME, RANK/RATE	**SQUADRON(S)**	**COMMENDATIONS**
Clegg, ARM2c Earnest Alwyn	VS-5	DFC
Cobb, Ens. Philip Walker	VB-3	NC
Cooner, Ens. Bunyan Randolph	VB-3	NC
Coons, ARM1c Ray Edgar	VB-3	DFC
Cowden, ARM2c Harold R.	VB-5	DFC
Craig, ARM1c Horace Henry	VB-3	DFC
Dawn, ARM3c Grant Ulysses	VB-3	DFC
Dickson, Lt. Harlan Rockey	VB-5, VS-5	NC, GS
Elder, Ens. Robert Martin	VB-3	NC
Forshee, ARM3c Lynn Raymond	VB-5	DFC
Gallagher, ARM1c William Earl	VB-3	DFC

(continued)

	USS *Yorktown* (CV-5) SBD Commendations Bombing Squadron Three (VB-3) Bombing Squadron Five (VB-5) Scouting Squadron Five (VS-5) (cont.)	
NAME, RANK/RATE	**SQUADRON(S)**	**COMMENDATIONS**
Godfrey, ARM3c Joseph Vernon	VB-3	DFC
Guest, Lt. William Selman	VB-5	NC
Hanson, Ens. Alden Wilbur	VB-3	NC
Henning, ARM2c Jack Charles	VB-3	DFC, AM
Holmberg, Lt. (jg) Paul Algodte	VB-3	NC
Horenburger, Lt. (jg) Carl Herman	VS-5	NC
Isaman, Ens. Roy Maurice	VB-3	NC
Johnson, AMM1c David Frederick, Jr.	VB-3	DFC
Lane, Ens. Charles Smith	VB-3	NC
LaPlant, AMM2c George Albert	VB-3	DFC
Larsen, Ens. Leif Walther	VB-5	NC

	USS *Yorktown* (CV-5) SBD Commendations Bombing Squadron Three (VB-3) Bombing Squadron Five (VB-5) Scouting Squadron Five (VS-5)	
NAME, RANK/RATE	**SQUADRON(S)**	**COMMENDATIONS**
Leslie, Lt. Cdr. Maxwell Franklin	VB-3	NC
Lynch, ARM2c Joseph Michael	VB-5, VS-5	DFC
McDowell, Lt. (jg) Henry Martin	VB-5, VS-5	NC, DFC
Merrill, Ens. Milford Austin	VB-3	NC
Neilsen, Lt. John Ludwig	VB-5	NC, GS
Phelps, ACRM Otto Russell	VB-5, VS-5	DFC
Schlegel, Ens. Paul Wahl	VB-3	NC
Sherwood, Lt. Gordon Alvin	VB-3	NC
Short, Lt. Wallace Clark, Jr.	VB-5, VS-5	NC, GS (2)
Shropshire, ARM2c Jack Alven	VB-3	DFC
Shumway, Lt. Dewitt Wood	VB-3	NC

(continued)

USS *Yorktown* (CV-5) SBD Commendations Bombing Squadron Three (VB-3) Bombing Squadron Five (VB-5) Scouting Squadron Five (VS-5) (cont.)		
NAME, RANK/RATE	**SQUADRON(S)**	**COMMENDATIONS**
Sobel, ARM1c Alvin Arthur	VB-5, VS-5	DFC
Straub, ARM1c Walter Dean	VB-5, VS-5	DFC
Till, RM3c Leslie Alan	VB-3	DFC
Trott, ACRM John W.	VB-5, VS-5	DFC
Weaver, ARM3c Sidney Kay	VB-3	DFC
Wiseman, Lt. (jg) Osborne Beeman	VB-3	NC
Zimmershead, AMM1c Clarence Eugene	VB-3	DFC

Note: Commendations listed only for *Yorktown* aviators present at Midway.

USS *Hornet* (CV-8) SBD Commendations Bombing Squadron Eight (VB-8) Scouting Squadron Eight (VS-8)		
NAME, RANK/RATE	**SQUADRON**	**COMMENDATIONS**
Bebas, Ens. Gus George	VB-8	DFC
Berthold, ARM3c William H.	VB-8	AM

USS *Hornet* (CV-8) SBD Commendations Bombing Squadron Eight (VB-8) Scouting Squadron Eight (VS-8)		
NAME, RANK/RATE	**SQUADRON**	**COMMENDATIONS**
Broughton, ARM2c John B., Jr.	VB-8	AM
Bunch, ARM1c Kenneth Cecil	VS-8	AM
Canfield, ARM1c Donald L.	VB-8	DFC
Carter, Ens. William Douglas	VB-8	DFC
Christofferson, Ens. Frank E.	VB-8	DFC
Clanton, ACRM John L.	VB-8	AM
Davis, Lt. Ray	VS-8	DFC
Devoe, Ens. Augustus, Jr.	VS-8	DFC
Ferguson, ARM2c George E.	VB-8	DFC
Fisher, Ens. Clayton Evan	VB-8	NC
Grant, Ens. Philip Farnsworth	VB-8	DFC
Griswold, Ens. Don "T"	VS-8	DFC
Johnson, Lt. Cdr. Robert Ruffin	VB-8	DFC

(continued)

USS *Hornet* (CV-8) SBD Commendations Bombing Squadron Eight (VB-8) Scouting Squadron Eight (VS-8) (cont.)		
NAME, RANK/RATE	**SQUADRON**	**COMMENDATIONS**
Kiley, ARM1c Clarence C.	VB-8	DFC
King, Ens. Joe W.	VB-8	NC
Kirkpatrick, Lt. (jg) Donald, Jr.	VS-8	DFC
Lynch, Lt. John Joseph	VB-8	NC
Manus, ARM3c David T.	VS-8	DFC
McCoy, ACRM Joseph G.	VS-8	AM
McEwen, ARM2c Richard C.	VS-8	DFC
Moore, Lt. Ben, Jr.	VS-8	NC
Mortensen, ARM1c Clyde S.	VB-8	DFC
Nickerson, Ens. Henry John	VB-8	NC
Parker, ARM2c Arthur M.	VS-8	DFC
Phillips, ACRM Ralph	VS-8	AM
Quillen, ARM3c Leroy	VB-8	AM
Riner, Ens. James Austin, Jr.	VB-8	DFC

NAME, RANK/RATE	SQUADRON	COMMENDATIONS
USS *Hornet* (CV-8) SBD Commendations **Bombing Squadron Eight (VB-8)** **Scouting Squadron Eight (VS-8)**		
Ring, Cdr. Stanhope Cotton	CHAG	NC
Ringressy, RM3c Alfred W., Jr.	VB-8	AM
Rusk, Ens. Philip James	VS-8	DFC
Stebbins, Lt. Edgar Erwin	VS-8	DFC
Stokely, ARM1c George D.	VS-8	DFC
Tappan, Ens. Benjamin	VS-8	DFC
Tepas, Ens. Paul Edmond	VS-8	DFC
Tucker, Lt. Alfred Bland, III	VB-8	NC
Urban, ARM3c John Stephen	VS-8	DFC
Vose, Lt. James Everett	VB-8	DFC
Walsh, ARM3c Thomas	VS-8	DFC
White, Ens. Harold	VS-8	NC
Whitney, Lt. Laurens Adin	VS-8	DFC
Woods, ARM2c Wilbur L.	VB-8	DFC

SOURCES

My interest in the Pacific dive-bombers first came at an early age, when I read Walter Lord's 1967 book on Midway, *Incredible Victory*. Twenty-five years after it was fought, Lord vividly described this crucial battle between aircraft carriers in which U.S. forces were "hopelessly outclassed" with "no right to win." I was therefore fortunate while writing this book to be able to read through many of the original interviews he conducted during the early 1960s with Midway veterans.

A wealth of knowledge and material was shared by leading naval aviation historians and archivists. Among those I must thank for their advice and contributions are historian and aviation author Barrett Tillman, Ron Russell of the Midway Roundtable historical group, Arnie Olson of the *Enterprise* Foundation, and oral historian William J. Shinneman. James C. Sawruk—one of the leading researchers of the Dauntless aircrews of 1942—kindly shared some of his notes and research and fielded various questions along the way.

Alex D'Amore was a key assistant in researching and copying various documents in Washington. Much credit is due to Dr. Edward Furgol of the Washington Naval History and Heritage Command center for suggesting this tireless pursuer of vital papers. Tim Frank of the Naval History Center was invaluable in tracking down various SBD documents and the research of Walter Lord. James Scott, a fellow naval historian, went out of his way to help collect requested documents during his research visits to Washington.

From Pensacola's Naval Aviation Museum, volunteers Bill Addison, Bob Ammann, and Theo Elbert in the Emil Buehler Library graciously scanned numerous pilot photos for use in this book. Video archivist Steve Heffernan allowed me to review the museum's collection of audiotapes for interviews with SBD pilots. Elizabeth Novara assisted with the Gordon W. Prange Papers at the University of Maryland's Hornbake Library. Naval aviation historian John Lundstrom kindly shared a Bureau of Aeronautics interview and helped me correct several facts while reading over the manuscript. In Midland, Texas, Keegan Chetwynd of the CAF Airpower Museum was key in helping to scan photos and reproduce recorded interviews with Dauntless veterans. Dr. Keith Huxen, the senior research director of the National World War II Museum in New Orleans, and Seth Paridon, his manager of research services, shared a few of the many thousands of World War II oral histories that Paridon and his team have tirelessly collected.

I am indebted to several key people who helped me shape the final manuscript. First is my friend and agent, Jim Donovan, who made sure that the narrative kept a proper pace throughout. I also want to thank my terrific editor at Penguin Books, Brent Howard, and his manuscript copy editor, Tiffany Yates, for their superb scrutiny of the names, facts, and dates.

Edith Weisheit allowed me to review her late husband's research on the *Hornet* Air Group at the Battle of Midway. Families of many of the Dauntless crew contributed stories, photos, logbooks, wartime diaries, and memoirs. Namely they were Janice Anderson-Gram, Terry Tereskerz, Jane Kirshenbaum, Mary Birden, Henry Weinzapfel, Richard Roll, Marlene Meckenstock, Dennis Rodenburg, Mary Mason, Patrick Lombardi, and Troy T. Guillory Jr.

Finally, I must thank those who were there for sharing their memories. Contributing author Mark Horan had the pleasure of getting to know dozens of these Dauntless aviators. In addition to allowing me to review his correspondence and photo archives, Mark added many valuable personal stories to this manuscript that he gleaned from his time with these veterans. Most important, I must thank those who aided me directly with stories, answers, photos, and other memorabilia. They were Norman Jack "Dusty" Kleiss, Stanley "Swede" Vejtasa, Jack Leaming, Edward Anderson, Harold "Hal" Buell, Achilles Georgiou, Ronald Graetz, Milford A. Merrill, John Iacovazzi, Willard "Rocky" Glidewell, Fred Bergeron, Kenneth Garrigan, Thomas Ball, Oral "Slim" Moore, and Ray Johnston.

To these men and all of the Dauntless warriors involved in the first six months of the Pacific War, this book is dedicated.

BIBLIOGRAPHY

INTERVIEWS, ORAL HISTORIES, AND CORRESPONDENCE

CAF AMERICAN AIRPOWER HERITAGE MUSEUM,
THE ORAL HISTORY ARCHIVE, MIDLAND, TEXAS:

Wayne C. Colley (VS-2): 27 July 1991 interview with William J. Shinneman, transcript

Lt. Cdr. Robert D. Gibson, USNR (Ret.), 10 July 1993, interview with William J. Shinneman, transcript

Norman J. Kleiss (VS-6): 4 March 2004, interview with Margaret Cawood, transcript

Stuart J. Mason, Jr. (VB-6): 9 August 2000 interview with William J. Shinneman, transcript

Oral L. Moore (VB-8): audiotaped interview, unspecified date

Tony F. Schneider (VB-6): audiotaped interview, unspecified date

Capt. Stanley W. Vejtasa, USNR (Ret.), 7 October 2000, interview with William J. Shinneman, transcript

CENTRAL CALIFORNIA WAR VETERANS ORAL HISTORY
PROJECT, CALIFORNIA STATE UNIVERSITY, FRESNO:

Donald L. Hoff (VS-6), 15 May 2010 interview with Valerie Nevens

MARK E. HORAN, PERSONAL INTERVIEWS
AND CORRESPONDENCE, AND OTHER ARCHIVES:

Floyd D. Adkins (VS-6), 23 October 1987

Edward L. Anderson (VB-6), 28 April 1987

Lt. Cdr. Richard H. Best (VB-6)

Capt. Harold S. Bottomley Jr. (VB-3)

Anthony W. Brunetti (VS-5), 21 August 1986

Harold L. Buell (VS-5, VB-5), 25 October 1986

William F. Christie (VS-5)

Capt. Ray Davis (VS-8), undated 1967 letter to Col. Robert E. Barde

Lt. Cdr. Joseph F. DeLuca (VS-6), 8 September 1987

Don L. Ely (VB-6), 3 January 1987

Edward J. Garaudy (VB-6), 30 December 1986

Capt. George H. Goldsmith (VB-6), 9 February 1987

Capt. Troy T. Guillory (VB-8), 27 April 1967 to Col. Robert E. Barde

Lewis A. Hopkins (VB-6), 28 February 1987

Harold L. Jones (VB-6), 22 December 1986

Cdr. Charles S. Lane (VB-3), 27 May 1987

John J. Lynch (VB-8), 1 June 1967 correspondence with Col. Robert E. Barde

John M. Lynch (VB-5, VS-5), 20 October 1986

Lt. Cdr. Stuart J. Mason (VB-6), 20 October 1987

John R. McCarthy (VS-6)

Capt. Vernon L. Micheel (VS-6)

Cdr. James F. Murray (VB-6)

Capt. Frank A. Patriarca (VS-6), 12 May 1987

Lt. Cdr. James W. Patterson (VB-6), 22 October 1986, 18 January 1987

Capt. Joe R. Penland (VB-6)

Capt. William R. Pittman (VB-6), 22 October 1986

Capt. Wilbur E. Roberts (VB-6)

Cdr. Eldor E. Rodenburg (VS-6), 1987

Capt. Tony F. Schneider (VB-6), 31 May 1966 with Col. Robert E. Barde

Lt. Cdr. Stephen Smith (VT-6)

Lt. Cdr. John W. Snowden (VS-6), 22 May 1987

James E. Vose, Jr. (VB-8), 9 January 1967 correspondence with Col. Robert E. Barde

WALTER LORD COLLECTION, INTERVIEWS DURING RESEARCH FOR *INCREDIBLE VICTORY* BOOK. OPERATIONAL ARCHIVES, NAVAL HISTORY AND HERITAGE COMMAND, WASHINGTON NAVY YARD, WASHINGTON, D.C. SPECIFIC QUESTIONNAIRES, INTERVIEW NOTES AND CORRESPONDENCE WITH SBD PILOTS AND GUNNERS THAT WERE REFERENCED:

Lt. J. Clark Barrett (VB-8)

Capt. Harold S. Bottomley Jr. (VB-3)

Eugene K. Braun (VB-6)

Capt. Norwood A. Campbell (*Yorktown* LSO)

Capt. Philip W. Cobb (VB-3)

Capt. Ray Davis (VS-8)

CWO-4 William E. Gallagher (VB-3)

Rear Adm. Wilmer E. Gallaher (VS-6)

Cdr. Joseph V. Godfrey (VB-3)

Capt. George H. Goldsmith (VB-6)

Capt. Troy T. Guillory (VB-8)

Capt. Alden W. Hanson (VB-3)

Rear Adm. Paul A. Holmberg (VB-3); also Holmberg narrative to Thaddeus V. Tuleja in Lord's collection, 9 June 1958

Ralph B. Hovind (VS-8)

Rear Adm. Roy M. Isaman (VB-3)

Rear Adm. Robert R. Johnson (VB-8)

Cdr. R. H. Konig (VT-3)

Cdr. Charles S. Lane (VB-3)

Capt. Harvey P. Lanham (VB-6)

Rear Adm. Maxwell F. Leslie (VB-3)

Lt. Cdr. Stuart J. Mason (VB-6)

John R. McCarthy (VS-6)

Cdr. Milford A. Merrill (VB-3)

Capt. Vernon L. Micheel (VS-6)

Cdr. Corwin F. Morgan (VT-8)

Cdr. J. S. Morris (VT-6)

Capt. Frank A. Patriarca (VB-6)

Lt. Cdr. James W. Patterson (VB-6)

Capt. Joe R. Penland (VB-6)

Capt. William R. Pittman (VS-6)

Capt. Wilbur E. Roberts (VB-6)

Cdr. Eldor E. Rodenburg (VS-6)

Vice Adm. Walter G. Schindler (*Yorktown*)

Capt. Tony F. Schneider (VB-6)

Lt. Cdr. John W. Snowden (VS-6)

Cdr. Thomas J. Wood (VB-8)

NATIONAL MUSEUM OF THE PACIFIC WAR, FREDERICKSBURG, TEXAS:

Frederick P. Bergeron (VB-3): 29 April 2004 interview

Richard H. Best (VB-6): 11 August 1995 interview

Lewis A. Hopkins (VB-6): 15 January 2004 interview

NATIONAL WORLD WAR II MUSEUM, NEW ORLEANS, LOUISIANA:

Cdr. Milford Austin Merrill (VB-3), interview with Seth Paridon

Capt. Vernon L. Micheel (VS-6), interview with Seth Paridon

Capt. Tony F. Schneider (VB-6), 2007 interview with Seth Paridon

Vice Admiral Ralph Weymouth (VS-3), interview with Seth Paridon

NAVAL AVIATION MUSEUM FOUNDATION, PENSACOLA, FLORIDA, ORAL HISTORY COLLECTION:

Evan Peter Aurand (VS-2) and Marion Carl joint interview, 1 May 1988

Admiral Ralph W. Cousins (VB-2) interview, 18 October 1988

Robert M. Elder (VB-3) interview, 9 January 1989

GORDON W. PRANGE PAPERS, INTERVIEWS AND CORRESPONDENCE WITH MIDWAY VETERANS FOR *MIRACLE AT MIDWAY* BOOK, UNIVERSITY OF MARYLAND, HORNBAKE LIBRARY, COLLEGE PARK:

Capt. Charlie N. "Tex" Conatser (VS-5) interview, 11 May 1966

Capt. Ray Davis (VS-8) to Robert E. Barde, 5 January 1967

Lt. (jg) Cleo J. Dobson (VS-6) diary, 1942

Robert Edward Laub (VT-6) interview, 13 May 1966

RADM Clarence Wade McClusky (CEAG) interview, 30 June 1966

Capt. Joe R. Penland (VS-6) interview, 18 May 1966

RADM Walter F. Rodee (VS-8) to Robert E. Barde, 18 October 1966

RADM Wallace C. Short (VS-5) interview, 24 May 1966

Lt. Cdr. Stephen Smith (VT-6) to Robert E. Barde, 3 February 1967

INTERVIEWS CONDUCTED BY JAMES C. SAWRUK. RELEVANT INFORMATION SHARED WITH AUTHOR VIA E-MAILS IN FEBRUARY 2012:

James H. Cales (VS-5)

Floyd E. Moan (VB-5)

Capt. Arthur J. Schultz Jr. (VS-2)

INTERVIEWS CONDUCTED BY MAJOR BOWEN P. WEISHEIT, USMCR (RET.). TRANSCRIPTS COURTESY OF EDITH WEISHEIT:

Walter F. Rodee (VS-8): 1981

Benjamin Tappan (VS-8): 1981

INTERVIEWS CONDUCTED BY THE AUTHOR:

Anderson, Edward R. (VB-6). Telephone interview, 12 January 2011

Armstrong, Robert B. (Nephew of VB-5 skipper Robert G. Armstrong). E-mail correspondence, photos, and biography of Armstrong provided to author on 6 March 2011

Bergeron, Frederick P. (VB-3). Telephone interview, 4 February 2011, and subsequent follow-up conversations and e-mail correspondence

Buell, Harold L. (VS-5). Telephone interviews, 9 January and 8 February 2011, and additional correspondence

Georgiou, Achilles A. (VB-6). Telephone interview, 2 March 2011

Graetz, Ronald W. (VT-6). Telephone interview, 14 January 2011, and subsequent correspondence and e-mail

Guillory, Troy T., Jr. (Son of VB-8 pilot). Telephone interview, 4 April 2012

Hoff, Donald A. (Son of VS-6 gunner). Telephone interview, 2 December 2012, and additional correspondence

Iacovazzi, John M. (VB-5, VS-5). Telephone interview, 25 January 2011

Johnston, Earnest Ray (VS-8). Telephone interviews, 3 June and 20 June 2011

Kleiss, Norman J. (VS-6). Telephone interviews of 5 January 2011, 27 September 2012, 2 December 2012, and additional correspondence

Leaming, Jack (VS-6). Telephone interview, 6 January 2011

Mason, Mary (daughter of VB-6 gunner Allen Brost). E-mail correspondence of 17 March 2011

Merrill, Milford A. (VS-6, VB-3). Telephone conversation, 15 January 2011

Moore, Oral L. (VB-8). Telephone interview, 2 June 2011

Tereskerz, Terry L. (Son of VS-8 gunner John L. Tereskerz). Telephone interview, 20 June 2011

Vejtasa, Stanley W. (VS-5). Telephone interview, 7 January 2011

WORLD WAR II DATABASE:

Gallaher, Rear Adm. Wilmer Earl. "Interview with Earl Gallaher," 4 June 1992, conducted by Jim Bresnahan. Accessed http://ww2db.com/doc.php?q=403 on 14 July 2012

OFFICIAL DOCUMENTS, STATEMENTS

Best, Lt. R. H, "Attack on Taroa Island, Maloelap Atoll, 1 February 1942 by nine bomber land planes."

Bombing Squadron Eight (VB-8) War Diary, April–June 1942.

Corl, Mach. Harry Lee. Statement of 15 June 1942.

CTF-17 to CINCPAC, "The Battle of the Coral Sea, May 4–8, 1942" (27 May 1942).

Dickinson, Lt. C. E., Jr. Bureau of Aeronautics interview of 10 July 1942, National Archives, courtesy of John Lundstrom.

Enterprise Air Group Action Reports: 7 December 1941 (including individual pilot statements); "Report of action on February 1, 1942 against Marshall Island Group."

Gallaher, Lt. W. E. Scouting Six Task Organization and Availability of Pilots and Aircraft, 23 February 1942 (Wake Island strike); Scouting Squadron Six action report, 25 February 1942 (Wake Island strike); Scouting Six Report of Attack on Marcus Island, 5 March 1942.

Hollingsworth, Lt. Cdr. W. R. Bombing Squadron Six action reports: 25 February 1942 "Attack on Wake Island" report; "Flight Leader's Report of Dawn Attack on Kwajalein Atoll, 1 February 1942"; "Flight Leader's Report of Attack on Maloelap at 1030, 1 February 1942, by Nine SBDs"; "Attack on Marcus Island," 4 March 1942.

McCauley, Cdr. James W. Navy Department Interview of 23 June 1945, rough transcript. Smooth transcript version of 27 July 1945 also reviewed. Office of Naval Records and Library, National Archives.

McClusky, C. Wade. "Battle of Midway." Recollections of 4 June 1942 mission as presented by Arnold Olson, Public Affairs Officers, USS *Enterprise* CV-6 Association. Accessed at http://www.cv6.org /company/accounts/wmcclusky/ on 4 January 2011.

Mitscher, Capt. M. A. "Report of Action—4–6 June 1942."

Quillen, Leroy, ARM3c, U.S. Navy. Statement of Bombing Squadron Eight On First Flight, June 4, 1942, Search in Plane 8-B-2 (June 5, 1942).

Shumway, Lt. D. W. "Report of Action, Period 4 June 1942 to 6 June 1942, inclusive." Bombing Squadron Three action report, 10 June 1942.

Strong, Lt. Cdr. Stockton B. Bureau of Aeronautics interview of 3 August 1943, Office of Naval Records and Library, National Archives, Record Group 38, Box 26. Courtesy of James M. Scott.

ARTICLES / MEMOIRS / REPORTS

"Alumnus Tells of Adventures at Charleston," *Alton Evening Telegraph*, August 8, 1942, 1.

Anderson, Edward Rutledge. "War Diary of Edward Rutledge Anderson, RM3/c U.S.N.R., Bombing Squadron Six, USS *Enterprise*." Courtesy of his daughter, Janice Anderson-Gram, along with her father's flight log.

Armstrong, Robert Bryan. "Armstrong, Robert Gordon. 1904–1980." Privately published biography of Captain Armstrong written by his nephew, August 2007.

Bridgers, John D., M.D. "On the Traveling Squad E-Base, Doolittle & Midway, 1941–1942." Privately published "Memoirs and Personal Remembrances." Accessed http://tkjk.net/Bridgers/NavyYears/OnTheTravelingSquad.html on 5 February 2011.

Brost, Allen J. Narrative of action with VB-6. Accessed http://www.veteraneyes.com/pages/allen_brost.php?section=island on 4 April 2011.

Childers, LCol. Lloyd, USMC (Ret), PhD. "Midway from the Backseat of a TBD." *The Hook*, Vol. 18, August 1990, 36–38.

Cressman, Robert J. "Blaze of Glory: Charlie Ware and the Battle of Midway." *The Hook*, Vol. 24, Issue 1 (Spring 1996), 24–29.

Cressman, Robert J. "Dauntless in War: Douglas SBD-2 BuNo 2106." *Naval Aviation News*, Vol. 96, Issue 5 (Jul/Aug. 1994), 24.

"Defense: Mr. Pacific." *Time*, January 6, 1961. Accessed http://www.time.com/time/magazine/article/0,9171,874242-3,00.html#ixzz1DGmMBQvx on 7 February 2011.

"Describes Sinking of Jap Aircraft Carrier in Pacific." *Joplin News Herald*, November 12, 1942, 7.

"Dive-bomber Pilots Hold a Reunion." *Joplin Globe*, July 1, 1942, 7.

"Edward Rutledge Anderson: The Anderson Family Book of Memories." Privately published in April 2013 by his daughters, Janice Anderson-Gram and Gretchen Wilkinson.

"Ensign's Absentmindedness Sends Jap Destroyer to Bottom." *Lowell Sun*, July 2, 1942, 49.

Esders, Cdr. Wilhelm G., USN (Ret.). "Torpedo Three and the Devastator: A Pilot's Recollection." *The Hook*, Vol. 18, August 1990, 35–36.

"Family Reunion on Father's Day." *Clovis News-Journal*, June 22, 1942, 6.

"Flier Describes Bursting of Bomb. Plane Carrier Hit by California Boy." *Reno Evening Gazette*, 16 June 1942, 1.

"Flier Describes Carrier Attack. Zeros Fail to Stop Him." *Reno Evening Gazette*, July 2, 1942, 6.

Forshee, Lynn R. *"Standby! Mark!" An Autobiography by WWII Naval Aviator*. Privately published, 2004. Accessed http://www.forshee.0sites.org/index.shtml on 12 January 2011.

Gallaher, Earl. "I Remember Pearl Harbor." Unpublished memoirs of World War II and Midway. Walter Lord *Incredible Victory* archives. Naval Historical Center.

Gee, Capt. Roy P. "Remembering Midway." Article written in 2003 for the Battle of Midway Roundtable.

Graetz, Ronald. "Memories from Navy Days." Memoirs of service with Torpedo Squadron Six, courtesy of Ron Graetz.

Hackett, Bob, Sander Kingsepp and Peter Cundall, "IJN Subchaser *CH-51*: Tabular Record of Movement." Accessed http://www.combinedfleet.com/Shisaka_t.htm on 21 August 2009.

"His Torpedo Plane Pierced by 68 Bullets at Midway. Pilot Stephen Smith Returns for First Visit in 14 Months." *Mason City Globe-Gazette*, July 6, 1942, 8.

Horan, Mark E. "The Last Flight of Charles Rollins Ware."

"John Doherty and Bombing Six." Accessed http://www.cv6.org/company/accounts/jdoherty/ on 8 January 2011.

"Kingsport, Va., Youth Vividly Tells of Jap Plane Attack." *Kingsport* (TN) *Times*, August 4, 1942, 1.

Kleiss, Capt. Jack "Dusty," USN (Ret.). "History from the Cockpit: Reflections of a World War II U.S. Navy Dive-bomber Pilot." *The Daybook* (Hampton Roads Naval Museum), 2012 Vol. 15, Issue 4.

Kleiss, Lt. (jg) N. J. "VS-6 Log of the War. Personal Diary, and *USS Enterprise* Orders of a Scouting Six SBD Dive-bomber Pilot, Pearl Harbor Attack through the Battle of Midway." Privately published.

Lane, Marica. "Veteran Recounts Service on USS *Enterprise*." *St. Augustine* (FL) *Times*, April 24, 2006. Accessed http://staugustine.com/stories/042406/news_3789710.shtml on 27 December 2011.

Lee, Clark. "Ex Indiana School Teacher Dive-bombs Japs, Likes It." *Charleston Gazette*, June 13, 1942, 1–2.

"Lieut. Tepas, Home After Crusoe Adventure, Is City's First to Win Flying Medal." *Portsmouth* (OH) *Times*, 17 December 1942, 1–2.

Linder, Capt. Bruce R. "Lost Letter of Midway." *Proceedings*, August 1999, 29–35.

Lundstrom, John B. and James C. Sawruk. "Courage and Devotion to Duty. The SBD Anti-torpedo Plane Patrol in the Coral Sea, 8 May 1942." *The Hook*, Winter 1988, 24–37.

Mason, Robert. "Eyewitness." *Proceedings*, June 1982, 40–42.

McCaul, Ed. "Dive-bomber at Midway." *Military History* 19(2): 42–48 June 2002.

McPherson, Lt. I. H. "I Fly For the Navy." *Salt Lake Tribune*, December 7, 1942, A-5–6; 9 December 1942, A-11; December 13, 1942, A-23;

December 20, 1942, A-19; December 27, 1942, A-15; January 3, 1943, A-21; January 10, 1943, A-15.

Murray, Cdr. James F., USN (Ret.). *Bombing Squadron Six in Action: A Radio-gunner Looks Back*. Unpublished memoirs, 1986, Naval Library.

———. "Midway: The View from a Bombing Six Rear Seat." *The Hook*, 17:1, Spring 1989, 40–47.

"Navy Gunner Gets Award, Tells of Lively Fight." *The Helena Independent*, November 25, 1942, 1.

"Nips Boasted Japan Bomb-proof Just as Tokyo Raid Was Begun." *Charleston Gazette*, April 24, 1943, 2.

"Oakland Flier Drifts 17 Days in Rubber Boat; Fails to Thumb Ride on Passing Jap Submarine." *Oakland Tribune*, 9 September 1942.

Orr, Timothy, Ph.D., and Laura Orr. "Jack 'Dusty' Kleiss and the Battle of Midway." *The Daybook* (Hampton Roads Naval Museum), 2012 Vol. 15, Issue 4.

Roberts, Rear Adm. Wilbur E., USNR (Ret.). "Air Raid on Pearl Harbor X This is No Drill." Unpublished memoirs of 7 December 1941, courtesy of Mark Horan Papers.

———. "Many Planes Heading Midway." Unpublished memoirs of 4 June 1942, courtesy of Mark Horan Papers.

Rodenburg, Dennis. *Eldor E. Rodenburg, Lieutenant Commander, U.S. N.R. World War II Dive-bomber Pilot and Landing Signal Officer*. Privately published. Courtesy of Dennis Rodenburg.

Schneider, Tony F. 1999 correspondence with Daniel Rush. Accessed http://www.cv6org/company/accounts/jdoherty/jdoherty–2.htm on 8 January 2011.

Tillman, Barrett. "Where Are They Now? Bob Elder." *The Hook*, Fall 1989, 12–17.

"Two Lisbon, N.D. Youths Honored. Tell of Sinking Enemy U-Boat and Big Jap Carrier." *Bismarck Tribune*, 25 June 1942, 1, 3.

"Wait Irked Utahn in Coral Battle," *Salt Lake Tribune*, June 21, 1942, 2B.

Woodson, ATC Richard T. "In the Rear Seat at Midway and Santa Cruz."

"Wounded Pilot Tells of Coral Sea Battle." *Salt Lake Tribune*, July 6, 1942, 6, 16.

"Yank Flyers Forced Down Aided by Island Natives." *News Palladium* (Benton Harbor, MI), August 27, 1942, 1.

VIDEO

Glidewell, Willard E. (VS-5). Oral history videotaped in 2006, Veterans History Project, Library of Congress.

Hilton, Hart Dale. University of Southern California Living History Project, 1978 videotaped interview.

Hoff, Donald L. "Vengeance at Midway." History Channel, *Battle 360*, Episode 2.

BOOKS

Ambrose, Hugh. *The Pacific*. New York: NAL Caliber, 2010.

Belote, James H., and William M. Belote. *Titans of the Seas: The Development and Operations of Japanese and American Carrier Task Forces During World War II*. New York: Harper & Row, 1975.

Buell, Harold L. *Dauntless Helldivers: A Dive-Bomber Pilot's Epic Story of the Carrier Battles*. New York: Orion Books, 1991.

Cohen, Stan. *East Wind Rain: A Pictorial History of the Pearl Harbor Attack*. Missoula, MT: Pictorial Histories Publishing Company, 1994.

Cressman, Robert. With Steve Ewing, Barrett Tillman, Mark Horan, Clark Reynolds, and Stan Cohen. *"A Glorious Page in Our History." The Battle of Midway, 4–6 June 1942*. Missoula, MT: Pictorial Histories Publishing Company, 1990.

Cressman, Robert. *A Magnificent Fight: Marines in the Battle for Wake Island*. United States Government Printing, 1993.

Cressman, Robert J., and Michael Wenger. *Steady Nerves and Stout Hearts: The* Enterprise *(CV6) Air Group and Pearl Harbor, 7 December 1941*. Missoula, MT: Pictorial Histories Publishing Company, 1989.

Cressman, Robert. *That Gallant Ship: U.S.S.* Yorktown *(CV-5)*. Missoula, MT: Pictorial Histories Publishing Company, 1985. Second printing, 1989.

Cummings, J. Glenn. *Trailing a Texas Eagle: The Life and Legacy of Lt. Commander Harry Brinkley Bass*. Virginia Beach: The Donning Company Publishers, 2010.

Dickinson, Clarence E. *The Flying Guns: Cockpit Record of a Naval Pilot from Pearl Harbor through Midway*. Washington: Zenger Publishing Co., Inc., 1942. Reprint, 1980.

Fisher, Cdr. Clayton E., USN (Ret.). *Hooked: Tales & Adventures of a Tailhook Warrior*. Denver: Outskirts Press, Inc., 2009.

Frank, Pat, and Joseph D. Harrington. *Rendezvous at Midway: U.S.S. Yorktown and the Japanese Carrier Fleet.* New York: The John Day Company, 1967.

Griffin, Alexander. *A Ship to Remember: The Saga of the* Hornet. New York: Howell, Soskin, Publishers, 1943.

Hoehling, A. A. *The* Lexington *Goes Down: The Last Seven Hours of a Fighting Lady.* Englewood Cliffs, NJ: Prentice-Hall, Inc., 1971.

Hoyt, Edwin P. *Blue Skies and Blood: The Battle of the Coral Sea.* New York: Paul S. Eriksson, Inc., 1975.

Johnston, Stanley. *Queen of the Flat-Tops.* New York: Bantam Books, 1942. Eleventh printing, 1979.

Kleiss, Lt. (jg) N. J. "Dusty." *VS-6 Log of the War.* Privately published.

Leaming, Jack. *Scouting Squadron Six: A Personal Story from the Radio-Gunner of 6-S-7.* Hawaii: Personal History Series, 2010.

Lord, Walter. *Day of Infamy.* New York: Bantam Books, 1957. Twenty-third printing, 1978.

———. *Incredible Victory.* New York: Harper & Row, 1967.

Ludlow, Stuart D. (Ex-lieutenant, AVS, USNR). *They Turned the War around at Coral Sea and Midway. Going to War with* Yorktown's *Air Group Five.* Bennington, VT: Merriam Press, 2003.

Lundstrom, John B. *Black Shoe Carrier Admiral: Frank Jack Fletcher at Coral Sea, Midway, and Guadalcanal.* Annapolis: Naval Institute Press, 2006.

———. *The First Team: Pacific Naval Air Combat from Pearl Harbor to Midway.* Annapolis: Naval Institute Press, 1984.

McEniry, Colonel John Howard Jr. *A Marine Dive-bomber Pilot at Guadalcanal.* Tuscaloosa: The University of Alabama Press, 1987.

Mears, Lieut. Frederick. *Carrier Combat: Battle Action with an American Torpedo Plane Pilot.* Garden City, NY: Doubleday, Doran and Co., Inc., 1944.

Mrazek, Robert J. *A Dawn like Thunder: The True Story of Torpedo Squadron Eight.* New York: Little, Brown and Company, 2008.

Nesmith, Jeff. *No Higher Honor: The U.S.S.* Yorktown *at the Battle of Midway.* Atlanta: Longstreet, 1999.

Ostlund, Mike. *Find 'Em, Chase 'Em, Sink 'Em: The Mysterious Loss of the WWII Submarine USS* Gudgeon. Guilford, CT: The Lyons Press, 2006.

Parshall, Jonathan and Anthony Tully. *Shattered Sword: The Untold Story of the Battle of Midway*. Washington: Potomac Books, 2007.

Prange, Gordon W., with Donald M. Goldstein and Katherine V. Dillon. *Miracle at Midway*. New York: McGraw-Hill, 1982.

Reynolds, Clark G., *The Fighting Lady: The New* Yorktown *in the Pacific War*. Missoula, MT: Pictorial Histories Publishing Company, 1993 (third printing).

Reynolds, Clark G., and E. T. Stover. *The Saga of Smokey Stover*. Charleston: Tradd Street Press, 1978.

Russell, Ronald W. *No Right to Win: A Continuing Dialogue with Veterans of the Battle of Midway*. New York: iUniverse, Inc., 2006.

Smith, Peter C. *Midway: Dauntless Victory*. South Yorkshire, England: Pen & Sword Maritime, 2007.

Stafford, Cdr. Edward P., U.S.N. *The Big E: The Story of the USS* Enterprise. New York: Random House, Inc., 1962.

Symonds, Craig L. *The Battle of Midway*. New York: Oxford University Press, 2011.

Tillman, Barrett. *The Dauntless Dive-bomber of World War II*. Annapolis: Naval Institute Press, 1976. Sixth printing, 1989.

———. Enterprise: *America's Fightingest Ship and the Men Who Helped Win World War II*. New York: Simon & Schuster, 2012.

Weisheit, Bowen P., Major, USMCR (Ret.). *The Last Flight of Ensign C. Markland Kelly, Junior, USNR*. Baltimore: The Ensign C. Markland Kelly Jr., Memorial Foundation, Inc., 1993. Second edition, 1996.

CHAPTER NOTES

PREFACE

1 Cressman, Robert J. "Dauntless in War: Douglas SBD-2 BuNo 2106." *Naval Aviation News*, Vol. 96, Issue 5 (Jul/Aug. 1994), 24.
2 Tillman, Barrett. *The Dauntless Dive-bomber of World War II.* Annapolis: Naval Institute Press, 1976. Sixth printing, 1989, 4–6.
3 Ibid., 8–12.

CHAPTER 1: "WE WOULD HAVE ONE HELLUVA CELEBRATION"

1 Tillman, Barrett. *The Dauntless Dive-bomber of World War II.* Annapolis: Naval Institute Press, 1976. Sixth printing, 1989, 1–6.
2 Ibid., 10.
3 Ibid., 10–11.
4 Ibid., 11–12.
5 Ibid., i.
6 Tillman, Barrett. Enterprise: *America's Fightingest Ship and the Men Who Helped Win World War II.* New York: Simon & Schuster, 2012, 25.
7 Lundstrom, John B. *The First Team: Pacific Naval Air Combat from Pearl Harbor to Midway.* Annapolis: Naval Institute Press, 1984, 5.
8 Leaming, *Scouting Squadron Six*, 15.
9 Stafford, *The Big E*, 7–8.
10 Donald Hoff oral history, 1–4.
11 Donald Hoff interview from "Vengeance at Midway," *Battle 360* video, Episode 2.
12 Stuart J. Mason oral history, 1.
13 Cressman, Robert J. and Michael Wenger. *Steady Nerves and Stout Hearts: The* Enterprise *(CV6) Air Group and Pearl Harbor, 7 December 1941.* Missoula, Montana: Pictorial Histories Publishing Company, 1989, 16.

14   Murray, Cdr. James F., USN (Ret.). *Bombing Squadron Six in Action: A Radio-Gunner Looks Back*. Unpublished memoirs, 1986, Naval Library, III–20.
15   Hoff oral history, 7–8.
16   Leaming, *Scouting Squadron Six*, 23–24.
17   Ibid., 20.
18   Cressman and Wenger, *Steady Nerves and Stout Hearts*, 15.
19   Ibid., 15.
20   Ibid., 11; Edward L. Anderson to Mark Horan, 28 April 1987.
21   Cressman and Wenger, *Steady Nerves and Stout Hearts*, 15.
22   Leaming, *Scouting Squadron Six*, 24.
23   Cressman and Wenger, *Steady Nerves and Stout Hearts*, 18.
24   Lord, Walter. *Day of Infamy*. New York: Bantam Books, 1957. Twenty-third printing, 1978, 23, 32, 47, 121. Other general sources for this section are: Jonathan Parshall and Anthony Tully, *Shattered Sword: The Untold Story of the Battle of Midway*, Washington, D.C.: Potomac Books, 2007, 6–13, 22–24; and Stan Cohen, *East Wind Rain*, Missoula, MT: Pictorial Histories Publishing Company, 1981, 12–14.

Chapter 2: "Our World Was Shattered"

Primary sources for this chapter were the *Enterprise* Air Group action reports for December 7, 1941, including individual pilot statements.

1   Cressman and Wenger, *Steady Nerves and Stout Hearts*, 27.
2   Ibid., 27.
3   Ibid., 29.
4   Dickinson, Clarence E. *The Flying Guns: Cockpit Record of a Naval Pilot from Pearl Harbor Through Midway*. Washington: Zenger Publishing Co., Inc., 1942. Reprint, 1980, 3; Cressman and Wenger, *Steady Nerves and Stout Hearts*, 17–18.
5   Dickinson, *The Flying Guns*, 1.
6   Ibid., 9.
7   Cressman and Wenger, *Steady Nerves and Stout Hearts*, 18.
8   Ibid., 31; War Diary of the U.S. Pacific Fleet, 10 December 1941.
9   Dickinson, *The Flying Guns*, 11–12.
10   Cressman and Wenger, *Steady Nerves and Stout Hearts*, 31.
11   Ibid., 14.
12   Ibid.
13   Ibid., 14–16.
14   Dickinson, *The Flying Guns*, 17–21; Lord, *Day of Infamy*, 147–48.
15   Cressman and Wenger, *Steady Nerves and Stout Hearts*, 16, 30.
16   Roberts, Rear Adm. Wilbur E., USNR (Ret.). "Air Raid on Pearl Harbor X: This Is No Drill." Unpublished memoir of 7 December 1941, courtesy of Mark Horan.
17   Cressman and Wenger, *Steady Nerves and Stout Hearts*, 22, 35.
18   Roberts, "Air Raid on Pearl Harbor," 4–5.

19 Cressman and Wenger, *Steady Nerves and Stout Hearts*, 37.

20 Ibid., 38.

21 Roberts, "Air Raid on Pearl Harbor," 6–8.

22 Ibid., 23.

23 Bresnahan, "Interview with Earl Gallaher."

24 Leaming, *Scouting Squadron Six*, 30.

25 Richard Halsey Best oral history transcription, 1–7.

26 Ibid, 7–12.

27 Armstrong, Robert Bryan. "Armstrong, Robert Gordon. 1904–1980." Privately published biography of Captain Armstrong written by his nephew, August 2007, 1.

28 Richard Best oral history transcription, 14–15.

29 McPherson, Lt. I. H. "I Fly for the Navy," *Salt Lake Tribune*, December 7, 1942, A-5, 6.

30 Lane, Marica. "Veteran Recounts Service on USS *Enterprise*." *St. Augustine Times*, April 24, 2006. Accessed http://staugustine.com/stories/042406/news_3789710.shtml on 27 December 2011.

31 Ibid.

32 Bresnahan, "Interview with Earl Gallaher"; Tillman, *Enterprise*, 36.

33 Bresnahan, "Interview with Earl Gallaher."

34 Ibid.

35 Cressman and Wenger, *Steady Nerves and Stout Hearts*, 23.

36 Cleo J. Dobson diary, 7 Dec. 1941 to 12 Jan. 1942.

37 Allen J. Brost narrative. Accessed http://www.veteraneyes.com/pages/allen_brost.php?section=island on 4 April 2011.

38 Tony Schneider to Daniel Rush 1999 correspondence. Accessed http://www.cv6org/company/accounts/jdoherty/jdoherty–2.htm on 8 January 2011.

39 Richard Best oral history, 16; Cdr. James W. McCauley, Navy Department Interview of 23 June 1945, rough transcript, 4.

40 Richard Best oral history, 16.

41 Cressman and Wenger, *Steady Nerves and Stout Hearts*, 46.

42 Ibid., 46.

43 Dickinson, *The Flying Guns*, 41.

44 Ibid., 44.

45 Cressman and Wenger, *Steady Nerves and Stout Hearts*, 47.

46 Leaming, *Scouting Squadron Six*, 37.

47 Bresnahan, "Interview with Earl Gallaher."

48 Cressman and Wenger, *Steady Nerves and Stout Hearts*, 49.

49 Kleiss, *VS-6 Log of the War*, 26.

50 Richard Best oral history, 17.

51 Ibid., 19–20.

52 Ibid., 19.

53 Ibid., 20.

54   Kleiss, *VS-6 Log of the War*, 26; McPherson, "I Fly for the Navy," December 7, 1942, A-5, 6.
55   Richard Best oral history, 21; Cressman and Wenger, *Steady Nerves and Stout Hearts*, 53; McCauley interview, rough transcript, 5.
56   Leaming, *Scouting Squadron Six*, 38.
57   Cressman and Wenger, *Steady Nerves and Stout Hearts*, 59–60; Lane, "Veteran Recounts Service on USS *Enterprise*."

Chapter 3: The Stuff

1   Orr, Timothy, Ph.D., and Laura Orr. "Jack 'Dusty' Kleiss and the Battle of Midway." *The Daybook* (Hampton Roads Naval Museum), 2012 Vol. 15, Issue 4, 8.
2   Orr, "Jack 'Dusty' Kleiss and the Battle of Midway," 8–9.
3   Ibid., 9.
4   Norman J. Kleiss oral history, 2.
5   Orr, "Jack 'Dusty' Kleiss and the Battle of Midway," 9.
6   Schneider oral history; Captain Schneider interview with Paridon, National World War II Museum.
7   Gallaher, W. Earl, "I Remember Pearl Harbor," 28–29, Walter Lord Papers.
8   Leslie, Maxwell F., to Thaddeus V. Tuleja, 21 July 1958, 8, Walter Lord Papers.
9   Weymouth interview with Paridon, National World War II Museum.
10   Captain Schneider interview with Paridon, National World War II Museum; Schneider to Rush, 1999.

Chapter 4: "I Was Really Upset"

1   Bresnahan, "Interview with Earl Gallaher."
2   Ibid.
3   Richard Best oral history, 21.
4   Ibid., 22.
5   Cohen, Stan. *East Wind Rain. A Pictorial History of the Pearl Harbor Attack*. Missoula, MT: Pictorial Histories Publishing Company, 1994, 62–63.
6   Richard Best oral history, 22.
7   Ibid., 22.
8   Kleiss, *VS-6 Log of the War*, 27; Kleiss, Capt. Jack "Dusty," USN (Ret.). "History from the Cockpit: Reflections of a World War II U.S. Navy Dive-bomber Pilot." *The Daybook* (Hampton Roads Naval Museum), 2012 Vol. 15, Issue 4, 12.
9   Hoff oral history, 13.
10   Anderson, Edward Rutledge. "War Diary of Edward Rutledge Anderson, RM3/c U.S.N.R., Bombing Squadron Six, USS *Enterprise*," 3–4.

11   "Edward Rutledge Anderson: The Anderson Family Book of Memories," privately published in 2013 by his daughters, Janice Anderson-Gram and Gretchen Wilkinson, 4–5.
12   Ibid., 6.
13   McCauley interview, smooth transcript, 3.
14   Brost narrative.
15   McCauley interview, smooth transcript, 4.
16   Hoff oral history, 14.
17   Dickinson, *The Flying Guns*, 56.
18   Ibid., 58–61.
19   Cressman and Wenger, *Steady Nerves and Stout Hearts*, 64.
20   Blair, Clay, Jr., *Silent Victory*, 92.
21   Dobson diary, 7 Dec. 1941 to 12 Jan. 1942; Kleiss, *VS-6 Log of the War*, 29.
22   Dobson diary, 6 February 1942.
23   Kleiss, *VS-6 Log of the War*, 29.
24   Murray, *Bombing Squadron Six in Action: A Radio-Gunner Looks Back*, I-4.
25   McPherson, "I Fly for the Navy," 9 December 1942, A-11.
26   Richard Best oral history, 38.

Chapter 5: "We Lost As Much As We Gained"

Primary sources for this chapter were the *Enterprise* Air Group action report and additional flight leader reports by Lt. Cdr. W. R. Hollingsworth and Lt. R. H. Best.

1   Richard Best oral history, 24; Dobson diary, 7 Dec. 1941 to 12 Jan. 1942.
2   Murray, *Bombing Squadron Six in Action*, I-4.
3   Ibid.
4   Dobson diary, 12–15 January 1942.
5   Murray, *Bombing Squadron Six in Action*, I-5.
6   Dobson diary, 12–15 January 1942.
7   Schneider oral history.
8   Dobson diary, 17 January 1942.
9   Ibid., 18 January 1942.
10   Ibid., 26 January 1942.
11   Richard Best oral history, 25.
12   Bresnahan, "Interview with Earl Gallaher."
13   Dobson diary, 26 January 1942.
14   Kleiss, *VS-6 Log of the War*, 45.
15   Dickinson, *The Flying Guns*, 71–72.
16   Murray, *Bombing Squadron Six in Action*, I-6.
17   Dobson diary, 14 January, 25 January 1942.
18   Richard Best oral history, 25.

19   Dickinson, *The Flying Guns*, 74.
20   Lundstrom, *The First Team*, 66.
21   Dickinson, *The Flying Guns*, 76.
22   Richard Best oral history, 26.
23   Dickinson, *The Flying Guns*, 84.
24   Lundstrom, *The First Team*, 70; Stafford, *The Big E*, 40.
25   Leaming, *Scouting Squadron Six*, 51.
26   Tillman, *Enterprise*, 49.
27   Bresnahan, "Interview with Earl Gallaher."
28   Leaming, *Scouting Squadron Six*, 52.
29   Kleiss, *VS-6 Log of the War*, 32.
30   Dickinson, *The Flying Guns*, 87.
31   Tillman, *Enterprise*, 50.
32   Leaming, *Scouting Squadron Six*, 52.
33   Kleiss, *VS-6 Log of the War*, 32.
34   Dickinson, *The Flying Guns*, 89.
35   Dobson diary, 1 February 1942.
36   Murray, *Bombing Squadron Six in Action*, I-7.
37   Ibid., I-7.
38   Richard Best oral history, 26.
39   Mason, Stuart James, Jr. Oral history interview of 9 August 2000 with William J. Shinneman.
40   Richard Best oral history, 26–27.
41   Schneider oral history.
42   Murray, *Bombing Squadron Six in Action*, I-7.
43   Kleiss, *VS-6 Log of the War*, 38; McEniry, Col. John Howard, Jr. *A Marine Dive-Bomber Pilot at Guadalcanal*, Tuscaloosa: The University of Alabama Press, 1987, 21.
44   Dickinson, *The Flying Guns*, 93.
45   Dobson diary, 1 February 1942.
46   Bresnahan, "Interview with Earl Gallaher."
47   Hackett, Bob, Sander Kingsepp, and Peter Cundall. "IJN Submarine Tender *Yasakuni Maru*: Tabular Record of Movement," 1998–2010. Accessed at http://www.combinedfleet.com/Yasukuni%20Maru_t.htm on 20 July 2011.
48   McPherson, Lt. I. H. "I Fly for the Navy," December 13, 1942, A-23; Tillman, *Enterprise*, 49.
49   Murray, *Bombing Squadron Six in Action*, I-8.
50   Dickinson, *The Flying Guns*, 99–100.
51   Murray, *Bombing Squadron Six in Action*, I-8.
52   Schneider oral history.
53   Schneider to Rush correspondence.
54   Schneider oral history.
55   Murray, *Bombing Squadron Six in Action*, I-9.
56   Leaming, *Scouting Squadron Six*, 53.

57   Murray, *Bombing Squadron Six in Action*, I-9.
58   Richard Best oral history, 27.
59   Ibid.
60   Lundstrom, *The First Team*, 62, 72.
61   Richard Best oral history, 27.
62   McPherson, Lt. I. H. "I Fly for the Navy," December 13, 1942, A-23.
63   Kleiss, *VS-6 Log of the War*, 38.
64   McPherson, "I Fly for the Navy," December 13, 1942, A-23.
65   Ibid.
66   McCauley interview, smooth transcript, 5; Brost narrative.
67   McPherson, "I Fly for the Navy," December 13, 1942, A-23.
68   Ibid.
69   "John Doherty and Bombing Six." Accessed http://www.cv6.org/company/accounts/jdoherty/ on 8 January 2011.
70   Ibid.
71   Kleiss, *VS-6 Log of the War*, 38.
72   Richard Best oral history, 27–28.
73   Ibid., 28.
74   Ibid., 28–30.
75   McPherson, "I Fly for the Navy," December 13, 1942, A-23.
76   "John Doherty and Bombing Six." Accessed http://www.cv6.org/company/accounts/jdoherty/ on 8 January 2011; Schneider to Rush correspondence.
77   Brost narrative.
78   Graetz, Ronald, "Memories from Navy Days," 9.
79   Dobson diary, 1 February 1942.
80   Kleiss, *VS-6 Log of the War*, 126.
81   Anderson, "War Diary," 7–8.
82   Ibid., 10, 13–16.
83   Stafford, *The Big E*, 45.
84   Lundstrom, *The First Team*, 74.
85   Stafford, *The Big E*, 46.
86   Dickinson, *The Flying Guns*, 103–5.
87   Richard Best oral history, 29.
88   Leaming, *Scouting Squadron Six*, 54.
89   Orr, "Jack 'Dusty' Kleiss and the Battle of Midway," 10.
90   Richard Best oral history, 29.

CHAPTER 6: ISLAND RAIDERS

The primary sources for this chapter were Scouting Six and Bombing Six action reports of 23 February 1942 (VS-6, Wake Island), 24 February 1942 (VB-6, Wake Island), 25 February 1942 (VS-6, Wake Island); "Report of Attack on Marcus Island," 5 March 1942 (VS-6); and "Attack on Marcus Island, 4 March 1942," (VB-6).

1 Dobson diary, 3 February 1942.
2 Murray, *Bombing Squadron Six in Action*, I-15; Anderson, "War Diary," 16.
3 McPherson, "I Fly for the Navy," December 13, 1942, A-23.
4 Dobson diary, 6 February 1942; Anderson, "War Diary," 17; Leaming, *Scouting Squadron Six*, 55.
5 Cressman, "Blaze of Glory," 24.
6 Dobson diary, 8 February 1942.
7 Murray, *Bombing Squadron Six in Action*, I-16; Anderson, "War Diary," 18.
8 Stafford, *The Big E*, 51.
9 Kleiss, *VS-6 Log of the War*, 56.
10 Dobson diary, 19 February 1942.
11 Leaming, *Scouting Squadron Six*, 57.
12 Dickinson, *The Flying Guns*, 114.
13 Bresnahan, "Interview with Earl Gallaher."
14 Leaming, *Scouting Squadron Six*, 55. Some books list Teaff as losing his left eye, but fellow pilot Cleo Dobson clearly wrote in his diary of Teaff learning to reuse his good left eye. Dobson also wrote, "It is his right eye that is gone." Dobson diary, 27 February 1942.
15 Bresnahan, "Interview with Earl Gallaher."
16 McPherson, "I Fly for the Navy," December 20, 1942, A-19.
17 Murray, *Bombing Squadron Six in Action*, I-18.
18 Dickinson, *The Flying Guns*, 116.
19 McCaul, "Dive-bomber at Midway," 43–44.
20 Stafford, *The Big E*, 54; McCauley interview, smooth transcript, 6.
21 Lundstrom, *The First Team*, 115.
22 Kleiss, *VS-6 Log of the War*, 60–61.
23 Dickinson, *The Flying Guns*, 119–20; Leaming, *Scouting Squadron Six*, 58.
24 Cressman, Robert. *A Magnificent Fight: Marines in the Battle for Wake Island*. United States Government Printing, 1993, 253–54.
25 Dobson diary, 24 February 1942.
26 Stafford, *The Big E*, 55.
27 Kleiss, *VS-6 Log of the War*, 65; Dobson diary, 25 February 1942.
28 Mason oral history, 3.
29 Ibid., 3.
30 Ibid.
31 Kleiss, *VS-6 Log of the War*, 65.
32 Murray, *Bombing Squadron Six in Action*, I-19.
33 Lundstrom, *The First Team*, 117; Ostlund, Mike. *Find 'Em, Chase 'Em, Sink 'Em: The Mysterious Loss of the WWII Submarine USS Gudgeon*. Guilford, CT: The Lyons Press, 2006, 52.
34 Kleiss, *VS-6 Log of the War*, 65; Dobson diary, 2 March 1942.
35 Murray, *Bombing Squadron Six in Action*, I-21.

36 Orr, "Jack 'Dusty' Kleiss and the Battle of Midway," 11.
37 Leaming, *Scouting Squadron Six*, 59–60.
38 Ibid., 60.
39 Ibid.
40 Kleiss, *VS-6 Log of the War*, 65.
41 Dickinson, *The Flying Guns*, 124.
42 Murray, *Bombing Squadron Six in Action*, I-21.
43 Stafford, *The Big E*, 55; Lundstrom, *The First Team*, 118–19.
44 Dobson diary, 4 March 1942.
45 Ibid.
46 Kleiss, *VS-6 Log of the War*, 65.
47 McCaul, "Dive-bomber at Midway," 44–45.
48 Leaming, *Scouting Squadron Six*, 61; Bresnahan, "Interview with Earl Gallaher"; Dickinson, *The Flying Guns*, 126; Lt. C. E. Dickinson, Jr., 10 July 1942 Bureau of Aeronautics interview, 4.
49 Dickinson, *The Flying Guns*, 127–28.
50 Leaming, *Scouting Squadron Six*, 62.
51 Ibid., 62–63.
52 Ibid., 63.
53 Richard Best oral history, 30–31; Dickinson, *The Flying Guns*, 129.
54 Leaming, *Scouting Squadron Six*, i.
55 Ibid., 64; Murray, *Bombing Squadron Six in Action*, I-23.
56 Leaming, *Scouting Squadron Six*, i, 66.
57 Ibid., 67.
58 Ibid., 67–68.
59 Ibid., 68–69.
60 Ibid., 69.
61 Lundstrom, *The First Team*, 121; McCauley interview, rough transcript, 14.
62 Dobson diary, 5 March 1942.
63 Dickinson, *The Flying Guns*, 133.
64 Lundstrom, *The First Team*, 121.

CHAPTER 7: ARRIVAL OF THE "NEW BOYS"

1 Leaming, *Scouting Squadron Six*, 69–74.
2 Ibid., 74–75.
3 Ibid., 76.
4 Ibid., 77–80.
5 Ibid., 81.
6 Cressman, *That Gallant Ship*, 68–69.
7 Richard Best oral history, 31.
8 Anderson, "War Diary," 24–25.
9 McPherson, "I Fly for the Navy," December 13, 1942, A-23.
10 Tillman, *The Dauntless Dive-bomber of World War II*, 58.

11   Bridgers, John D., M.D. "On the Traveling Squad E-Base, Doolittle & Midway, 1941–1942." Privately published "Memoirs and Personal Remembrances." Accessed http://tk-jk.net/Bridgers/NavyYears/OnThe TravelingSquad.html on 5 February 2011.

12   Ambrose, *The Pacific*, 30; Bridgers, "On the Traveling Squad E-Base, Doolittle & Midway, 1941–1942."

13   Bridgers, "On the Traveling Squad E-Base, Doolittle & Midway, 1941–1942."

14   Anderson, "War Diary," 25–26.

15   Murray, *Bombing Squadron Six in Action*, I-26.

16   Gee, "Remembering Midway" 2003 article.

17   Russell, *No Right to Win*, 128–29.

18   Rodenburg, Dennis. *Eldor E. Rodenburg, Lieutenant Commander, U.S.N.R. World War II Dive-bomber Pilot and Landing Signal Officer.* Privately published, 1.

19   Ibid, 2–3.

20   Mears, *Carrier Combat*, 19–20.

21   Ibid., 24.

22   Ibid., 26.

23   Ibid., 29–30.

24   Lundstrom, *The First Team*, 145.

25   Bridgers, "On the Traveling Squad E-Base, Doolittle & Midway, 1941–1942."

26   Tillman, Barrett. "Where Are They Now? Bob Elder." *The Hook*, Fall 1989, 12.

27   Ibid.

28   Ibid.

29   Murray, *Bombing Squadron Six in Action*, I-27.

30   Rear Admiral Lewis Hopkins oral history, interview of 15 January 2004, for Nimitz Museum.

31   Richard Best oral history, 32; Murray, *Bombing Squadron Six in Action*, I-27.

32   Murray, *Bombing Squadron Six in Action*, I-27.

33   Anderson, "War Diary," 28.

34   Lundstrom, *The First Team*, 149.

35   Ibid., 150.

36   Anderson, "War Diary," 29; Murray, *Bombing Squadron Six in Action*, I-28.

37   Benjamin Tappan interview with Weisheit, 1; Bridgers, "On the Traveling Squad E-Base, Doolittle & Midway, 1941–1942."

38   Lundstrom, *The First Team*, 150; War Diary of Bombing Squadron Three, 18 April 1942.

39   Schneider oral history.

40   Murray, *Bombing Squadron Six in Action*, I-28.

41   Ibid., I-28; Richard Best oral history, 33–34.
42   Anderson, "War Diary," 30–31.
43   McCaul, "Dive-bomber at Midway," 44–45.
44   "Nips Boasted Japan Bomb-proof Just as Tokyo Raid Was Begun." *Charleston Gazette*, April 24, 1943, 2.
45   Bridgers, "On the Traveling Squad E-Base, Doolittle & Midway, 1941–1942."
46   Anderson, "War Diary," 32.
47   Dickinson, *The Flying Guns*, 134.
48   Rodenburg, *Eldor E. Rodenburg*, 5; Ambrose, *The Pacific*, 30.
49   Ambrose, *The Pacific*, 7–9, 19–21.
50   Lundstrom and Sawruk, "Courage and Devotion to Duty," 32.
51   Patterson to Lord, "Short History of William R. Pittman's Experiences Through the Midway Battle," 1, Walter Lord *Incredible Victory* research collection, Naval Historical Center.
52   Kleiss, *VS-6 Log of the War*, 72.
53   Cressman, "Blaze of Glory," 27.
54   Ambrose, *The Pacific*, 31–32.
55   Rodenburg, *Eldor E. Rodenburg*, 5; Ambrose, *The Pacific*, 35.
56   *Enterprise* War Diary, 30 April 1942.
57   Lundstrom, *The First Team*, 287–88.

CHAPTER 8: "SOMETHING BIG WAS IN THE WORKS"

1   Dobson diary, 2 May–4 May 1942.
2   The key sources for the Japanese planning of the Midway operation are: Parshall and Tully, *Shattered Sword*, 47–69; Belote and Belote, *Titans of the Seas*, 80–83; and Symonds, *The Battle of Midway*, 90–105.
3   Dobson diary, 11 May 1942.
4   *Enterprise* War Diary, 13 May 1942; Richard Best oral history, 35–36.
5   Mears, *Carrier Combat*, 76–77.
6   Ibid., 77.
7   Anderson, "War Diary," 36–37.
8   Hopkins oral history.
9   Richard Best oral history, 36.
10   Dobson diary, 20 May 1942; Kleiss, *VS-6 Log of the War*, 80.
11   Dobson diary, 21 May 1942.
12   VB-8 war diary, April 1942.
13   Griffin, Alexander. *A Ship to Remember: The Saga of the* Hornet. New York: Howell, Soskin, Publishers, 1943, 80–87.
14   Kleiss, *VS-6 Log of the War*, 80.
15   Reynolds, Clark G., and E. T. Stover. *The Saga of Smokey Stover.* Charleston: Tradd Street Press, 1978, 28.
16   Ibid., 29.

17 Fisher, *Hooked*, 73.
18 Lundstrom, *Black Shoe Carrier Admiral*, 217.
19 Symonds, *The Battle of Midway*, 379–86.
20 Parshall and Tully, *Shattered Sword*, 12–13; Lord, *Incredible Victory*, 12–14.
21 Lundstrom, *Black Shoe Carrier Admiral*, 230.
22 Forshee, *Standby, Mark!*, Chapter 12.
23 Ludlum, *They Turned the War Around*, 117; Conatser interview with Barde, 11 May 1966.
24 Murray, *Bombing Squadron Six in Action*, I-32.
25 Lanham to Lord questionnaire, Naval Historical Center.
26 Dickinson, *The Flying Guns*, 136.
27 Patterson to Lord, "Short History of William R. Pittman's Experiences through the Midway Battle," 2, Naval Historical Center.
28 Dobson diary, 27 May 1942.
29 Mason oral history, 4.
30 Griffin, *A Ship to Remember*, 94–96.
31 Statements of Ens. A. A. Devoe and Ens. F. C. Auman, 29 May 1942; Tillman, *The Dauntless Dive-bomber of World War II*, 58.
32 Richard Best oral history, 37.
33 Ibid., 37–38.
34 Tillman, *The Dauntless Dive-bomber of World War II*, 59; Bottomley 1966 questionnaire to Lord, Naval Historical Center.
35 Godfrey 1966 narrative of Midway to Lord, 1, Naval Historical Center.
36 Lane to Lord questionnaire, Naval Historical Center.
37 Tillman, *The Dauntless Dive-bomber of World War II*, 59.
38 Kleiss, "History from the Cockpit," 12.
39 Ibid., 12–13.
40 Ibid., 13.
41 Holmberg narrative of Midway experiences, 2, Naval Historical Center.
42 Lundstrom, *The First Team*, 322.
43 John Lynch to wife, 2 June 1942, Naval Aviation Museum, Pensacola.
44 Bridgers, "On the Traveling Squad E-Base, Doolittle & Midway, 1941–1942."
45 Holmberg narrative of Midway experiences, 3, Naval Historical Center.
46 Cressman, *That Gallant Ship*, 123.
47 Tillman, *The Dauntless Dive-bomber of World War II*, 62.
48 Lane to Lord questionnaire, Naval Historical Center.
49 Fisher, *Hooked*, 65, 76.
50 Roberts, "Many Planes Heading Midway," 3.
51 Richard Best oral history, 38.
52 Dickinson, *The Flying Guns*, 138–40.
53 Kleiss, *VS-6 Log of the War*, 82.
54 Bresnahan, "Interview with Earl Gallaher."

CHAPTER 9: "GOD, THIS IS IT!"

1   Kleiss, "History from the Cockpit," 13.
2   Hopkins oral history; Rear Adm. Walter F. Rodee to Robert Barde, 18 October 1966.
3   Murray, "Midway: The View from a Bombing Six Rear Seat," 41.
4   Conatser interview with Barde, 11 May 1966; Lundstrom, *The First Team*, 331.
5   Dickinson, *The Flying Guns*, 141; Kleiss, "History from the Cockpit," 13.
6   Kleiss, "History from the Cockpit," 13.
7   Childers, Lt. Col. Lloyd, USMC (Ret.), Ph.D. "Midway from the Backseat of a TBD." *The Hook*, Vol. 18, August 1990, 36.
8   Capt. Joe R. Penland interview with Robert Barde, 18 May 1966; Capt. George Goldsmith to Mark Horan, 9 February 1987.
9   Griffin, *A Ship to Remember*, 123.
10 Gee, "Remembering Midway" 2003 article; Wood 1966 questionnaire to Lord, Naval Historical Center.
11 Fisher, *Hooked*, 77.
12 Tillman, *The Dauntless Dive-bomber of World War II*, 66.
13 Dickinson, *The Flying Guns*, 143.
14 Symonds, *The Battle of Midway*, 253–54; Mrazek, *A Dawn Like Thunder*, 112–13.
15 Murray, "Midway: The View from a Bombing Six Rear Seat," 41.
16 Harold L. Jones to Mark Horan, 22 December 1986.
17 Dickinson, *The Flying Guns*, 143.
18 Capt. Frank A. Patriarca to Mark Horan, 12 May 1987.
19 Ambrose, *The Pacific*, 47–51.
20 Patterson to Lord, "Short History of William R. Pittman's Experiences through the Midway Battle," 2, Naval Historical Center.
21 Murray, "Midway: The View from a Bombing Six Rear Seat," 41.
22 Hopkins oral history; Stuart J. Mason to Mark Horan, 20 October 1987.
23 McClusky, C. Wade. "Battle of Midway." Recollections of 4 June 1942 mission as presented by Arnold Olson, Public Affairs Officers, USS *Enterprise* CV-6 Association. Accessed http://www.cv6.org/company/accounts/wmcclusky/ on 4 January 2011.
24 Best oral history, 39.
25 Tappan interview with Weisheit, 9; Gee, "Remembering Midway" 2003 article.
26 Moore oral history.
27 Lundstrom, *The First Team*, 334.
28 Fisher, *Hooked*, 78.
29 Gee, "Remembering Midway" 2003 article; Troy T. Guillory to Mark Horan.
30 Lundstrom, *The First Team*, 334.

31   Tillman, *The Dauntless Dive-bomber of World War II*, 66.

32   Ibid., 67; Schneider oral history.

33   Graetz, Ronald, "Memories from Navy Days," 12.

34   Lundstrom, *The First Team*, 336.

35   Rodenburg, *Eldor E. Rodenburg*, 6.

36   Orr, "Jack 'Dusty' Kleiss and the Battle of Midway," 11.

37   Rodenburg, *Eldor E. Rodenburg*, 6–7; Rodenburg to Horan, 1987 correspondence.

38   Murray, "Midway: The View from a Bombing Six Rear Seat," 42; Penland interview with Barde; Capt. Tony F. Schneider, 2007 interview with Seth Paridon, the National World War II Museum oral history collection; Roberts, "Many Planes Heading Midway," 1.

39   Richard Best oral history, 39.

40   Fisher, *Hooked*, 79.

41   Weisheit, Bowen P., Major, USMCR (Ret.). *The Last Flight of Ensign C. Markland Kelly, Junior, USNR*. Baltimore: The Ensign C. Markland Kelly, Jr., Memorial Foundation, Inc., 1993. Second edition, 1996, 14; Mrazek, Robert J. *A Dawn Like Thunder: The True Story of Torpedo Squadron Eight*. New York: Little, Brown and Company, 2008, 126; Symonds, *The Battle of Midway*, 251.

42   Mzarek, *A Dawn Like Thunder,* 127.

43   Ibid, 128; Tappan interview with Weisheit, 28.

44   Woodson, "In the Rear Seat at Midway and Santa Cruz."

45   Rodee interview with Weisheit, 2; Russell, Ronald W. *No Right to Win: A Continuing Dialogue with Veterans of the Battle of Midway*. New York: iUniverse, Inc., 2006, 136.

46   Lundstrom, *The First Team*, 345–47.

47   Ibid., 347; Gee, Capt. Roy P., USN (Ret.). "Remembering Midway." Battle of Midway Roundtable, 2003.

48   Tappan interview with Weisheit, 25, 32; Tillman, *The Dauntless Dive-bomber of World War II*, 68; James E. Vose to Col. Robert E. Barde, 9 January 1967, 1.

49   Wood correspondence of 21 February 1967 to Lord, Naval Historical Center.

50   John J. Lynch to Col. Robert E. Barde, 1 June 1967; Fisher, *Hooked*, 80.

51   Lundstrom, *The First Team*, 347–48.

52   Symonds, Craig L. *The Battle of Midway*. New York: Oxford University Press, 2011, 389–90; Mitscher, Capt. M. A., "Report of Action— 4–6 June 1942."

53   Symonds, *The Battle of Midway*, 390–91.

54   Ibid., 390–91, 255–260.

55   Hovind to Lord questionnaire, Naval Historical Center; Rodee to Barde, 18 October 1966.

56   Tillman, *The Dauntless Dive-bomber of World War II*, 71.

57 Godfrey 1966 narrative of Midway to Lord, 4, Naval Historical Center; Charles S. Lane correspondence with Mark Horan, 27 May 1987.

58 Tillman, *The Dauntless Dive-bomber of World War II*, 71. Gunner Lloyd Childers stated in an account of Midway on the launch order that "VT-3 took off last." Childers, Lt. Col. Lloyd, USMC (Ret), Ph.D., "Midway from the Backseat of a TBD," *The Hook*, Vol. 18, August 1990, 36; Holmberg narrative of Midway experiences, 5, Naval Historical Center.

59 Tillman, *The Dauntless Dive-bomber of World War II*, 71.

60 Bridgers, "On the Traveling Squad E-Base, Doolittle & Midway, 1941–1942."

61 Vice Adm. Schindler questionnaire to Walter Lord.

62 Tillman, *The Dauntless Dive-bomber of World War II*, 71; Lundstrom, *The First Team*, 349.

63 Holmberg narrative of Midway experiences, 6, Naval Historical Center; Gallagher interview notes with Lord, 19 April 1966, Naval Historical Center.

64 Lane correspondence with Horan; Austin Merrill interview with Paridon, National World War II Museum.

65 Bottomley 1966 questionnaire to Lord, Naval Historical Center.

66 Tillman, *The Dauntless Dive-bomber of World War II*, 72.

67 Captain Vernon Micheel interview with Seth Paridon, National World War II Museum; Patterson to Lord, "Short History of William R. Pittman's Experiences through the Midway Battle," 3, Naval Historical Center.

68 McClusky, "Battle of Midway."

69 Hoff, "Vengeance at Midway," *Battle 360* video, Episode 2; Tillman, *The Dauntless Dive-bomber of World War II*, 70.

70 McClusky, "Battle of Midway."

71 Anderson, "War Diary," 40–41.

72 Dickinson Bureau of Aeronautics interview, 10 July 1942, 6; Dickinson, *The Flying Guns*, 145–46; Hoff, "Vengeance at Midway," *Battle 360* video, Episode 2.

73 Lundstrom, *The First Team*, 345–47; Symonds, *The Battle of Midway*, 266–69.

74 Statement of ARM3c Leroy Quillen, U.S. Navy, Bombing Squadron Eight, on first flight, June 4, 1942, search in plane 8-B-2. (Taken 5 June 1942.)

75 Lundstrom, *The First Team*, 343–44.

76 Murray, "Midway: The View from a Bombing Six Rear Seat," 42; Tillman, *The Dauntless Dive-bomber of World War II*, 68; Robert Edward Laub interview with Robert Barde, 13 May 1966; McPherson, "I Fly for the Navy," January 10, 1943, A-15.

77 Stephen B. Smith to Robert Barde, 3 February 1967.

78 "Oakland Flier Drifts 17 Days in Rubber Boat; Fails to Thumb Ride on Passing Jap Submarine," *Oakland Tribune*, 9 September 1942.

79 Parshall and Tully, *Shattered Sword*, 214–16.

80 Tillman, *The Dauntless Dive-bomber of World War II*, 70.
81 Capt. Schneider 2007 interview, National World War II Museum.
82 Gallaher, "I Remember Pearl Harbor," 24.
83 Hoff, "Vengeance at Midway," *Battle 360* video, Episode 2; Hoff oral history.
84 Richard Best oral history, 40.
85 McCarthy interview notes with Lord, 19 April 1966, Naval Historical Center.
86 Tillman, *The Dauntless Dive-bomber of World War II*, 72; Lundstrom, *The First Team*, 351.
87 Lundstrom, *The First Team*, 351; Parshall and Tully, *Shattered Sword*, 221.
88 Cressman, *That Gallant Ship*, 126.
89 Esders, Cdr. Wilhelm G., USN (Ret.). "Torpedo Three and the Devastator: A Pilot's Recollection." *The Hook*, Vol. 18, August 1990, 35.
90 Childers, "Midway from the Backseat of a TBD," 37.
91 Ibid., 37–38.
92 Esders, "Torpedo Three and the Devastator: A Pilot's Recollection," 36.
93 Cressman, *That Gallant Ship*, 127.
94 Tillman, *The Dauntless Dive-bomber of World War II*, 73.
95 Leslie to Captain William H. Ashford, correspondence of 9 September 1947, Naval Historical Center.
96 Bresnahan, "Interview with Earl Gallaher"; Parshall and Tully, *Shattered Sword*, 224–27.

Chapter 10: Five Minutes of Glory

1   Pittman narrative of Midway to Lord, 3, Naval Historical Center.
2   Floyd D. Adkins correspondence with Mark Horan, 23 October 1987.
3   Capt. Joe R. Penland interview with Robert Barde, 18 May 1966; Schneider questionnaire to Lord, 1966, Naval Historical Center; Capt. Schneider 2007 interview, National World War II Museum.
4   Schneider letter to Colonel Barde, 31 May 1966, Naval Historical Center; Capt. Schneider 2007 interview, National World War II Museum.
5   Schneider questionnaire to Lord, 1966, Naval Historical Center.
6   Tillman, *The Dauntless Dive-bomber of World War II*, 74.
7   McClusky, "Battle of Midway."
8   Dickinson, *The Flying Guns*, 150.
9   Ibid., 151–53.
10 Snowden 1966 questionnaire to Lord, Naval Historical Center.
11 Kleiss, "History from the Cockpit," 14.
12 Dickinson, *The Flying Guns*, 151; Tillman, *The Dauntless Dive-bomber of World War II*, 76.
13 Richard Best oral history, 40–41.
14 McClusky, "Battle of Midway"; Wildenberg, *Destined for Glory*, 209; Richard Best oral history, 41.

15   Gallaher, "I Remember Pearl Harbor," 25.

16   Patterson to Lord, "Short History of William R. Pittman's Experiences Through the Midway Battle," 3, Naval Historical Center.

17   Tillman, *The Dauntless Dive-bomber of World War II*, 77.

18   Ibid., 179; Adkins to Horan correspondence.

19   Adkins to Horan correspondence.

20   Ibid; Patterson to Lord, "Short History of William R. Pittman's Experiences through the Midway Battle," 3.

21   Patterson to Lord, 3.

22   McClusky, "Battle of Midway."

23   Tillman, *The Dauntless Dive-bomber of World War II*, 77; Cressman, Robert. With Steve Ewing, Barrett Tillman, Mark Horan, Clark Reynolds, and Stan Cohen. *"A Glorious Page in Our History." The Battle of Midway, 4–6 June 1942*. Missoula, Montana: Pictorial Histories Publishing Company, 1990, 102; Gallaher, "I Remember Pearl Harbor," 25; Bresnahan, "Interview with Earl Gallaher."

24   Parshall and Tully, *Shattered Sword*, 234.

25   Cressman, et al, *"A Glorious Page in Our History,"* 102; Rodenburg to Lord.

26   Kleiss, *VS-6 Log of the War*, 88; Orr, "Jack 'Dusty' Kleiss and the Battle of Midway," 10.

27   Snowden 1966 questionnaire to Lord, Naval Historical Center.

28   Parshall and Tully, *Shattered Sword*, 234–35.

29   Hoff, "Vengeance at Midway," *Battle 360* video, Episode 2.

30   Ibid; Cressman, et al, *"A Glorious Page in Our History,"* 102; Parshall and Tully, *Shattered Sword*, 235.

31   Hoff, "Vengeance at Midway," *Battle 360* video, Episode 2.

32   Dickinson, *The Flying Guns*, 152.

33   Ibid., 153–54; Dickinson Bureau of Aeronautics interview, 10 July 1942, 7.

34   Dickinson, *The Flying Guns*, 155.

35   Ibid., 156–57; Joseph F. DeLuca to Mark Horan, 8 September 1987.

36   McCarthy interview notes with Lord, 19 April 1966, Naval Historical Center.

37   Roberts, "Many Planes Heading Midway," 6.

38   Ibid.

39   Richard Best oral history, 41.

40   Murray, "Midway: The View from a Bombing Six Rear Seat," 42.

41   Ambrose, *The Pacific*, 53.

42   Buell, *Dauntless Helldivers*, 86; Captain Micheel interview with Paridon, National World War II Museum.

43   Ambrose, *The Pacific*, 54; Buell, *Dauntless Helldivers*, 86.

44   Bombing Squadron Six action report, 10 June 1942; Penland to Lord questionnaire, Naval Historical Center; Penland interview with Barde, 18 May 1966.

45 Hopkins oral history; Anderson, "War Diary," 42.

46 Patterson to Lord questionnaire from 1966, Naval Historical Center; McPherson, "I Fly for the Navy," January 10, 1943, A-15.

47 Goldsmith to Horan correspondence.

48 Mason oral history, 4.

49 Parshall and Tully, *Shattered Sword*, 248–50.

50 Richard Best oral history, 41.

51 Ibid., 42; Tillman, *The Dauntless Dive-bomber of World War II*, 78.

52 Lord interview notes with Roberts, 19 April 1966, Naval Historical Center; Roberts, "Many Planes Heading Midway," 12. According to Roberts, Murr Arnold told him the pictures were confidential and he took the film. Roberts was at this time on the cruiser *Portland* after abandoning ship from *Yorktown*. He had taken his "water-soaked film to the ship's photo lab to see whether it could be salvaged. After processing, the emulsion was peeling from the edges of the film, but in the centers of several frames there were images of the three burning carriers."

53 Smith, Peter C. *Midway: Dauntless Victory*. South Yorkshire, England: Pen & Sword Maritime, 2007, 146.

54 Mark Horan research.

55 Murray, *Bombing Squadron Six in Action*, II-9.

56 Mark Horan research and interviews with Best.

57 Murray, "Midway: The View from a Bombing Six Rear Seat," 42; Richard Best oral history, 42.

58 Murray, *Bombing Squadron Six in Action*, II-8.

59 Richard Best oral history, 42.

60 Cressman, et al, "*A Glorious Page in Our History*," 104; Symonds, *The Battle of Midway*, 304–05.

61 Parshall and Tully, *Shattered Sword*, 241, 257–58.

62 Richard Best oral history, 42; Parshall and Tully, *Shattered Sword*, 253–54, 276, 280, 286–87.

63 Leslie to Lord correspondence, 8 March 1966, Naval Historical Center.

64 Tillman, *The Dauntless Dive-bomber of World War II*, 73; Wildenberg, *Destined for Glory*, 210; Gallagher 1966 questionnaire to Lord, Naval Historical Center.

65 Parshall and Tully, *Shattered Sword*, 236–37.

66 Leslie to Lord correspondence, 8 March 1966, Naval Historical Center.

67 Holmberg, 15 April 1966 narrative of Midway attack to Lord, 2, Naval Historical Center.

68 Tillman, *The Dauntless Dive-bomber of World War II*, 75; Holmberg to Thaddeus V. Tuleja of 9 June 1958, Walter Lord collection, 7–8; Leslie to Lord correspondence, 8 March 1966, Naval Historical Center.

69 Smith, *Midway: Dauntless Victory*, 147.

70 Parshall and Tully, *Shattered Sword*, 237–38.

71 Godfrey 1966 narrative of Midway to Lord, 3, Naval Historical Center; Hanson account of Midway published in Bellevue, Washington, newspaper, supplied to Lord, 3, Naval Historical Center.
72 Godfrey 1966 narrative of Midway to Lord, 3, Naval Historical Center.
73 Fred Bergeron oral history.
74 Ibid.
75 Ibid.
76 Isaman to Lord questionnaire, Naval Historical Center.
77 Cobb 1966 questionnaire to Lord, Naval Historical Center.
78 Smith, *Midway: Dauntless Victory*, 143.
79 Ibid., 143.
80 Lane to Horan correspondence, 27 May 1987.
81 Parshall and Tully, *Shattered Sword*, 238, 251.
82 Tillman, "Where Are They Now? Bob Elder," 13.
83 Tillman, *The Dauntless Dive-bomber of World War II*, 75.
84 McCaul, "Dive-bomber at Midway," 42–43.
85 Leslie to Lord correspondence, 8 March 1966, Naval Historical Center.
86 Tillman, "Where Are They Now? Bob Elder," 13.
87 Gallagher 1966 questionnaire to Lord, Naval Historical Center.
88 Wildenberg, *Destined for Glory*, 164–67, 214.
89 Ibid., 167.
90 Tillman, *The Dauntless Dive-bomber of World War II*, 78.

CHAPTER 11: THE DEADLY FLIGHTS HOME

1 Tillman, *The Dauntless Dive-bomber of World War II*, 78.
2 Cressman, et al, *"A Glorious Page in Our History,"* 107; Cressman, *That Gallant Ship*, 129.
3 Holmberg, 15 April 1966 narrative of Midway attack to Lord, 2–3, Naval Historical Center.
4 Tillman, "Where Are They Now? Bob Elder," 13; McCaul, "Dive-bomber at Midway," 45–46.
5 Cressman, *That Gallant Ship*, 131.
6 Kleiss, *VS-6 Log of the War*, 89.
7 Gallaher to Lord 1966 correspondence, Naval Historical Center; Gallaher, "I Remember Pearl Harbor," 27.
8 McClusky, "Battle of Midway;" Tillman, *The Dauntless Dive-bomber of World War II*, 79.
9 McClusky, "Battle of Midway."
10 Ibid.
11 Patterson to Lord, "Short History of William R. Pittman's Experiences Through the Midway Battle," 3; Cressman, et al, *"A Glorious Page in Our History,"* 108.
12 Hoff oral history, 33–35.
13 Richard Best oral history, 42–43.

14   Murray, "Midway: The View from a Bombing Six Rear Seat," 43–44.

15   Ibid., 44.

16   Dickinson, *The Flying Guns*, 157.

17   Ibid., 157–58.

18   Ibid., 160–61; Dickinson Bureau of Aeronautics interview, 10 July 1942, 13. Dusty Kleiss also caught a glimpse of this devastating explosion on *Kaga*. See Kleiss, "History from the Cockpit," 14.

19   Cressman, et al, *"A Glorious Page in Our History,"* 109.

20   McCarthy to Lord 1966 correspondence, 1, Naval Historical Center.

21   Ibid.

22   Horan, "The Last Flight of Charles Rollins Ware."

23   McCarthy to Lord 1966 correspondence, 1–2, Naval Historical Center.

24   Ibid., 2–3.

25   Ibid., 3.

26   Ibid., 4.

27   Ibid.

28   Ibid., 4–5.

29   Ibid., 5.

30   Ibid. Charlie Ware's mother would remain in contact with the mothers of Carl Peiffer and Jim Shelton until 1946 as the grieving mothers wrote to each other every few months.

31   Kleiss, *VS-6 Log of the War*, 89.

32   Cressman, et al, *"A Glorious Page in Our History,"* 109.

33   Ibid., 109–10; Horan interview with Wilbur Roberts.

34   Patterson to Lord questionnaire, Naval Historical Center; Goldsmith to Horan, 9 February 1987.

35   McPherson, "I Fly for the Navy," January 10, 1943, A-15.

36   Patterson to Lord questionnaire, Naval Historical Center; Goldsmith 1966 narrative of Midway to Lord, 1, Walter Lord *Incredible Victory* research collection, Naval Historical Center. Although Patterson made no mention of his own wounding to Lord, Goldsmith notes the wounding of his rear gunner in three accounts (Goldsmith to Lord, 1 March 1966; interview for an article shortly after Midway, published in McPherson, "I Fly For the Navy," January 10, 1943, A-15; and Goldsmith to Horan, 9 February 1987).

37   Edward L. Anderson to Mark Horan, 28 April 1987.

38   Mason oral history, 4.

39   Cressman, et al, *"A Glorious Page in Our History,"* 110.

40   Mason oral history, 4.

41   Ibid., 4.

42   McPherson, "I Fly for the Navy," January 10, 1943, A-15.

43   Ibid; Roberts, "Many Planes Heading Midway," 9. In Roberts's written account, he states that Steinman's lip was ripped by a shard of aluminum, shrapnel from their own SBD, which ended up in his mouth.

44 Rodee interview with Weisheit, 3; Fisher, *Hooked*, 81; Russell, *No Right to Win*, 113.

45 Griffin, *A Ship to Remember*, 138; Cressman, et al, *"A Glorious Page in Our History,"* 113.

46 Guillory to Horan; Lynch to Barde, 1 June 1967.

47 Wood 1966 questionnaire to Lord, Naval Historical Center.

48 Vose to Barde, 9 January 1967.

49 Cressman, et al, *"A Glorious Page in Our History,"* 114; Lynch correspondence with Barde,1 June 1967.

50 Cressman, et al, *"A Glorious Page in Our History,"* 114.

51 Kenneth White letter shared on Battle of Midway Roundtable, Topic 265-02, August 2003; ARM3c Leroy Quillen statement, 5 June 1942.

52 Lynch to Barde, 1 June 1967.

53 Gee, "Remembering Midway," 2003 article.

54 Buell, *Dauntless Helldivers*, 86; Captain Micheel interview with Paridon, National World War II Museum.

55 Cressman, et al, *"A Glorious Page in Our History,"* 109; Hopkins to Horan, 28 February 1987; Anderson, "War Diary," 42.

56 Goldsmith 1966 narrative of Midway to Lord, 1, Naval Historical Center.

57 Ibid.

58 Cressman, et al, *"A Glorious Page in Our History,"* 114; Anderson to Horan, 28 April 1967.

59 McCarthy to Lord 1966 correspondence, 6, Naval Historical Center.

60 Ibid., 7.

61 Ibid.

62 Ibid., 7–8.

63 Esders, "Torpedo Three and the Devastator: A Pilot's Recollection," 36.

64 McCarthy to Lord 1966 correspondence, 8–9.

65 Ibid., 9–10; Cressman, *That Gallant Ship*, 139–41.

66 Dickinson, *The Flying Guns*, 162–63.

67 Ibid., 163–65; DeLuca to Horan, 8 September 1967; Dickinson Bureau of Aeronautics interview, 10 July 1942, 18.

68 Dickinson, *The Flying Guns*, 166; DeLuca to Horan.

69 Dickinson, *The Flying Guns*, 168.

70 Lundstrom, *The First Team*, 372–73.

71 Bridgers, "On the Traveling Squad E-Base, Doolittle & Midway, 1941–1942."

72 Patterson to Lord questionnaire, Naval Historical Center.

73 Ibid.

74 Ludlum, *They Turned the War Around*, 131.

75 Goldsmith to Horan, 9 February 1987; Goldsmith to Lord, 1 March 1966. It is interesting to note that in both of these accounts, given twenty-four and forty-five years after Midway, Goldsmith wrote that

the deflected Japanese bullet had come to rest in the mouth of his own gunner, Jim Patterson. As previously noted, however, Tex Conatser told his squadron intelligence officer that Steinman, the gunner for Roberts, was the one who had been wounded in the mouth. In an account given to a correspondent only months after the battle at Midway (McPherson, "I Fly for the Navy," January 10, 1943, A-15), Bill Roberts stated that the bullet had glanced off an instrument panel, and went through Steinman's lower lip and into his mouth. In the absence of direct statements on this event from either Steinman or Patterson, the fresher 1942 versions of this incident have been used in favor of Patterson being the bullet receipient.

76   Lundstrom, *The First Team*, 373.
77   Murray, "Midway: The View from a Bombing Six Rear Seat," 44.
78   Ibid.
79   Richard Best oral history, 43.
80   Rear Adm. Clarence Wade McClusky interview with Robert Barde, 30 June 1966.
81   Tillman, *The Dauntless Dive-bomber of World War II*, 80.
82   Ibid., 80; Cressman, et al, *"A Glorious Page in Our History,"* 115.
83   Kleiss, "History from the Cockpit," 15.
84   Ambrose, *The Pacific*, 55–56; Micheel to Lord.
85   Anderson to Horan, 28 April 1987.
86   Anderson, "War Diary," 44–45.
87   Mason oral history, 5.
88   Ibid., 5; Anderson to Horan.
89   Mason oral history, 5; Stuart J. Mason to Mark Horan, 20 October 1987.
90   Braun 1966 questionnaire to Lord, Naval Historical Center.
91   Murray, "Midway: The View from a Bombing Six Rear Seat," 44; Smith letter to Barde, 3 February 1967.
92   "His Torpedo Plane Pierced by 68 Bullets at Midway. Pilot Stephen Smith Returns for First Visit in 14 Months," *Mason City Globe-Gazette*, July 6, 1942, 8.
93   Smith letter to Barde, 3 February 1967; Murray, *Bombing Squadron Six in Action*, III-23.

CHAPTER 12: THE JAPANESE STRIKE BACK

1   Holmberg, 15 April 1966 narrative of Midway attack to Lord, 3, Naval Historical Center.
2   Ibid; Merrill correspondence to Lord.
3   McCaul, "Dive-bomber at Midway," 46–47; Lundstrom, *The First Team*, 387; Lane to Lord questionnaire, Naval Historical Center.

4   Hanson account of Midway published in Bellevue, Washington, newspaper, supplied to Lord, Naval Historical Center; Robert M. Elder interview with Barrett Tillman, National Naval Aviation Museum, 9 January 1989.

5   Ludlum, *They Turned the War Around*, 134.

6   Bridgers, "On the Traveling Squad E-Base, Doolittle & Midway, 1941–1942."

7   Patterson to Lord questionnaire, Naval Historical Center.

8   Lundstrom, *The First Team*, 388.

9   Fisher, *Hooked*, 84.

10   Tillman, "Where Are They Now? Bob Elder," 13.

11   Esders, "Torpedo Three and the Devastator: A Pilot's Recollection," 36.

12   Cressman, *That Gallant Ship*, 141; Leslie to Lord correspondence, 8 March 1966, Naval Historical Center.

13   Tillman, *The Dauntless Dive-bomber of World War II*, 82–83.

14   Holmberg, 15 April 1966 narrative of Midway attack to Lord, 4–5, Naval Historical Center.

15   Gallagher 1966 questionnaire to Lord, Naval Historical Center.

16   Childers, "Midway from the Backseat of a TBD," 38.

17   Ibid.

18   Gallaher, "I Remember Pearl Harbor," 27; Captain Micheel interview with Paridon, National World War II Museum.

19   Lane to Horan, 27 May 1987; Bottomley 1966 questionnaire to Lord, Naval Historical Center.

20   Godfrey 1966 narrative of Midway to Lord, 4, Naval Historical Center; Hoff oral history.

21   Murray, "Midway: The View from a Bombing Six Rear Seat," 45; Murray, *Bombing Squadron Six in Action*, II-11.

22   Hanson narrative to Lord, 3, Naval Historical Center.

23   Lundstrom, *The First Team*, 391–94.

24   Ludlum, *They Turned the War Around*, 137.

25   Ibid., 137; Bridgers, "On the Traveling Squad E-Base, Doolittle & Midway, 1941–1942."

26   Lt. Cdr. Robert D. Gibson, USNR (Ret.), interview by William J. Shinneman, 10 July 1993, transcript, the Oral History Archive, American Airpower Heritage Museum, Midland, Texas, 6–7.

27   Goldsmith 1966 narrative of Midway to Lord, 2, Naval Historical Center.

28   Ludlum, *They Turned the War Around*, 131.

29   Tillman, *The Dauntless Dive-bomber of World War II*, 84.

30   Ludlum, *They Turned the War Around*, 137–38.

31   Ibid., 138.

32   Bridgers, "On the Traveling Squad E-Base, Doolittle & Midway, 1941–1942."

33   Ibid.

34   Gibson interview with Shinneman, 7.
35   Lord interview notes with Roberts, 19 April 1966, Naval Historical Center; Roberts, "Many Planes Heading Midway," 10–11.
36   Patterson to Lord questionnaire, Naval Historical Center; Goldsmith 1966 narrative of Midway to Lord, 1, Naval Historical Center; Goldsmith to Horan, 9 February 1987.
37   Goldsmith to Horan.

Chapter 13: The Flying Dragon Strike

1   Hanson account of Midway published in Bellevue, Washington, newspaper, supplied to Lord, Naval Historical Center.
2   Don L. Ely to Mark Horan, 3 January 1987.
3   Jones to Horan, 22 December 1986.
4   Frank Patriarca interview with Mark Horan; Ambrose, *The Pacific*, 57; Buell, *Dauntless Helldivers*, 87.
5   Braun 1966 questionnaire to Lord, Naval Historical Center.
6   Hoff oral history, 224–25.
7   Oral Lester Moore oral history, CAF Museum.
8   Gee, "Remembering Midway," 2003 article.
9   Ibid.
10   Tillman, *The Dauntless Dive-bomber of World War II*, 84; Reynolds, Clark G. *The Fighting Lady: The New Yorktown in the Pacific War*. Pictorial Histories Publishing Company, 1993 (third printing), 1–2.
11   Ludlum, *They Turned the War Around*, 139–40.
12   Ibid., 141.
13   Ibid.
14   Forshee, *Standby, Mark!*, Chapter 13.
15   Christie recollections to Horan.
16   Gallaher, "I Remember Pearl Harbor," 28.
17   Tillman, *The Dauntless Dive-bomber of World War II*, 85; Gallaher, "I Remember Pearl Harbor," 29.
18   Tillman, *The Dauntless Dive-bomber of World War II*, 85; Lundstrom, *The First Team*, 414.
19   Gallaher, "I Remember Pearl Harbor," 29.
20   Gallaher to Lord, 1966 correspondence, Naval Historical Center; Tillman, *The Dauntless Dive-bomber of World War II*, 85; Gallaher, "I Remember Pearl Harbor," 29–30.
21   Kleiss, "History from the Cockpit," 15; Kleiss, *VS-6 Log of the War*, 89.
22   Buell, *Dauntless Helldivers*, 87; Ambrose, *The Pacific*, 58; Micheel interview with Mark Horan.
23   Tillman, *The Dauntless Dive-bomber of World War II*, 85.
24   Ibid., 86.
25   Richard Best oral history, 44.
26   McCaul, "Dive-bomber at Midway," 46–47.

27 Braun 1966 questionnaire to Lord, Naval Historical Center.

28 Murray, *Bombing Squadron Six in Action*, II-13.

29 Murray, "Midway: The View from a Bombing Six Rear Seat," 45.

30 Ibid., 45; Murray, *Bombing Squadron Six in Action*, II-21.

31 Tillman, *The Dauntless Dive-bomber of World War II*, 86.

32 Richard Best oral history, 44.

33 Lane to Horan, 27 May 1987.

34 Hanson newspaper account, Naval Historical Center.

35 Lane to Lord questionnaire, Naval Historical Center; Murray interview with Mark Horan. Murray originally believed that the number twelve Dauntless he saw lose its bomb before diving belonged to Ensign Stephen Hogan. Bombing Six's SBDs, however, did not have numerals painted on their wings' undersides as Bombing Three did.

36 Harrington and Frank, *Rendezvous at Midway*, 217; Cobb 1966 questionnaire to Lord, Naval Historical Center.

37 Bottomley to Horan.

38 Parshall and Tully, *Shattered Sword*, 326.

39 Kleiss, *VS-6 Log of the War*, 90.

40 Hanson newspaper account, Naval Historical Center.

41 Bresnahan, "Interview with Earl Gallaher"; Gallaher, "I Remember Pearl Harbor," 30.

42 Kleiss, "History from the Cockpit," 15.

43 Gee, "Remembering Midway," 2003 article.

44 Ibid.

45 Fisher, *Hooked*, 87–88; Parshall and Tully, *Shattered Sword*, 329.

46 Fisher, *Hooked*, 88; Cressman, et al., *"A Glorious Page in Our History,"* 139.

47 Richard Best oral history, 44.

48 Murray, "Midway: The View from a Bombing Six Rear Seat," 45; Richard Best oral history, 44.

49 Micheel to Walter Lord 1966 correspondence; Gallaher, "I Remember Pearl Harbor," 31.

50 Murray, *Bombing Squadron Six in Action*, II-15.

51 Gallaher to Lord 1966 correspondence, Naval Historical Center.

52 Gallaher, "I Remember Pearl Harbor," 31.

53 Lane to Horan, 27 May 1987.

54 Fred Bergeron oral history.

55 Murray, "Midway: The View from a Bombing Six Rear Seat," 45–46.

56 Ibid., 46.

57 Murray, *Bombing Squadron Six in Action*, II-21.

58 Tillman, *The Dauntless Dive-bomber of World War II*, 86; Lundstrom, *The First Team*, 418.

59 Prange, Gordon W., with Donald M. Goldstein and Katherine V. Dillon. *Miracle at Midway*. New York: McGraw Hill, 1982, 253.

60   Ibid., 254. Like the other SBD crews at Midway, O'Flaherty and Gaido had no direct knowledge as to Midway's true defenses, although they would have known that additional aircraft were used to bolster the island. Under the duress of torture, the numbers they created to please their captors turned out to be fairly accurate. Mark Horan interviewed James Cales, a 1942 SBD gunner who later became a pilot who was taken as a POW. Cales had a similar incident of inventing numbers while under torture—figures he created that surprisingly would prove to be accurate.

61   Ibid., 254. Both O'Flaherty and Gaido were single, thus the lighter must have been borrowed from a shipmate before the flight. Although naval intelligence would learn of the murders of these two VS-6 aviators, this fact was kept closely guarded during the war to protect the secrecy of the broken Japanese codes. At war's end, O'Flaherty's family was notified that he had been executed. This information comes from letters obtained from the family by Mark Horan that were shared with the family of Charlie Ware and other VS-6 pilots who did not survive Midway.

62   Kleiss, VS-6 Log of the War, 126–27.

63   Wood 1966 questionnaire to Lord, Naval Historical Center.

64   Ibid.

65   Ibid.

66   Guillory questionnaire to Lord, Naval Historical Center. Additional details of the rescue related by pilot Harold Lowe to Troy T. Guillory Jr., son of the VB-8 pilot.

67   Tillman, The Dauntless Dive-bomber of World War II, 87.

68   Moore oral history.

69   Lane to Lord questionnaire, Naval Historical Center.

70   Snowden 1966 questionnaire to Lord, Naval Historical Center.

71   Kleiss, VS-6 Log of the War, 90.

CHAPTER 14: "THE LITTLE DEVIL WAS MOST DIFFICULT TO HIT"

1   Capt. Schneider interview with Parison, National World War II Museum; Schneider letter to Colonel Barde, 31 May 1966, Naval Historical Center.

2   Schneider oral history; Capt. Schneider interview with Parison, National World War II Museum.

3   Troy T. Guillory to Col. Robert E. Barde, 27 April 1967.

4   Wood 1966 questionnaire to Lord, Naval Historical Center; Guillory questionnaire to Lord, Naval Historical Center; Cressman, et al., "A Glorious Page in Our History," 142–43.

5   Guillory questionnaire to Lord, Naval Historical Center.

6   Tillman, The Dauntless Dive-bomber of World War II, 88.

7   Dickinson, The Flying Guns, 183–84; Anderson, "War Diary," 45.

8   Penland to Lord questionnaire, Naval Historical Center; Capt. Joe R. Penland interview with Robert Barde, 18 May 1966.

9   Richard Best oral history, 45; Cressman, et al., *"A Glorious Page in Our History,"* 149; Best interviews with Mark Horan.

10   Cressman, et al., *"A Glorious Page in Our History,"* 149.

11   Ibid.

12   Ibid.; McClusky interview with Barde, 30 June 1966.

13   Cressman, et al., *"A Glorious Page in Our History,"* 149; Christie to Horan.

14   Gallaher, "I Remember Pearl Harbor," 32.

15   Cobb 1966 questionnaire to Lord, Naval Historical Center.

16   Fred Bergeron oral history.

17   Gee, "Remembering Midway," 2003 article.

18   Cressman, et al., *"A Glorious Page in Our History,"* 149.

19   Lynch to Barde, 1 June 1967.

20   Fisher, *Hooked*, 92.

21   Linder, "Lost Letter of Midway," 33; Fisher, *Hooked*, 95–97.

22   Cressman, et al., *"A Glorious Page in Our History,"* 150.

23   Rodenburg, *Eldor E. Rodenburg*, 8.

24   Hanson account of Midway published in Bellevue, Washington, newspaper, supplied to Lord, Naval Historical Center.

25   Hopkins oral history; Anderson, "War Diary," 48; Lane to Lord questionnaire, Naval Historical Center; Lane to Horan, 27 May 1987.

26   Kleiss, *VS-6 Log of the War*, 90.

27   Ludlum, *They Turned the War Around*, 143.

28   Fisher, *Hooked*, 97; Wood 1966 questionnaire to Lord, Naval Historical Center.

29   Jones to Horan, 22 December 1986.

30   Linder, "Lost Letter of Midway," 33.

31   Johnson to Lord questionnaire, Naval Historical Center.

32   Russell, *No Right to Win*, 142; Fisher, *Hooked*, 92; Tappan interview with Weisheit, 43.

33   Johnson to Lord questionnaire, Naval Historical Center.

34   Fisher, *Hooked*, 92; Johnson to Lord questionnaire.

35   Linder, "Lost Letter of Midway," 33.

36   Mzarek, *A Dawn Like Thunder*, 168–69; Russell, *No Right to Win*, 129; Fisher interviews with Mark Horan.

37   Cressman, et al., *"A Glorious Page in Our History,"* 151.

38   Russell, *No Right to Win*, 120; "Lieut. Tepas, Home after Crusoe Adventure, Is City's First to Win Flying Medal," *Portsmouth* (OH) *Times*, 17 December 1942, 1–2.

39   Hanson account of Midway published in Bellevue, Washington, newspaper, supplied to Lord, Naval Historical Center; Godfrey 1966 narrative of Midway to Lord, 8–9, Naval Historical Center.

40   Lane to Lord questionnaire and Davis 1966 questionnaire to Lord, Naval Historical Center; Ray Davis to Col. Robert E. Barde, undated letter circa 1967.

41   Rodenburg, *Eldor E. Rodenburg*, 8.
42   Adkins to Horan, 23 October 1987.
43   Gallaher to Lord 1966 correspondence, Naval Historical Center; Gallaher, "I Remember Pearl Harbor," 32.
44   Anderson to Horan, 28 April 1987; Edward Garaudy to Mark Horan, 30 December 1986.
45   Hopkins oral history.
46   Mears, *Carrier Combat*, 61.
47   Gee, "Remembering Midway," 2003 article.
48   Cressman, et al., *"A Glorious Page in Our History,"* 151.
49   Ibid., 151.
50   Kleiss, *VS-6 Log of the War*, 91.

Chapter 15: "I Wish I Had Just One More Bomb"

1   Schneider oral history; Captain Schneider interview with Paridon, National World War II Museum.
2   Gee, "Remembering Midway," 2003 article.
3   Ibid.
4   Cressman, et al, *"A Glorious Page in Our History,"* 154.
5   Fisher, *Hooked*, 99.
6   Cressman, et al, *"A Glorious Page in Our History,"* 154; Lundstrom, *The First Team*, 423.
7   Cressman, et al, *"A Glorious Page in Our History,"* 154.
8   Ibid.
9   Linder, "Lost Letter of Midway," 34.
10   Cressman, et al, *"A Glorious Page in Our History,"* 154.
11   Ibid., 155; Fisher, *Hooked*, 99; Christie to Horan.
12   Ibid., 155; Fisher, *Hooked*, 99.
13   "Ensign's Absentmindedness Sends Jap Destroyer to Bottom," *Lowell Sun*, July 2, 1942, 49.
14   Cressman, et al, *"A Glorious Page in Our History,"* 155.
15   Linder, "Lost Letter of Midway," 34.
16   Ibid., 34–35.
17   Garaudy to Horan, 30 December 1986.
18   Fred Bergeron oral history.
19   Rodenburg, *Eldor E. Rodenburg*, 8–9.
20   Cressman, et al, *"A Glorious Page in Our History,"* 154.
21   Forshee, *Standby, Mark!*, chapter 14.
22   Ibid., 144–45.
23   Ibid., 145.
24   Patriarca questionnaire notes to Lord, 1966, Naval Historical Center; Lundstrom, *The First Team*, 424.
25   Ludlum, *They Turned the War Around*, 145.

26 Cressman, et al, *"A Glorious Page in Our History,"* 156.

27 Ibid., 156; Lane to Horan, 27 May 1987.

28 Cdr. Jamie S. Morris to Walter Lord, 20 June 1966; Forshee, *Standby, Mark!*, chapter 14.

29 Ludlum, *They Turned the War Around*, 145; Kleiss, *VS-6 Log of the War*, 91.

30 Hanson account of Midway published in Bellevue, Washington, newspaper, supplied to Lord, Naval Historical Center.

31 Ely to Horan, 3 January 1987.

32 Jones to Horan, 22 December 1986.

33 Garaudy to Horan, 30 December 1986.

34 Hanson account of Midway published in Bellevue, Washington, newspaper, supplied to Lord, Naval Historical Center; Lane to Lord questionnaire, Naval Historical Center; Cressman, et al, *"A Glorious Page in Our History,"* 156.

35 Lane to Horan, 27 May 1987.

36 Cressman, et al, *"A Glorious Page in Our History,"* 156.

37 Prange, *Miracle at Midway*, 339; Cressman, et al, *"A Glorious Page in Our History,"* 156.

38 Tillman, "Where Are They Now? Bob Elder," 13; Kleiss, *VS-6 Log of the War*, 91; Vose to Barde, 3.

39 Lundstrom, *The First Team*, 424.

40 Woodson, "In the Rear Seat at Midway and Santa Cruz."

41 Cressman, et al, *"A Glorious Page in Our History,"* 156–57.

42 Hovind to Lord questionnaire, Naval Historical Center.

43 Parshall and Tully, *Shattered Sword*, 376–77.

44 Rodee to Barde, 18 October 1966; Christie to Horan.

45 Griffin, *A Ship to Remember*, 151–52.

46 Per his son Terry Tereskerz; William Roy recollections in Battle of Midway Round Table, 17 April 2004. Accessed http://www.midway42.org/Backissues/2004/2004-01.htm on 20 June 2011.

47 Lynch to Barde, 1 June 1967.

48 Fisher, *Hooked*, 99–101; Cressman, et al, *"A Glorious Page in Our History,"* 162.

49 Christie to Horan; Griffin, *A Ship to Remember*, 152–53.

50 Tillman, *The Dauntless Dive-bomber of World War II*, 88.

51 Ludlum, *They Turned the War Around*, 146.

52 Garaudy to Horan, 30 December 1986.

53 Kleiss, *VS-6 Log of the War*, 92; Dobson diary, 6 June 1942.

54 Cressman, et al, *"A Glorious Page in Our History,"* 162.

55 Forshee, *Standby, Mark!*, chapter 14.

56 Fisher, *Hooked*, 101.

57 Orr, "Jack 'Dusty' Kleiss and the Battle of Midway," 11.

58 Anderson, "War Diary," 50.

EPILOGUE

1 Dickinson, *The Flying Guns*, 194–95.
2 Ambrose, *The Pacific*, 61.
3 Tillman, *The Dauntless Dive-bomber of World War II*, 89; Prange, *Miracle at Midway*, 273; Captain Schneider interview with Paridon, National World War II Museum.
4 Tillman, *The Dauntless Dive-bomber of World War II*, 90.
5 Lundstrom, *The First Team*, 429–30; Tillman, *The Dauntless Dive-bomber of World War II*, 89
6 Murray, *Bombing Squadron Six in Action*, II-20.
7 Mason oral history, 5.
8 Ibid.
9 Lanham to Lord questionnaire, Naval Historical Center.
10 Murray, "Midway: The View from a Bombing Six Rear Seat," 46.
11 Ibid.
12 Murray, *Bombing Squadron Six in Action*, II-26.
13 Ambrose, *The Pacific*, 62; Stafford, *The Big E*, 103.
14 Kleiss, *VS-6 Log of the War*, 108; Forshee, *Standby, Mark!*, chapter 15.
15 Goldsmith to Horan, 9 February 1987.
16 Mears, *Carrier Combat*, 67, 76–77.
17 Horan, "The Last Flight of Charles Rollins Ware."
18 Murray, "Midway: The View from a Bombing Six Rear Seat," 47.
19 Bresnahan, "Interview with Earl Gallaher," 4 June 1992; Cressman, "Blaze of Glory," 24.
20 Murray, *Bombing Squadron Six in Action*, II-29–30.
21 Hoff oral history, 46–47.
22 Murray, *Bombing Squadron Six in Action*, III-2.
23 Ibid., III-39.
24 Ibid., III-18.
25 Fred Bergeron oral history.
26 Leaming, *Scouting Squadron Six*, 110.
27 Kleiss, "History from the Cockpit," 16.

INDEX